DR. WAYNE W. DYER

"As I wrote this book I persistently kept my mind focused on being helpful and practical instead of theoretical. I want you to be able to apply today what you are reading in these pages. As a professional counselor I always knew precisely what formula it took to get people to change. First, I would get people to identify behaviors that were not working for them. Second, I would get them to see the payoffs, or the "neurotic dividends," for these self-destructive behaviors. Finally, we would attempt to come up with intelligent, practical new behaviors to help them change.

"This is the formula I have used in writing this book. First, identify what it is that you may be doing in a given area of child-rearing. Then look at your payoffs for continuing to treat your children this way. Finally, find out how to use new techniques that just might bring about your desired result."

What Do You Really Want For Your Children?

"Dyer brings his philosophy home with specific advice for parents on how to help kids realize their potential... and like all his other books, he makes it sound so easy!"

St. Petersburg Times

Other Avon Books by
Dr. Wayne W. Dyer

PULLING YOUR OWN STRINGS
YOUR ERRONEOUS ZONES

DR. WAYNE W. DYER

What Do You Really Want For Your Children?

AVON BOOKS ◬ NEW YORK

To my children and stepchildren, *Tracy, Stephanie, Skye, Sommer* and *Serena.* The very special loves of my life.

To my mother, *Hazel Irene Dyer,* who, through many hardships, always celebrated every day of her life and taught me to do the same....I Love You.

To the mothers of my children: *Judith Arlene Matsura,* who is a living example of integrity; and...

Marcelene Louise Dyer, Mother and Wife, who is "No-Limit" parenting in action....I Love You.

All of you have provided me with the real-life examples to write about this glorious business of raising children and have helped me to answer in the pages of this book, WHAT I REALLY WANT FOR ALL MY CHILDREN.

Grateful acknowledgment is made for permission to reprint excerpts from David Elkind's *The Hurried Child,* copyright © 1981. Used by permission of Addison-Wesley Publishing Company.

AVON BOOKS
A division of
The Hearst Corporation
105 Madison Avenue
New York, New York 10016

Copyright © 1985 by Dr. Wayne W. Dyer
Published by arrangement with William Morrow and Company, Inc.
Library of Congress Catalog Card Number: 85-10652
ISBN: 0-380-69957-5

The William Morrow edition contains the following Library of Congress Cataloging in Publication Data:

Dyer, Wayne W.
  What do you really want for your children?

  Includes index.
  1. Child rearing. 2. Parenting. 3. Child psychology. 4. Conduct of Life.
I. Title. HQ 772.D95   1985   649'.1   85-10652

First Avon Books Printing: December 1986

Contents

Contents

7

I Want My Children to Celebrate Their Present Moments 235

8

I Want My Children to Experience a Lifetime of Wellness 269

Average children do things right . . .
No-limit children do the right thing.
                                        —Eykis

Introduction

There are many provocative quotations about the raising of children, none of which has ever struck me with more force than the words of John Wilmot, the Earl of Rochester back in the seventeenth century. "Before I got married I had six theories about bringing up children; now I have six children and no theories." There is a powerful amount of truth in that statement. Nothing renders us less "all-knowing" than having the responsibility of raising children on a daily basis. It is with these words in mind that I have written the book you hold in your hand. I have no theories for you. I offer you my own common-sense applications, which have come from my experiences with children, from my contact with thousands of skillful parents, from being around children all my life, and from my great love for them.

When I was teaching at St. John's University in New York many years ago, and my daughter was only three years old, her friends would knock on the door and ask politely of my wife, "Can Wayne come out and play? Please?" There I was, a thirty-year-old college professor, playing "horsey" and chasing the little ones around the block. At parties when all of the adults would congregate in a smoke-filled room, drinking cocktails, I was often off playing games with the children. I have been blessed with beautiful children and stepchildren of my own. I can honestly say that I have often preferred the company of children to adults, that I love to wrestle, tease, play, and be around, children of all ages.

When I was traveling in Europe, I once played soccer with a group of non-English-speaking children in a mountain village in Switzerland. I spent several exhausting hours in the company of twenty young children, and though we could not communicate with words, there was a mutual sharing and love, a respect and perfect enjoyment that transcended the need for a verbal language. The laughter, the determination, the wondrous excitement for living that unspoiled children share is a universal trait.

In the crowded train stations of Japan and Hong Kong I played with Oriental children, getting them to laugh and squeal with delight over a game of finger wrestling, or "who can make the funniest face." In Germany, I taught an entire neighborhood of tiny tykes, all screeching in delight, how to catch and throw an American Frisbee. When you have a love affair with children, it matters little what language they speak. The language of love is so powerful that the words become unnecessary. In writing this book

I have been able to strongly identify with the words of Carl Jung, a brilliant contributor to the field of human awareness, when he said:

> From the beginning I had a sense of destiny, as though my life was assigned to me by fate and had to be fulfilled. This gave me an inner security, and, though I could never prove it to myself, it proved itself to me. I did not have this certainty, it had me.

My strong love and affection for young people has owned me all of my life; it was only a matter of time before I decided to write about this wonderful love affair with the children of the world.

My books have all been a part of this participatory destiny that I allude to in the previous paragraph. *Your Erroneous Zones* was my effort to teach everyone the common sense of managing one's own emotions, and *Pulling Your Own Strings* was a natural follow-up on how to deal more effectively with others who would attempt to victimize you in any way. *The Sky's the Limit* was an extension of these principles. It offered ideas for going beyond simply managing one's own emotions and dealing more effectively with others, into the area of no-limit living—that is, living the highest functioning life possible for a human being based upon the ability to choose one's own greatness. In *Gifts from Eykis,* I wrote my parable for our time, a story of one woman from another world who gives us the "reality-only" wisdom and simple truths to apply to our own personal lives, and to the healing of our planet. It was inevitable that I write *What Do You Really Want for Your Children?* It is the natural way to go for me. This book offers the same basic no-nonsense approach to the most important task facing all of us: the raising of children in such a way as to leave our world in the hands of people who can not only manage it and themselves effectively, but who can finally make this world a place of peace and love forever.

As I wrote this book I persistently kept my mind focused on being helpful and practical instead of theoretical. I want you to be able to apply today what you are reading in these pages. As a professional counselor I always knew precisely what formula it took to get people to change. First, I would get people to identify what it was that they were doing which could be labeled self-defeating, to simply identify the behaviors that were not working for them.

Second, I would attempt to get them to see the payoffs, or the "neurotic dividends," for these self-destructive behaviors. Finally, we would attempt to come up with intelligent, practical, and implementable new behaviors to help them to change. That is the essence of effective counseling, and it is the formula that I have used in writing this book. First, identify what it is that you may be doing in a given area of child rearing. Then look at your payoffs for continuing to treat your children this way. Finally, find out how to use new techniques that just might bring about your desired result.

I have not written a standard book about the raising of children. All of the concepts, ideas, strategies, techniques, or whatever you choose to call them apply to all ages and all situations involving children. They are universal to the helping of young people to become independent, no-limit people.

Throughout the pages of this book I will be presenting the specific skill areas of no-limit living. These areas fall almost exclusively in the "how you feel" domain. I will emphasize those that will carry you and your children through any troublesome situation. If you cannot figure out how to adjust your carburetor, at least you can look it up or take it to a carburetor expert. But, if you find yourself immobilized by your out-of-control anger, or your child is hopelessly nervous, there is no instruction manual on anger control, nor is there a "nervous system repair garage" available. The answers must come from within you and within your child. The key to being a no-limit person has very little to do with mastering a set of cognitive skills. Instead, it has almost everything to do with knowing how to be at the controls of your own emotions. You and your children become to your own life as a great painter is to his masterpiece, shaping, shading, designing as you choose.

I have written this book to help you out *now*. You will not find neat little categories for what to do at every stage of development, because your child is unique *now*, and therefore resists compartmentalization. I want to help you now to get started on turning the direction from "many limits" to "no limits." Whether you are a parent, grandparent, teacher, neighbor, caretaker, stepparent, friend, minister, counselor, social worker, or any other caring person who wants to help young people, I want you to be able to use this book now. I wrote it believing that you can pick it up today, regardless of whether you are expecting your first child, or are parents of six teenagers, or anyplace in between. I never intended to write a book about starting from the beginning, because today is the only day you have, and your children are precisely the age they are, and you must deal with that particular reality. I do not believe that you must start them out in a certain way, and if you do not, then it is too late once they pass through a particular developmental stage. I know that it is possible to change at any given moment, regardless of one's previous history. I am convinced that you can begin right now on a course of no-limit parenting, and change your child's life beginning right now. I have changed self-defeating behavior patterns in myself by simply making the decision to do so, and by exercising the will and self-determination to make the decision stick. So, too, can you apply any of the principles in this book and make them work, if you have the will to work with children in a new light.

There have been books written on the subjects of single parenting, children of divorce, the preteen, guilt and parenting, infancy, you and your teenager, menopause parenting, and every conceivable subcategory you can think of. I had one single objective in mind when writing this book. How can I help you, regardless of your current situation, *now*, to influence your children in a positive no-limit way, to raise them to become all that you want for them? I have kept uppermost in mind the need to be specific, to use concrete examples, and to make it practical rather than theoretical. You will find some duplication in the pages of this book. Many times a point made in one chapter on creativity will apply equally in the area of discipline or promoting a positive self-image. Rather than attempting to disguise it, I deliberately repeated the principle when it seemed to be called for in my writing.

In order to help bring about positive results with children— or with anyone, for that matter—you must repeat, repeat, and repeat again. You must constantly reiterate something until it becomes a positive habit. When you think about it, that is precisely the way you *learned* self-defeating habits, by constant repetition. So when you see an example or a principle reused later on in the book, try not to think of it as a writer's repetition, but simply as a reminder, right here where you are reading, that the same principle that applied in an earlier section applies here as well. I have done it deliberately to reinforce the need as it arose in my writing.

I did not edit out all the duplication, because I believe in it and I know it is necessary in order to help you to make these techniques work for you. Just as children do not ever fit into neat little categories as many who have written about the two-year-old, the preadolescent, or the adolescent might have you believe, neither do the principles of parenting fit into tightly wrapped packages. There is much overlap in the various "wants" that I have used to title the ten chapters of this book, and I will not pretend that something said in one place must never be repeated in another. It simply does not come out that way in reality, and it did not come out that way in writing about that reality either.

The book you are holding evolved in very much the way a young child evolves into adulthood. In the early chapters I was very careful to guide you through the pages, taking you step by step, using clinical examples. I assumed that you could not be left alone and that you needed constant supervision. As I wrote, I became more personal, sharing private stories, using personal examples, and straying from clinical case studies into more everyday human situations. I was letting you, the reader, in on my beliefs and strategies. I kept it specific, but not at all nurturing, simply offering you my strong beliefs and applications on this glorious subject of raising no-limit children. In the later stages I asked you to stretch more, much as you might ask such stretching of your adolescent. I took on the subjects of wellness, creativity, higher needs, and a sense of purpose, almost as if you were now in an advanced stage of your parenting development.

I went beyond simply asking you to help your own child, to a plea for you to help all of the children everywhere as well. I can see this progression in the book, and rather than editing it out, I have left it as I wrote it: from infancy, through the toddler years, into preadolescence and the teenage years, and finally into adulthood. The same evolution that your children must traverse whether they like it or not, so too did I traverse as I wrote about this vital subject. You will realize this progression in the book.

In the past few years I have received thousands of letters from people who genuinely care about children. I want to share a portion of three of those letters from people who asked me to keep in mind some important truths while writing this very book. First, Bonnie Kippen, from Carney's Point, New Jersey, wrote to me, saying:

Dear Dr. Dyer:

While reading *Your Erroneous Zones* I realized exactly what I want to do. I want to see my three smallest children—ages eight, seven, and six—educated without all the approval-seeking brainwashing that myself and various schools have used to all but destroy my fourteen-year-old. The middle girl, age eight, is already on her way in the same direction. I've watched them all start out bright and eager, enjoying preschool and kindergarten as a satisfactory experience, only to be pressured into conformity. One is so indoctrinated that her teacher describes her as a "sweet" child and a "good influence on the class." Horrors! My seven-year-old son resisted in first grade and now, this obviously gifted, secretly frustrated treasure has been branded as troubled and a proverbial handful. The youngest, almost six, was consistently criticized for being a disruption because she tried to do things that were "not part of the day's lesson" or "unrelated to what we must accomplish in kindergarten." She was the most resistant and stubborn about her opinions, but her teacher couldn't accept it when I suggested that the child might have an opinion. The teacher told me that kindergarten children are too young to have formed any opinions about anything and that even if they did it wouldn't matter because the school system knew the best way to structure her education. Do you know of anywhere that I can get them educated without all the nonsense? Is there maybe an experimental school somewhere that applies the sort of freedom and self-love techniques that you espouse in combination with sound academic goals to develop not only well-educated but also well-adjusted students?

Thank you,
Bonnie Kippen

Bonnie's concerns as a parent and her very real determination to keep her children from becoming indoctrinated into sameness by "approval-seeking brainwashing" was a real inspiration for my writing.

Several months later, I spoke to a group of teachers on Long Island, as a keynoter for the opening day program. A teacher, Marilyn Chiaramonte, of Rockville Centre, New York, wrote to me afterward. Her letter said in part:

Please repeat in your parenting book ad nauseam the importance of loving the child for himself and not for what we expect

him to be. I see so many damaged, hurt, scarred, walled egos in
my classes every term that I spend most of the term just loving
and accepting these kids, most of whom are truly beautiful human
beings and just do not believe it because they've never been told.
You can knock down an inflated ego with a few well-placed
words. But it takes a lifetime to boost up an ego that's broken by
well-meaning parents who don't want to ''spoil'' the child.

I hope your presentation touched many of the teachers at
Lawrence who've sort of given up on teaching, maybe even life. I
can think of no other way to better start the school year. I look
forward to the publication of your parenting book and will probably use it in my parenting classes.

I kept your words in mind, Marilyn, as I wrote this book, and
I too feel many of the concerns you have expressed in your
thoughtful letter.

Then, as I was putting the finishing touches on this manu-
script, a letter came to me from a woman in Seattle. Her name is
Chloe Robinson. She had written to me previously, after hearing
me speak several months earlier. This time she sent me the following letter, which she had sent to her children and her grandchildren. I have included it here in its entirety, because I believe
it gives a powerful message to all of us who care about children,
and it helps to answer the question that is the title of this book,
What Do You Really Want for Your Children?

To My Children and Grandchildren,

As the year comes to a close, I want to tell each of you how much
I love you and how special you are to me.

In this existence that we call life, I have learned two things: that
each of us is special and unique in the universe and that love is
the most powerful device that we have in our lives.

Our contribution to this planet should be that of becoming all that
we can become as a person and allowing each and every other
person that same privilege. If we do this through love and caring
and by being a nonjudgmental person, when we leave this place,
as we all will, it will be better because of our having been here.

Our mission in life should be to be as happy and as positive as we
can possibly be. It is our God-given right, and unless we are truly

happy with ourselves and love ourselves as the unique and special individuals that we are, we can never totally give of ourselves to others and make this planet the beautiful, loving, and peaceful place that we would wish it to be.

Self-love is not selfish. It is the most positive and perfect way that you can thank God for your life. If you love yourself and know that you are perfect in God's eyes, then you will be able to radiate this message to others and reinforce in them that they, too, are perfect. That is the only way that everyone can achieve this elusive thing that we call happiness.

Happiness, in itself, does not exist. It is an illusion. Only by being happy within ourselves can we find it. If you search the world until you die, you will never find it. You will not find it in material things, excitement, other people, wishing for it, buying it, or by any other means. It is totally personal and comes from within.

The wonderful thing is that it is there for everyone, and no matter who you are or what your circumstances, you must realize that it is your gift. You are entitled to it, and there are no strings attached. You must never depend on another person to "give" you happiness; that places too much of a burden on both of you. If you are truly happy inside yourself and allow the other person that same right, then you automatically bring happiness to each other without even trying, and it is a bonus because it is not expected or anticipated . . . it just is.

Our responsibility to this planet, ourselves, and others is to be as positive as we can possibly be. This does not mean being unrealistic; it only means that no matter what the circumstances and how they affect us, we maintain our inner calm, our unwavering knowledge that we are unique and that there is nothing that can shake our belief in ourselves if we don't allow it to.

We must face each situation in our lives with dignity and love and allow the other person that same right.

Life is not a game of there having to be a winner and a loser. We are all winners. Only when we perceive ourselves or others as winners or losers do we place a label on something that isn't really there. Let yourself be a winner in life and allow the other person to be a winner too. In that way, everyone wins.

We are each unique from the day of birth. Small children need the protection of their parents until they are old enough to take care of themselves physically, but we should, from the day each baby is born, recognize that a baby is a human being, exactly as we are, in a tiny body. They are not "apprentice people."

Life is wonderful and beautiful; God intended it to be that way. It is only through our own attitudes about ourselves and others that we allow it to become less than perfect.

Our bodies are made up of billions of cells, and in order for us to maintain perfect health, each of these cells must operate at its optimum level. If we have sick or weak cells, then our healthy cells must work harder to counteract this negative situation so that the body as a whole can be healthy.

Our planet is like a body, and each of us is one of the cells. It is our responsibility to this body that we call our planet to be a healthy, happy cell that radiates nothing but goodness and positiveness. Only in this way can we help counteract the sick or weak cells and make our world perfect and beautiful in every way. There is no room for negative thinking and selfishness. Only by being the best that we can be, and allowing others the same right, can this be accomplished.

We must each strive to become a loving, nonjudgmental person and to give every other person, no matter how much he or she differs from us in looks, behavior, or beliefs, the right to also become a loving, nonjudgmental person. This is the only way our planet will survive.

I expect to live a long and fulfilling life and to continue to grow and learn, but if I were to be gone tomorrow, this is what I would like to leave as my message to each of you.

I love each of you and accept you exactly as you are. I want and expect nothing more from you than your right to be happy and fulfilled as a unique person. I, in turn, will try to become the very best person I can be so that you will never have to look on me as a burden or feel any responsibility for me other than sharing with me your love and your self as a person if you so choose.

There is nothing that you will ever do that will disappoint me or make me love you less than I do. You have my unconditional love and the sure knowledge that this will never change. We are all on our own paths even though our lives are intertwined with each other's.

All I hope for and expect from you is that you exercise your God-given right to be happy and become the very best that you can become and allow that same right to everyone else with no reservations or conditions.

Au aloha oe nui loa [I love you very much].

> Aloha [Love],
> Makuahine a Tutu Koloe
> [Mother and Grandma Chloe]

I trust that you will find this book useful from the opening pages through the letter that is the appendix. Some time ago my mother, to whom this book is partially dedicated, wrote me the following poem. It too summarizes beautifully the feeling I want to convey as you begin reading this book, of which I am so proud.

WAYNE

A mother can but guide . . .
    then step aside—I knew
I could not say, "This is the way
    that you should go."

For I could not foresee
    what paths might beckon you
to unimagined heights
    that I might never know.

Yet, always in my heart
    I realized
That you would touch a star . . .
    I'm not surprised!

—HAZEL DYER

You can help your own children to touch their own stars if you follow that important advice. *Guide, then step aside*. It is the message of this book. It is your own destiny as a caring person who genuinely loves all those "little stars."

1

What Do You Want More Than Anything for Your Children?

There is no wealth but life.

—JOHN RUSKIN

Just for the fun of it, take a poll of all the parents you know, asking them the question that I have used as the title of this very first chapter: *"What do you want more than anything for your children?"* While you are at it, ask yourself and your spouse (if you have one) the very same question and see what you discover as you begin reading this book. While you may receive a wide variety of responses, I suggest that if you categorize the answers, you will find that the most significant responses gravitate around a central theme.

In my experience, when asking parents this leading question, and giving them time to consider the importance of such a profound question, the answers tend toward the ones you will find in the following list.

I want my children to be happy, and free from hang-ups in life.

I want them to know how to enjoy life and appreciate every day as a miracle.

I want them to feel successful and significant as people regardless of what they do.

I want them to have positive feelings about themselves and about life.

I want them to grow up knowing how to avoid having the inevitable problems defeat them in any way.

I want them to avoid being depressed and miserable.

I want them to avoid growing up to be neurotic.

I want them to have a strong sense of inner peace that will sustain them through difficult times.

I want them to value the now: to take pleasure in life's journey, avoiding overemphasis on a destination.

I want them to know that they are the designers of their lives, that they have the power to choose and change their lives.

I want them to be sensitive and responsible to, and have a reverence for, nature and humanity.

I want them to find and explore their potential and feel satisfied and challenged with a purpose in life.

I want them to feel loved and loving.

I want them to find the opportunities that are hidden in life's inevitable painful experiences.

I want them to be on friendly terms with health—physically and mentally.

These are the typical answers, condensed into a few simple sentences, that I have received in response to this question. Parents do not seem to be obsessed with having their children become rich and famous, or with wanting them to have problem-free lives. They are not absolutely determined that their children should have idyllic jobs, a beautiful home, a marriage to a perfect "10," and a storybook family life as portrayed on television and in the movies. Parents seem to be realistic in their goals for their children. They know that things will not bring happiness, and they do not want to teach their children to accumulate things in a search for happiness. We all seem to have come to the realization in recent years that acquisitions, position in life, accumulation of wealth, and some of the more traditional barometers of a successful life are no longer appropriate. We have all heard too many stories of "successful" people who are addicted to tranquilizers, who must visit their shrinks regularly, who view depression as "only normal," who consider suicide as a solution to life's problems, or who are so busy pursuing "more" that they have no time for enjoying life.

People have become wary of those undesirable accompaniments to success, and want their children to develop instead a kind of serenity and happiness that will carry them through even the toughest of times. I am quite confident that you want your children to grow into contented, highly functioning, no-limit adults who will be able to handle all of life's difficulties without allowing themselves to be so overwhelmed by them that they are either defeated in some way, or so badly bruised that they come to rely on external measures such as pills, therapy, or even surgery to cope with life. In short, you want your kids to grow up to be no-limit people in every single aspect of their lives, and to enjoy life without developing a sour attitude or a defeatist posture.

You want them to be positive about their lives, rather than grumblers. You want them to *feel* successful rather than having some external factor determine their degree of success.

The Ability to Enjoy Life

Think for a moment about the greatest priority in life. Imagine for yourself, and for your children, that you were all bequeathed the ability to enjoy life regardless of the circumstances around you. If someone abandoned you, nevertheless you would still know how to enjoy life. If you were faced with a serious illness or about to go through a difficult tax audit, you would still be able to enjoy life. Disappointments would come and go, yet because of your inherited gift, you would always know how to enjoy life. Given this imaginary ability, it would be impossible for you to ever be a burden to anyone else; therefore, you would be as *un*selfish as is humanly possible. Naturally, if you could always enjoy life, you wouldn't have a set of expectations for other people to provide enjoyment for you, regardless of what they chose at any given moment. What a miraculous gift this ability to enjoy life at all times would be.

You do have this capacity! It need not exist only in your imagination. You can make it very real for yourself and inspire this marvelous quality in your children. After reviewing your objectives for your children and considering all the possibilities of things you might provide for them, it almost always boils down to this one wish: "I would love for my children to always have the ability to enjoy life." If this sentence describes what you would like to provide for your children, you can make it a priority beginning today. If you offer this wonderful gift to your children, and give it to yourself at the same time, your reward will be children that grow and mature into the highest-level functioning human beings on our globe. The people who genuinely make a difference in the world are those who are not preoccupied with their own personal happiness, but who instead simply take it for granted as a precondition of their humanity. The people who feel successful, and in fact achieve at the highest levels, are those who are able to ignore the need to have someone provide them with happiness injections. The truest definition that I know of a no-limit person is simply *a person who knows how to enjoy life, especially when those around him are going mad.*

Assuming that most parents want to cultivate this kind of a general attitude of enjoying life for their children, then what goes wrong between what we genuinely wish to provide our children and the reality we face each day? Why are there so many adults and young adults popping tranquilizers in order to make it through the day? (Approximately 100 million prescriptions for Valium and Librium are filled annually in the United States alone.) Why do we need to take pills to go to sleep, to stay awake, to relieve tension, to give us energy, to send away miseries, to slow us down, to speed us up, and on and on? Why are so many people filled with stress? Why do suicide rates continue to rise, especially among young people, and why are visits to "shrinks" a way of life? Why such widespread use of drugs and alcohol to get high? Why so much anger and hostility in our world? Why do people resort to desperate measures in order to be heard? If we want children to be able to enjoy life, then where have all these desperately unhappy people come from? Why has hate become more rampant than love? Why are so many people living in fear in the supposed safety of their own homes? Why do so many children become drug addicts, criminals, cult followers—or, at best, impolite and inconsiderate to strangers?

The fact is that most of us do not know how to go about helping children to learn how to enjoy life because we have not learned that simple secret ourselves. We cannot teach what we do not know. We go on and on in the same vicious cycle that was handed to us, and our own children become the victims of our parental ignorance. We often think that we know what it is that constitutes a successful person, and we spend time browbeating our young people into submissively becoming what we think they *should* become. We look at our own errors and vow to avoid their repetition in our children. We assume that having lived longer gives us wisdom that a young person should welcome. And nothing could be further from the truth. Learning how to enjoy life is an attitude. It is a central belief system that we either learn or we don't. We often forget this, or we don't have this inner conviction ourselves, and consequently we cannot provide it for our young people. A central premise of this book, and of all that I have ever written, is that you must be able to model what you are attempting to teach.

Being an Example

Imagine going to your dentist and having him give you a lecture on the importance of oral hygiene, while all the time smiling at you through rotting front teeth. Or, visualize yourself talking to your doctor and having him tell you about the evils of nicotine addiction while blowing cigarette smoke in your face. Your initial reaction would be "This person is a phony." The same kind of logic applies to the teaching of attitudes about life. If your goal is to assist children in developing an appreciation for life, and the ability to *always* enjoy life, then you must begin this task by first working on yourself and modeling this kind of an attitude in all of your interactions.

If you are constantly putting yourself down, living on a day-to-day basis with low self-respect, and literally demonstrating to children that you do not think very highly of yourself, then you are hardly in a position to help any child raise his self-esteem. YOU MUST LIVE BY EXAMPLE! It is essential to show children a portrait of a person who has self-respect if you want it to rub off on them. It is important that you have your own life together if you are going to provide an authentic example for children.

There is no better answer to a child's negative attitude than a positive example. You can look up the answers in all the baby books ever written, but to a child who has no motivation, there is no better answer than a motivated person. The angry child is best answered by a calm person. The prejudiced child is best answered by a tolerant loving person. The lackadaisical child is best encouraged by an enthusiastic person. While all of your attributes are not necessarily going to rub off on children, the best place to begin in the business of raising children to become all that they can become, is by doing the same for yourself, and proudly displaying this example wherever possible.

Even if you are not a person who has conquered your own erroneous zones, and you see yourself as having a great deal of work to do, you can begin to work on the comments you make in front of children. For example, you can try to eradicate any and all sentences that reflect your own inability to enjoy life. Eliminate such mutterings as the following:

"It's so depressing—we can never get ahead."

"Things never seem to work out for us."

"How can I ever enjoy myself with all the troubles you cause me?"

"Some people have all the luck."

"Life is a penalty box."

When you work each day at eliminating the kinds of sentences that reflect an inability to enjoy life, you will be providing an example, a real live personal model, of at least one person who is not ever going to be defeated by life. New sentences which you can practice each and every day, especially when things do not seem to be going as you would like them to be, and even if you do not believe them yet, include:

"It's just a minor setback. We'll get over it real fast."

"We can find something positive in this for all of us."

"Your troubles are your own, and I'm not going to get depressed because of them."

"People make their own luck."

"Life is a banquet."

In each of the five sentences above, you can see the difference between a parent who is constantly providing a pessimistic example and one who looks at the bright side in the same situations. If you want your children to develop the ability to enjoy life at all times, and you see a lot of negative attitudes creeping into their personalities, begin the task of reversing those attitudes by first looking at yourself. You will not be able to eliminate all self-defeating behaviors and attitudes in children by simply changing yourself and doing nothing more, but you can make a huge dent in that negative armor by giving children a consistent example of one person who refuses to be one of life's victims.

As you think about providing a live example of a person who knows how to enjoy life, not only for your children's sake, but for your own as well, remind yourself about what really counts in life. Far too often we place an extreme value on learning rules, obtaining knowledge, achievement, acquisitions, and external rewards, such as a career slot and the ability to make money. All too often we have modeled these as the most important values a person can possess, at the expense of the far more consequential qualities of simply being able to be happy.

What You Know vs. How You Feel

At any given moment in your life, what is more important: what you *know* or how you *feel*? It is impossible to separate them entirely, but generally speaking, what is it that has priority, your knowledge or your feelings?

We are all aware that when we feel bad we become less effective and have difficulty performing our "duties" effectively until we somehow correct the bad feelings we are experiencing. Feelings, or emotions, are the most significant side to our lives, yet we almost totally ignore them as we overemphasize the acquisition of knowledge in both our homes and our schools. Educators have faced this dilemma for centuries. The "affective" (feelings) versus the "cognitive" (knowledge) approach is the technical label for the controversy as it applies to education. Schools spend better than 95 percent of their funds and energy on the cognitive side. Parents spend almost the same amount of their energy and time in developing the cognitive domain, and we all know in our hearts that our emotions take precedence in virtually all of life's important situations.

Learning to manage our own emotions, to have self-confidence and self-esteem, to avoid being depressed, afraid, stressful, anxious, worried, guilty, jealous, shy, and the like are primary skills that no-limit people possess. These skill areas in the affective domain are absolutely essential to a full and happy life, the kind of life that allows you to always appreciate and enjoy it, yet we ignore the affective skills, dismissing them as trivial or things that we should already know. Few of us can really manage our own emotions, and even fewer of us are capable of teaching our children how to avoid the pitfalls of an ineffective education in the affective domain.

People who have nervous breakdowns do not suffer from a poor education. Often they are quite capable of creating or solving complex rhyming schemes of esoteric poetry. People who take pills to cope with life have often mastered quadratic equations. Shy people often score in the highest percentiles in reading and writing skills. People who lack love and confidence are quite capable of winning a spelling bee. Angry, hostile people can usually master the requirements of their jobs and even figure out the complex circuitry in electronic equipment. Fearful people are usually able to add and subtract, and often have perfect school attendance records. You begin to see that the really important skills are ignored in the name of acquiring an education. I strongly believe in learning cognitive skills; the more you know in all areas, the better are your chances of being a no-limit person throughout your life.

The principal goal of parenting is teaching children to become their own parents. You want children to rely on their own inner signals, to be able to think for themselves, to avoid costly emotional letdowns, and to know that they have the skills and the ability to use them, to lead happy and fulfilled lives without the need to consult you forever. You are to be their guide for a while, and then, you will enjoy watching them take off on their own. To accomplish this, you will want to be well versed in the specifics of no-limit living, and to be helpful in allowing children to make choices and acquire as many cognitive skills as they desire, while always possessing the abilities to be at mastery in the affective areas as well.

In this affective domain, where "how I feel" is of paramount importance, there are many specifics as well. They may not categorize as neatly as addition or sentence diagramming, but they are easily as significant. And, best of all, when you and your children get these qualities of no-limit living down pat, you will never ever forget them. In fact, you will take them with you wherever you go, and in every single task you undertake throughout your life, whether you are cleaning out your closet, working in the garden, changing a diaper, mending a dress, appearing in traffic court, or making love. These are tools that you take with you to all jobs and all of life's experiences. And you need not ignore them any longer.

The Affective Domain

A major premise of this book is that you want children to live happy, neurosis-free lives. You want to help them to internalize specific skills and attitudes that will serve them throughout their lives in such a way that they will know how to live at mastery. You also start with the awareness that they are not going to learn these skills and attitudes in a classroom. Schools do not have a curriculum for developing no-limit people; in fact, they often work in opposition to these objectives. Children will have to acquire their no-limit beliefs out there in the real world. Herman Melville, the well-known nineteenth-century author of *Moby Dick,* whose works most of us have been required to read at one time or another, said it this way: "A whale ship was my Yale College and my Harvard." A clever way of saying that one learns by doing, and not by attending lectures in a prestigious university. Your children will need a whale ship of their own if they are going to learn to navigate their own emotional destiny.

Living fully in the "how I feel" realm is extremely rewarding. In this affective domain, there are no rules to memorize, no examinations to take, no grades that appear on a report card. The rewards are a happy, fulfilled life regardless of what tasks you undertake. The rules are flexible and varied, and the examinations are the ways in which you handle your everyday real-life situations. This is not classroom education for an artificial environment, or a method for making a lot of money later in life. In this part of your life, each and every setting, each and every human being you encounter, each moment of life is an opportunity to demonstrate your skills and abilities. This is the realm of your being in which you use your knowledge and skills all the time; you need not wait until you are working in the marketplace to see why you studied a specific subject. Each and every day of your life you will see the beautifully rewarding reasons why you practiced so hard in learning these skills and attitudes.

Our goals, then, are quite simple. We must maximize our skills in teaching our children to be as powerful and as healthy as they can possibly be, within the area of their lives that we are calling the "how you feel" dimension. We want our children to learn the specifics of no-limit living, and we can help them to attain these high-level skills through our own parenting efforts. As a wonderful spin-off goal, perhaps we will become equally powerful and healthy, the affective corner of our world.

What are the components of no-limit living? Throughout this book, each chapter will focus on specific traits which constitute the highest functioning available to people in our culture, and show how to help our children internalize this particular trait. I call those who exhibit all of these traits consistently "no-limit people," largely because they have no internally imposed limitations on themselves, and refuse to permit outsiders to place any limits on them either. Others who have studied human behavior in the past have used such descriptors as "self-actualized," "inner-directed," "fully-functioning," "conscious," and "awakened." It does not matter how we refer to no-limit people, as long as we know what we are talking about. A no-limit person is one who has high levels of self-respect and self-confidence, regardless of the situation. This person has great enthusiasm for himself, and feels a sense of belonging to the world. He will seek out the unknown and wander around in the mysterious, seeing life as a miracle rather than as a bother.

For the most part, the no-limit person operates on inner signals, trusting himself and willing to take risks. He experiences anger at times, but is never immobilized by it and is not a person who is out of control of himself at any time. He is not a complainer but a doer instead, and never whines to others about his bad luck. Our no-limit person does not use up his time being worried about what will happen; instead, he focuses on what he can do to avoid problems. Similarly, he is not occupied by guilt and anxiety about the past. He knows how to learn from the past without being upset and depressed about things that are over and done. He is a person who feels a strong sense of purpose and mission in life, and no one can take this inner fortitude away from him. He perseveres in his mission, and obstacles only serve to intensify his resolve.

Our no-limit person is motivated by higher qualities such as aesthetic appreciation, love, respect, justice, world peace. He is much more likely to be concerned about global issues, rather than narrowly defining himself within a neighborhood, country, family, or ethnic group. He is occupied with all of mankind, and not focused on his own personal selfish motives. This is a person who is concerned with ideas rather than acquisitions; with helping the world to be a better place, rather than with a career slot in a prestigious law firm. He knows that his own happiness comes from within, and therefore does not waste his life pursuing things which he has always possessed, such as happiness, love, success, and fulfillment. He brings these qulities *to* his life, rather than asking them *from* life.

No-limit people take a cooperative approach to life. They do not feel in competition with others, and seldom compare themselves to measure their own progress. They are inner-directed, and see themselves as unique in all the universe; therefore, they see the folly of comparison. They seek truth rather than being occupied with winning approval or being right. They are able to live in the present moment and therefore are not obsessed with what will happen in the future or with redoing what has already happened. They know that one can never be approved of by everyone, and because of their strong inner convictions, they are unconcerned with trying to impress others, or with chasing accumulations in the name of being on top. No-limit people avoid being judgmental and see the inherent right of everyone to choose his own path so long as it does not interfere with the rights of others to do the same.

Living life as a peak experience with a high sense of appreciation is the trademark of the no-limit person. Such people do not seek out highs with artificial substances; instead, they genuinely are high on everything life has to offer. They do not know about being bored or disinterested. They are the appreciators of life, and it is difficult to find things that do not fascinate them. They are unpretentious, able to take joy in virtually anything. From athletics to operas, from hiking to reading poetry—they love it all. They fulfill the ancient dictum of Terence: "I am a man: nothing human is alien to me."

No-limit people live a healthy lifestyle, stay in shape, and are not tempted to be unhealthy, not because they are superior to others, but because they have an inner light that tells them how bad it feels to be fat, or out of shape, or drugged, or consuming foods that are toxic to their bodies. They combine a healthy mind with a healthy body as a way of life, rather than to be "in" socially. They reject addictions to poisonous substances just as an animal would turn away from a glass of Scotch whiskey, because it would be unnaturally stupid in their minds to poison their own bodies.

These are people who have developed a strong sense of humor, who are fun to be around, who waste no time in blaming others for their shortcomings, and who are highly motivated from within. The absence of blame is manifested in their unwillingness to find fault with others for the things that are not going well in their own lives. Their inner-directedness helps them to put responsibility for their lives on themselves, to seek out their own answers and take responsibility as independently functioning people for their own objectives in life. They do not rate themselves as successes or failures; instead, they accept failure as a part of learning and are willing to try almost anything that interests them. They are not conformists and will easily get around petty rules and customs that seem to bother others so drastically. These are people who have their own creative imaginations, and they look within to determine how a task might be attempted. They are not obsessed with winning—be it the approval of others or defeating others—yet they are always labeled as winners by those who categorize people in these ways.

No-limit people are free from depression and unhappiness in their lives, because of their own unique attitudes about life. They look to the positive side while others see the negative. They think affirmatively about their own abilities to get the job done, instead of thinking in terms of impossibility. Their enthusiasm keeps them from going down emotionally, and their ability to count their blessings instead of their sorrows is a trademark of no-limit human beings. In short, we are talking about people in charge of their lives who have that wonderful capacity at almost all times to be able to enjoy life while others might choose madness.

This brief portrait is offered here in the first chapter to give you a glimpse of what I am talking about when I say that you can raise children to be no-limit people. Young, unspoiled children have virtually all of these qualities as a part of their natural inheritance. Too often they lose sight of these natural qualities as they pursue happiness and success. They need to learn to apply their own inner capacities for the same. It is only natural to be happy, healthy, inner-directed, sensible, fulfilled, successful, and on and on. These are normal human qualities which get pushed aside in the pursuit of external measures of success.

I am operating from the premise that we all have a no-limit person within us and that we have mixed it all up as we try to fit into our cultural slots in life. The great irony of life is that there is no way to happiness; happiness is the way. Similarly, there is no path to success; success is an inner attitude that we bring to our endeavors. If you chase love it will always elude you; you must let love chase you. If you demand security, you will always feel insecure. If you chase after money, you will never have enough. You must let money serve you.

All of these ironies are seldom internalized by neurotic people. Most people spend their lives chasing happiness, security, and love, never stopping to realize that they could have all they wanted of these qualities if they stopped chasing and brought these attitudes to their life's work and play. Children seem to know this. They have these wonderful qualities in vast amounts. We must allow children what is their birthright as no-limit children: to grow into no-limit adults. Yes, they need our guidance, and certainly they need us to help them avoid becoming self-destructive in their youthful enthusiasm for life, but we must always keep in mind that we have as much to learn from our children as we have to offer them. We do not want to ruin our parenting efforts by assuming that it is our role to mold these young people into what we think is right for them. They are virtually perfect in terms of no-limit skills and attitudes. What we must be careful, exceedingly careful, to ensure, is that we do not take these qualities out of them in our zeal to have them become ''successful'' by our external measures of that concept.

As we explore what we are doing as parents, keep in mind our objectives. We are attempting to refine and encourage our children in the direction of their own dreams and endeavors, so that they might become all that they are potentially capable of becoming, while simultaneously recognizing that they are already perfect creations. We must come to understand that they will not always agree with us, that they will want to march to their own drummer much more often than we like, that they will take a contrary view of what is right for them more often than they will agree with our beliefs about what is good for them, that they have their own inner lights that are obscured from our sight, that their vision will hardly ever match ours, that their calling will not always be our calling, and that their beliefs may vary widely from our own.

This wonderful quality of total no-limit happiness that we want to activate in our children will not come without a struggle. The struggle, however, need not be with the parents who are willing to enjoy all of their children's efforts to become what is right for them, as judged by them. Not us! *Them!* There is no greater challenge in the world than that of being a parent. We must leave the helm to our young people while we take satisfaction as temporary navigators. Our reality dictates that they will take over, and so will their children someday in turn. It is their destiny. If we can see the importance of raising them so that they will not have any limits, so that they will grow into highly functioning, self-fulfilled people, we might all be surprised to find that the problems which we have not been able to eradicate—such as poverty, hunger, war, crime, environmental pollution, and on and on—might better be handled by a generation of people who are functioning at a personally masterful level. Perhaps, just perhaps, if they are not obsessed with their own petty problems, and if they feel a sense of belonging and purpose, they will be even better equipped to take on the big problems. An ancient Chinese proverb goes like this:

> If you think one year ahead—sow a seed.
> If you think ten years ahead—plant a tree.
> If you think a hundred years ahead—educate the people.

Imagine a world full of educated parents who are raising their youngsters to become fully functioning no-limit people—a generation of emotionally stable, highly motivated people who no longer think in the destructive terms that have dominated our world up until now. John Ruskin wrote, "That country is the richest which nourishes the greatest number of noble and happy human beings." This is indeed a possibility: educating the people and creating whole nations where the majority of the population are noble and happy human beings. I can think of no greater legacy!

2

I Want My Children to Value Themselves

The no-limit person is self-fulfilling; has great enthusiasm for himself, with no regrets or reservations. No time or need to be conceited. Recognizes that love and respect come to the person who cultivates them; is genuinely loved and respected by all who can return his original openness to them; does not worry about others rejecting him.

The greatest evil that can befall man is that he should come to think ill of himself.

—GOETHE

Of all the judgments and beliefs that each one of us own, none is more important than the ones we have about ourselves. As a parent, our primary concern ought to focus on what our children think of themselves, rather than attempting to shape their attitudes toward other people, things, and events.

Our beliefs about ourselves are the single most telling factors in determining our success and happiness in life. While many may believe that talent, opportunity, money, IQ, loving families, or positive outlooks are the real barometers for determining one's success potential, it seems that these are all secondary to the possession of a healthy positive self-portrait. Your child's self-image is a direct result of the kind of reinforcements he or she receives from you on a daily basis. If you want to have a fairly accurate predictable indicator of what kind of adults your children will turn out to be, ask yourself, "What do they think of themselves?" Remember not to ask, "What do I think of them?" or "What do their friends, teachers, grandparents, or neighbors think of them?" Do they have the confidence that they can successfully complete any task before they attempt it? Do they feel good about the way they look? Do they feel intelligent? Do they think of themselves as worthy? These are the questions you must be concerned with, and if you feel that your children lack self-worth or feel unattractive, stupid, incapable, or unhappy with themselves, there are some very positive steps that you can take to change their self-pictures to reflect a more worthwhile and positive image.

As you think about the self-esteem of your children, keep in mind that the barriers we erect to our own growth and happiness almost always are internal barriers. The lack of love in a person's life is the internal fear that he or she does not deserve love. The absence of achievement is most often due to a genuine belief that one could never achieve at a high level. The absence of happiness stems from the internal sentence that "Happiness is not my destiny." Consequently, the job of motivating your children to have greater aspirations in life is essentially the task of working on their self-pictures in all areas of their young lives. Any place where you find negativity, pessimism, or indifference about their own dreams or abilities, you have an assignment for self-portrait improvement to work on. Once you see a child's self-image begin to improve, you will see significant gains in achievement areas, but even more important, you will see a child who is beginning to enjoy life more.

You will see happier faces, more excitement, and higher expectations for themselves. The only authentic barrier to a child's own greatness is his fear of his own greatness. Eliminating those fears is the avenue to take in working on the self-images of your children.

The importance of a positive self-image cannot be overstressed. It is not an accident that the subject of self-image is presented in the opening pages of this book. It is the single most significant attribute of a no-limit person. When a child grows up to love himself, to be self-confident, to have high self-esteem, and to respect himself, there are literally no obstacles to his total fulfillment as a human being. Once a strong self-portrait is in place, the opinions of others will never be able to immobilize your child. The young person who feels confident as he approaches a task will not be undone by failure, but instead will learn from it. The child who respects himself will respect others, since you give to others what you have inside to give away—and, conversely, you cannot give away what you do not have. Similarly, the young person who has learned to love himself will have plenty of love, instead of hate, to give away.

Self-Image

There is no such real-world attribute as a self-image. In fact we have many images about ourselves concerning virtually everything we think or do in our lives. We have our own opinions of ourselves regarding our musical abilities, athletic prowess, sexuality, cooking, mathematical skills, and everything we do as human beings. Children have multiple self-images as well, and these are constantly shifting between highly positive and fearfully negative. These images are not sterile, measurable facets of our personalities. On one day we may feel quite capable as a tennis player, and on the next we may feel like a novice. In the morning your child may feel like a macho man with the girls, and after lunch he may revert to being a shy introvert.

The most significant areas for you to concern yourself with in a child's overall self-portrait are spelled out below. Keep in mind as you read about these areas, and attempt to implement some of the suggestions for keeping these images high in your child's eyes, that these are not stable, specific, measurable attributes that lend themselves to precise calculations. All human beings are unique. They cannot be categorized into foolproof slots or reduced to computerized data. In addition to being unique, children are ever-changing entities. Just when you think you have one figured out, he or she will surprise you by being something quite the opposite of what you imagined. This is as it should be. We are talking about human beings here, not pieces of software. Children are dynamic, ever-changing, unique. We must never forget this as we try to help them to have positive expectations for themselves, and healthy self-images that will help them to become all that they want for themselves during their brief visit on this spinning globe. As we keep in mind a child's uniqueness, here are the general components of that self-portrait.

Self-Worth. This is a term which describes your child's own general personal view of himself as a human being. It begins with how the significant other people in his life view him. If you see and treat your child as worthy, important, and attractive, then your child will generally come to believe the same things about himself; thus the early seeds of self-worth are planted. Your child's self-worth becomes internalized as he tests himself in the world, and he adopts attitudes of worthiness or worthlessness as he treks through the maturation process, with an eye on your reactions.

While it may sound too simple for those of you who have become accustomed to complex psychological explanations, the fact is that *you are worthy because you say it is so.* Teach children to look within, and encourage them to see themselves as worthwhile, even when they fail. If they are always encouraged to see themselves as worthwhile, as having value, as being significant and important regardless of any particular performance, then they will have self-worth.

The word *self* in self-worth is crucial. While it is formed in infants and toddlers as a result of the way they are treated by significant others, it becomes incorporated as a kind of habitual self-picture very, very early. The child learns to view himself as others around him view him, and then, as he matures, he takes the controls for his self-worth into his own hands. We can assist our children in having positive self-views as worthy human beings. It is our responsibility to do all that we can to keep children from assessing themselves as worthless—*ever!* A child who comes to view himself as having no worth will live out these expectations in virtually everything he undertakes.

Studies of human beings who have spent their lives as criminals, chronic underachievers, delinquents, drug addicts, or simply maladjusted people have, without exception, stressed that they all seem to reflect an inner attitude of "I'm really not worthwhile, no one ever thought of me that way, and I just don't think of myself as very important." We all know that having self-worth is important, yet even as concerned, caring parents we often interact with our children in such a way as to promote a lowered self-worth picture. I will elaborate on many of the parental patterns that encourage low self-worth assessments in our children in the next section of this chapter.

Self-Confidence. While self-worth is, generally speaking, a yes or a no proposition, depending upon what a child decides to believe about himself as a total human being, self-confidence has many areas for consideration. You can be self-confident in one moment and shaky in the next. Your child can be bursting with self-confidence in the home, but become a nervous wreck as he prepares to give an oral book report in school. A child can possess great self-confidence around his mother, and tremble at the sight of his father. *Self-confidence is measured in behavioral terms, while self-worth is assessed in attitudinal ways.* Teaching your child new behaviors is the avenue for building and sustaining the self-confidence.

The components of self-confidence include: the willingness to become a risk taker, the ability to challenge oneself, the capacity for courage and assertiveness. All of these themes revolve around one key word: *action.* You build confidence by doing; not by worrying, thinking about it, talking about it, but by doing. You need not look for a complicated formula to determine if your children are lacking in self-confidence. Put as simply as possible, if your child is immobilized or otherwise unable to act the way he would prefer to act, then you have work to do in the self-confidence arena.

Self-confidence is not a term that describes a total human being. A child is *not* either self-confident or not. All of us are more confident in some areas than in others, and certainly our children are not exceptions. What we must keep in mind in helping children to gain self-confidence in all areas of their young lives is the importance of their becoming persons who challenge themselves, who are willing to take risks, and who have no immobilizing fear of failure. Too often, because of our own fear of failure, or our own unwillingness to take risks, we encourage children to be as they are rather than as they can be. This is a very important concept in helping to build self-confidence. If you treat your children as they are, then they will stay that way and consequently have very low levels of self-confidence. If you treat your children as if *they already are what they are capable of becoming,* then you will be doing them a large favor in this self-confidence endeavor. I once overheard a mother telling her young child at the swimming pool, "Don't you go near that water until you know how to swim." Over and over she admonished her child for getting too close to the water, saying, "You'll drown if you're not careful! How many times have I told you that you can't swim!" These are the reinforcers of lowered self-confidence, and they can be reversed and stated in a positive way just as easily. You can say to your child, "You'll have to get in the water if you want to swim," or "Swimming is really great fun. Of course you can swim—give it a try. Put your head in the water and see what happens—why not try it!" A caring parent does not want her child to develop fears of failure or an attitude that he or she cannot do things. While you obviously must watch a young child around a pool with extremely cautious eyes, you will discover that a child will learn to swim much faster if he is encouraged to get in the water and go for it than if he is admonished for his innate desire to take a risk. Remember, self-confidence is learned by *doing.* The more experience your child has in as many new areas as possible, the more he will gain a sense of confidence about himself.

Treating your child as if he already is what he can become is the greatest self-confidence booster there is. Instead of reminding a child of how little he has achieved, you look at him and talk as if he were a great achiever. "You are one sensational basketball player!" instead of "You never make your jump shot because you don't practice enough." "You are really a mathematical genius waiting to flower," rather than "You've never been good at math—your father isn't, either." The important self-confidence builder here is in talking to your children as if they were already achieving their potential, and conveying to them that you believe in them, as opposed to being a parent who points out flaws and constantly reminds children that they are limited in their abilities.

We are going to focus on assessing how children view themselves and on helping them to have positive self-portraits. Their self-worth image is largely an attitude about themselves. Their worth as human beings must be a given, not something that they have to prove. You are worthy because you exist, and anyone with life is a worthy creation. I will offer some specifics in this area in later sections of this chapter. Also, we want to focus on their self-confidence image, which is based upon their willingness to become doers, rather than critics. Action oriented people take risks and try new things even if they fail. They understand that no one ever learned to ride a bicycle by watching others, or became a dancer by simply watching movies of dancers. You gain confidence as a person by doing, and I am going to offer many suggestions for helping your child to see himself as a self-confident person. Your role as a parent is absolutely crucial.

Before we, as parents, can adopt new techniques for helping our children to think highly of themselves, we must look at the ways in which we inhibit their positive self-pictures. If we are inadvertently contributing to our children having low self-worth and an absence of self-confidence, then we must first work at eradicating these negative reinforcers. We want to be positive influences, yet we often fail to see the negative influences of our practices because they have become so natural that they are almost habitual.

How We Inadvertently Lower Self-Confidence and Self-Worth in Our Children

Here are some of the more common practices that contribute to lowered feelings of self-worth and a depletion of self-confidence in our children.

Telling our children that they are bad *boys or girls.* Children who believe they are bad when they have only *behaved* badly, begin to assess their worth as a person based upon these judgments. A child who spills milk on the table and is told, "You're a bad boy—that's the fourth time this week you've been so clumsy,'' will soon internalize the sentence: ''When I am clumsy, I am a bad person.'' The child's internal sense of self-worth is lowered, and with repeated messages that reflect his badness as a total person for mistakes or bad behavior, he soon thinks of himself as unworthy.

Telling our children that they are good *boys or girls only when they behave properly.* Here again, the difference between *behaving* properly or nicely and *being* a good person is not distinguished. It is just as detrimental to a child's sense of self-worth to believe that he is good only because he behaves well as it is to believe that he is bad because he sometimes behaves badly. With the constant reinforcement of statements like ''You're a good boy—Mommy loves you when you pick up your clothes,'' the child soon internalizes ''I am only good as a person when I please Mommy and Daddy.'' The child who always hears that he is good when he behaves in appropriate ways, will have a lowered sense of self-worth whenever he fails to behave in the ways that his parents have dictated. Every child in the world will spend a great deal of his childhood doing things that his parents do not think of as good.

Constantly catching children doing something wrong. This approach to parenting says, ''I will look for the things that my children are doing wrong and remind them about that behavior all the time.'' Children who are only talked to or noticed when they are doing something wrong soon come to doubt themselves and believe that they are disliked. In schools, administrators who are always catching children doing things wrong soon set up an atmosphere of distrust and an us-against-them approach to running the school. Children in schools of this type quickly come to perceive teachers and administrators as the enemy.

Using pet names for children which contribute to a lowered sense of self-regard. Calling a child *shorty, dumbo, turkey, klutz, nerd, spaz, fatso,* or any name which is not designed to promote positive self-regard is a way of creating a lowered sense of self-worth. These become daily reminders of how clumsy he or she is, or how incompetent, or unattractive, and while they may seem like meaningless little pet names to you, they actually are repetitive reinforcers to the child of apparent flaws. Negative connotations in nicknames or the ways in which you address your children become embedded in their self-picture. We can recall vividly how much we hated being reminded of any faults when we were children, and how those words stuck with us as we developed our own portraits of ourselves. Words are like little birds in the nest. Once you let them out, they can never be taken back. Negative words, phrases, and nicknames are lasting mementos that we seldom erase from our own self-portraits.

Viewing children as "apprentice people" who have not really arrived yet as total human beings. This attitude is characterized by treating children as if they are always *preparing* for life—telling them that someday they will know why they are expected to do what you are asking of them. "When you grow up, you'll understand why I'm always bugging you." "Someday you'll appreciate what I'm telling you." "You're too little to know why; just do it because I say so." This type of message conveys to a child that he isn't whole, that he is incomplete, and therefore he should view himself as only a partial person.

Treating children as part of one big whole unit, rather than as individuals. Constantly comparing a child to brothers and sisters, or to you when you were a child, or to other children in the neighborhood, gives him a feeling of not being special and unique. If a child is treated like a piece of a puzzle, rather than as a whole unique special person, he will soon begin to assess himself in this way. Lowered self-esteem comes from believing that I am not special and unique, and this kind of self-assessment comes from hearing sentences like "Who do you think you are, someone special?" "You're no different from everybody else around here!" "Why can't you be like your sister?" "Why, when I was a child, we always did what our parents said, or else!"

Refusing to give children responsibility. Doing and thinking for children will contribute to lowered self-worth and undermine their self-confidence. You will create opportunities for children to develop a lot of self-doubt by constantly sending messages showing that you do not think they can do things correctly, or that they should not try because you believe it is too difficult for them. Do not ignore the plea of the young child: "I can do it myself, Daddy." As self-doubt grows, the child begins to think of himself as unworthy of important tasks; consequently, the amount of confidence he internalizes is reduced. The more things you refuse to allow your child to attempt, the more blurs you are helping to ultimately place on his own self-picture as a worthwhile and confident human being.

Criticizing your children when they make mistakes. Criticism contributes to lowered self-assessments. The more criticism a child receives, the more likely he is to avoid trying the things which engendered that criticism. Such sentences as "You've never been very good at athletics," "That's the third time you've missed practice—I guess you'll never learn to be responsible," "You look fat in that dress," or "You're always mumbling" are the tools that children use to carve out a poor self-image. There are many ways to help motivate a child to more effective behavior, and criticism is perhaps the least useful and the most damaging technique available. The more you rely on external criticism, the greater the chance that your child will internalize these very same kinds of assessments and, before long, develop a self-picture that is based upon—you guessed it—being critical of himself.

Speaking for your child, instead of allowing him or her to respond in the age-typical ways that a child will use. Speaking for your children as if they are incapable of expressing themselves contributes to self-doubt and lowers self-confidence. It also teaches them to rely on others to do their talking for them. When you speak for them you send a silent message: "I can say it better and more accurately than you can; you're too young to really know how to express it, so doubt yourself and rely on me, your all-knowing, omnipotent parent."

Modeling to your children that you are not confident and worthy. Offering such a model provides them with a poor example for building self-esteem. The more you grumble around your children about your unfortunate lot in life, the better example you provide of a person with low self-esteem. Your children will incorporate the example that you provide for them. When you complain constantly around little people, you teach them to be self-complainers. If you demonstrate to your girls that you feel victimized as a woman and that you have no strong feelings of your own worthiness, you will teach them to feel like victimized girls with no self-worth of their own. As a father, you can teach your boys to be chauvinistic and inconsiderate of females by acting that way yourself in the home.

Talking about your children in front of them as if they weren't there. This behavior teaches them to regard themselves as unimportant people or, even worse, as simply part of the furniture. "I don't know what we're going to do with Brian—he seems to get worse every day." "Sally just doesn't listen in school, and she's really no different here at home." Meanwhile Brian and Sally are receiving messages from their parents, which they internalize as "Gee, they act like I'm not even here and I don't count, the way they talk about me to others." The less regard you have for your child as a feeling, significant total human being, the less regard he will have for himself.

Keeping your distance from your children, and refusing to touch, kiss, hold, wrestle, or play with them. By maintaining a physical distance from your children, you will teach them to doubt their own lovability. Children who are not fondled and physically loved begin to internalize the notion that they are not worth being held and loved. They begin to see themselves as unattractive, and ultimately they will doubt themselves as lovable, worthwhile humans. Children who are deprived of touching show severe signs of maladjustment, and the total lack of such loving contact can actually be fatal. Similarly, if you fail to tell your child "I love you," he will not have these important words turning over in his own mind to remind him that he is worth being loved. By shunning these three valuable words you encourage your child to wonder about his own worthiness as a loving, loved person.

These are some of the more common ways in which adults inadvertently contribute to lowered self-esteem. Before looking at some principles and techniques to use for the purpose of raising your child's self-esteem and self-confidence, it is extremely important for you to understand what kinds of payoffs you receive when you adopt some of the self-image destroying attitudes and behaviors mentioned above.

What Are Your Payoffs When You Contribute to a Lowered Self-Image in Your Child?

Everything you do has a payoff! Everything! While that payoff is not always to your best advantage, and often the rewards are neu-

rotic in nature, nevertheless there are always dividends that accrue to you for all of your behavior. If you as a parent are interested
in helping your children to raise their self-esteem and self-confidence, then you must look within yourself to find out exactly what
it is that you are getting out of any behavior which does not meet
your objectives for your children. If you understand your motives, you can then make new choices to avoid the unhealthy payoffs. The most common psychological payoffs to you as a parent,
for behaving in ways toward your children that contribute to a diminished self-image, are summarized in the following list.

□ An obedient, self-effacing child is easier to handle.

□ When you dominate your children by thinking and speaking
for them, it gives you a feeling of superiority. You have a
captive audience that must listen, and dominance over your
children allows you to have the power that is very likely lacking in other areas of your life.

□ You really don't have to take responsibility for your child's
growth and development as a healthy human being when you
can blame any and all failures on his "poor attitude and low
self-image." This is a convenient way to abdicate parental responsibility and give yourself a built-in excuse.

□ By constantly correcting, advising, and generally keeping
your child dependent, you can rule by fear and remind yourself how "right" you are. Being "right" is very important to
parents, and by maintaining a child in low self-confidence, you
have the opportunity to be right almost all the time. It is *his*
fault, *he* won't try anything, *he's* a scaredy-cat, *he* has no
confidence in himself—all are convenient postures to keep you,
as a parent, right.

□ You can avoid the risks that always go with establishing a
loving relationship, even with your own children. If touching,
holding, kissing, and being physically demonstrative are difficult for you because of your own self-doubts, then you can
use this excuse: "That's just the way I am; I can't help it."

□ It is easier to treat everyone in a family the same way. By
comparing your children with each other and encouraging them
to all act, think, and feel the same way, you avoid the conflicts that go with having individuals around. "Everyone gets

the same treatment" really means "I only have to deal with one personality, even though there are five people in this house."

The neurotic dividends that you receive for these attitudes toward your children revolve around the theme of avoidance: avoidance of risk, avoidance of responsibility, avoidance of change. When you stop avoiding these three essential ingredients of effective parenting, you will find yourself adopting new attitudes and behaviors toward your children. A healthy person is willing to take risks throughout life, both as a child and as a parent. Similarly, the no-limit person takes responsibility rather than blaming others, and this, too, is an essential component of being both a parent and a healthy child. Finally, the no-limit person understands that one cannot always take the easier route in dealing with people. As parents, we must often take the more difficult path rather than doing what is most convenient at the moment. So, too, children must learn to accept difficult challenges, rather than avoiding them.

In order to reduce our reliance on these unhealthy motives for keeping children in the lowered self-esteem range, we must adopt a new set of clear and meaningful principles for helping children to think of themselves as important, significant unique human beings. If we want high levels of self-confidence and self-esteem, we must always be aware of these basic principles and try each day to interact in ways consistent with them, by adopting new techniques and strategies for raising a child's self-image to the highest levels imaginable.

Basic Principles for Building Self-Esteem in Your Children

Below are seven principles that you can use as guideposts for raising your child's self-esteem. All of your interactions as a caring parent can be consistent with these principles. Specific examples of how to implement these principles will follow.

1. *You must model self-respect.* Just as you must provide an example of a person with a positive self-image, you must also show your child, through behavior, that you respect yourself and are entitled therefore to be treated respectfully. A child must believe down to his soul that you genuinely think of yourself as a respected human being. This means first of all carrying yourself in a way that gives you personal dignity, with all that this implies; it also means that you never tolerate disrespect from anyone in front of your child, and particularly when that disrespect comes from your child.

You are unique in all the world, a very special creation who is dignified, important, and a special human being. You want your child to feel this way about himself or herself as well—not in a conceited manner, but in a way that shows that disrespect is simply intolerable. Consequently, you must teach children that disrespect is not permitted in your everyday interactions with them. You must provide the example first by eliminating disrespectful self-behavior around your children. Crass language directed at yourself, by yourself, is eliminated, and you meet any disrespectful language directed at you with this sentence: "I have too much respect for myself to listen to such talk. I will not tolerate you talking to me in this manner, now or ever again. Do we understand each other?" No nonsense, no endless bickering; just a simple sentence declaring you as a respectable human being, and then removing yourself or your child for a cooling-off period. The basis for your refusal to hear such talk is that "I have too much respect for myself to listen to such talk!"

When children hear this often enough, they will begin to expect the same kind of treatment, and before long they will adopt the same behavior that they see modeled for them. The importance of this principle can be summed up in these words: *If you want your child to respect himself, give him an example of a person who does the same, and never, ever waiver from that position.* You do not have to demand that a child respect you; instead, you demonstrate that you think of yourself in this way and therefore his disrespectful behavior is simply not registering. Once you begin providing examples of a person who has high self-esteem and enormous self-respect, you will see a significant change in your children's self-pictures as well. When children see a shining example, it is easier for them to incorporate high self-esteem behaviors into their own lives.

2. *Treat each child as a unique individual.* Each of your children is a special person not like his brothers or sisters, or any other

person with whom you might compare him. Respecting a child's uniqueness means more than simply avoiding comparisons. It is a genuine acceptance of that person as a unique creation who has unlimited potential within him to become anything that he might choose for himself throughout his life. It means respecting him or her as total and complete *now,* and always being conscious of his unique attributes. A child who is treated as unique in all the world begins to see himself the same way. A child who is allowed to be different, to dance to his own special music, to be unlike everyone else without being criticized, to be in fact anything he chooses as long as he does not interfere with anyone else's right to uniqueness will have a great deal of self-confidence and high levels of self-esteem.

3. *A child is not his actions.* He is a person who acts. To promote high self-esteem you must be aware of the difference between these two conflicting notions. A child who fails is not a failure; he has simply acted in a way which has given him an opportunity to grow. A child who does poorly on a mathematics quiz is not a dunce; he is simply performing in mathematics at a given level at this particular time in his life. You can teach your child to grow from mistakes and to never fear failure as long as he understands that his worth does not come from how well he performs a given task on a particular day. *You are worthy because you say it is so, because you exist.* No more, no less. Self-worth cannot be validated on the basis of performance; it must be a given and something that you convey every day. Always remind children, especially after they fail at something, that they are valuable regardless of their performance. If you want to hit home runs you must be willing to strike out. When you do strike out, as we all do on a regular basis, you are not a worthless person any more than you are a worthy person because you have hit a home run. "I am a person who acts; I am not my actions" is what you must always reinforce with children if you want them to have positive self-assessments.

4. *Provide opportunities to be responsible and make decisions.* Children with high self-esteem are those who are given the opportunity to be decision-makers right from the very beginning of their lives. Children need to take on responsibilities, rather than have their parents do things for them. They learn confidence by

doing, not by watching someone else do it for them. They need to feel important, to take risks, to try new adventures, and to know that you trust them, not so much to do something without error as to simply go out and give it an effort. Children who learn early to be decision-makers—to pick out their own clothes, to decide what to eat, to play with whomever they choose, to be responsible without endangering themselves—learn very early to like themselves and feel positive about who they are. They begin very early to trust themselves with the daily age-typical tasks that make them feel proud and worthwhile.

5. *Teach enjoyment of life each day.* Children who live in a positive environment learn to be positive about themselves. To raise self-esteem it is essential to provide a positive approach to life as a way of thinking for your children. Give them regular examples of "counting your blessings" reactions when they feel down. Show them with your own example that you are grateful for being alive, that this is a wonderful place to live, and that this is the greatest time in the history of mankind to be alive. There is something positive to be realized in all of life's situations. Having to wash the dishes is a time to be grateful for having food to eat and dishes to wash. Fixing a flat tire is a time to appreciate having a car when you consider all of the people in the world who do not have cars. Even more basic is the satisfaction of doing any job well, no matter how simple or repetitive it may be. A disappointment or a setback gives us new strengths and helps us to develop tools for handling problems. This kind of thinking about and reacting to everything will help children to adopt similar attitudes toward themselves.

6. *Provide praise rather than criticism.* Children who are criticized learn to do the same thing to themselves, and ultimately become persons with low self-regard. Praise is a wonderful tool in the entire process of child rearing. Remember, nobody (including yourself) enjoys being told what to do or being criticized. Parents often believe that they are providing help to their children when they constantly correct and criticize them, assuming that they will grow from these remarks. But ask yourself: Do you like being corrected? Do you grow when you are constantly criticized? In truth, we tend to stay the same when we are criticized; we want to defend what we have done, and our innate stubbornness refuses to permit us to accept the criticism we are receiving. Behind virtually all criticism is the sentence "If only you were more like me, and living life as I see it, you would be a lot better off." But no one, even your child is exactly like you. Praise them for attempting a task, even if it was unsuccessful, and for taking risks. Create an environment in which your children know that you are with them in their efforts, rather than looking to criticize them, and you will have taken a step in building a positive self-image.

7. *We become what we think about: Our thinking determines our self-image, which in turn determines our feelings and our behavior.* Philosophers from ancient times until today have reminded us of this truth, and it impacts profoundly on a child's self-picture. Marcus Aurelius, the Roman emperor, said it this way: "A person's life is what his thoughts make of it." Ralph Waldo Emerson, an American philosopher of the nineteenth century, said, "A person is what he or she *thinks* about all day long." Keep in mind that your children from the earliest moments of existence have thoughts that are shaped by your input.

What your children think about can be shaped in a positive way by you, their most significant person. Do they believe in themselves? Do they see people every day who believe in themselves? Do they approach a task believing that they can do it, or do they feel that they will fail before beginning? Do your children think in positive goals? Do they have exciting pictures in their heads of what can be accomplished in life? Their thinking will determine what their life will be. If that thinking is negative and pessimistic, the self-image will reflect that negativism. Think about this as you read on for some specific strategies to use in your daily life for helping to raise your children's self-esteem and self-confidence. They will become what they think about, and you can be a positive force for thinking or a negative force. Whatever they think about themselves will become a positive predictor of their success in life. It is crucial to look for behaviors and attitudes that will help them to think about themselves in the most positive and self-fulfilling ways imaginable.

Strategies for Raising a Child's Self-Portrait

Strategies for raising a child's self-portrait include new attitudes, dialogues, and behaviors on your part as well as your child's. Be-

low are some suggestions, for use with children of all ages, that
will have a positive effect on encouraging children to view themselves in more exalted ways.

*Encourage children to be risk-takers rather than always tak-
ing the safe road.* Children who avoid risks will always have a
lowered sense of self-esteem because they will never feel any genuine sense of accomplishment. While it may not seem that risk-
taking is related to self-esteem, remember that attitudes like "I'm
lousy at everything" or "I can't do that—I might look stupid if I
fail" come from being afraid to try new things and being afraid to
fail. Give your children exercises in success if you want them to
have self-confidence. Encourage them to do things they have never
done before, and give them plenty of praise for attempting new
projects. Remind them frequently that failure is normal and that
failing at a task is not equivalent to failure as a person. Encourage
your child to swim two laps of the pool underwater and praise his
effort, rather than telling him that it is too dangerous. Avoid saying, "Watch out—you might not make it." Instead, say, "Go
ahead—try it." Remember that all of their "Watch me, Mommy
and Daddy!" behavior, and the subsequent praise they are looking for, will help them to internalize that they are courageous and
worthy, and ultimately they will not require anyone to watch them
in order to feel positive about themselves. They need those reas-
surances and that approval from you when they are young, in order to build a self-image that does not require constant approval
as adults. Encourage their efforts to expand themselves and try
new things, and be sure to take a few seconds to watch and tell
them how fantastic they are in your eyes. It is great for their self-
image—you can count on it.

Discourage children from any and all self–put-downs. Whenever you hear them saying, "I can't do anything," "I'm lousy at
spelling," "I'm just a klutz," "I'm ugly," "I'm too skinny," "I
can't ride a two-wheeler," you are being given a clue to help raise
their self-esteem. While it is not helpful to give a long lecture at
such moments (or any moments, for that matter), you must always respond with positive reinforcement at these moments of self-
repudiation. "You can do anything you put your mind to." "You
can figure out that math if you work on it." "You'll do well on
the test if you get some help with your spelling—come on, let's

take a look at it." "You are not a klutz—I've seen you fix lots of things around here." "You are gorgeous and just right." "Why not try it rather than think you can't do it." Use simple, direct positive self-esteem statements that counteract the negative statements. After children have heard these things often enough, they will incorporate more positive statements. Whenever I hear someone in my family say, "I can't" do something, I will also overhear another family member remind him or her that "Success comes in cans, not in cannots." A simple little slogan, but a very effective one to get a child to try something, rather than resorting to lowered expectations of his own abilities.

Make an effort to reduce the emphasis on external measures of success. The relentless pursuit of grades, rewards, money, merit badges, being number one, and material objects is a sure way to lower a child's self-esteem. Remember, self-esteem comes from the self, not from acquisitions and approval. A child who grows up believing that he is worthwhile only if he gets good grades, will always feel inferior when an average grade appears on his report card. And every child will perform at an average or below pace at some times in his life. You cannot always be number one, or always win a contest, or always get the merit badge, or always make the honor roll, but you can always think of yourself as an important, worthwhile person. A child's self-esteem must come from his own self-evaluation. He must feel like an important person even if his grades are lower than he expected or he didn't get a medal in a race. You can reinforce inner rather than outer measures of success in children throughout their lives by reducing the high premium you have placed on achievement and competition. Asking a child, "Are you satisfied with yourself?" rather than "What did you get on your report card?" Asking, "Do you think you are improving in spelling?" rather than "Did you win the spelling bee?" Ask, "Did you feel excited about playing in the game and improving your skills?" rather than "Did you win?"

Children who understand that they will still have self-esteem without the external rewards are on their way to their own measures of success, while children who relentlessly pursue the external measures of success are on the way to tranquilizers, ulcers, and lowered self-esteem. The simple truth is that no one is always number one in comparison with others, but anyone can always be number one in his own eyes, when the yardstick for that measure is within. Going out and running a 10-kilometer race and finishing it can be an indication of number-one status for the inner-directed person, while the outer-directed person must win every race in order to feel positive self-esteem. And in the history of man, no one has ever won every race.

Work at reducing complaining and whining behavior in a child. A complaining child is really saying to you, "I don't like who and where I am at this moment." Positive self-esteem means a positive approach to all of life, even when things are not going the way you would like them to go. A person with high self-esteem thinks too much of himself to go around complaining about anything in life. Such people are doers rather than critics, and they know how to accept things that are not going their way. When children persistently complain, and you let them get away with it, you are literally reinforcing lowered self-respect. You want children to grow into fully-functioning persons with high self-regard, and this must be accompanied by an absence of complaining and faultfinding in their young lives. Practice greeting any complaints or whining with new statements and new behaviors. If you hear such typical whines as "I hate going to Grandma's," "Mommy, Billy made a face at me," "Are we having hamburger *again?*" or "I hate doing the dishes," you can respond with new tactics that will help your children to become more positive about life as well as about themselves. "We're going to have a good time at Grandma's—let's plan a game to play there." "Why should you pay attention to Billy's face?" "Hamburger is terrific, but tonight we are calling it minced steak a la maison." "Doing dishes is your responsibility. All of us have things to do that we'd rather not, but you can make it fun." Also, practice ignoring whining and complaining. If children do it in front of you regularly, it is because they want you to react and give them some attention for their annoying behavior.

Teach children that you will not reward annoying behavior with attention. Remember, you want children to have high self-regard, and a whiner is showing contempt for himself and his world by disapproving of everything. By being positive, by not reinforcing whining, and by ignoring complaints when they are persistent, you will help children to deal effectively with their world, rather than complaining about it. And that is the measure of a child who has high positive self-esteem: the ability to deal effectively with his world rather than simply complaining about it.

Always focus your criticism on a child's behavior instead of his value as a human being. The simple statement "You are a bad boy!" is an attack on a child's worth. The effective statement "You have behaved badly" puts the focus on behavior which can be adjusted. Try to show your disapproval with children's behavior when they do things for which they need to be corrected. "You're stupid," "You're lazy," "You're no damn good," "You're clumsy," "You're irritating," are statements designed to lower a child's self-esteem. Simple substitutes which place the emphasis on the ineffective behavior would be "You've behaved in a stupid way," "You're acting lazy today," "This kind of behavior will not be tolerated," "You were looking at the ceiling when you were running and that's why you fell," "The way you are cracking your gum is very irritating." Children should never believe that they are inherently bad.

Encourage children to be excited about everything in life and to always avoid trapping themselves with the "I'm bored" routine. Children who are *genuinely* bored have low self-esteem. I emphasize *genuinely* here because most statements of "I'm bored" really mean "I want *you* to do something with me." When this ruse is used, the child has learned that he cannot be creative enough to find out how to use his time in an exciting way, and so the responsibility is now on Mommy or Daddy. At these moments, it is up to you to decide if you want to take on that role. There is nothing wrong with doing things together and putting some excitement in both your lives. However, a genuinely bored child is showing a kind of contempt for himself and his surroundings. Always remind children (and yourself) that boredom is a *choice*. There are dozens of things to do in any given moment: reading, running, exploring, playing, thinking, meditating, fishing, hiking, snowball making, and on and on.

Any time children feel bored and use this as a means to attempt making others feel guilty, you will lower their self-esteem by taking over for them. This is the time to teach them. I used to say to my daughter when she would tell me that she was bored, "I will give you a list of twenty things you could do in this moment, rather than choose to be bored. I do not know how to be bored; I have so much to learn and see in life that I do not know what you mean by bored." Statements of this kind, spoken with good-natured humor, always reinforce that *you*, little person, must take responsibility for not being bored. Your dad does not even know how to be bored, and he is not biting your hook by feeling guilty for not entertaining you sufficiently. A child who learns how to do zillions of things at any moment—who can read a book, or go for a walk, or just think, or invent a new kind of ice cream, or experiment with an old transistor radio—learns how to be alone. And make no mistake about this: A bored child is one who does not enjoy being alone, and that is because *he does not enjoy the person he is alone with*. This is a terse but accurate statement of low self-esteem. If you love yourself, you have no problem in being alone with yourself. Having time to themselves to be creative is something you can encourage in children, rather than taking it away by thinking up entertaining things for them to do, or by turning on the television to be babysitter, or—even worse—using up your energy playing *Chutes and Ladders* because you feel too guilty to teach your children not to choose boredom. Children with high self-esteem can do many things, and they do not have to rely on someone else to do things for them.

Encourage children to choose independence rather than dependence. A dependent child who is discouraged from becoming independent by a clutching parent, will develop low self-esteem habits. Once again, the source of a child's self-worth becomes located in the person upon whom he is dependent; thus he is unable to feel competent and capable on his own. While infants are naturally dependent and need as much nurturing as can be mustered in order to internalize feelings of confidence, as they begin to explore their world they must be encouraged to try things on their own: to stumble now and then, to reach beyond their grasp, to feel the excitement of holding a rattle alone, to know the joy of feeding themselves. Every child in the world has said, "I'll do it myself." Children want to feel independent in order to have a strong sense of self-esteem, and you can encourage them to be this way by reducing any ownership claims you make on your child and by encouraging them to think independently. "What do *you* think?" "Why not go to a synagogue even though we are a Catholic family? Check it out for yourself." "Who would *you* vote for in the election?" "You can try asparagus, even if Mommy dislikes it." "You do the problems first; *then* I'll check them." Independence breeds self-esteem, while dependence encourages lowered self-regard.

Teach children to be nonjudgmental. Children who learn to hate must store that hate within themselves in order to call upon it when someone they have been taught to hate appears. Obviously, children who store hate inside must have hatred for themselves, since they are the container for that contempt. A person who criticizes others, who harbors prejudices and hatred, must feel very insecure about himself to have to resort to such tactics to feel better about himself. The process of being judgmental and prejudiced comes from a need to make others look small in order to feel positive about oneself. This is the tactic of someone who has little self-regard. When you genuinely like yourself, you are never threatened by anyone who is different from you; in fact, you welcome such a person into your life.

Teach your children to be receptive to every person and every idea. Correct them when they "slip" and refer to old people in a derogatory way. "I wonder why you need to put down older people to make yourself feel important. They have a right to be who they are, just as you have a right to be who you are." No lecture, no punishment, no criticism—just a simple statement of integrity that will encourage them to think about their own prejudgments. Similarly, "Do you really think all Russians are bad just because of what you see and hear on television? Why not learn to explore new ideas and new people, rather than simply hating them?"

When you see children beginning to form opinions about everyone and everything without the benefit of any knowledge or study, encourage them to become more open and inquisitive. Remember that to simply have an *opinion* about a profound subject such as poverty, hunger, nuclear war, prostitution, religious wars, or anything else, is really quite trivial. But, to have a *commitment* to ending these problems is a profound statement about yourself. Teach children to make commitments rather than to simply have opinions. And also, teach them the shallowness of having opinions based on prejudices and a noninquiring mind.

Encourage children to be honest with themselves—in fact, to be brutally honest. Children lower their opinion of themselves every time they deceive themselves. The self-deceptive child invents a whole world in order to fool others, and consequently makes the opinions of others the reason for his invented self. Encourage honesty with statements such as "I don't mind if you didn't win your soccer game because the other team was better today. We all have to lose sometimes. Even if the officials were bad, you don't have to blame them for the loss." Or "You got a D in spelling because you haven't mastered spelling yet, not because the teacher is bad. I really think you'll need to spend more time on spelling and less time on blaming." Or "You are terrific even if you are late for school, but it is still your responsibility to get there on time, and it is not the fault of the alarm clock."

A child who learns to be honest with himself will have self-respect, and this can be taught if *you* place a premium on honesty at all times. Do not talk about cheating the government on taxes and then reprimand a child for stealing. Do not lie and then be stunned when your child does the same. Create an environment where it is all right to tell the truth, and where a child will not be punished for being honest. Lying is a reflection of low self-regard, and you cannot create a truthful environment in your home by practicing it. The more your child learns that he does not have to distort his world to gain acceptance in your eyes, the more you will be helping him to get along in the world, and in his own inner world as well.

Be aware of the importance of appearance to young people. Work constructively *together* at a self-improvement program for children that will aid them in becoming as attractive and healthy as is possible. Run a mile a day *with* children to get them started on an exercise program. Refuse to buy junk food and sugar products if children have a weight or complexion problem. Better yet, refuse to buy them at all, and help your children to avoid developing such problems. Show them by your example and behavior that you want them to think of themselves as attractive and healthy. Once a child begins any kind of exercise or weight-reduction program you will notice an improvement in his or her self-image. The act of doing something constructive, regardless of how inconsequential it may seem, is a sure-fire way to raise self-esteem. Your participation in this kind of activity will guarantee that children will stick with it. Simple, day-to-day goals for self-improvement are great inner morale boosters—and, after all, self-esteem is really nothing more than high inner morale.

Encourage children to think in healthy ways rather than in sick ways. Reinforce their abilities to cure their own colds, to get rid of their own aches and pains, to think positively about their own bodies, and to make being healthy a lifelong commitment. When children complain about being sick, do not reinforce their illness. A sickly-thinking child is a child who has no faith in his own ability to be healthy. Eliminate such statements as "You'll catch a cold if you don't dress warmly," "Here, take this medicine—you know how allergic you are," "Don't you feel well today, dear?" "Mommy will kiss your boo-boo and make it better." Instead, try to encourage children to think about their capacity to be well, and do not reward them with attention for being sick. "I bet you'll never catch a cold—you're so strong and healthy." "Let's wait for symptoms before taking a pill and try not thinking sick today." The child who always thinks he is sick has learned that the healing powers of the world are in pills, Mommy's kisses, pity, and doctors' advice. But the truth is that the body is the hero, and that only your body can cure disease. By thinking sick you discourage self-healing. By thinking well, and reinforcing wellness attitudes, you will be helping children to feel better about themselves and to avoid a lot of unnecessary illness.

Catch children doing something right, and remind them on a regular basis of how terrific they are. Eliminate trapping them by asking leading questions which encourage them to lie, especially when you know something they do not know you know. A mother of my acquaintance inadvertently saw her daughter taking a cab to school one morning after the mother had specifically told her to avoid wasting her money this way. All day she planned how to "trap" her, and when the teenager arrived home from school, the mother asked, "So how did you get to school this morning?" Immediately the girl was placed in a position of either lying or being admonished. Instead, the mother might have tried, "I saw you get into a taxi this morning, after we both agreed that this was a wasteful use of money, especially since we are all short of cash this month. Was there some particular reason you had to break our agreement?" This kind of an exchange encourages honesty, and allows the child to state her case without being forced to lie or feel terrible. After this kind of an exchange look for your daughter to be doing something right. "Mary, you're terrific—I'm really happy that you're cleaning up the kitchen. Thanks so much for helping out." The more you spend your energy catching them being good, the more good you will promote between you and your children, and the more positive a sense of self-worth you give them. Help them to change self-defeating behaviors by being honest with them and by giving them an opportunity to be honest easily, and then catch them doing things right. They will soon develop an "I'm all right" image, which is what you really want for your children.

Treat children as though they have arrived as total, complete human beings, rather than as though they are on their way to something or someplace in the future. When you talk with them, eliminate sentences which show you view them as apprentice people. Two-year-olds talk like two-year-olds; do not correct them in anticipation of what they will say when they are adults. Enjoy their two-year-oldness. If they wet the bed at three, this is not a reflection of a serious social problem that will afflict them when they live in a dormitory in college. It is age-typical behavior, and should be viewed as such. Four-year-olds like to tease and be silly. Eight-year-olds like to get dirty or play with Cabbage Patch dolls, and eleven-year-olds enjoy punching each other. These are whole behaviors, to be enjoyed for what they are, and ought not to be seen as stepping-stones to mature adult behavior. You will do children and yourself a large favor if you enjoy some of their age-typical behaviors with them. Play dodge ball in the yard, tackle each other, share treats from the ice cream vendor. These kinds of activities are the normal, fun, natural things that young people do, and ought to be seen in just those terms. Do not concern yourself that they will become fighters because they like to punch and fool around; instead, enjoy them for the period of their development which they are experiencing at this moment. Treat children as complete, fully-arrived human beings who have as much to teach you as you have to teach them. The less criticism they receive for being children, the more they will naturally enjoy themselves and see themselves as worthy and significant persons. A healthy self-image is flowering in children who accept themselves for what they are now, and who have significant others who do the same, rather than worry about what the children will or won't turn into at some future time.

Give children an opportunity to be unique and special persons. If athletics is preferred over music and you thought your child would be a musician, do not push; allow him to have his own interests. If she shows signs of being an actress and you had hopes of her going to law school, back off. Allow your children to be the unique people they are, rather than giving them your expectations to meet or comparing them with others in the family. Acceptance by you as a parent for what they are and what they enjoy in life is a big factor in building a healthy self-image. Parents who push children into thinking and believing as the parents do, and pursuing the goals that the parents have preset for them, are encouraging the children to doubt their own choices and inner signals. Self-doubt creates a lack of self-confidence. The healthiest thing you can do for children is to give them some guidelines on their choices, but always convey that you personally will not be upset or in any way immobilized by the choices that they make.

Rollo May, the great expert on human behavior, said this about the importance of making your own choices in life: "The opposite of courage in our society is not cowardice, it is conformity." You do not want your children to conform because it pleases you. You want them to think for themselves and to attempt their own personal challenges with your blessings. This means suspending any notions that they have to grow up to please you. They must look within, have confidence in that person they are consulting inside, and know that you will not judge them harshly or in any way for following their own inner lights. Give them the right to be who they are and they will have confidence galore in themselves. Otherwise they will be filled with guilt and self-doubt for having disappointed you.

Hold them, touch them, kiss them, be physical with them. They will learn to love themselves if they feel loved by you, and they cannot get that feeling of being attractive unless they actually experience it with you, the most important person in their young lives. A woman once told me that it just wasn't natural for her to be kissy and touchy with her children, and she asked me what to do. She was shocked at my answer. "Fake it!" I told her. "Touch them anyway. Even if it is unnatural for you now, you will grow to love it yourself." Being touched and held by a parent is crucial in the development of a young child's self-image. They need to feel loved, really loved a lot, in their young lives. They need to feel beautiful, important, attractive, and wanted. If you have trouble with this, then do it anyway and remind yourself that it is good for both of you. The more you do it, the more natural it will become, and before long, you will find yourself doing it automatically. In a letter written by author George Eliot (Marian Evans Cross), in 1875, she told her friend, Mrs. Burne-Jones:

> I like not only to be loved, but also to be told that I am loved. I am not sure that you are the same kind. But the realm of silence is large enough beyond the grave. This is the world of light and speech, and I shall take leave to tell you that you are very dear.

I say tell them that you love them every day. And even more important, show them that they are lovable by grabbing them, hugging them, kissing them, and demonstrating that they are really terrific. The more you do it, the more you are sending them wonderfully important messages about their own value, and soon they will love themselves as you love them, and that is our goal after all.

If you want them to feel attractive, beautiful, competent, and healthy, then show them a person who lives that way. Children are proud of having attractive parents. They love you to feel beautiful, and it gives them an image that they can adopt for themselves. Do not just talk about being healthy. Give them an example of a healthy, cheerful, exercising human being of normal-weight, and it will be natural for them to see themselves in the same way. If you are fat, smoke, drink, and generally allow yourself to be run-down, you are inadvertently contributing to your children's diminished self-concepts. They want to love themselves as healthy human beings, and they need a model on which to base this love. And guess what? You are that model. Do you like what you are teaching your children by your own looks, healthy habits, and exercise regimen? If not, go to work on yourself and you will be helping them and yourself in the process.

Listen carefully to your children. Be attentive and honest with them at all times, for attention and integrity are the cornerstones of the honest and respectful attitudes you want them to have about themselves. Show them that you are genuinely interested in them, even if you only give them a few moments a day. Become a learner in their lives. Ask about their school, their friends, their activities each day. For the very young ones, listen as they reveal their fantasies with their dolls or playthings. Show them that you care enough to hear their stories, and they will think they are significant people just because you listen to them each day.

Be involved in their age-related activities. Spend a few moments throwing a ball, catching, dribbling, jumping, batting, learning the alphabet, and so on. Avoid team sports until their skills are developed, and do not allow someone else to convince them that winning is everything. Spend time with teenagers, showing interest in their activities and attending their functions. Convey to children that you enjoy watching them in their activities—not as a snoop, but just because you get excited about their interests. When they see you caring, they feel more important, and that is what a healthy self-image is based upon.

Encourage them to have their friends "hang out" at your home. Show them that their friends are welcome and that you see them as important. Children who know that their friends are welcome in their home receive a message from their parents which says, "I know that you have good judgment in making friends, and if you like them, that is good enough for me. I trust you and welcome your friends here." This is a wonderfully powerful signal for letting children know that you believe in them. And if you believe in them, they will believe in themselves.

Read aloud with them at all ages. Give them the precious currency of your life, your time. Share your favorite stories with them, tell them about what happened to you when you were a child, tell them how wonderful they were as babies. All attention of this kind is a self-image booster. They know that you care, and they learn to care, for you and for themselves.

Be supportive of their efforts to be independent, rather than viewing their independence as a threat to your superiority. Encourage them to take jobs after school, to earn an allowance, to do things for themselves, to choose their own meals in a restaurant, to decorate their own rooms, or to do anything else that gives them a sense of belonging and independence as a person. The more independent they feel as they go through their young lives, the more confidence they will have in themselves. They should not have to ask permission for every little undertaking, or find out if Mommy would approve or not before doing everything. They must learn to budget their money, select well-made clothes, cook and clean, take care of their own belongings, schedule their time for work and leisure, be courteous with thank-you notes and gifts to others, eat a balanced diet, get sufficient sleep, and so on.

Help your children to develop positive self-pictures in their heads. Positive imagery is a powerful force in the building and maintenance of a healthy self-concept. Children who learn to picture themselves as successful, to have constructive images of themselves overcoming difficulties, are far more likely to believe in their abilities than those who cannot imagine themselves as successful. What kinds of pictures do your children have in their heads about themselves?

Children who are unable to imagine themselves doing things like getting up in front of the class and giving an excellent book report, or passing a test, or cooking a meal, or going on a date, will not persevere to accomplish these goals. Assist children to create positive images of success about themselves in any undertaking in their young lives. Just the correct picture in the mind will create confidence for a child, and soon, positive imagery will become a habit, replacing the negative imagery. These pictures can be created by you working with your children and deliberately helping them to imagine themselves in a successful way in any undertaking. This is a tremendously useful strategy in helping children to gain self-assurance. It is also a strategy that you can use, and model for your children in your own life. A picture in your mind is worth a thousand hours of practices. Help children to evoke effective internal pictures, and not only will you be helping them to achieve success, but you will be aiding them in developing a stronger sense of self-assurance as well. The mind is a powerful tool, and it can picture anything you choose. When children talk in negative "I can't do it" terms, think first of a positive picture, and then ask them to practice that picture over and over again. If their minds can conceive it, they can make it a reality, and the picture in their minds will stay there forever. *The subconscious cannot distinguish between a picture and reality.* Once the picture is there it will stay there as if it were reality, and before very long, that success picture, that image of being capable, will become a reality.

Teach children to avoid self-destructive/self-talk. Whenever you hear them verbally abusing themselves, help them to correct that. The ways in which a child talks to himself reflect his self-concept. Children who constantly complain, telling themselves that they are worthless and that they cannot do certain things, are in fact creating a self-fulfilling prophecy. By correcting self-talk to make it more positive, you will be teaching new self-image habits to children. If they instantly say something negative, such as "We're all going to be cramped into the car if everybody goes to the restaurant, and it won't be fun," gently remind them that having a lot of people along can be more fun. "Think about the good side, how much fun we will all have, and remember that we all get to be even closer to the people that we like when there are more of us." Not a lecture, just a little self-talk exercise in being positive. I constantly remind my children about not saying things that are predictions of a negative outcome, because that will in fact make it come true. The way that we talk to ourselves is nothing more than a habit, and negative self-talk is just a habit that has been reinforced. Positive self-talk can become a habit if you assist your children in this endeavor, by first modeling it yourself and then reminding them to look out for thoughts that will bring about something they do not want in the first place. A child who has positive self-talk is saying something about how he views himself. Here is an example of a brief dialogue which changes the focus from negative to positive self-talk:

Mother: We're all going to the beach for a picnic.
Sally: The last time we went I was miserable. We got sand in everything, and there was no place to get a drink.
Mother: I had a great time. This time we'll take some drinks with us and all have a lot of fun.
Sally: I know I'll have to watch the baby again. I won't have any fun at all.
Mother: We'll all watch the baby. She has such fun playing in the sand, I'm sure you'll have a good time if you give it a try. Try thinking about the fun part.

While Sally may or may not cease her verbal complaining, she will soon get the message that Mother is expecting to have a great time and that she is thinking positively about the afternoon at the beach. Sally's negative thinking has always produced some attention from Momma in the past, usually something that will keep the focus on Sally at the expense of everyone having to listen to her negative predictions and angry outbursts. Positive self-talk will become a habit with Sally if her mother is persistent and refuses to be baited by Sally's attempts to get attention by sabotaging everyone else's good time.

It is impossible to spoil a child under the age of eighteen months with too much love and attention. You cannot give them too much love as infants. The more you hold them, pick them up when they cry, coo with them, and meet all their needs, the more you are helping them to feel secure and loved from the first moments of life. Do not be afraid that you will spoil them by picking them up too often when they cry out as infants. They need to feel secure and safe; it will aid them in developing a strong sense of their own worth later on in their lives. Pick them up often, kiss them all the time, hold them, make them feel comfortable, change their diapers often, keep them content and happy as infants. You will see a positive payoff for this kind of loving attention when they are young. The self-image is formed by the love that the parents provide for the infant. In addition to providing as much physical contact as possible—holding them, rocking them, sitting with them, and talking gently to them—try to perform these seemingly trivial actions, which are crucial in the development of a secure baby.

□ Respond instantly to infants' distress calls. They have no alternative to crying to let you know they are hurting inside, and there is no one else to give them comfort if you refuse. Research shows that infants with low distress anxiety are much more secure with themselves as they mature.

□ Remember that people are more important than things. Remove things that might be destroyed and make your home a place that a child can enjoy in safety.

□ Provide night-lights for tots. They will not become dependent on them for a lifetime; they will simply feel safer and more secure when they wake up in the middle of the night if they can see something familiar. They will learn soon enough about darkness as they develop the mental capacity to comprehend what light and dark really are.

□ Insist on car seats and seat belts at all times. No excuses. This is a signal to your children that you care about them, and they will learn to care about themselves as a result.

□ Avoid junk food, excess sugar, and too much salt in your children's meals. Convey to them from the beginning that you love them enough to want them to develop lifetime habits of being healthy. If you do it early, they will do it for a lifetime because you have shown them with your behavior that you care. When you care for them, they care for themselves, and that is what a healthy self-concept is all about.

A child's self-image is the most important factor in his or her happiness and fulfillment. Children who believe that the world is a good and miraculous place, and that they are special and loved, have a tremendous advantage over children who are doubting and negative. The garden of being a no-limit person blooms from the early seeds that you plant in a child's mind about who he is and what he can become. When you send highly charged positive signals to children, they begin to have an expectation of happiness and success, they become eager to meet new people rather than being judgmental of or intimidated by others, they enjoy challenges, and—most important—they are loving, open, and generous toward others. By way of contrast, children with low self-value are constantly seeking approval and are full of self-doubt and fear of others. They feel insecure in the world because they view it as a tricky place. They are often dependent and prejudiced, unable to give love away because they have none within themselves to give.

Your child's self-image ought to be of great concern to you, and it is something that you have a great deal of input in creating. The Japanese culture indulges its children because they are expected to succeed in school and work and then support and indulge their aging parents. The Japanese have been immensely successful in this regard. They work at developing a child's self-perceptions in such a way that the child comes to expect to be happy and successful. This is something that all of us as parents can reflect upon. The child who sees himself as a successful, attractive person, and who has this image reinforced through his young life, will not disappoint himself. We know that his view of himself is the key to his realizing his own potential. Henry Ford summed it up this way: "Whether you think you will succeed or not, you are right!" The answer is what you think about yourself, and this is what we must convey to our children.

3

I Want My Children to Be Risk-Takers

The no-limit person seeks out the unknown and loves the mysterious. He welcomes change and will experiment with almost anything in life. He views failure as a part of the learning process. Success comes naturally in the fulfillment of life projects and practice at things he deeply cares about.

Nothing endures but change.

—HERACLITUS

Everything is changing. Change is as basic a component of our reality as night and day. Everything will always be changing. This is a prediction I can make with absolute certainty. As human beings, we are constantly in a state of change. Our bodies change every day. Our attitudes are constantly evolving. Something that we swore by five years ago is now almost impossible for us to imagine ourselves believing. The clothes we wore a few years ago now look strange to us in old photographs. The things we take for granted as absolutes, impervious to change, are, in fact, constantly doing just that. Granite boulders become sand in time. Beaches erode and shape new shorelines. Our buildings become outdated and are replaced with modern structures that also will be torn down. Even those things which last thousands of years, such as the Pyramids and the Acropolis, also are changing. This simple insight is very important to grasp if you want to be a no-limit person, and are desirous of raising no-limit children. Everything you feel, think, see, and touch is constantly changing.

The important question to ask yourself is not whether you like change. It simply does not matter if you like it; change will go on independent of your opinion about it. The real issues are, how do you teach children to handle this phenomenon called change, and how do you deal with it in your everyday life? The child who grows up to accept change as a way of life, to welcome change as a part of being a highly functioning person, is on the road to a wonderfully fulfilling life.

On the other hand, the child who is intimidated by change, who avoids new experiences, who fears failure and consequently stays only with the familiar and the "safe" way is destined for an unawakened life. It appears that it is unhappy people who most fear change. If you raise your children to avoid or fear change, you are raising them to be full-blown neurotics who are unable to handle the world as it is, an ever-changing phenomenon. And you are giving them a ticket to a dull, unfulfilled life. Teaching your children to welcome change involves adopting new attitudes and behaviors in your everyday dealings with them. It also involves you coming to grips with your rigid thinking and actions and looking closely at the risks involved in raising children to welcome rather than dread change. Learning to embrace change begins with you examining your own attitudes and behavior toward the unknown for you and your children.

Learning to Welcome the Unknown

When we are very young, we often look at ourselves and the world through the eyes of someone who has been taught to think incorrectly. We want to be strong, yet we think of ourselves as weak. We have great fantasies of ourselves as accomplished actors or athletes and yet we view ourselves as untalented in everyday situations. We want to be successful yet we see ourselves as only average, or even as failures. In order to match the inner vision with the outer reality more accurately, it is necessary to help children to think of themselves as in *total* control of themselves. Fears and wariness must come to be viewed by children as self-imposed limitations; otherwise they will always blame external circumstances for their inability to achieve their inner dreams of greatness. Young people often fear their own greatness, and while they would love to become heroes, and can even envision themselves doing so in imaginary circumstances, the self-pictures of their limitations severely restrict their real accomplishments.

It is imperative for parents to help their children to look more authentically at their possibilities for greatness. A child cannot maximize his potential for greatness if he is afraid of the unknown, or encouraged to be fearful of new ideas, adventures, experiences, or people.

Parents spend a great deal of time training children to avoid the unknown, by encouraging them to adopt the adult point of view without question. We teach them to be obedient and to never question an authority figure. We encourage them to eat the same kinds of foods, to see the same kinds of movies, to attend the same religious services, to hold the same political leanings, and to adopt our prejudices—be they against a racial minority, an avocado, a religion, or a particular fad in fashion. Any unwillingness that children of any age have toward attempting new things, meeting new people, exploring new ideas, or wandering into unknown territory is in fact an inhibitor to their own greatness, as well as a severe barrier to their being a no-limit neurosis-free human.

Melissa, a friend of mine, and a parent of a seven-year-old girl named Tammy, was upset that her daughter seemed so fearful around other children and wanted to encourage her to become more outgoing and adventurous. After talking with Melissa for an hour, it became evident to me that she had raised Tammy to be exactly what she disliked most in herself. Melissa had been taught to never question her father or grandfather. She had been told that athletic activities were inappropriate for a little girl, and that feminine activities were such things as sewing, flower arranging, and cooking. Caring for her man was supposed to be her purpose in life. As a young girl, Melissa was afraid of many things, including the dark, boys, getting dirty, loudness, and the like. As an adult she was extremely soft-spoken and meek.

I pointed out to Melissa that she was repeating the same scenario with Tammy, helping to create in her daughter the very same reactions to the world that she hated in herself. If she wanted to see Tammy become more positively assertive, she would have to break the chain of thinking that had victimized her, as well as her parents and grandparents before her. I encouraged her to allow Tammy to try new things. I asked her to erect a basketball hoop in their yard for Tammy. I suggested that she and Tammy dig the hole for the pole, pour the cement, put up the backboard, and do all of the dirty work involved in making this a reality. I encouraged her to get Tammy acting out some fantasies, such as taking trips without a map, going to a church of a different denomination than the rest of the family attended, questioning her father when he said things that she did not agree with—in general, becoming a challenging human being who is heard and who thinks in new and adventurous ways rather than continuing to be a shy little girl who fears everything that she knows nothing about and consequently avoids new activities.

In a few months' time Melissa began to see a dramatic change in Tammy's approach to life. She watched in amazement as Tammy told her authoritarian father, "I'm not afraid to compete with the boys in school anymore, even if you think I should be." Tammy began to try things that she had never done before. She cooked an entire meal for the family one night, something that her parents thought was impossible for someone so young. She made two new friends in the neighborhood by going right up to the house and introducing herself, something that she had feared immensely only a few months before. Today, some six years later, Tammy is an assertive, unfrightened girl who has turned her young life around because her mother encouraged her to seek out the unknown rather than to be frightened by it: to be sensibly cautious, but to avoid going through life with blinders on, shunning all of the wonderful new adventures that are waiting for anyone who welcomes, rather than fears, the unknown.

If you stop and think for a moment, you will realize that any person who fears the unknown has placed the largest restriction to his own appreciation of life directly upon himself. If you only do what you are familiar with, you will pretty much ensure that you will stay exactly the same for the rest of your life. The person who invented the wheel did it because he believed in trying something new, rather than staying with the familiar. All inventors are willing to wander off into unknown territory. Similarly, the person who will invent a cure for cancer will be someone who is willing to face the unknown rather than to run away from it. As a parent, look first at your own attitudes and behavior toward the unknown. Do you seek out new activities, or only stay with the familiar? If you are an avoider of the unknown, it is quite likely that you will encourage your children to follow the same route in life. Be on the lookout for things you tell your children that encourage them to avoid the unknown.

Ask yourself this question as you proceed with this chapter and head toward some specific ways to help children to embrace, rather than fear, change and the unknown: "How do I know when something is alive?" The answer is "If it is growing, then it is alive." A plant that is dried up is technically dead only because it is no longer growing. The same is true of human beings. If they are not growing, then they are drying up physically and emotionally, and spiritually. If children fear the unknown, then they are not growing, since people cannot grow and still stay exactly as they are. Growth means change, and change means testing yourself out in new arenas with a strong inner sense of excitement rather than fear. This must be our objective as we look at our children: to help them to shift from a fearful mentality about the unknown to one of warmly embracing—with sensible caution, but with unabated enthusiasm—anything that sparks an interest inside them. You can help them to welcome rather than to dread change, whether it is going away to a new camp, a new taste sensation called squid, trying out for the soccer team, or taking a course in statistics or existentialism. The fear of the unknown is often based upon an even more devastating prospect in the minds of young people who have not been taught to become no-limit people: the fear of failing. This, too, must be confronted in a new light by the parents of the world.

Becoming Sensible About Failing

William Saroyan had this to say about failure: "Good people are good because they've come to wisdom through failure." Does that surprise you? If you have given any thought to how we learn, I'm sure you are not at all surprised by this notion about coming to wisdom through failure. We learn very little by success. In fact, success tends to make us comfortable and complacent. When we find something that we do quite easily, it is a natural tendency to continue, and the more successful we are at it, the less likely we are to change and, ultimately, to grow. A reversal on the old aphorism would be "Nothing fails like success."

In 1927, Babe Ruth hit sixty home runs, more than anyone in the history of baseball. He also set another record that year: He struck out more than anyone in the history of baseball. The truth is, if you want to hit home runs, you must be willing to strike out. There is no way around this simple lesson of life. If you want your children to experience the exhilaration of success, then you must encourage them to learn how to fail—and, in fact, to fail a lot.

The important distinction here is the difference between failing at a task and being a failure as a person. No one is a failure as a person. Each person, by virtue of his aliveness, has inherent value and dignity. No one is guaranteed that he will never experience failure, and the more you want to experience a feeling of success in your life, the more you are going to invite the lesson of failure. We learn by our failures! We remain complacent through our successes. We must begin to teach our children that failing is not only acceptable, but that it is an absolute requirement if they are to be no-limit people. It is this insight about failure that leads virtually all great innovators to pursue their work with a kind of obsession. Thomas Edison, who dabbled in the unknown almost all of his life, was inspired to say, "Show me a thoroughly satisfied man and I will show you a failure."

Take the fear out of failure, and help children to understand the difference between failing at a task and being a failure as a person. To accomplish this, we must take a look at our obsession with achievement. The no-limit person is not one who never fails; instead, he is a person who dusts himself off after falling, and learns what obstacles to avoid in the road. The person who shuns failure will lie in the road and whine or, even worse, stay off the road in the first place, content to take a safe, well-known course throughout life, avoiding failure and personal fulfillment at the same time.

Young people who are afraid of failing are usually obsessed with achievement. They tend to evaluate their personal worth and success in terms of external achievement. Consequently, children begin very early to believe it is important to acquire gold stars in everything they do. The grade becomes more important than what is being learned, and students who pursue the grades will avoid anything that might give them less than an A or B on a transcript. Take the easy courses, cheat on examinations, stay away from the difficult teachers. These become the watchwords of young people obsessed with the externals. Or they work so hard for a grade from a difficult, perfectionistic teacher that they exhaust themselves by staying up late to create projects and reports designed to please the teacher rather than educate the student.

Whatever they do, they feel that they must not fail anything. Winning the game becomes more important than being physically fit and athletically skilled. The trophy is the most important thing; therefore they do whatever they have to do to get on the team, beat the other guy, or become number one. Getting into the right college becomes more important than having knowledge. Beating the opponent becomes more important than learning to help each other out on this planet. Because they believe that you are nothing if you are not number one, they do whatever they have to in order to have the recognition of others. Inner rewards are considered meaningless. Instead it is the money, the power, the merit badge, the trophy, the diploma that really have meaning.

Pursuit of external symbols of success is the reason why young people today consume more tranquilizers than any generation in the history of our country. It explains why suicide rates are increasing dramatically, even among youngsters seven and eight years of age. Young people who have been taught to evaluate their worth on external measures and who have avoided failure symbols all their lives are unable to deal effectively with real-world exigencies as they grow up. When you teach children that the external symbols of success are the most important part of living, you are teaching them to look outside themselves for their successes. You are teaching them to look for happiness in things, rather than carrying happiness around with them and bringing it to any human enterprise.

The no-limit youngster can take joy in weeding a garden, reading a book, playing catch with an old baseball mitt, or kicking a soup can around the back yard. The "many-limits" youngster, who has been taught to chase success symbols, is relegated to the bench of his neighborhood organized team until the score is so lopsided that he can maybe get into the game because the results have already been determined. His coach believes that winning the game is more important than learning to play and enjoying the thrill of participation. "Watch out for failure," some coaches and "many-limits" parents tell their youngsters, all the time forgetting that all winners are people who have struggled, who have failed a lot, and who have learned how to benefit from their failures and work hard at their game, or their musical instrument, or their dance routine, never comparing themselves with others, only being fulfilled in the pursuit of their own inner excellence and their own inner signals.

The more we teach achievement at the expense of inner satisfaction, the more we teach youngsters to take the easier path and to avoid a failure label. Yet, when we take just a cursory look at greatness in any human being in any profession, we are looking at people who have failed, and failed, and failed again and again, learning something new each time. When a reporter asked Thomas Edison how it felt to have failed 25,000 times in his effort to create a simple storage battery, his reply was unique to great no-limit spirits: "I don't know why you are calling it failure. Today I know 25,000 ways not to make a battery. What do you know?"

You will want to learn from the unfortunate parents who have seen their children break down in the face of extreme competition, taking to drugs or even suicide attempts because they did not measure up to some external yardstick of success. You will want to take note that too many children label themselves as losers because they believe that failure is a disease, and when it catches up to them, they succumb to the toxic elements of the disease. If we are "bad" people because we lose, then we are all bad people. No one can win all the time, not even the most talented or hardest working among us.

I have talked with parents who believed all that rah-rah stuff about winning, being number one, and pushing their children throughout their young lives. One parent told me that his daughter came home from school in the second grade saying, "I have to get all A's in school or else I won't get into the right college." In the second grade! Seven-year-old children need to be laughing, enjoying life, trying everything that comes along, and being happy, complete young people, rather than experiencing fear that they will not get into the college of their choice. This same father, who so proudly boasted about his children all attaining external excellence in their lives, had high blood pressure, a hint of a serious ulcer, a severe drinking problem, and was always worried about not having enough money. He seldom experienced failure in the traditional sense, but he certainly was not an example of someone who had inner peace. He was a mess, and he was teaching his children to be like him. While he relentlessly chased after success, he forgot the important measure of real success. Christopher Morley put it this way: "There is only one success—to be able to spend your life in your own way." If we train our children to go after achievement and ignore inner satisfaction, then we are teaching them to take the easy path, to be more concerned about the opinions and rewards bestowed upon us by others, and consequently to avoid any hint of failing. This is our national malady. Put more succinctly by William James, the psychologist and philosopher, "The exclusive worship of success is our national disease." Failing is not a bad thing; it is the only way to learn anything. Learning to fail, which means being willing to try almost anything that you would like to try based upon your own inner signals, involves being willing to take risks. Risk-taking is the third component of learning how to welcome rather than to fear change. The first component is seeking the unknown, and the second is realizing the necessity of failure.

Risk-Taking

You may have fallen into a trap by now in your life. The name of this device, which will devour your innards and leave you empty, is called security. Too many of us spend our energy looking for this elusive thing that will give us a secure feeling of being taken care of for the rest of our lives. Perhaps you have come to believe that if you are careful enough, save your money, and accumulate a lot of ''stuff,'' including a home, a car, furniture, and a bank account, then you will have a secure position in life. This is all nonsense! It is the kind of thinking that leads you into a safe, predictable, and yes, unfulfilled life, pursuing an illusion called security until the end of your days, and always coming up empty. Plain and simple, there is no such thing as external security, and only insecure people strive for it.

We are making a mistake when we seek security and safety in possessions. Yet, our concept of security in contemporary America too often masquerades as money, a home, a job, a diploma, or a protective spouse with these attributes. These are all externals, and are incapable of providing anyone with security. External security is a myth. These things come and go depending upon any number of variables over which you, as an individual, have absolutely no control. Moreover, even if you have these things in abundance in your life and feel absolutely certain that they will never disappear, you still have no more security than the penniless beggar on the street.

External security does not exist; it never has and it never will in a dynamic society. There is a different kind of security which, if you get it, and teach your children to have it, will eliminate forever any obsession with the illusory kind. Inner security, the sense of faith in oneself to be able to handle any circumstance, the willingness to believe in oneself, to know that the only real security lies within oneself—that is what we want children to come to know. Henry Ford, who amassed great wealth in his lifetime, was once quoted as saying, ''If money is your hope for independence you will never have it. The only real security that a man can have in this world is a reserve of knowledge, experience, and ability.'' When you have this philosophy as a way of living your life, and you teach children the difference between these two approaches to attaining security, you will be encouraging them to become risk-takers, rather than to be obsessed with the illusion of being secure and safe.

Children who believe in the concept of inner security look within themselves for the answers to what to be in life, rather than seeking those answers in things. They will not be afraid, for instance, to go off to a new summer camp, because they feel confident that they are capable of handling potential problems. They will know that the solution to homesickness does not lie in asking their parents to solve the problem for them. They will know that they can deal with being away from home because they know how to rely on themselves. They will know that they have the ability to figure out what to do if a bigger kid picks on them. They will look within rather than outside themselves to find solutions. This kind of mentality, when supported throughout a lifetime, encourages a child to have the only kind of security there is: the abiding faith in oneself for resolving problems. However, if a child comes to believe in the elusive external security, he will try to buy his way out of problems, or have his parents do it for him. Self-reliance, when fostered within a child for a lifetime, encourages risk-taking rather than fearing it, and creates a kind of inner security which tells the child realistically that *"If I am going to get where I want to be in life, I can't rely on anyone but myself in order to make it happen, since I am the only person that I am absolutely certain will be with me at all times, whenever these problems in life crop up. If I am all I've got, then I want to be certain that I can call upon me at any time."* This is the essence of becoming a risk-taker.

In helping children to become risk-takers, we need to emphasize that they exercise a sensible amount of caution. Risk-taking should not involve a life-or-death decision. It does involve following one's own inner dictates and not becoming one of the sheep. As mentioned earlier, the opposite of courage is not so much fear as it is conformity. Being just like everybody else, and doing primarily what others say, is the kind of cowardice I am speaking about here. A child who is more concerned with fitting in and doing what he is told will never become a risk-taker, nor will he ever view himself as a no-limit person. I am talking about learning to avoid the easy path, to try things that might seem difficult without being afraid of what others will think, to stand up for what you believe in, rather than quaking in fear of being laughed at or bullied by someone else.

Toward the end of this chapter you will find some specific exercises that can be used with children to help them to become sensible risk-takers. I have always encouraged my oldest daughter, Tracy, from the earliest years of her life right through her teens, to look within herself for answers and not to be afraid to take risks or face change. Here are a few examples from her life.

Tracy at two years of age:

Tracy: Daddy, Billy doesn't like me—he told me he hates me . . . [sobbing]

Daddy: What does it matter what Billy thinks. Do you like you?

Tracy: Of course I like me. Why shouldn't I?

Daddy: I can't think of a reason. Even if Billy doesn't like you now, you are still fantastic if you think so.

A child's awareness that she need not be hurt if someone does not like her, that she need not allow other people's opinions to rule, can begin when the child first starts to talk, and should be reinforced throughout her life. An exchange like the preceding one with two-year-old Tracy is much more constructive than saying to your child, "Well, what did you do to Billy? Let's go see if we can get him to stop being mad at you" or "Billy's a bad boy; *I* like you, and that's what is really important."

Tracy at eight years of age:

Tracy: I'm afraid to move into that new neighborhood. All my friends are here. What if I don't like it, or what if I don't make any new friends?

Daddy: Have you ever had trouble making friends before?

Tracy: No, but this is a whole new city we're moving to.

Daddy: Why do you suppose you're so good at making friends?

Tracy: I guess it's because I've always just done it without worrying about it.

Daddy: Exactly. You make friends because you must take a little risk to meet someone new, and you do it. And when we get to the new city, you'll probably do the same thing again.

While these are tiny little exchanges, they reinforce Tracy's belief that she has the power within her. If she thinks about her own skills and abilities, and takes a few small risks, then she will have what she wants and will not be able to continue to think in disaster terms.

I always encouraged Tracy to take risks as a teenager. When she contemplated running for class vice-president she seemed nervous. I talked to her about the worst thing that could possibly happen to her if she ran and lost. As she thought about it, she said, "I guess the worst thing that could happen is that I wouldn't be vice-president. Since I'm already not vice-president now, and I'm all right, I guess I'll give it a shot." She ran for vice-president and lost, but when I talked to her about it, she was in good spirits.

I reminded her that there were five hundred people in her class and that only a handful had decided to run. Those six or seven people were the ones who thought of themselves as leaders and had the confidence to take the risk of rejection. I reminded her that how we view ourselves will ultimately determine whether we are leaders or followers in life, and that she should feel proud that she viewed herself as a leader.

To take the risk, to attempt something, and to be one of the small handful, says so much more about you than whether you actually win or lose the election. While we may not memorialize the second-place finishers in an election, (but all first-place "winners" have had many second-place finishes) those who participate are far ahead of those who sit back and say to themselves, "I could never win anything, so I just won't even run."

Learning to welcome rather than fear change means becoming familiar with the unknown, welcoming failure as a way of life, taking risks each and every day, and, finally, creating a picture that is based upon having a vivid, creative imagination that allows a young person to view himself or herself in a no-limit way. All of those risks that children learn to take come from the willingness to picture themselves in new and more effective ways. To be able to welcome change, children must have permission to imagine themselves as portraits of greatness.

A Creative Imagination

Young people often fear change because they have not been encouraged to have a creative, positive imagination about what that change might bring about. We must be careful to avoid stifling the imaginations of youngsters of all ages. Little children enjoy telling creatively imaginative stories about what might happen to them in a given situation. Encourage this kind of inner picturing. A child who is encouraged to have a positive imagination will not be afraid of change nearly as much as a child who is discouraged in this activity. Remember, when storing away images, children cannot distinguish a picture of something from the real thing. After a while, the mind is unable to distinguish the image from the reality. Consequently, the more positive pictures children image, the more likely they are to be capable of handling virtually any situation in life.

You can help children to become much more effective at dealing with the fear of the unknown, the fear of failing, and the fear of taking risks by encouraging them to talk about *all* of the possibilities that might come about as a result of a change. You will find that many of their images are quite positive. Reinforcing them is your primary responsibility in helping them to become no-limit people.

For example, a child who is going from a middle school to a high school will be entering foreign territory for the very first time. If you ask him to imagine what it will be like, you will likely hear a combination of awful and very positive thoughts. When Larry, a thirteen-year-old neighborhood boy who was entering high school in the fall, was asked to do just this, he gave some of the following images (I have included positive reinforcers for creative imaging from the parent as well):

Larry	Parent
I could get lost—the place is so huge.	Picture yourself finding your way or asking someone for directions, just like I do when I can't find an address while driving.
I may not have enough time to get around between classes.	How about going through a trial run before classes start? And what would so terrible about being late?
I won't know anybody in the school.	Imagine yourself with lots of friends around you and maybe you can make it happen.
I won't be treated like a little baby anymore, that's for sure.	You can just see yourself as a person finally in charge of himself all day instead of standing in line and being told what to do every minute. It must feel great.
I can even pick my own courses.	You are going to be making a lot of important decisions for yourself in high school.
In a couple of years I may be able to drive to school after I get my license.	Just picture yourself behind the wheel, actually driving to the school. Wow, what a great thought!

I trust you get the picture! Allowing Larry to think positively with a creative imagination, while all the time giving him positive reinforcement, will help him to change his attitude. This same kind of exchange can be used in dealing with a nursery school child who is leaving the house for the first time, as well as with the college student on her way to the big time with a dormitory to live in. The importance of creative imaging and positive reinforcement for having an imagination is the crucial point. The old song says, "Imagination, it's funny, it makes a cloudy day sunny," and it is absolutely true. A cloudy, fearful attitude can create anxieties about a change, while a positive imagination can literally make things work out—first in the mind, where it is stored away as fact, and then in reality, because the child has already practiced it.

William Blake wrote some of the most important words I have ever read on this subject. Think about them in relation to this entire business of helping children to imagine themselves in positive rather than negative terms. "Man's desires are limited by his *perceptions; none can desire what he has not perceived.*" Children must first perceive something about a change of any kind, and their desires are indeed limited by what they picture for themselves. Parents have a great deal to do with what their children picture. It is reinforcement of those early pictures that children are looking for as young toddlers. If you mock or discourage their pictures, they will soon either stop picturing or imagine bad things. Encourage them to visualize themselves in as many positive ways as possible, even if they do not agree with you at the moment or seem to be fighting what you are reinforcing. The essential thing is for you to continue reinforcing positive images at all times. Soon they will sink in and your children will become positive visualizers as a matter of habit.

Before looking at some of the positive strategies you can employ in helping your children of all ages to welcome instead of fear change, it is important first for you to see some of the specific kinds of things that all parents do at times which actually encourage children to fear change. Look through this list (which could go on for fifty pages, but is condensed to give you an idea of how often this negative reinforcement regarding change occurs) and see if you recognize yourself doing these things. This list can be a place for you to start by realizing what you are creating in your children when you think and behave in these ways.

How We Discourage a Positive Attitude Toward Change

▢ Being *overly* cautious with continuous reminders about the dangers of life. "Don't go near the water!" "Stay away from *that* kind of child!" "You're not big enough yet to climb a tree or to play football." "You'll get a boo-boo if you try that."

▢ Discouraging your children from trying foods with admonitions such as "You won't like it—I know you hate anything with tomatoes in it," "You've never liked Mexican foods," "In this family we don't eat things that are cooked rare," "We are all meat-and-potatoes people in this family and we just don't go in for gourmet foods."

▢ Keeping your children from experiencing any religious ideas or ceremonies other than those which your family has always known.

▢ Exposing your children to only one political point of view with statements such as "We are all Democrats in this family, always have been, always will be" or "There is only one political party for us, and that's the Republican."

▢ Encouraging babies to believe they are totally helpless, by not allowing them to have minor struggles early. This is done by rescuing them prematurely when they are crawling and run into an obstacle, rather than waiting to see if they can crawl over it, or by picking them up and "saving" them when they experience a minor frustration.

▢ Not allowing young children to believe they have power over themselves. "He can't help himself; he's only two and he can't get into his chair by himself." "Mommy will do it for you." "You're too little to feed yourself." "You can't dress yourself yet—you have to wait until you're big like Daddy."

▢ Encouraging your children to conform to current fads because everyone else is doing it.

▢ Discouraging your children of all ages from challenging any ideas, and telling them instead that "The teacher is always right," "You don't question your father," "The law is the law," or "Just do it, and don't ask questions."

▢ Encouraging fearful attitudes. "Watch out for the monsters under the bed if you don't go to sleep *now!*" "All strangers are bad." "The bully is someone to stay away from." "The bogeyman will get you if you don't do what I say!"

□ Being a fearful person yourself and presenting this example to your children.

□ Ridiculing the dreams of your children with admonitions to "Be realistic."

□ Being the referee in all disputes between your children.

□ Resolving your children's disputes with neighbors by coming to the rescue whenever there is any kind of difficulty.

□ Taking the easiest route in life and encouraging your children to do the same.

□ Having prejudices toward other people, talking about your hatreds in the home, and encouraging children to adopt those same hatreds.

□ Encouraging overdependency on you, their parents, throughout their childhood years. Making them ask permission for virtually anything they do or even think.

□ Planning your children's days and lives for them at all times. Scheduling their activities so that they have no time left to think or act for themselves.

□ Living your life through your children's accomplishments and encouraging them to feel guilty when they do not want to include you in their activities.

□ Refusing to entertain an opposing point of view and therefore modeling this kind of thinking for your children. Always assuming you are right in any dispute with younger people.

□ Forbidding all adventurous activities such as going to camp, going to a mall, participating in a hike in the wilderness, taking a long bicycle ride, or anything else that youngsters might do that involves any risk.

□ Putting labels on your children such as "You're not athletic," "You're not talented in music," "You have big bones; it's not your fault," "You're the klutz of the family," "You're not the serious one—you're the clown and always will be."

□ Being rigid about insisting on high grades in all subjects, achievement at all costs, and top performance in everything, thereby making grades and winning the most important facets of life.

□ Judging children, and only giving love based on their performances in everything they do.

□ Emphasizing money. Rating what things cost as highly important.

□ Dismissing anything you know nothing about as "weird," and not allowing children to discover any of these so-called weird things, such as yoga, wok cooking, meditation, Buddhism, break dancing, MTV, or dirt-biking.

□ Forbidding any discussion of sex, and labeling it forbidden until they are "old enough" or married.

□ Programming sex stereotypes such as "Girls take baths; boys take showers," "Boys always call girls for a date; girls wait and hope," "Boys play sports; girls sew their uniforms."

□ Condemning failure and punishing anything which smacks of having tried and failed.

□ Reminding children of their limitations, and presenting to them an example of a person who fears his or her own greatness. "You're only a little country boy and don't forget it."

□ Constantly correcting children when they speak ungrammatically, make a mistake in money transactions, or say something which doesn't jibe with your interpretation of how it is.

□ Looking for them to be doing something wrong and always reminding them of their past mistakes. Reinforcing negative behavior by refusing to forget past mistakes, theirs and yours. Providing a negative example of a person who berates himself for any past errors.

This list could literally be endless. However, the point is clear. Now that you have read some of the more common ways in which you might be encouraging children to fear change and avoid the unknown, let's look at your payoffs, the hidden reasons for doing this. Once you know what it is that you get out of thinking and behaving in these ways, it will become possible for you to look for new, more life-enhancing ways in which to interact with your child.

The Psychological Support System for Discouraging Risk-Taking

Keep in mind that behavior that you repeat is behavior that in some ways gives you a psychological reward. The types of behavior that encourage children to avoid the unknown and resist change are essentially self-defeating and neurotic. The discussion that follows points out some of the rewards to you for encouraging negative thinking and behavior. As you read through the following list, consider which statements might apply to you.

You view life as risky and the world as a dangerous and suspicious place. If you are not independent, you will cultivate children who are dependent, shy, fierce hangers-on and who desperately need you. As a dependent adult you encourage children to be the same. It is easier for you to teach your children to be afraid of new experiences, since this is all that you know and it makes you feel important to have your child clinging to you, rather than teaching him to explore his world at his own level.

You do not want to concern yourself with behavior that is unlike your way of being in the world. For you, conformity is a virtue at home, at school, and on the assembly line of life. Therefore, your life is easier if your child also learns conformity. A windup doll or a robot might do just as well in your household.

You prefer to live your life by habit rather than by using your thinking capacity. Children who fear change are often encouraged to do only what they are told to do, just as their parents have always done. This is the least challenging and easiest path to take. It is a lazy approach to parenting, since creative energy is suppressed.

You feel secure as one of the majority. You are content to do things as everyone else does them, to think like the herd, to be part of the crowd. It is your way to avoid criticism from others and to have a safe life. Staying with the majority, who fear change, is indeed its own payoff, although it is a cowardly approach to life. Remember what Andrew Jackson said: "One man with courage makes a majority." But thinking like the majority of other people is, indeed, the easiest and least courageous approach you can encourage in your child.

You are more concerned with being right than with being happy. By teaching children to stay only with the familiar and to avoid change and the unknown, you manage to feel right. It is difficult to provide any evaluation in areas where we have never been before, so we encourage children to stay with the situations in which we can provide them with a grade of "right." Being right is reinforced in familiar territory only, so anything else is discouraged.

By staying away from change, you avoid risks and ever failing at anything. If you believe that failure is bad, then you want to avoid anything that might cause failure. Since failure is so loaded with stigma in our achievement-oriented culture, we do all that we can to be winners in our own minds. Often this means avoiding any and all risks at all costs, and encouraging children to do the same.

By impeding the imaginations of children who like to dream, you may feel that you can keep them from encountering any setbacks in their lives. You encourage them to set their heights low, to stay with the familiar, to avoid risks, and to also avoid any disappointments. As parents, it is hard to witness our children being disappointed, so we often tell them to lower their sights. It makes us feel better to believe they are content. Content, perhaps; but fulfilled and a no-limit person, never. The price is often too high for us as parents, so we keep them from dreaming about their own greatness in the name of avoiding frustration. (Of course, most of the frustration we fear so much is our own, not our children's.)

You keep your children from wandering into new and unknown territory with the excuse, "If it was all right for me, then it is good enough for my children." This attitude is convenient, since it keeps you from having to try new things. It also frees you from any responsibility that you might have to accept if your children turn out "different." Doing things the way you have always done things certainly paves a safer and easier path, but progress and growth are impossible if you never change the way you have always done things.

These are the major payoffs that you recieve for not teaching children about the inevitability of change and the potential rewards of exploring the unknown. If you can see how self-defeating these attitudes and behaviors are for you and your children, and if you recognize that your children will not be able to grow into fully functioning no-limit people if the same old attitudes are repeated generation after generation, then begin to look at some new ways of thinking and behaving with your children. What follows is a chronicle of some new and exciting ways to encourage children to welcome rather than fear change, and to wander around in unexplored territory rather than staying forever in the same old patterns. Remember that a no-limit person seeks out the new, loves the mysterious, and wants to see change for the better. These are some of the ways that your children, if exposed regularly to these ideas, will become welcomers of the unknown, not just now, but always.

Ideas for Encouraging Children to Seek Out, Rather Than Fear, the Unknown

Blend a sensible approach to being careful with an encouragement of questions, new ideas, new territories for exploration, and the sense of life as an adventure rather than a path to conformity. In today's world it is absolutely necessary to warn your children of the real dangers which exist, and to have them behave in strictly cautious ways when it comes to getting into cars with strangers, not swimming without a partner, not walking the streets after dark, and so on. However, one can become overly cautious to the point of viewing all the world as a sinister and dangerous place that is always to be feared.

In any society there are real dangers and too many casualties. However, the child who is fearful of the unknown will never be able to develop either the necessary skills to cope with danger or the ability to distinguish a dangerous situation from something new and exciting. All strangers are not bad, and if we never talked to any stranger, then of course we would never meet anyone new in our lives. Obviously, very young children must be watched by a responsible adult at *all* times, but as they begin to grow, they must be encouraged to distinguish perilous situations for themselves, since they cannot go through their lives being supervised and observed every single moment. A sensible integration of caution with encouragement to trust their own instincts whenever they even suspect a problem, mixed together with encouragement to try new things, will help your children to grow in no-limit ways. Otherwise, they will grow up to be fearful children who never look within to make decisions themselves about what constitutes danger and what doesn't.

Encourage children to try new foods, and try to prepare various meals that you yourself do not particularly enjoy. Why should your children grow up disliking cabbage simply because it does not meet your own personal taste preferences? Take them to restaurants that specialize in Indonesian, Indian, Greek, Mexican, Thai, Chinese, and other kinds of ethnic taste treats. Expose them to all kinds of foods as very young children, and they will grow up with a multitude of options. Many people are limited to only a few specific meals throughout their entire lives because of food prejudices which were ingrained as young children. The more taste sensations a child is introduced to, and the fewer times he hears you say things like "I hate carrots" or "Indian food is too spicy," the more opportunities he will have for expanding himself in this dimension. No-limit people are those who have options in life, not those who have been restricted by unnecessary prejudices passed along through generations of family members who unthinkingly have placed limitations on each other. Life is far more enjoyable to those who can eat virtually anything and are willing to try something that they have never experienced before. Many Americans visiting Europe and Asia look for a franchised fast-food restaurant that is decorated exactly like the one around the corner from their homes and serves the same well-done hamburgers and french fries. Meanwhile, they miss learning what people of other cultures are like and they are limited by their own self-conditioned attitudes for a lifetime.

Make an effort to have children visit as many different places of worship as possible. Expose them early to the great ideas of religious thinkers from around the world and throughout human history. No one ought to have a monopoly on religious thinking and behavior. Obeying the commandments that are practiced by Christians need not conflict with learning the teachings of Buddha or Confucius or Mohammed or Moses. Young people need to be exposed to all religious ideas and then encouraged to make up their own minds about what particular institution they will join, or even if they want to belong to any one particular sect. No-limit people make their own choices, rather than growing up believing in only one particular point of view through a family conditioning process. We want children to think for themselves, to behave toward others based upon an ethical set of principles that they carry within them. Remember the admonition from the Bible, ''The kingdom of Heaven is within.'' If they are restricted in their religious thinking, and so conditioned to believe that they will only get into heaven if they join the Baptist, or Catholic, or Moslem institution, then you are going against the basic principle of an internal kingdom of heaven. Encourage them to determine their own ethical thought processes, rather than making robots of them by having them believe only as you and your family have for generations.

Try to avoid all political labels for yourself and your children. Allow them to be exposed to all points of view and to develop their own set of beliefs based upon having an awareness of all points of view. Do not tell them that we are all Democrats or Republicans or Socialists or anything else; let them learn for themselves what the differences are. Encourage them to vote not for a party but for an individual that appeals to them as a thinking person. The ''party'' is nothing more than a collection of individuals who band together to promulgate a particular point of view. A person who votes for whomever the party picks has no mind of his own, and instead is a non-thinking robot who lets others decide for him what lever he should pull on Election Day. This is true of those who vote only for the union candidate, or the business candidate, or the female candidate, or the black candidate, or any other candidate with a group label. Teach your children to think for themselves and give them an example of a person who does the same. Help them to shun labels and to develop a sense of their own uniqueness in making decisions. It is appropriate to repeat here what Sören Kierkegaard, the Danish theologian, said in this regard: ''Once you label me, you negate me.'' You do not want your children to be merely predictable labels, with no opinions or commitments of their own. The surest way to make certain this does not happen is to encourage each child to be an individual first—a leader, not a follower.

Encourage infants to become explorers right from the very beginning. A baby who is assisted with every tiny struggle will soon get the measage: "A big person will do it for me, so why should I give it a try?" When the baby is trying to feed himself by thrashing around with a spoon, hitting his nose and forehead, just wait a few moments. Wait until you catch a baby doing something right, and then give positive reinforcement. Applaud and clap your hands when his food finally hits his mouth, and watch him smile. Let toddlers dress themselves if they want to, even if their clothes are inside out now and then. Allow babies to work a bit when they are crawling over a pillow on the floor, or trying to pick up a toy with their newly developing fingers. Teach them perseverance early and reward them early for it. Every child in the world says, "I can do it myself, Daddy," almost every day, until and unless he is thoroughly indoctrinated to believe that he does not have a mind of his own and that only Mommy or Daddy can do it for him. How many times I have heard parents say absurd things, such as "Eat this now—don't you think I know when you are hungry?" or "Wear this coat outside—don't you think I know when you are cold?" Teach them from the beginning that they can explore their own tiny life space without constant interruption from a big person rescuing them and teaching them to give up almost before they even start walking.

Teach them, by example and by regular positive reinforcement, that one need never be a slave to a current fad or fashion. While they certainly might be encouraged to enjoy the contemporary fads, they should also learn that they need not be bound by them or have to feel "out of it" if they forsake these contemporary passing trends. When they absolutely "must" have the current popular blue jeans, ask them why they really want them: because they will look attractive wearing them, or because they simply want to be "in"? Talk to them about the importance of choosing their own clothes based upon what they want rather than what everyone else is wearing. Discourage conformity in dress, or anything else, simply for the sake of conforming. Teach them through your example not to slavishly adhere to the so-called correct labels, the presumed proper etiquette, the "in" designer, or anything else dictated by "experts." The need to conform is a means of staying only with the familiar or the majority, and it keeps you thinking, acting, and dressing just like everybody else. If you are raising children to be just like everybody else, what do they really have to offer? When they want something that everyone else is wearing, ask them directly, "Do you want this in order to be just like everybody else, or do you genuinely like the way it looks on you?" Then if they want it, encourage them at any age to contribute something toward the purchase of it.

When children have disputes, let them know that you are aware that there are two sides. Spinoza once said, "No matter how thin you slice it, there will always be two sides." Keeping this in mind, be wary of telling children to obey all laws, to always do what they are told, that the teacher is always right, or that they should always respect their elders. You do not want a blindly obedient child in place of a no-limit person. No-limit persons find themselves on the opposite side of authority figures a great deal of the time, and so will your children. Encourage them to ask "Why?" Do not berate them for questioning established practices, and do not tell them to do a thing just because everyone else does it.

The changes that have brought improvement to our world have not come about because of individuals who simply took an acquiescent attitude. Change is fomented in the world by people who challenge established practices when they are no longer appropriate. Do not take that spark out of your child, unless you want him or her to grow into a conforming, dissatisfied adult. Teach your child that there is no difference between simply conforming for the sake of being like everyone else, and being a nonconformist simply for the sake of being different. The nonconformist who simply wants to be on the other side of the fence is still being controlled by the will and behavior of others, this type of nonconformity is just as neurotic as conformity for the same reasons. Teach your children to honestly look within themselves, and to agitate for improvement whenever they see an injustice. There are times when it is more effective to go along than to resist. The no-limit person is not against fighting; he is against useless or senseless fighting.

When Laurie, a fifteen-year-old algebra student, was having difficulty with her teacher and was threatened with removal from the classroom, I encouraged her to look at her own senseless fighting. I pointed out that she was defeating herself by trying to reform her algebra teacher, and that she would be much better off to quietly work at her algebra and simply forget about her personality difference with her teacher. As she worked on ridding herself of her hatred for her teacher, she soon was able to concentrate on getting through algebra without further troubles. After all, her goal was to pass algebra and move on. She was surprised a few months later when I also encouraged her to argue through the student council and the school administration for the removal of an unfair dress code. In the algebra case, she was senselessly fighting her own objectives, while the dress code was a true injustice which she felt needed to be reversed. Teach your children of all ages that asking "Why?" is terrific, that fighting against injustices or for your own point of view is sensational, but that useless fighting, in which they will only end up the victim, is simply a waste of time.

Do not create monsters in the minds of young children to temporarily quiet them. Fearful children become more fearful of the unknown as they grow older. Besides, it is as frightening for a two-year-old to fear monsters as it is for you to hear strange noises in the woods on a dark evening or to imagine a sixty-foot giant waiting to gobble you up. To them that monster is really you. Fearful tactics provoke fearful attitudes toward life and a suspicious nature in a child. Children who fear the dark (a symbol of the unknown) because of your taking advantage of their naiveté could be fearful for a lifetime.

The world is a beautiful place, and change is a wonderful experience; tell your little children these things, always remembering to be positive and hopeful. "There are no monsters in real life; no one is going to get you. You're a big boy/girl—come on, we'll go back there and look together." These are the ways you can fight those early fears. Often these fears are learned from bigger brothers and sisters, or from scary movies, or from the news. Teach them very early to be explorers and not to have irrational fears, and they will cultivate these attitudes for their entire lives. You must show them that you are not a fearful person. Show them that you take sensible precautions, but do not talk about bogeymen, scary creatures, and the like. Show them a brave person who is not timid when it comes to standing up for yourself, and you will do more to help them to overcome any fear they might have learned.

Positively reinforce any dreams or goals that children have, regardless of how impossible they might sound to you. The young man who tells you he wants to become a doctor, but has a string of D's and C's on his report card, does not need a realistic lecture on not aiming too high. Instead, support him with words such as "Go for it," "Why not—it's never too late for anything," or "I'm sure if you put your mind to it, you could accomplish anything you really want." Even if you are absolutely positive that a child is not going to reach his goals of becoming, say, an astronaut—perhaps because of height, or aptitude in science, or whatever—never, but never, discourage him from aiming high. The worst that could happen is that he would reevaluate his objectives as he encounters some difficulties. However, he might surprise you someday. I cannot tell you how many English teachers I have had through my educational career who told me that I would never be able to write for the public unless I drastically changed my style. But the more I found myself writing in my own commonsense, nongrandiose style, the more I found that my teachers were wrong. Children need to know that the words "It's impossible" are not a part of your vocabulary, and that you are supportive of their dreams regardless of how absurd they might sound to you at the moment. Imagine how Mr. and Mrs. Wright must have felt when Wilbur and Orville told them about wanting to fly, or Edison's parents when he dreamed of lighting the world without flames. How about Henry Ford's parents when he idealized about motorized cars replacing horses? Let them dream; encourage their goals to be high and farfetched. Do not take the wind out of their sails. Encourage them to talk more to you about what they might do and explore how it could be accomplished. Do you honestly think that whoever out there will someday invent a cure for cancer or multiple sclerosis will make it happen if he or she is told, "Don't be silly! We've always had these diseases, and you certainly aren't going to change that fact. Now, be realistic and behave like everyone else."

Encourage children of all ages to try the more difficult road now and then. Let them know that you will not be disappointed when low grades result from attempting a difficult subject or electing to learn from the teacher who is known as a great scholar but a hard marker. If they want to dive off the high board, teach them to do it safely, and then let them give it a try. Give them praise for trying hard things, such as advanced mathematics, economics, a solution to a complicated puzzle, a swim underwater across the pool, or climbing a tree. Furthermore, show them that you too are willing to try difficult things in your life, and do not shy away from a tough course, confronting an unruly neighbor, or standing up for yourself with an obnoxious salesperson. The more you illustrate directly to them that you too will take a chance at failing, and that you do not always take the known path, the more you will be providing them with the fortitude to explore unknown territory.

Watch out for letting your prejudices toward others show. We are only prejudiced toward what we are ignorant of, since being prejudiced means literally to prejudge without experience. These attitudes will encourage children to stay away from those that they are taught to hate, and before long, they will have many lifetime limits. No-limit people do not prejudge anyone; in fact, they do not judge anyone at all. They have an accepting attitude toward those who are different in any way. The more you promote a sense of acceptance, exploration, and being around those who are different from you in any respect, the more you will be doing to assist your children in their growing process. Additionally, you will be doing a great deal to remove the barriers that keep people apart. Teaching tolerance and love of others, if practiced on a larger scale, could end the horrible results of so much hatred in our world. But, the only way to change the world is to start with yourself and your children. Gordon Allport, who wrote the definitive work on prejudice, concluded: "Mothers of prejudiced children, far more often than mothers of unprejudiced children, held that obedience is the most important thing a child can learn." The lesson is obvious. Teach them to be inquisitive, to ask why rather than saying, "Yes, sir" or "Yes, ma'am" unless you want your own prejudices to infect them as they do you.

Keep in mind that the business of parenting is to teach children to become their own parents. It is important to aid them in becoming independent and learning to think for themselves. Try to help them in this process by not monitoring their young lives to such an extent that they must seek your permission for everything they think or do. It is important to have some specific areas in which they ask permission at various ages of their lives, and these things of course are dependent upon your own personal views about each child's readiness for handling more and more responsibility. This readiness will vary with each child. However, it is important to help them to look within for their own guidance and not to fear their own judgment. Requiring a child to ask permission to stay overnight at a friend's house at the age of ten is obviously responsible parenting. However, if the child must ask permission to ride his bicycle over to a friend's or to buy something with his own money at the same age, then perhaps you are not allowing him to take some responsibility for his young life. The more areas in which you can sensibly allow your children to take responsibility, the more they will become familiar with that unknown territory called independent thinking. Do not assume that they cannot handle responsibility before giving them a chance. If they mishandle opportunities to take some personal responsibility, then of course you can withdraw these privileges. Even at an early age they must be given an opportunity to think and act for themselves within reasonable limits. A two-year-old need not ask permission every time she wants to play with a toy or eat a healthy snack. A five-year-old can generally be relied upon to use proper judgment in taking a nap, in choosing his friends, and certainly in deciding what interests him as a human being. Ten-year-olds are often perfectly capable of preparing their own breakfasts, washing their own clothes, cleaning their own rooms, choosing their own playmates, and making many other decisions as well. Teenagers are capable of running their lives if they have your proper guidance and if they know that these opportunities can be withdrawn if they are abused. Asking permission to do anything is characteristic of a very childlike attitude, and while some permission must be obtained at various age levels, it is still an important policy to stop incessantly monitoring and thinking for children. If you do not, they may either resent you for your constant interference in their lives, or become nonthinking robots who consult you for every activity of the day, or do nothing until ordered.

Encourage sensible independence and you will find children becoming accustomed to change and the unknown, largely because they are given unwritten, unspoken permission to test their own judgment in this world. Do not schedule their days for them in the summer months, and give them an opportunity to think and plan for themselves. Have some vital interests of your own, rather than living your entire life through and around your children. Allow them the pleasure of deciding what they like. Become a learner sometimes rather than a teacher 100 percent of the time. The child who has his entire day planned is not a person who is becoming equipped to handle the unknown or to deal effectively with change. I have heard parents telling their children, "At nine o'clock you can ride your bike, but you must be back here at ten thirty because we are having visitors. Then you will have lunch at noon with Aunt Molly and me, and you must be here for the two o'clock trip we are taking to the mall. At four thirty you can talk to your father, who will be calling to talk, and then you will have dinner at six o'clock sharp. After dinner we are going to the movies, and then I want you in bed at eight thirty sharp because I want you up early to start the wonderful day I have planned for you tomorrow." This kind of scheduling approach to a young person's life teaches him that he has no mind of his own, and that if he wants to know how to enjoy himself he can simply ask his parents, since he is unable to decide such vital things on his own. This is not an endorsement of abandoning your children and ignoring them. A sensible blend of helping them to think for themselves, some strong interest in their well-being, and caring enough about them to be concerned about where they are is what I am advocating. Teach them that they must have some responsibility over their own lives and that it is all right to schedule a big part of their own lives without constant interference from anyone.

Live your life through your own accomplishments and enjoy those of your children. Do not become so involved in their young lives that you become a burden to them as they grow up. While it is wonderful to enjoy your children's accomplishments, to attend their dance recitals, and to go with them to their athletic events, it is also important that the children be allowed to experience these things for what they bring to *them*. Be an excited spectator, but be sure that their experiences are for them and that yours are for you. Demonstrate to your children that you have important interests, just as they do. If they become emotional when you leave, explain in an understanding yet firm manner that you also like to play, just as they do, and that you have your own interests and want to have time alone with your friends. Then do it! You will be a far better parent and person if you feel satisfied, purposeful, and significant, rather than trapped at home in expectation of the needs of your youngsters. As a human being who is fulfilled, feels important and useful, and enjoys life to the fullest, you give children the best example you could give them. You become a real live model of a no-limit person. Give them an everyday model of what they can be, even if they fight you in order to get you to change your mind and give in to their demands. They need an example of a self-fulfilled, happy person, not someone who lives life through children and who will later feel stressed by the empty nest syndrome.

Avoid giving your children descriptors which will limit them throughout their lives. A child who is constantly reminded that she is not athletic will soon paint that kind of picture for herself in her mind. Soon the picture will become her reality, and then her behavior toward athletics will reinforce the picture she has of herself. Consequently, she will avoid any athletic activity and justify her behavior with "I'm just not athletic. I never have been— it's just my nature. I can't help it." Encourage your children to try everything in life, to practice in areas where they feel deficient, and to avoid those self-descriptors which inhibit their enjoyment of life, to say nothing of lowering their own expectations for themselves. Each person is intrinsically capable of excelling in any area of human endeavor if he or she is willing to persevere. Never allow your children to think for a moment that you personally believe that they cannot do anything because of some self-description. Whenever you hear them using "I'm not talented," or "attractive," or "good in math," or whatever, challenge it with "You've chosen to think of yourself this way; would you like to change it?" Let them know that while they may be uncertain themselves, you know better.

Replace "Do your best" with simply, "Do." "Your best" is an illusion, since one never knows what his best is at any time in his life. Besides, one need not achieve at a high level in every single area of human endeavor. Enjoying life is far superior to being graded on your performance in life. Children should not be placed in a position in which their worth depends on how well they perform. While it is nice to pick out a few things in which to excel at a high level, it is far more sensible and healthy to try lots of things, and to simply do them, rather than having to achieve at the highest possible level. Children who know in the back of their minds that they must *always* excel will avoid trying rather than face possible failure. They may also experience a great deal of frustration and anxiety in constantly striving to attain their elusive "best."

Achievement as an indication of success is a low-level means of self-evaluation. Substituting quality and personal fulfillment for the external measures of achievement provides much higher levels to attain. Moreover, the external measures of success will follow your child throughout life if he learns to advance confidently in the direction of his own dreams and stop chasing someone else's definition of success. Success, like happiness and love, is an inner process. You bring it to what you do, rather than trying to take it from your activities. Teach children to enjoy life and to feel fulfilled in whatever they do, and success as I am presenting it here, will chase after them for a lifetime. The alternative is to have them always chasing it in the form of more and more achievements. Consequently they will suffer from the disease called "more" for a lifetime, and success will always just elude them.

Take off the pressure in this whole business of having to win at everything, and instead teach them to do anything and not to be afraid of losing. While high grades are certainly nice, knowledge is far more significant. While trophies are fun to accumulate, being a participant in the exciting athletic contests of life is far more beneficial. Too much pressure for winning and success, for getting on the team, or for pleasing some external judge and winning medals puts pressures on young people that they often cannot handle. Moreover, it teaches them that outer rewards are the basic ingredients of being a successful person. Nothing could be further from the truth. Being serene within yourself, feeling a sense of purpose and mission, being able to laugh and enjoy life—all of the variables that I mentioned in the first chapter—are the real ingredients of a no-limit person, and none of these qualities comes from external sources.

Try to take the price tag off life for your children. Young people who learn to idolize money will only pursue those things which money can buy, and that is a very limited way to go in life. Teach inner values, emphasize the inner glow that comes from admiring an object rather than always asking how much it costs or stressing what you paid for it. Those people who are trained to think about money and evaluate life in monetary terms, seldom think about anything else. While it is certainly healthy to teach the value of money, it is also equally important to teach that value is determined not by money but by how much you personally enjoy an activity or object.

Try to create an open environment within your family. Be open to discussions about everything and anything. Try to eliminate any taboos in your relationships with your children. They are curious about sex, as we all are, so make it okay to discuss any component of sex. Be more open about their teenage likes. Take in a concert performed by the currently popular rock groups and learn firsthand what all the fuss is about. They are no more "weird" than the silly fads you subscribed to in your teenage years. Encourage your children to enjoy their youth and to ask you questions about anything that troubles them. Let their laughter remind you of what you used to be. An open, honest environment, free from the judgments that so often discolor the relationship between parent and child, is the key to helping your children to be open and inquiring about life, rather than closed and fearful of the unknown. Have open discussion sessions at the dinner table or some other specified time, when you exhibit open-mindedness. Show them that you do not treat their young views as inferior simply because they have not lived as long as you have. In fact, if you think about it, you have simply had a longer time to reinforce your prejudices and so it may be far more difficult for you to be objective about new things than it is for your children. Do not stifle their inquisitiveness with your own rigid thinking, and work hard at allowing them to express their ideas. Listen attentively.

Make an agreement with your children that you will not correct them in public, and that you expect comparable treatment yourself. No one enjoys being corrected in public. Children who are always being publicly corrected soon develop a fear of speaking and being made to look foolish. This fear manifests itself when children refuse to try new things, to speak up for themselves, to become assertive. The parent who constantly corrects a child's grammar, who reminds him constantly of factual errors, who tells him in front of strangers that he has miscalculated a price, is creating a kind of avoidance tension as well as creating resentment and anger. If you feel that you are doing it for the child's own good, then gently remind him when he does not feel embarrassed around others. A person who is always being monitored and who knows that a reprimand is about to be delivered soon loses respect for the person doing the reprimanding, and eventually withdraws from any communication. *No one likes being corrected in public!* Keep this in mind, and do not do it because you think you know what is best for the children. Instead, be like a friend to them, and if you must help them by correcting them, at least give them the courtesy of doing it privately. And of course you must insist on the same courtesy yourself.

Be a reinforcer of positive rather than negative behavior. Catch them doing things right. Compliment them when you see positive behavior, and forget about trapping them when they are doing something that you believe is wrong. Positive reinforcement helps children to welcome change; negative reinforcement teaches children to be fearful of change. Suspicious, fearful children who know that they are expected to do something wrong will not disappoint you for very long. They will do those things that get your attention if that is what you reinforce, so think hard about not being the "I caught you doing something wrong" adult.

Use storytelling with young children. Tell a story up to the point where the hero faces danger; then allow the child to make up the endings, and talk about why he chose his own particular version. Give children an opportunity in your creative stories to have themselves become adventurers and to welcome new surroundings, rather than taking the safe route. The storytelling method can spur children's imaginations to new heights, and little children love to participate in a new story. Play a new game such as "I'm a new friend; ask me questions to find out who I am and what I like to do."

Put into practice what you know is right for children. You want them to be creatively alive, searching out new territory, exploring the world, and viewing each day as a miracle. You want them to be comfortable with change and to take risks, rather than to have a bored approach to life. To the suggestions I have offered here in this chapter I am quite sure that you could add your own invaluable list that would have equally beneficial results. A wonderful summary for this chapter on helping your children to welcome change and seek out the unknown is offered by Goethe, one of the most creative thinkers and philosophers of all time: "Treat people as they are, and they remain that way. Treat them as though they were what they can be, and we help them become what they are capable of becoming."

Treat children as though they already have achieved their own greatness, as if they are no-limit people who welcome change and are unafraid of the unknown. Do it enough and they will actually be all that they ever dreamed of becoming.

4

I Want My Children to Be Self-Reliant

The no-limit person pursues his own individual destiny by his own best internal lights. He feels every moment of life as one of free personal choice. He never wastes time blaming anyone for his own faults or the woes of the world. He depends on nobody else for his own identity or self-worth.

We forfeit three-fourths of ourselves in order to be like other people.

—ARTHUR SCHOPENHAUER

Our inner world is very different from our outer world. Inside of us, deep down where we all must live with ourselves, is a universe of crucial experiences. That inner world, consisting of our emotions or feelings, is different for every individual. Our inner world is where we must be totally honest with ourselves, and where pain does not go away just because something on the outside seems to get fixed.

In order to have a fully developed inner sense of peace, each human being must learn how to take command over what he thinks, how he responds to his feelings, and ultimately how he behaves. Our uniqueness as a human being is the core of our inner world. This idea is beautifully expressed by Friedrich Nietzsche:

> At bottom every man knows well enough that he is a unique being, only once on this earth; and by no extraordinary chance will such a marvelously picturesque piece of diversity in unity as he is, ever be put together a second time.

The development of our inner world as a self-accepting human being involves taking total responsibility for that inner world, and eliminating the inclination to blame others for our life conditions. Inner-directed human beings come to rely on their own inner signals and shun the tendency to be externally motivated in any way. They learn to avoid the need for approval from everyone else, and instead look inside for self-approval based upon a code of ethics and a strong determination to remain unique. These components of inner development are often ignored in our parenting undertakings, but they must not stay on the sidelines if we truly want to raise children as no-limit people.

One of the most important lessons for children to learn is the necessity of taking total personal responsiblity for their inner development. They must learn early that no one else is capable of controlling what goes on inside of them. The world creates many circumstances over which we have little or no control. Each person must learn from the very beginning that his inner world belongs to him only, and that everything he thinks, feels, and ultimately does as a human being is within his power to control. This is the ultimate freedom that you can give to your children: *the knowledge and belief that they can control their own inner worlds*. Once they have this belief, and begin to live their lives based upon this fundamental premise, they will be on the road to no-limit living for their entire lives. If they fail to get this basic understanding ingrained, they will become blaming, complaining, whining, approval-seeking individuals who do not believe that they have the capacity to make choices. They will remain dependent rather than becoming independent, not only as children but forever. This, then, is a major lesson on the pathway of no-limit living.

Blaming is a way of life for many people in our culture, and it is particularly endemic among children who have been around those adults who are faultfinders. Children learn fast, and blaming is one thing that they master at a very early age if it is a part of their environment. You can either reinforce a blaming mentality in children, or you can assist them in taking total responsibility for what goes on in their lives, and in learning to eagerly accept that responsibility as well. This means trying to ensure that they do not feel they are being persecuted or punished for taking total responsibility for their own inner development. It also means that you will positively reinforce their taking responsibility and help them eliminate blame for their life conditions. In order to accomplish this objective, you must see the advantages of having them grow to assume total responsibility for themselves. Try to keep an open mind about this entire business of inner development and how it is controlled by the ways in which children are taught to think!

They Feel as They Learn to Think

Children begin to assume total responsibility for their own inner development as they learn to rid themselves of the words "It's not my fault," "Don't blame me," "I couldn't help it," and the like. All of us have a very private life within ourselves. We live with that private person continuously, and that private person always knows when we are lying or exaggerating, when we are fooling others by blaming someone else for our mistakes, and when we are feeling sad or joyous. That inner world holds the key to becoming a no-limit person. How that inner self is developed depends largely upon how easy it is for us to be honest with ourselves and those around us. That inner world I am describing contains all of our feelings. It is that special place within each of us where we can find peace if we are at peace with ourselves. We can have privacy there if we are comfortable with ourselves. We can feel healthy if we have no ill thoughts or feelings toward ourselves. This very private inner world is uniquely ours to develop, but we can do it much more readily if we have helping people on our side.

The person who has a highly developed inner world is basically one who has eliminated blame from his life entirely. When children are free enough to take responsibility for their own thoughts, feelings, and behavior, they will also be free enough to understand as well that they do not have to assume responsibility for anyone else's inner world. So, while there are some hardships that a young person must endure in assuming responsibility for how he thinks and feels, there are many more advantages to becoming a person with a highly developed inner world. The big advantage, of course, is in not having to feel guilty, angry, or afraid when others refuse to be responsible for their own inner selves.

The most important lesson in becoming a highly evolved inner-developed person is to learn right from the very beginning that each person is capable of using his mind in any way that he wants to, regardless of what is going on in the outside world. The mind is the inner self; people and events are the outer world. We control our thoughts; the world simply exists. We control our thinking mechanism; other people act as they are going to no matter what we think. Children must learn that they can control their thoughts and consequently their inner development no matter what is taking place around them, and that those thoughts determine their internal feelings and external actions. It is impossible to control that entire inner world if blame is an ingredient in the mental process. Blaming others for conditions in your life is nothing more than excuse making. Whatever you feel, each and every moment of your life, is the result of how you perceive your world and the people and events in it. If you feel depressed, you have been victimized by your own depressing thoughts. If you feel frustrated, then you are choosing to think frustrating thoughts. If you are growing a worry ulcer, it is because you have used your mind to think worry thoughts, or because you have chosen to think of the world as a worrisome place. If you feel joy and satisfaction, it is also because of your thinking mechanism.

Each one of us, therefore, is free to think in any way we

choose. We often encounter people who make it difficult to adopt this way of thinking as a habit, particularly as we are growing up. Your children must be reminded that any blame they may assign to others does not change their reality; they are still choosing their own inner experiences. Just because they blame someone else for their feelings does not alter reality. Whatever they choose to believe, be it blame or self-responsibility, the truth is still there. Others do not make them unhappy; it is what they think of what others are doing that determines their state of mind. The important lesson we want to teach children at all stages of their development is that *you feel as you think.* William James put it this way: "The greatest discovery of my generation is that human beings can alter their lives by altering their attitudes of mind."

Children who learn to accept responsibility for themselves learn how to live no-limit lives. Children who learn to blame, shun self-responsibility and try to circumvent reality by blaming external events or other people.

How Blame Works

Most children love to blame someone else for their problems in life largely because they have been taught that accepting self-responsibility is going to have a negative result with their parents. When you notice children using typical blame sentences like "It's not my fault," "I can't do anything about it," "My teacher flunked me," or "Jimmy made me do it," you must examine your own previous attitudes. Have you punished them in the past when they acknowledged responsibility for a behavior?

The child who spills milk as a two-year-old, and receives a response of anger and frustration, believes that he is a disappointment and interprets the anger and frustration as rejection. Consequently, he will look for any excuse to avoid that kind of reproach, since children want to be loved. A healthy reaction to a glass of spilled milk is simply "That's okay—we all spill things sometimes. I know you did not do it on purpose. Let's get it cleaned up." Then follow up with a hug and a big kiss, regardless of how many times it has occurred in the past week. The child who receives a glare, or a slap, or criticism for his clumsiness in front of others, learns that he must avoid responsibility for the mistake.

"Billy did it; I was just sitting here," "The glass was slippery; it wasn't my fault," "Mary was pinching me" are some of the creative excuses he will haul out of his rapidly forming blame arsenal. The fact is that the milk spilled. Period. No amount of anger or lecturing is going to unspill it. More important, the child was responsible for spilling it. Even if he tries to abdicate that responsibility, he still spilled the milk in reality. What you want to do is help him to say, "I spilled it. I didn't mean to do it." No blame is necessary in this environment of simply expressing truth and getting on with life. Even if the spill was intentional, to gain attention, the child can be given a sponge or paper towel to clean up the mess for which she is responsible. This example may not sound significant, but after a few hundred times the child whose actions meet with angry outbursts will blame someone else for them and will become a person who is always looking outside himself to explain why things did not work out. This child develops into the person with excuses similar to the following: When he does poorly on an examination in school, "The teacher was unfair—she tested us on material that we didn't read. *She* gave me a failing grade." When he loses a tennis match, "The wind did it, and besides, he gave me bad line calls." When he has a fight with his girlfriend, "She never listens to me! It always has to be her way." When he loses a job, "No one could work with my supervisor—he was always picking on me. Besides, he hates all Italians."

The focus for failure and life difficulties is transferred to everyone but the self. Self-questioning asks: "What is it about me that always makes me lose these close tennis matches?" "Why couldn't I get along with her? I have to work on my quick temper." "I keep losing jobs. What could I do to prevent that?" The young person who learns to blame others for even the most insignificant things, is always looking for someone else to blame so that he can appear innocent. Teach children at all stages of their development that most of the things that happen to them in their lives are generally in their own hands, and that *everything* they feel inside is entirely in their control. In the examples above, the young boy who is growing into a man and blaming everyone else for his failures could be something quite different. He could have been taught from the very beginning that there is nothing wrong with saying, "I did it; it's my fault. I'll work on not doing it anymore." He could have learned that self-responsibility is one of the greatest assets that a no-limit person can acquire, since it keeps you in charge of your life, rather than letting others have control.

Children who blame teachers for academic difficulties are giving that teacher permission to control their lives. Similarly, when they encounter difficulties with love and friendship and are depressed for long periods of time over a lover's or friend's behavior, they have given up the control of their lives. Help children to assume responsibility for themselves from the earliest days of their existence. You are doing them a favor when you encourage them to acknowledge their shortcomings, to admit their mistakes, to be unafraid of contrary opinions. Help them to be responsible people by loving them for their errors, telling them that it is okay to make mistakes, and letting them know that they are loved even if they do get jelly on the carpet, or fail a biology course, or wet the bed, or anything else that they do as human beings. You are showing them how much you love them when you talk to them about not blaming a sister for their mistakes, or not trying to take the focus off themselves when they are obviously the one who is responsible for burning the pan. People burn pans in this life. It happens. The more a child learns to say, "Okay, I was careless. I'll replace it if I can save up the money. I did it and I'm sorry," the stronger he will be. When you also can say, "You are much better off for admitting it. It's not the end of the world because you burned a pan"—rewarding them verbally for honesty, rather than punishing them—you are encouraging them to be honest, and are reinforcing inner strength. A lifetime of fearing self-responsibility produces a person who blames everyone for everything in his or her life. Ultimately such people become adults who blame the economy for their lack of fortune, the stock market for their lack of fiscal security, the anxiety attack for their own anxious thinking, employers for their inability to keep a job, bad luck for their illnesses, in a never-ending array of excuses that create a self-deception as a way of life. Avoid blaming, and be a person who works with children to teach them responsibility for their own inner development, understanding the importance of the word *choice*. Use it regularly in the beautiful job of assisting children to develop into self-reliant humans.

They Are Always Making Choices

Virtually everything in life is a choice. Even if children have learned to blame others for their problems, they are still making choices.

If they do not admit it, that still does not change the fact that they have chosen to be exactly where they are in their young inner lives. A giant parental task is helping children to understand this business of making choices: reinforcing the knowledge that they have a free will as their birthright, and reminding them that they must maintain the ability to choose how they will think in life.

As you think, so will you feel and behave, and your ability to think whatever you choose is the paramount lesson of this entire chapter. You too must believe that you are a person who can make choices, and be an example for children of a person who lives accordingly. You must show your children that you take responsibility for how you feel in your life. If you find yourself upset at the way a clerk has talked to you, and you continue with outbursts of anger at home, you are demonstrating that a store clerk has control over your emotional life at home. Practice being a different kind of example for both yourself and your children. You have the power to think anything you wish when a person is rude to you. Do not allow the behavior of others to ruin your day. Let children hear you say something like "I allowed her rude treatment to upset me at the time, but I refuse to go on being upset over something that happened hours ago. I am not going to think about it any longer." This shows that you can choose to think in a more productive and fulfilling way. Work at letting children know that you are not a person who blames others for your own upsets, and you will be teaching them to think likewise.

The power of regarding yourself as a person with a free will to choose how you think will rub off on children almost immediatley. You are teaching them the truth of their reality. They *do* choose how they feel. When a child tells you that a friend hurt her feelings, be sympathetic, and teach her to be truthful with herself. "I know you are hurt right now because of what Karen said, but don't you think you are making her opinion of you more important than your own opinion of yourself?" This kind of a response puts the focus where it belongs: on the child who is choosing to be upset because of what Karen has said. Karen didn't make her upset. You must know and recognize this. There was a choice made to *be* upset. Do not deliver a lecture, but do interact from the perspective of a person who knows that no one else has the power to upset another person, and help your child to see that how she is thinking at this moment is a choice.

As you proceed in teaching children about their own abilities to make choices, begin to expand this in many different dimensions of their lives. Help them to take responsibility for their illnesses by seeing that these, too, are the result of the choices that they make. (See Chapter 8 for a detailed treatment of thinking and health.) They make choices to be tired at almost any time in their lives. Thinking sickly is a choice. All depression, anxiety, stress, and relationship difficulties fall in this choice-making category. The more you encourage them to see themselves as free-willed choice-making individuals, the more you help them to take control of their inner lives. The ability to say to oneself, "I chose it," is the freedom not to choose self-defeating thoughts and actions in the future. Children can grow believing that there is a genius residing within, that they can choose to think virtually anything they wish. Children can grow up recognizing that this wonderful power of making choices is what gives them freedom. You want children to be in control of their entire inner development as human beings. If they give that control to anyone else, they are literally slaves, and there is no such thing as a well-adjusted slave.

Children will not like the emphasis on choice making at first because it takes away their ability to blame others for their own problems. If a child is upset because his father is verbally abusive, and you commiserate about the situation, stating that the father is being cruel and gets that way when he drinks too much, you are putting the source of his upset on his father's behavior. This gives the child a reason to feel bad, and it *prevents* a solution to the child's anguish, since his father is not likely to either stop drinking or refrain from picking on him.

Teach children that at moments like these they have a choice. Yes, admittedly, it is a difficult choice, but still a choice nevertheless. Children need to know that they can work on their own inner thoughts at these unpleasant moments, and learn how to turn the father's verbal assaults into something other than their own inner despair. "You can tell yourself something quite different while your father is yelling at you. This is his problem, but you are telling yourself that he is right, that you are a twerp, and therefore you are making his opinions of you count more than your own. How about practicing some new thoughts when your father starts yelling? Perhaps you could internally file it away someplace where you won't hurt yourself with it so much." This kind of logic is crucial for young children to learn very early in their lives. They do have choices. No matter how badly someone treats them verbally, they still must know that it is their own thoughts about that treatment that makes them upset, not the treatment itself. Teach them that they control their inner lives, that they always have a choice to think what they choose, and ultimately you are helping them get on the path to no-limit living. Otherwise, they will be victimized for a lifetime by the thoughts, feelings, and behaviors of other people. When you teach them that they have choices about their own inner development, including their emotions, then you are gearing them toward becoming inner-directed people. This business of inner-directedness is at the heart of being a self-fulfilled person.

Note: Obviously, young children who are physically or sexually abused by anyone are in no position to be told to "think differently." They must be *immediately* removed from such circumstances, and the offending adult treated for the sickness that he or she possesses. While ex-victims of sexual or physical abuse can subsequently be helped to think in less self-defeating ways about their earlier experiences, the only intelligent first responses are immediate removal and counseling.

Choosing Inner Rather Than Outer Direction

The pressures to be an outer-directed person are everywhere in our culture. Being outer-directed means that the controls of your life are located outside of yourself, so consequently you become dependent upon external forces and other people in making significant decisions. It is important to help your children become as inner-directed as possible, and to have the courage and perseverance to resist external control in their lives.

Obviously, infants and very young children need a great deal of external control over their lives. This does not mean that they cannot learn very early to begin to consult their inner signals in making some determinations about their own young destinies. Babies, if allowed, will make choices every day. They decide what toy to hold, whom they want to go to, what foods they like, and what to smile at. If you allow them a large measure of choice making from the very beginning, they will develop a sense of control over themselves and their environment. If you do not, and you fail to encourage choice making throughout their lives, they may substitute blame and faultfinding for that control.

As children mature they have a different set of developmental tasks that will reflect their general direction in life, pointing toward either inner or outer control. Young toddlers can be taught to put the locus of control more and more within themselves as they naturally become less physically dependent. The two-year-old who learns to make decisions about what clothes to wear is learning that internal choices are useful, rather than relying on an adult every time he changes a piece of clothing. Two-year-olds also know with whom they like to play. Respecting that choice is a step toward helping them develop inner direction. They know how to feed themselves, when they are tired, when they want to sit quietly, or when they want to play with the older children. They do not need to be told that they are too young for this or that; they can try things as long as reasonable caution is observed.

The growing toddler has thousands of opportunities every day to make choices. If those opportunities are discouraged and all decisions are made by big people, then inner-directedness is being squelched as well. This is not an endorsement of nondiscipline. Effective discipline involves placing reasonable limits on children at their various ages of development, but only for the safety and welfare of the child, not to show who is boss. Ultimately, the goal of discipline is to create children who become self-disciplined persons with inner controls. You do not want children always looking to you, or any other authority figure, for discipline. Your objective is to have them learn to discipline themselves without ever having to consult anyone else. As I sit here at this typewriter in this very moment, I am exercising a great deal of self-discipline. I would love to be outside on the beach, swimming, playing tennis, laughing with my children, or making love with my wife, but I am sitting here facing this typewriter. Imagine if I had to still rely on someone to say to me, "Wayne, you have to sit down and write this afternoon, and I will not let you out of your room until you do." Silly, of course, but an example of precisely what I am discussing in this section on inner development and internal directedness.

We must have the discipline to make ourselves do the things that bring a sense of purpose and meaning to our lives. We cannot rely on anyone else to do it for us. This is your goal in disciplining youngsters. Help them get to the point where they make their own disciplinary decisions. You can only reach this goal by allowing them to experience as much inner-directedness as is humanly possible throughout their developing years. You should only take over for them when it is absolutely necessary.

During their formative years you will have thousands of opportunities to allow your children to become more inner-directed. They can begin by making everyday decisions about what they eat, how much they sleep, what they wear, and with whom they play. Later, as school-age children, they can decide what they will study, what they would like to do a report on, and who their friends will be. Eventually they will make more adult kinds of decisions about the extent to which they will use alcohol, whether they will wear seat belts while driving, whom they will date, and how they will decorate their rooms.

Outer-directed people tend to develop external habits in their lifetimes. Children who learn to blame others for their emotional downs will look to something equally outside themselves to alleviate their problems, such as drugs and alcohol. Naturally, if you believe that something outside yourself made you down, you will reach for something outside yourself to get back up. Inner-directed persons know they are responsible for making themselves down, and never blame anyone else for their thinking. Consequently, inner-directed youngsters will look within for the ability to come back up. They will shun drugs in favor of more positive self-rewarding thoughts and actions. They know that they have the power within themselves to get back up and need not rely on externals for fortification. Being up becomes an attitude, an approach to life that is based upon feeling in control. Inner-directed persons know that all of the controls are within, and act that way in a crisis rather than looking for an external method. Inner causes of feeling high on life are located just there, inside, and therefore they are not merely temporary.

The problem with becoming an externally directed person is that the opinions of other people take on an entirely new meaning. They become literal shackles that keep the young person a prisoner to those opinions. The inner-directed young person learns very early how to deal more effectively with that monster demon called approval seeking, one of the great inhibitors to a person's total inner development.

Curbing Their Need for Approval

Children do not *need* the approval of others in order to feel positive about themselves. While it is certainly nicer to have approval than disapproval, and there is nothing unhealthy about seeking approval, there is something very unhealthy about needing that approval. The person who needs approval goes into a state of emotional collapse without it. He becomes immobilized when his friends disagree with him, or when anyone directs disapproval in his direction. Be aware of the importance of becoming not only an inner-directed person who trusts himself, but also one who is able to handle disapproval without any hint of immobilization.

Everyone is going to get a lot of disapproval in their lives. In fact, the people who love you the most will send you huge quantities of disapproval on a regular basis. You simply cannot please everyone all of the time. You cannot please anyone all of the time, either. Consequently, disapproval is something that every single one of us will encounter every single day of our lives. There is no escaping it. Yet I can say with certainty that the need to be approved of by almost everyone for almost everything that we do is perhaps the single most prevalent cause of unhappiness and disease in our culture. Somehow we have inculcated in our youth the notion that disapproval is a terrible thing. Our psychology textbooks have told us for decades now that young people *need peer-group approval* to become healthy, productive adults. I disagree. Young people need to learn very early, and have it positively reinforced every day, that peer-group approval is something that comes and goes depending upon what group you are in, what day it is, the outcome of the football game, what you are wearing, the opinions of other contemporaries elsewhere, and on and on through an endless list of transitory factors. While peer-group approval is nice, it is not a prerequisite to being a self-reliant no-limit person. To achieve this, one needs to approve strongly of oneself. It is important to listen intently to the opinions of others, but to understand that no one will ever get the approval of everyone he meets, so one ought to stop being concerned about it and look within for that approval. In fact, the more one approves of oneself in a nonconceited manner, the far greater chance he has of attaining that elusive peer-group approval. People generally gravitate toward those who have a strong sense of self-worth, rather than toward those who are consumed with being approved of by everyone else. It is a paradox that approval comes the most to those who are the least concerned with it. And, conversely, those who constantly seek approval are those who receive the least of it.

From the earliest years on through adolescence and into adulthood, people need to learn that approval seeking is a waste of time and that it will only make them neurotic if it is pursued as a need. Children must learn that being depressed because one of their friends dislikes them is tantamount to giving that friend's opinion total control over their own inner emotional world. When young children are hurt because they have incurred some disapproval, it is a clue to help them to see that this disapproval is quite normal, that they will encounter a lot of it in their lives, and that their own self-picture is far more important than the pictures of others, since they have to live with their own pictures all the time, while the pictures of others come and go on a constant basis.

Suppose you believe that peer-group approval is absolutely essential, and your teenage daughter seeks your advice on how to be liked. Your reaction to her will be "I must see what I can do to help her get some peer-group approval, since this is obviously what she needs." From this particular stance, you will then set about helping her to become an apple-polisher. "Lisa, maybe your friends will like you better if you change your hairstyle or your clothes. Or perhaps you should try to become more like the rest of the kids; then you would fit in and maybe you wouldn't feel so bad. How about taking each one of them some money—then you'll get their approval." You see how absurd it is to have a child believe that the approval of others is a need. A far healthier no-limit approach would be to say, "Lisa, there will be many times when others will disapprove of you. I know you are feeling hurt, but maybe it's more important for you to be Lisa than to be something that they want just so they will approve of you. Are you happy with you? Because that's all you really have, you know—and that's a lot. In fact, it's everything." You can also suggest that she evaluate her peers' data to see if there is any worthwhile message in it about her behavior, not about her *worth*.

You can explore with Lisa the difference between wanting and needing approval. Help her to see that needing approval just makes her a slave to the opinions of others, and that as she becomes confident within herself, approval will flow her way in large amounts without any expenditure of effort on her part. Help her to work on her own self-confidence and stop putting the focus on what everyone else is thinking.

Most young people of all ages are constantly seeking the approval of others because we have placed such a premium on being just like everyone else, and fitting in at all costs. Somehow the socialization process has become more important than helping young people to grow up believing in themselves. The results of this constant search for the approval of others can be seen in the vast numbers of people who seek out therapists, who consume tranquilizers, who try to fit in at all costs, and who lack any measure of self-dignity or confidence in themselves. Children can learn to respect the opinions of others, and still not be consumed with winning the approval of everyone. We must allow children to grow up to be separate and unique. Robert Frost, the wonderful no-limit poet, said "The best things and best people rise out of their separateness; I'm against a homogenized society because I want the cream to rise." If everyone is the same, constantly striving to be just like everyone else and to win the approval of everyone they meet, there will be no cream. We will all be a mixed blend of homogenized pap.

The process of teaching children not to need the approval of others can begin very early. When they whine about someone calling them names, rather than chastising the name-caller, respond to them with "Even if he does think that you are stupid, does that mean you are?" Get them to see from the earliest moments of their lives that being called a name, or being thought of as stupid, is only meaningful if you internalize it. Teach them to ignore those kinds of taunts, and not only will you be helping them to toss away that neurotic need for approval, but you will also be helping them to have to endure less taunting later on in their lives. You see, people only call others names if it succeeds in getting them upset. When it is ignored, the taunting goes away. And why wouldn't it? Who wants to hurl abuse at someone who is not paying attention?

There is a tremendous irony involved in approval seeking. The more you seek approval, the less likely you are to get it, since no one enjoys being around an approval seeker. The same is true of love, success, and money. Anything in life that you chase will always elude you until you become more involved in your own life projects. Then love, approval, money, and success will chase you. If you want approval, you must stop chasing it and become a person who is approved of. Infants who are given very heavy doses of approval, who are loved unconditionally, who are picked up and cuddled all the time, have the greatest opportunity to be free from the need for approval later in their lives. It is almost as if they get filled up with so much approval as toddlers that they do not need it anymore as adults. The more approval they get as youngsters, the less inclined they will be to demand it as adults.

As children go through their own maturational processes, they will encounter disapproval a great deal. There will be times when it will be almost overwhelmingly difficult not to give in and agree with your child that the people who are withholding their approval are the real causes of his or her temporary unhappiness. Do not give in to this pressure! Always be sympathetic to what a child is experiencing inside, but never for one moment allow children to believe that the source of their inner turmoil is located in anyone but themselves. In showing them that you understand how they feel, you are providing a compassionate model of a caring person, but if you slip, and put the blame for their hurts on those friends, teachers, bosses, neighbors, lovers, or anyone else, you teach them to give up the control of their inner lives.

Here are a few examples of ways to interact with youngsters who feel that they must have the approval of others in order to be happy. Communicate sensible empathy with their feelings, but always put the emphasis on their ability to handle a problem from within, without always requiring the approval of others.

> I know you are hurting now, but you are making your teacher's attitudes too important. Perhaps we can figure out a way to help her to be more considerate, but if she won't give in, you do not want to allow her to be the cause of your pain.
>
> It is very difficult to have a fight with your girlfriend, but I'm proud of you for standing up for what you believe and not allowing her to manipulate you. And you do not want to let her manipulate you inside, either.
>
> Of course Sammy next door thinks you are a sissy—he thinks that about lots of kids. But what do you think of you? Are you a sissy just because Sammy thinks so?

I see that you are depressed over the things that some of the kids said about you. Why do you think we all give other people so much power over us? Do you think that maybe they said those things to get you to react just like this?

Inner development is just as important as outer physical development. The biggest inhibitors to achieving a highly evolved sense of inner peace are the inclination to blame, the abdication of responsibility for what one is experiencing within, and the need to have everyone else approve of you for everything that you do. What follows are some of the typical ways in which adults interact with children to discourage a strong sense of inner growth, and some of the more typical ways in which children behave that give evidence that inner development is being constrained in the name of fitting in or just getting along. Next are the more common payoffs that you receive for these behaviors, along with some highly specific suggestions for helping to teach children to ultimately become totally responsible for their own inner development.

Typical Child and Parental Behaviors Which Inhibit Inner Development

Here are some common examples of adult–child behaviors which foster learning disabilities in the area of inner development.

□ Providing excuses for children which they can readily adopt as their blame techniques. "You're too young to understand." "You couldn't really help it." "It wasn't your fault—you just got in with the wrong crowd." "Your teacher just doesn't understand how sensitive you are." "You have too many pressures on you now, so you really couldn't concentrate."

□ Focusing attention on who is at fault rather than on providing solutions. "I want to know who broke this dish!" "Somebody left fingerprints on the wall, and I am going to find out who did it!" "This house is a mess—which one of you did this?" "Nobody is going to watch TV until I find out who left the water running in the kitchen."

◻ Encouraging tattling by children, and then taking their word as a basis for meting out punishment.

◻ Punishing children for telling the truth, thereby making lying and blaming much more sensible alternatives, in their eyes, for the future.

◻ Being a person who uses excuses and blames others. "I never got anywhere in life because of—my spouse, my parents, the economy, or whatever." "It wasn't my fault that I got a traffic ticket." "I couldn't help it—I just got fat because my mother always made those wonderful desserts."

◻ Using "It's not my fault" as a regular part of your vocabulary.

◻ Using pills and medicines for all sorts of pains and troubles, and encouraging your children to believe that pills will make them better.

◻ Encouraging children to blame each other for their problems, fights, and difficulties. Always settling their arguments for them, and disbursing blame to the appropriate child.

◻ Providing children with genetic excuses. "You're just like your grandfather." "Your mother couldn't spell, so it's no wonder you can't either." "You sound just like your father when you whine like that. I guess you got it from him."

◻ Doing their homework for them because it is too hard for them to tackle.

◻ Putting the major emphasis in life on being right. Encouraging children to never admit to being wrong by never doing so yourself.

◻ Being concerned with impressing others in your dress, purchases, and lifestyle.

◻ Encouraging children to become apple-polishers and win the approval of others at the expense of their own integrity, particularly when the apple-polishing can result in improving their grades, getting a job, making more money, or achieving some other external gain.

◻ Doing anything to avoid a confrontation with your children. Letting them rule the house with their unruly behaviors and attitudes and saying nothing to them for fear of having a scene or upsetting them.

□ Being fearful of providing necessary disciplinary actions, thereby giving your children an example of a person who needs their approval. Encouraging them to avoid responsibility for their actions by pretending that they have been behaving properly when you know that just the opposite is true.

□ Not allowing them to state their own opinions and stand up to you for what they believe, by being overly authoritarian and rigid.

□ Using labels with them which ultimately become cop-outs. "You're not an athletic person." "You've always been shy." "You inherited deficient math genes." "You have always been lousy in the cooking area." "You never liked music."

□ Demanding that they respect you and parenting out of fear.

□ Forbidding the question "Why?" by saying, "I am your parent and that is why you must obey me."

□ Making them ask permission for everything they think, say, feel, and do throughout their lives.

□ Forcing them to apologize when they really do not mean it.

□ Being unable to handle an opposing point of view and becoming upset when children disagree with you.

□ Making grades more important than knowledge.

□ Using external sources as the ultimate authority. "It's the rule." "It's in the Bible." "Your teacher said so." "The law is the law and you do not challenge it."

□ Deciding who their friends will be and forbidding them to play with certain types of people.

□ Thinking and acting for them when they are very small and assuming that they do not have minds of their own. Treating them as apprentice people who have not really arrived yet as total human beings.

□ Refusing to listen to their suggestions. Conversely, they will then refuse to hear your suggestions about anything as well.

□ Never eliciting their opinions about home and family matters. This could include purchases, decorating, vacations, meals, and the everyday decisions that go into living together with them.

□ Telling them, "You're only a child, and someday you will have a family of your own to make decisions for."

□ Forcing them to consult etiquette guides and to live up to standards that others have written for them.

□ Making the acquisition of awards, trophies, and merit badges, and membership in honor societies, more important than what the awards and honors signify.

□ Living your life through the accomplishments of your children and achieving your own personal status via the external route of your child's life.

□ Ignoring their inner development. Making fun of feelings like anxiousness or shyness, or their attempts to express their individuality. Preferring instead that they please others, cope, and do what everyone else is doing.

This list might go on for three hundred more pages. I trust the message is becoming clear. You can do a great deal for children of all ages in helping them to become more responsible for their own inner development as human beings. You can assist them in reducing their propensity toward blaming and approval seeking, and help them to understand that they can make many more choices about the kind of people they want to be than they might have ever considered previously. In order to help them to become choice-making, nonblaming people who have no fear of assuming rightful responsibility for all of their inner experiences, you must take a look once again at your own psychological support system for doing just the opposite. Once you fully realize what it is that *you* as a parent get out of encouraging this external thinking and blaming, perhaps you can then begin to adopt some of the more specific suggestions that follow.

The Psychological Support System That You Receive for Raising Outer-Directed Children

The purpose of blame is to relieve the blamer of responsibility. How did he learn that responsibility was a burden? The fact that blame changes nothing in reality (the catsup is still in a puddle on the table, the account is still overdrawn, the new dress is still torn, the gas tank is still empty) does little to deter the neurotic blamer, because the big need is to be relieved of responsibility for anything negative. There is a fear of disapproval, loss of love, withdrawal of parental or other sources of care. The payoffs for you as a parent, self-defeating though they are, include the following facts:

Outer-directed children want others to make choices for them, and this gives you an element of control over their lives. Controlling children can be a power trip for the person who has little control over his own life. Making the children ask permission and look to you as their boss provides an authority status that may elude you elsewhere. The no-limit person does not need to control anyone in order to feel powerful.

Children who are outer-directed are a captive audience. They are little; you are big. You get to make the decisions; they carry them out. This routine is a strong support system for not allowing children to develop a large measure of choice over their own destinies. The problem is that they stay that way as adults and thereby avoid responsibilities for virtually a lifetime. You can actually sacrifice their independence and maturity for the sake of temporarily feeling important by maintaining all of the controls of their lives, without ever intending to do so.

Children raised to become approval seekers are kept in a "safe" category for a lifetime. Likewise, you get the safe option as a parent. The child who does what he is told, who tries to please everyone else, is a child who is "fitting in" as he is supposed to. This may make for obedient children, but it offers the child no opportunity to grow, to be unique, to make a contribution to his society.

By teaching children to blame others, you are giving them a cop-out for a lifetime. This is the easiest approach to child rearing. It is void of all risks, and it wins you the approval of most of the people who are blamers (nearly everyone). Children will pass the buck and assign responsibility to others for all of their failings and shortcomings while you sit back and agree with them about how tough and unfair this world is. As you are sitting back commiserating about the sorry state of affairs in the world, and how bad everyone else is, you will accomplish nothing, while the world passes you and your children by.

When you raise children to believe that they have no choices in life, you encourage them to stay dependent on you well into their adult years. The more you convince them that they must have you to make decisions, the longer you can extend the period of dependency. While this may make you feel important, it prevents you and your children from participating in a no-limit kind of life.

These are the major psychological payoffs for teaching children to be nonchoosing blamers. While you obviously do not do it deliberately, the effects are the same. Eliminate some of these payoffs and in their place substitute a gloriously exciting feeling of accomplishment in helping each child to become an independent, fully functioning person, who feels strong deep down inside and who has a wonderful sense of being the captain of his own ship, rather than steering a course through life dictated by a navigational plan filed by you. Enjoy their preparation to be their own captains, and find joy in watching them take off on their own. You can take pride and pleasure in their feelings of power as they grow up to be responsible for their entire inner development, recognizing blame as a foolish enterprise for weaklings too scared to own up to their own mistakes. To help you aid them in making choices, ridding themselves of the need for approval and eradicating that insidious blame and faultfinding from their lives, you can try some of the actions described in the following section.

Action Strategies for Helping Children to Be Nonblamers and Inner-Directed

In all of your interactions with children, regardless of their ages, try to eliminate excuses and cop-outs. Begin to insert the words "You chose it" or "It was something that you brought on yourself." For example, instead of saying, "You couldn't really help it—you just got a bad teacher this year," try saying, "You will always get teachers that you disagree with. What kinds of adjustments can you make to have things go more smoothly for you in school?" Put the responsibility for everything that is going on in your child's world on his shoulders, at least to the extent that he experiences it within himself. Teach him to be a choice-maker in the way that he perceives his world, and you will be teaching him to have inner responsibility. Instead of saying, "Your teacher is making you upset," say instead, "You make yourself upset over the way your teacher treats you." It may seem like a small point, but if instead you do the opposite and reinforce to your children that other people are responsible for the way that they feel, you will ultimately teach them to become blamers. With your very young children, do not say, even kiddingly, "Let's hit that bad chair for giving you a boo-boo!" Instead, remind them that the chair was just doing what it was supposed to be doing—that is, sitting wherever it was left. "I guess you will have to watch out for that chair next time" is a response that puts the responsibility for boo-boos where it belongs—that is, on the person who got the bruise, not the inanimate object he ran into.

Eliminate the "who's at fault" syndrome in your home, and insert a "let's find a solution" pattern. Finding out who is to blame and assigning blame points is a senseless activity that only teaches children to become blamers. Instead of looking for problems, look for solutions. When Jennifer complained to her mother about the fact that one of her brothers was messing up her room and breaking her dolls, the mother took a nonblaming approach. Instead of looking to find who was at fault and creating a scene, she asked Jennifer, "What is the solution to putting an end to this kind of thing?" Jennifer also brought the subject up at the dinner table in a nonblaming, nonfaultfinding request. "I really don't care who has been breaking my dolls," she said, "but I would like everyone to stay out of my room. I promise not to go into anyone else's room without permission, and I'd like everybody to ask me, too." Then she asked each person for a verbal agreement and got it. Her mother had helped her to devise a solution, rather than to simply blame her brothers and then have the behavior she disliked so much continue.

Blame solves nothing, but solutions are there if you can get past the notion of finding fault. Instead of having family fights about what the little children do to the bigger children, and vice versa, teach them to think in more creative, solution-oriented ways and you will also be teaching them a far more valuable lesson—that is, to eliminate all tendencies to simply pass out blame points, since they change nothing.

Eliminate the inclination of children to become tattletales by removing yourself as the source of their behavior. A child who constantly runs to his parents to tell on other children is a child who is learning to become a blamer and a non-choice-maker. When you listen to the tattling, you are reinforcing an outer-directed-ness; that is, "Mommy will take care of things for you. I know you can't do it, so just come tattling to Mommy whenever you see something that I should know about." This posture also encourages children to become spies and to win approval through subversive means. No one likes a squealer, and the person who most dislikes a squealer is a squealer himself. A child must learn to fight his own battles and this means taking a few lumps along the way.

At the swimming pool, I have seen parents having their vacation time wasted away with a constant barrage of "Harold splashed me, Mommy!" "Michael pushed me under the water!" "Sammy was running and you said no running." "Mary stuck her tongue out at the lifeguard." "Theresa pulled Mikey's bathing suit down." The little tattletales are gaining attention by attempting to ruin Mommy's time at the pool. The unconscious message to the children is that Mommy isn't really entitled to relaxation time. She has taught all of the children that her time is unimportant and that her role in life is to monitor the age-typical teasings of young children and then to rescue them from their own normal selves by enlisting the aid of a few tiny spies in her life quest to be a rattled mother.

The best response to tattletales is an honest statement about how you feel about tattletales. "I am not interested in having you tattle on others. If you get splashed, figure out your own response to it. If Theresa pulled down Mikey's bathing suit, turn your head if you do not want to see Mikey naked." A few statements which tell children that they are going to have to learn how to play together without constant adult attention, will encourage them to become masters of their own worlds, rather than spies and informants.

A sensible approach to safety is obviously to be considered in this area. A child who is actually hurting a baby or throwing darts at his sister must be reported, but if this kind of extremely dangerous behavior between siblings is going on regularly in your home, then you have to look carefully at the source of such activity. Children should not have access to dangerous materials, and a child who deliberately hurts other children or animals is demonstrating a very serious personality problem, which must be monitored and treated without delay. However, most tattling does not fall into this category. Usually it is a ploy to get the attention of the adult, an approval-seeking strategy that teaches the tattler to look outside himself for the solutions to minor problems, rather than looking within and learning to fight his own battles.

Teach children that the "truth" is something that you respect, and that blaming and lying are not going to be rewarded. If a child knows that he is going to be punished for telling the truth, and punished in such a way that will make his life miserable, then he is very likely to lie or to place blame on someone else. A child learns very early whether he will be accepted and loved when he owns up to his mistakes. If you spank a three-year-old when he says, "Yup, I punched the baby in the nose," and then you withhold love, he will soon learn to say to himself, "This truth stuff only gets me a lot of misery, and Mommy hates me to boot." So the next time the baby cries and you ask your three-year-old, "Did you punch the baby?" he is likely to respond, "Nope, the teddy bear did it" or "I didn't see what happened."

A child can be told very sternly that a baby cannot be hit; you can make it a very firm response. But then, and most important, you must put your arms around your three-year-old, let him know that you understand that he gets frustrated with the baby, and that you love him very much, but that hitting just cannot be permitted. Giving a hug and a kiss after disciplining may sound like sending confusing messages, but it is not at all a conflicting response. Children need to know that you love them even when they behave badly. A hug, a kiss, but a firm reminder that certain behavior is intolerable, teaches a child that owning up to the truth is not all bad. If punishment is called for, always do it with love, the most effective teacher of all. Bear no grudge, have no anger, give no silent treatment; simply teach children that the truth is all right, and that "I love you even when you do things that cannot be tolerated." This applies to children of all ages. Let them know that we all make mistakes, that you are not offended or surprised by anything they do, and that you still care very much for them, but do not allow them to blame others and get away with it.

Stop your own blame trip as of right now. Accept the fact that you are precisely where you have chosen to be in life. Stop blaming your spouse for your unhappiness, your parents for your lack of motivation, the economy for your financial status, the bakery for your excess weight, your childhood for your phobias, and anything else to which you assign blame points. You are the sum total of the choices you have made in your life. Even if you think your parents made mistakes with you, accept the fact that they were human beings doing what they knew how to do at the time, given the unique conditions of their lives. How can you ask any more of anyone? Forgive them and make peace with everyone in your past, and provide your children with an example of a person who blames no one. Show them that you can take responsibility by being honest in front of them. "I am where my choices have led me" is a good response to your children when they ask you about your own life situation. And as life situations come up which encourage you to blame, try to change yourself in front of them. Stop blaming the tax laws for your financial condition. Tell them, "I simply have not made the best financial choices for myself, but I am working at changing that now." Instead of telling them that as a youngster you never had a chance to get a solid education, tell them, "I made other choices as a young person, but now I intend to correct any educational deficiencies I have, because it is never too late." Statements like this provide children with examples of a person who is not a blamer, a person who can make choices to correct the mistakes of the past.

Encourage children to believe that they have control over their own bodies, particularly their illnesses. You must make decisions about the extent to which you rely upon physicians, drugs, over-the-counter medications, and the like. It is important to help children to realize that their attitudes have a great deal to do with how much sickness they have in their lives. The most recent research points dramatically to the ability of the mind to act as a healer. Look into the literature on mind over illness, but even if you are skeptical, it is important for your children to know that they can, in fact, control to some degree the health of their bodies. Every time you tell them to take a pill for a headache or a cramp, you send them the message that they have no power over their own ability to work on the headache or cramp. Encourage them to examine their own attitudes about their illnesses.

Headaches, backaches, cramps, blood pressure, aches and pains of all kinds, ulcers, skin disorders, fatigue and many other conditions are affected by attitudes. Raising children to think of themselves as healers, and to shun medicines unless absolutely necessary, teaches them to avoid the hypochondria that is prevalent among many-limits people. Do not pass out a pill right away when they complain about a common ailment. Instead, help them to examine how their own thinking may be contributing to their pains. Talk about the power of the mind in this regard, about how we often bring on illnesses at convenient times. Encourage them to read up on these issues, and become familiar with them yourself. With your very young children, try to avoid a "going to the doctor" mentality for every little ailment in life. Children who are always encouraged to go to the doctor tend to do so for a lifetime, always looking to the doctor or his magic medicines to cure them, when in fact in a large number of cases the doctor or medicine is not the cause of the healing. *The body is the healer*; that magnificent perfect creation is capable of healing itself in many many instances. The element of choice over one's own health is an attitude that you can cultivate in your children, raising them to believe in their own powers and to use the miracles of modern medicine and the many highly skilled physicians in our world only when necessary, and not as a way of life. (See Chapter 8 for a more thorough treatment of this subject.)

Stop making references to children which encourage them to believe that they inherited their personality traits and talents, or lack of the same. When a child behaves in the same self-defeating manner as his father or a departed grandmother, remind him of the kinds of choices he is making, instead of giving him excuses. "You are failing mathematics because you have given up on yourself in this subject area. You have not chosen to seek out additional help, and you spend no time studying, but most important, you really believe that you cannot do mathematics problems. Once someone believes she cannot succeed at something, she will do everything she can to prove herself right. What do you think we can do *now* to improve your mathematics?" An inherited personality trait is the greatest excuse in the world, since one can never alter his or her chromosomes. Forget the father who failed mathematics, or the grandmother who failed at everything, and help this child to become all that it is possible for her to be.

Be as helpful as you can in assisting your children to help themselves. Keep this sentence in mind when they ask you to do things for them.

If they get into trouble in school, teach them to accept the consequences of their behavior. If they are repeatedly late, help them to be more punctual. Work out together a program for helping them to get out of bed in the morning and off to school on time, but if they continually go back on their agreements, refusing to commit themselves to more punctual behavior, then let them take the consequences of that behavior. If they have to attend summer school because they had to drop a class in high school due to excessive tardiness, then ultimately they will have to do just that. While it may pain you to see them being irresponsible, keep in mind that only through their own experiences will they learn to adopt more self-enhancing behaviors. No matter how much it may pain you internally, they still must learn from experience, just as you did. And while continually rescuing them from their self-defeating behavior may make you feel a bit relieved temporarily, eventually your children will pay for the price for your soft heart. I can remember my mother forcing me to go back to a grocery store owner in the neighborhood and return a squirt gun that I had stolen as a ten-year-old. I was as scared as I could be. I begged her to let me off this one time, but she was unrelenting. "Stealing is immoral," she informed me, "and you are going to face up to what you have done." I went to the market, returned the stolen squirt gun, faced the music by having to work bagging groceries for free, and never again in my life even considered stealing anything. This is true for homework, fights with other children, irresponsible schoolwork, and anything else at any and all ages. Help them to help themselves. Be as concerned and loving as you can be, and always teach them that they make choices and that being a no-limit person involves taking responsibility for the choices one makes in life.

Shift the emphasis in life from being right to being effective. Do not provide children with an example of a person who must always be right, a person who can never admit he has made a mistake, or a person who never changes his mind even when he is confronted with the absurdity or error of the position he has taken. Always having to be right means never admitting to ignorance of something. Teach your children to simply say, "I don't know" or "I'll look it up." A child who cannot say, "I don't know," begins to exaggerate or lie when asked any question. I have seen many children who have learned that making up something is better than admitting that you do not know the answer. These children have been exposed to adults who do exactly the same thing. If you ask this kind of rigid-thinking adult, "How far is it to the Rialto Theater?" that adult will start to give directions even if he does not know where the theater is located or has never heard of the theater. Being seen as knowledgeable and right is more important than simply saying, "I don't know," for this person. Children of such parents will give answers to any question even if they know nothing about what they are saying. Similarly, if such a child does give an answer, he will argue unendingly about the rightness of his position, even when it is obvious to everyone around him that he does not know what he is talking about. Teach children to say, "I don't know," and to admit when they are wrong about something. Teach them through your own example that being right is not really that important. Show them that you can admit to your mistakes, and that you are much more concerned with making sure that it does not happen again than with being right.

If you allowed an insurance policy to lapse, don't try to demonstrate to everyone that it was not your fault. Simply vow to make sure that it does not happen again. Forget the excuses to yourself and your children: "They didn't mail the statement. It must have been lost in the mail. The cat ate the notice. They should have reminded me." Instead, correct your error immediately and learn from it. Admit to everyone, especially the younger ones, that you are responsible for your own insurance, and that if you do not have insurance you are going to suffer the consequences. This kind of thinking will help you to raise children who do the same. Once they see that you do not need to make excuses and be right, then they will have a model to emulate. Soon you will see their excuses and need-to-be-right responses diminish. Always let them know that being wrong and learning from it is far more sensible than appearing to be right but knowing inside that you are a phony.

When children experience hurt feelings, or are feeling badly because of the opinions of others, show them with pure logic that the source of their discomfort is located within because they have made a choice to be upset. Here is a simple dialogue which illustrates the point.

Mother: You look upset, David. Is there anything wrong?

David: Mike and Allen made me feel bad.

Mother: How did they do that?

David: They were laughing at me because in the baseball game I struck out with two men on base.

Mother: Are you upset because you struck out, or because the other boys were laughing at you?

David: Everybody strikes out in a game. I just feel stupid because they were making fun of the way I swung the bat.

Mother: Suppose they had laughed at the way you swung the bat, but you didn't know that they had laughed. Would you still be upset?

David: Of course not. How could I be upset about something I didn't know about?

Mother: It's impossible, of course. I guess it really wasn't Mike and Allen's laughing that upset you, so much as what you told yourself about their laughing.

David: I guess I didn't really have to pay any attention to their dumb laughing in the first place.

Mother: You always have a choice, David. No one else can make you upset unless you allow it, and in this case you let their laughter get the best of you.

The logic needs to be brought home whenever possible. Other people will react to you in any way they choose, and if you did not know about their reactions, then you could not be upset about them. It is only when you learn about the opinions of others, and then make those opinions more important than your own, that you find yourself upset. Teach children to make their own opinions paramount in life, to choose how they react rather than giving others that kind of power over their inner lives.

Teach children to consult themselves about what they enjoy in life, and to forget about what everyone else is thinking and doing. In choosing their clothes, ask them what they prefer, rather than focusing on what is in style. The more they consult their own inner signals to determine what they like and dislike in life, the more inner-directed they will become. The more practice they have at looking inward, the more self-confidence they will acquire. Self-confidence is the cornerstone upon which one builds an inner-directed choice-making personality. The more they rely on what others are thinking or doing, the less they depend upon themselves. Children are extremely vulnerable to this kind of external approval-seeking thinking. They are observing all the time, and they are keenly aware of what others are doing. Help them to observe carefully, but to choose based upon what they feel is appropriate for them. Buying something simply because everyone else is wearing that label is a kind of approval seeking that teaches them to consult others rather than themselves in their dress. This insidious disease can creep into many other areas of their lives. When they ask, "How does this look on me?" respond with your honest opinion, but always ask, "What do you think of the way it looks on you?" Give them practice throughout their lives in making their own choices, and when they are very, very young, applaud them for the choices they make. "You look sensational in that dress, and you picked it out all by yourself—wow, you are really something!" can be said to a two-year-old who picked her own dress for a party. Positive reinforcement to a child for having a mind of her own is crucial at the earliest stages. Subsequently she needs continual practice at using that mind, rather than someone else's, throughout her life.

Demonstrate to children that integrity has greater value than taking the easy route and pleasing others. A child with integrity has a major head start in life on the child who is an apple-polisher. Integrity is located within, and so is the approval that comes with living one's life in this manner. Always trying to please others means that approval is gained from without, and it is the road to being neurotic and unfulfilled in life. Teach your children to take the road that is proper for them. If the school principal expects them to obey rules that they really do not believe in, then reinforce that there are ways to get the rules changed, and be proud of their serious efforts to fix things that have always been a certain way. Telling a child, "Just do what you're told and forget about always challenging the rules and regulations. After all, no one else is complaining," is really asking that child to ignore his or her own integrity. Instead, a statement such as "I know that you think it is stupid to be told what you have to write about on your own research report. How do you think you might get your teacher to see your point of view?" is doing the child a much bigger favor.

Be positive toward children when they challenge established authority and silly rules. A reminder, *Growth is impossible if a person always does things the way everyone has always done things*. Children feel as strongly about stupid rules as adults do, and if you simply tell them to ignore their consciences and just go along and cope, then you are teaching them to be slaves rather than no-limit people. It takes a courageous person to challenge something that he feels in unjust, regardless of how meaningless his concerns may seem to you. Help children to figure out ways to challenge and change rules and policies that conflict with their inner beliefs without belittling them for having those views in the first place. Tell them, "I am proud of you for standing up for what you believe," rather than "Shut up and get along like everyone else," or, even worse, "Forget about it and do what you're told." They want to feel as if they can make some choices and display some element of control over their own world. You certainly do not want them to enter adulthood as people who just take whatever is handed to them. They need practice at being assertive and challenging outdated policies. This is true in the home when they have to accept an unreasonable bedtime simply because you want them out of your hair, in church when they are told to believe without question what they are being force-fed, on the playground when a bully is enforcing his will on everyone, or anywhere else where they encounter rules and laws which *they* feel are unjust.

Examine your approach to discipline, keeping in mind that it is not always possible to have everything run on a basis that pleases everyone, especially the children. If you are waiting on them hand and foot, and they are showing disrespect, you must alter your behavior toward them. By being their servant and taking abuse, you are sending a message to them that says, "I will reward you for treating me in this manner." You must take responsibility for helping them to be responsible with your approach to discipline. Children who refuse your requests to empty the garbage will continue to do so if you ignore their recalcitrance out of fear. A confrontation is inevitable, but it need not take the form of a violent verbal explosion. Simply placing the garbage can in a child's room or even on the bed after several attempts to have her listen is a very effective way to get her to see that you mean business. Similarly, if you make your children's lunches every day and they are remiss in their responsibilities, or smart-mouthed to you, then you can simply withdraw that privilege and let them fend for themselves at lunchtime. I can remember hearing "I forgot" for what seemed like a thousand times from my daughter. Then one day, when "I forgot" to pick her up at the mall and she had to walk home in the 95-degree heat, she got the message.

Once again, you must be a model of what you are attempting to teach. You can show children with your own behavior that you will not take any abuse, but you need not argue about it. Be firm with your behavior; loving, but firm always. This will teach them that you really mean business and that you are not going to be drawn into a senseless argument about anything. If you ignore a child's self-destructive behavior because you are afraid of his reaction or are simply trying to avoid an unpleasant argument, then you are doing him a giant disservice as his parent. Children need to learn to be responsible human beings, and ignoring their irresponsible behavior is simply reinforcing what you dislike. Forget the endless words, and concentrate on demonstrating what you want with new and effective behavior of your own.

A word about the crass, often abusive language and behavior that teenagers direct toward parents is in order here. Do not be shocked when your teenager treats you in a way that you feel is disrespectful. Virtually all teenagers go through a two- or three-year period wherein they talk in a nasty manner to their parents (particularly their mothers) and show signs of disrespect. While I do not condone such behavior, nor do I believe that you must simply put up with it because they are going through a phase, I also think it is important for you to understand the source of it. A teenager is generally most disrespectful around people he knows he can trust. This may sound contradictory, but nevertheless it is true. A teenager knows that his mother is going to love him regardless of how he behaves. He knows that Mom, despite being hurt, will still love him. Mom then becomes the safe person on whom to try out some of his own self-doubts and angry feelings. The risk is miminal. If he tried it on his teachers, friends, neighbors, or strangers, he would find himself in deep trouble, forced to suffer the very real consequences of being abusive to others. But Mom, good old Mom, will love him even when he is at his most crass and unruly. It is almost a sign of love, even though it is misdirected, and it will most certainly pass quickly. In short, a teenager will try out those behaviors around the people she trusts the most never to withdraw their love. Mom is the easiest target, and Mom should know that it is really a veiled compliment. Your daughter trusts you enough to try out her worst side in front of you. It is a sign of love in reverse, and yet it is still painful. As a mother, you too have choices, and you certainly need not put up with being abused. But first you must understand that it is quite normal to the developing adolescent who feels like an adult trapped in a child's body. Whatever you do, do not think that it is a sign that you have failed as a parent. Actually it is quite the opposite. You have provided your child with a model of a person she can trust enough to exhibit her yukkiest side to, without fearing total disapproval or the withdrawal of love. Once you understand this, then you can take some creative steps to minimize your involvement in your adolescent's outrages. You can remove yourself as a target, refuse to argue, give the child a bit more space. But whatever you do, you do not have to internalize the assaults as a reflection on you as a failure as a parent. That is simply an erroneous assumption, and one that will lead you to even more anguish than your adolescent is already providing.

These, then, are some suggestions for major changes that you can begin to implement today in order to help children of any age to become more inner-directed and self-reliant. At all stages of their lives children must learn that they are responsible for what goes on inside them. A child is the only one who experiences his inner world, and he has many, many choices to make about what that world will be like for him. Teach children that they have choices to make, that their thinking does truly effect what they experience, and that they can choose to be just like everybody else and merely fit in, or become their own independent, fully-functioning persons. They must believe deep down within them that blame is simply a waste of their life energy, that regardless of who is at fault, reality is not going to change simply because they have assigned blame someplace. Teach them to consult their own inner lights, rather than to try to please everybody else and live their lives as approval seekers, as blamers rather than responsible doers. Back in the nineteenth century, Nathaniel Hawthorne wrote, "Every individual has a place to fill in the world and is important in some respect whether he chooses to be so or not." You are responsible for helping children to make the no-limit choice to think and *be* important. You can make a difference, and do not ever believe for a single moment that you cannot. As always, the choice is yours to make.

5

I Want My Children to Be Free from Stress and Anxiety

The no-limit person knows that worrying only inhibits performance, and he sees nothing in life to complain about. He never manipulates others with guilt or allows them to manipulate him. He has learned to avoid anxious thinking. Is as happy alone as with anyone else. Seeks out privacy. Cultivates the art of relaxation and recreation. Is expert at attaining total relaxation at will.

The world is perfect; there is no anxiety in it . . . anyplace. There are only people thinking anxiously.

—EYKIS

Every day you hear about people having anxiety attacks. You have seen the statistics on the phenomenal increases in the use of tranquilizers, uppers, downers, sleeping pills, antistress tablets, antidepressants, and drugs for every kind of so-called anxiety attack. We are relying more and more on external elixirs to rid ourselves of something that does not even exist.

Anxiety does not attack! People choose to think anxiously about their world and then look for a pill to rid themselves of this mysterious thing called anxiety. Our children are being raised in an atmosphere of anxious thinking that is taking its toll dramatically. Suicide rates among young children are increasing at a frightening pace. Increasing numbers of children are requiring psychiatric services to help them to cope more effectively with "the complexities of growing up in the modern world." Children are growing into adults who have higher and higher blood pressure readings, increased incidence of ulcers and coronary problems, and migraine headaches. They are the participants in an entire new industry called "stress management," and many of the stress experts are blaming the stress rather than the stressful thinking.

You can raise children to be completely free from the ravages of an anxious life. Your children need not be part of the statistical picture mentioned above. Being a no-limit person means being free from anxiety at *all* times in one's life. Raising your children as no-limit persons means raising them to believe that they have control over anxiety. It means teaching them to take responsibility for how they use their minds. It means teaching them how to think in ways that will not end up poisoning their insides with the physical or mental manifestations of anxiety and stress. Take a close look at the process of child raising to ensure that they never utter the absurdly incorrect words, "I'm having an anxiety attack," or even believe that such a thing is possible.

Children can be guaranteed a lifetime without anxiety, provided you are prepared to encourage them to believe that they have a large measure of control about what they carry around inside themselves. With healthy thoughts, and an amalgamation of common sense and appropriate reinforcement, your child will not end up consuming Valium in order to cope with the problems of life, or be in a therapist's office endlessly discussing his childhood and how to overcome it. Your children will not grow up to be neurotics reaching for an antidepressant or antistress tablet at the first sign of a problem. In order to be certain that you are raising your children to be free from this anxiety neurosis, you must first look at precisely what it means to be free from these inner torments that we have come to label as anxiety.

What Is Freedom from Anxiety?

Anxiety is a way of thinking! The results of anxiety are felt in our inner worlds. In order to be free from anxiety in our inner life we must think in nonanxious ways. Perhaps the greatest place we can arrive at as human beings is what I call effortless perfection or inner serenity. The Japanese culture calls this experience of total inner peace *Shibumi*. It is difficult to write about this state of serenity because it is a unique experience for every individual. The essence of achieving this kind of inner perfection lies in a view of the world as a perfect place. It means thinking in terms of harmony, peace, love, and perfection, rather than looking at the world as a hostile, ugly, hateful place. Inner perfection involves making peace with oneself, vowing to avoid fighting life, and instead joining with the natural forces of our universe and enjoying each moment as a miracle. It means shunning attachments to old ideas that wreak havoc within ourselves and within our entire universe. There is a kind of acceptance of our world, a love of ourselves as human beings, a respect for all that is alive and ever lived, a refusal to think in a hostile manner, and a daily commitment to making our world a better place. While this may sound like a philosophical approach to life that is rooted in idealism and ignores the everyday realities of our world, I suggest that it is nothing of the sort. In fact, I firmly believe that inner perfection is there for each one of us to recapture. Yes, I said *recapture!*

As tiny unspoiled infants we come into our world full of inner perfection. In our earliest months we do not judge. We simply exist, and our basic needs for survival are met—or, we simply fail to survive. Young unspoiled children represent the nearest form of inner perfection. Watch a playground full of young children as they run everywhere, laugh at everything, and appreciate all that is there for them. Think back to your own childhood and remember how you were fascinated by a caterpillar, how you could spend hours lost in play beside a lake or watching frogs on lily pads. Remember how you rode your two-wheeler for the first time and felt the freedom of moving on it. Remember the fascination of studying a colony of ants, your first sailboat ride, the smell of grass after mowing, a fresh snowfall, dressing up in your parents' clothes, the taste of a toothpick made from a wild-growing stiff weed, or the dizzying smell of a magnificent blooming lilac tree. Virtually everything you did as a child proved that life was a miracle for you and that everything in it was there for your pleasure. You did not analyze it, you did not worry about it, you did not try to categorize it. You simply lived it, free from anxiety, and free from worries about the future. You had this state of mind for a while in your lifetime, and you can recapture it any time you wish. You can also make sure that your children of all ages not only recapture that kind of inner peace but retain it for a lifetime of serenity rather than neurotic anxiety.

The achievement of inner peace is a journey. It is a manner of traveling throughout your brief time here on this planet. The path that you take is your choice to make, and the way that you think while on your path is a result of how you exercise your own free will. You can teach children how to think in ways which will help them to maintain that natural ability to have inner serenity. In writing about how to teach children to keep their natural inner peace for a lifetime, and to live on their own paths in as harmonious a manner as is possible for them, I think only of the word *love*.

I have written earlier about the necessity for self-love and how to help your children to be more self-loving. Love is also the answer here in this section on inner peace. Self-respect as opposed to self-contempt is crucial, and I will not reiterate this point in this chapter, but ask you to look back over Chapter 2 carefully. There is also the love that you can give to children and the love that you can teach them to give back to everything and everyone they encounter here on earth. This love is not necessarily demonstrated with hugs and kisses (although they are pretty nifty) but with an attitude that you cultivate in your reactions to children, and which can be reinforced every day in the manner in which you help a child relate to his world and the people in it.

Freedom from anxiety, then, is an attitude, or a way in which you and your children are always practicing a loving approach to life. It is a total acceptance of the world and a nonjudgmental approach to life. It is a commitment to living fully rather than complaining about life. It is all about this thing called happiness, which Aristotle described this way: "Happiness is the meaning and the purpose of life, the whole aim and end of human existence." To accept this kind of happiness you must first remind yourself that happiness is an inner experience that you bring to life, rather than something that can be extracted from the people and experiences of life. Secondly, this all-important happiness or inner contentment is already there within each of us, and only needs to be nurtured in a nonanxious manner in order to continue for a lifetime. I am talking here about cultivating a *habit* of happiness as opposed to a *habit* of anxiety. The ways in which you relate to children are major factors in helping them to cultivate this habit. Nonanxious children become nonanxious adults and stay that way for a lifetime if they know how to think nonanxiously from the beginning. You can show them the way to get on the right path and stay there. It begins with eliminating the big three culprits responsible for the seeds of anxiety: guilt, worry, and immobilizing stress. These are three big uglies in the production of anxious human beings. You must understand them and vow to rid them from both your own life and the lives of your children.

No More Guilt

Guilt means feeling bad about something said or done in the past. To the extent that it is a tool to motivate improved behavior, *learning from the past* serves a useful purpose. But guilt is not learning from the past. Guilt means to be immobilized in the present over something that has already occurred. It is a tool used by adults to help make children feel bad so that the adults can control their behavior. Whatever an adult's intentions may be in reinforcing feelings of guilt in children, its negative manifestations—immobilizing panic, sleeplessness, fear, introversion, shame, loss of self-esteem, and lack of initiative—are all too often the reaction.

When you use guilt to prod children of any age into behaving as you would like them to, or to feel bad about something that is already over, you are taking a big step toward helping them to become anxious thinkers, filled with the physical manifestations of anxiety. Guilt is experienced *within* the child. Although it may get you the temporary results you are seeking, the internalizing of guilt feelings is a powerful anxiety producer for the child. When you pretend to cry with your three-year-old and force her to give you a kiss because she cannot stand to see you feeling bad, you have introduced a high feeling of anxiousness to her mind by creating what may seem like a harmless game to you. She has learned very early that she has no choice over whom she kisses, and that her own unwillingness to give you a kiss or a hug ought to be abandoned in favor of making you feel better. She learns that her own feelings are to be abandoned and that your hurt feelings must be assuaged even though she must go against her own wishes at the present moment. As an adult, would you like to be forced into kissing anyone simply because he or she would feel bad if you did not do it? Would you like to make the opinions of others more important than your own when it comes to passing out affection at any given moment of your life? Of course you wouldn't. Imagine how anxious you would feel if you could not decide whom you wanted to kiss—if it was left up to others, and all they had to do was push certain buttons and you would automatically provide kisses and hugs to whoever wanted them. This is the anxiety-producing effect that a minimal guilt experience provides for a young child, and it is something to be on guard against throughout all the developmental years of your children's lives.

The preteen who is convinced that God is going to dislike him if he does not go to church every Sunday is taught to feel guilty when he goes against *your* values. He is not being allowed to make a choice, since guilt through fear is being used. If you withhold love from a teenager because she does not keep her room clean or because she chooses a boyfriend of whom you disapprove, you are teaching her to become immobilized and upset over your reactions to her. The adolescent boy who is warned, "Someday you will pay for the way you are treating me," when he is making some normal choices to become independent, is being taught to experience inner doubt and anxiety over his own choices, and that being your victim is far more important than becoming a no-limit person.

Guilt comes in many varieties. Parents can manipulate children with it, and children become experts at doing the same to their parents. The game gets played out with small stakes at the beginning, when little children are manipulated into performing their parents' wishes, and gradually it becomes an all-encompassing means of communicating. Everyone in a family can experience the ravages of guilt when it becomes a regular tool of communicating. Children soon grow up to distrust what they think, and to only behave in ways which will keep their parents from imposing their own guilt on them. They take the course of study that others want for them, rather than becoming people who exercise free choice. They attend the religious services that their parents impose on them since they do not want to see their parents hurt. They choose the friends that a parent wants for fear of hurting the parent's feelings. In short, they become miniatures of their parents. They become consumed by the fear of retribution in the form of guilt. They soon know everything that you disapprove of, and they begin to live their lives not as free-thinking people but as programmed computers, long after their parents have relinquished control over their lives and even after their parents have left this earth.

Guilt is a weapon of the weak. It is used exclusively as a manipulator. Its purpose is to get others to live their lives as we feel that they should, or to feel badly about how they have behaved in the past so that we can control them now and in the future. Avoid any discipline technique which has internal pain and anguish for children as its major purpose. A guilty child is a manipulated child who soon learns to abandon his own inner voice in favor of doing what he is supposed to do to make sure that you do not feel bad. A guilty child learns to become an irresponsible child as well. Think a moment about this entire business of guilt. Suppose a child's behavior is being controlled by the guilt feelings he experiences as a result of the way you interact with him. Here are the internal results of such a strategy.

First, the child feels bad inside and experiences anxiety about the way he is treating you. Second, he uses up his present moment to simply feel bad about what he did, or about how he disappointed you. Third, because he is feeling bad he is unable to use his present moment in any other way (he becomes immobilized) to correct his behavior or to learn from his mistakes. Remember, learning from the past is just that, while feeling bad about the way you have behaved is called guilt. Do not confuse the two, because they are opposite responses. Benefiting from one's mistakes by learning from the past is a highly functional no-limit way to learn. Feeling guilty and being manipulated by that guilt keeps you immobilized in the very moments that you could be doing something about the offensive behavior. Therefore, guilt becomes an irresponsible choice to offer children. It means that they will learn to simply sit around and feel bad whenever they do things that they dislike. It means that they will become victims rather than free-choice individuals, always being pushed around by their emotional reactions to others. And, worst of all, it means that they will not benefit and grow, but will instead become guilt users themselves.

If you use guilt on children on a regular basis, it will not be long before they start using it on you. "Thanks a lot, Mom, for forgetting to buy some lunch meat for me. I guess you really don't care about me." "I never get to go anywhere, but Danny gets to do everything. I guess you've always liked him better." "You never think of me. It's always you and Dad who get everything." "I only got seven presents, and everybody else got eight. I knew you liked them better." "I must be adopted—I know my real parents would never treat me this way." These kinds of guilt-producing sentiments flow commonly from children who have grown up with guilt. A child who uses these tactics is learning to manipulate others, to be exceedingly irresponsible, and to have a great deal of anxiety in his life. He will become a manipulator because he is learning to use the sensitive feelings of others to get those people to behave as he wants them to. He will become irresponsible because he will simply use guilt (and feel guilty) as a substitute for doing something constructive to correct a situation. He will feel anxious because he will internalize the opinions of others and make them the source of his own behavior, or help others to feel bad, both of which are nonloving acts. Anxiety is always present within us when we behave or force others to behave in nonloving ways. So you see, you become a three-way loser when you make guilt a part of your parenting lifestyle.

The alternatives to guilt are remarkably simple and easy to employ. They involve having enough respect for your children as complete human beings to never want them to experience the inner torment that goes with guilt feelings. To avoid guilt techniques, you must use constructive interaction that will help your children to learn from their mistakes. You must give them love when they make an error rather than ask them to feel stupid, foolish, or terrible inside. You must not remind them of their mistakes once they have set themselves on a new course. A great number of specific examples and strategies to help you to abandon guilt techniques are offered at the end of this chapter.

The basic change away from using guilt must come from within you. You must see the dangers of producing guilt-ridden children. You can make a commitment to work at your own guilt, and to stand up to those who would otherwise manipulate you with their desires. You can become a model of a human being to your child, a model who not only refuses to help children internalize guilt feelings but who has removed them from his or her own life as well. As with everything else about helping children to be no-limit people, you must live by example as much as possible, and honestly demonstrate to them that you are working on yourself to be a no-limit person. If you do not want them to be full of anxiety in their lives, then guilt must go. So too must the second of those demons that produce anxious rather than happy children.

Farewell to Worry

The second component of the anxious-thinking person's repertoire is worry. Just like guilt, worry can only be experienced now, right here in the present moment. Worry is a means of using up the present moment in being consumed about something in the future, over which you have no control. To worry is to manufacture anxiety. It is not to be confused with being concerned about the future or with planning carefully to avoid trauma. Worry is not simply thinking about the future. Worry is not making plans, nor is it spelling out your objectives for the future. Worry is anxious thinking about the future. The physical results of worry—high blood pressure, stammering, anxiety, loss of self-assurance, and physical immobilization—are quite the same as those of guilt. Children who grow up learning to be worriers are children destined to live with anxiety.

There is much more that you can do to ensure that children are not being programmed to be worriers. The worrying child is one who is consumed with fears about his performance in life. Worriers are children who are told that they must be perfect, please their parents, win at everything they do, and be judged by reputation instead of character. The worrier is often pushed to be perfectionistic, is afraid of failing, and believes that life is not to be enjoyed, but instead must be analyzed, studied, and compartmentalized. The child who learns to spend his time worrying will not easily let go of this way of life. Worriers find pleasure in worrying even when they have everything in order. In these moments they will worry about not having anything to worry about.

Like all neurotic behavior, worry is a *habit*. It is a learned response generally picked up from models of people who are worriers. The habit of worry (which is really the habit of anxious thinking over the future) can be reversed by teaching children to think in more healthy, productive no-limit ways.

Imposing external criteria upon children, stressing the need for them to achieve at all costs, encourages them to think in worrying ways. Constantly worrying in front of children gives them a negative example to follow. Continuous worried talk about bills, war, getting old, unemployment, the weather, social standing, how the party will turn out, the tidiness of your home, personal appearance, and on and on will teach them exactly how to become effective worriers. They will pick it up even if you dislike it yourself. Vow to stop all anguishing in front of children, and to work at becoming an effective human being, rather than someone who simply worries as a way of life.

Worry also takes the form of complaining. Many children have learned to complain about life rather than to do something creative to terminate their difficulties. "I don't want to go on that trip." "I hate going to parties." "I don't want that babysitter." "I'm not going to take that teacher for science." "I hate going to Grandma's and seeing all my cousins." These kinds of "I hate the world" sentiments are often a disguise for children who are worried about the outcome of such events, or worried deeply about how they will be viewed by others. The complaining child, who finds fault with the world rather than enjoying everything that life has to offer, is often a child who has learned to substitute worry and complaining for living. This behavior will persist into adulthood if left unchecked, or if it is encouraged by the caring adults in his environment who have a similar mind set.

Eliminating worry means developing a more peaceful, accepting, serene attitude toward life. There is an old saying that I have used many times in working with worriers: "I'm an old man, and I've had many troubles, most of which have never happened." The truth is that almost everything you ever worry about turns out just fine. Worry about losing your job and ultimately you may in fact lose it. Then what? Almost always the person finds another job that suits him better, pays higher, and is more fulfilling. And all the worry? It was wasted energy. Virtually everything that we or our children worry about turns out to be a senseless waste of time. If you can teach children to use the time they would ordinarily spend worrying to work on the object of their worry, you will be helping them toward a much less anxious style of life.

When you study great thinkers and innovators in every field of human enterprise, you find that they are seldom worriers. This is true because a person who uses up the precious currency of his life (his time) worrying, has an empty bank account when it comes time to do something. Great leaders are doers, not worriers. They spend their time actively engaged in what they are about in life, rather than worrying about the results. At this moment of my life, sitting here at my typewriter composing this chapter, I could be doing something else. I could be worrying about whether the public will like it, whether my editors will want to change it around, whether it will be criticized by the so-called "child experts," if it all fits together nicely, if I am being too personal, whether I will make money on it, if I will run out of typing paper, whether my typewriter will break, if my children will get into college, whether a nuclear explosion will burn up my first draft, whether my sun sign is properly aligned with Uranus for good writing vibrations, whether the pimple on my cheek will clear up, or even whether I will develop hemorrhoidal tissue from sitting here hour after hour. If I were to choose any of these things to worry about, I would not have to write at all—I could just worry.

That is precisely the point of the futility of worry. It keeps you so occupied worrying that you cannot get anything done, and even if you do manage to sneak in some work between worry sessions, you cannot enjoy it. Instead of being occupied with any of the above concerns, I look at it this way. The public will decide whether or not they like this book about raising no-limit children. If they buy it, or borrow it from the library, then that alone will determine what they think. But I will never even get to know that if I do not discipline myself to write each day. Furthermore, everything else will take care of itself; the sun will align itself however it is ordained, as will any blemishes. I force myself to avoid worry by taking action in the direction of *my own* dreams and endeavors. And I learned a long time ago that worry is just a great big waste of my life. Everything I have ever worried about turned out exactly as it was going to despite my worry moments to the contrary.

Your children are entitled to learn this valuable lesson about worry. They need help in developing strategies for becoming doers rather than worriers. They cry out for you to teach them how to avoid all those internally troublesome moments that they spend in useless worry. They need to have the pressure taken off their internal selves to always achieve, always be a winner, always be perfect, and always focus on the future. *Now is all there is and all there ever will be.* A now moment used up worrying is a lost moment in the sense of being happy and fulfilled. All of those wasted moments of worry soon add up to a lifetime of anxiety that will ultimately destroy the worrier. Both guilt and worry are tremendous anxiety producers in children, and in combination with stress and tension they create an anxious person who spends time consuming tranquilizers rather than devouring life. A look at this stress is in order before examining some specific ways to rid ourselves and our children, once and for all, of this senseless anxiety.

No More Type A Toddlers

A major cause of anxiety (anxious thinking) is the inclination to think in stressful ways. You may have read or heard of studies about stress in which various life choices result in increased stress. These studies assign stress points to occurrences like a move to a new location, a divorce or breakup, a tax increase, changing jobs, having a baby, a political change, and the like. All such occurrences are theoretically linked to additional stress. The fact is that people who experience stress in their lives are those who have learned to think stressfully. There is no stress in our world. The world just is!

People perceive the world in their own unique way, and then they learn to think in stressful ways that multiply their internal upsets. Events do not cause stress; thinking does. My old friend

Earl Nightingale once said, "Each of us must live off the fruit of his thoughts in the future, because what you think today and tomorrow, next month and next year, will mold your life and determine your future. You are guided by your mind." Children are no exception. They too must grow up believing that they are the sum of their own thoughts. They cannot blame external events for any stress they are experiencing within, since it is caused by their own way of perceiving their world.

In 1974, Meyer Friedman and Ray Rosenman published a book entitled *Type A Behavior and Your Heart.* They gave us a new phrase for an old problem. A Type A person is described as one whose life pattern is marked by a compelling sense of time urgency, "hurry sickness," aggressiveness, and competitiveness, usually combined with a degree of free-floating hostility. These people are not in a minority. They comprise more than fifty percent of American males and a growing number of females. The amazing statistic from this book that made a difference in my own life is that "One American male in five dies of a heart attack before the age of sixty. Well over ninety percent of them are Type A's." If this is true in our adult population, then we are grooming people for Type A behavior in childhood. Our stress-producing environment must be shifted to a less anxious approach to life. Examine closely your style of dealing with children so as to avoid encouraging Type A behavior, while simultaneously helping them to fit into our world in a positive no-limit manner. I quote to you directly from *Type A Behavior and Your Heart*: "Actually a continuous frenzied pace almost ensures later disaster in every field of human activity." This is warning enough, from two prominent doctors who have studied this phenomenon in depth. Your children are in danger if they are raised with the anxiety-provoking thinking I am describing in this chapter.

Children can become Type A people very early, and it is up to us as caring adults to be on guard against including high levels of stressful thinking in their young lives. The following five characteristics describe the Type A person; they are presented to help you to begin to introduce nonstressful thinking into the lives of children, regardless of their present age.

1. *Intense striving.* This behavior is demonstrated by children who are constantly pushing to excel and are never able to enjoy a present moment. Such children must do extra-credit reports all the time, and are meticulous about every detail of their young lives. They cannot relax without feeling guilty, or find it impossible to simply rest and enjoy themselves. Be careful to provide a solid assortment of relaxation, play, and work activities for children. Do not place such an overemphasis on homework, achievement, awards, winning, and making money that there is seldom a moment to just enjoy life. Do not push your children into the Type A category. The results of pursuing excellence at the expense of enjoying life are manifested in young children by speech problems like stammering and stuttering, intense withdrawal into their own worlds, and an inability to get out and act like children. Very young children who are pushed beyond their limits will stop smiling, whine regularly, and find it difficult to be cheerful. They often become sickly, developing such ailments and problems as asthma, allergies, stomach aches, excessive crying, bed-wetting, nightmares, depression and withdrawal, acne and rashes, frequent colds, vomiting and low stamina.

Children of all ages need to laugh, play, enjoy, and stop striving all the time. They need to be able to relax, act silly, put on skits, be a littly nutsy, and in general not have a perpetually serious approach to life. Children who can laugh and be silly are developing healthy internal resistance to the heavy pressures that are going to be there for them. They do not need the adults in their lives to put additional pressure on them by always monitoring their behavior, giving them grades on everything they do, and making demands that they strive to be something better. There is absolutely nothing wrong with not being better or with not always having goals. Simply living and knowing how to enjoy life are sufficient. The more pressure there is to always excel, to always strive for something better, the more you will see the internal signs of anxiety and the external manifestations of a child who is not allowed to simply be an age-typical child. Learn from your children. Watch their natural ability to enjoy life, and begin to apply some of their unique approaches to no-limit living rather than asking them to join you in the rat race, and justifying it by saying, "I want them to have more." Sometimes, more is less, especially when it takes its toll in the form of an anxious life and physiological deterioration.

2. *Competitiveness.* A Type A person is exceedingly competitive, always looking over his shoulder, assessing his performance compared with how someone else is doing. This puts the control of his life in other hands, rather than within him, where it belongs. It is nice to feel competitive, and to engage in healthy competition, but it is a poor way to assess where one is going in life. Overly competitive persons are always looking at the performance of others to determine their own worth.

If you must always have competition in order to feel happy or worthwhile, then you are doomed to a lifetime of unfulfillment. You see, you are alone virtually all the time. You are alone with your thoughts and feelings at all times. No one else can experience what you are feeling within yourself. Children are exactly the same. They need to learn to enjoy competing without being neurotic about it. To do so, they must be able to be alone with themselves, free from the need to measure their actions against the performances of others. They must learn to assess their own value and exploits based on guidelines which are independent of what others are doing.

In business, the most successful leaders know that ultimately they must consult themselves. In the so-called dog-eat-dog world of competition, the genuine leaders are those who feel confident about themselves, without always having to concern themselves with what others are doing. When the competition of a tennis match is over, it is over, and the no-limit person does not carry around a win or a loss as a badge of his self-worth for that day. On the court he is a dynamo, running everything down and competing fiercely, but when it is over, he leaves it there and enjoys the real thrills of learning to hit improved forehands and backhands, sweating and exercising for the pure joy of being healthy, and improving his skills in many areas of his game. When you lose a tennis match, what have you really lost? A game—period. Examine how much anxiety you are encouraging in children by forcing them to evaluate themselves based upon the external barometers of competitiveness, rather than the inner measures of self-worth and positive feelings about one's own performance.

3. *Deadline Urgency.* Children can grow up believing that deadlines are more important than enjoying life. They can become neurotics very early by insisting on excessive attentiveness to a timepiece, a calendar, or some other externally imposed measure. Children who must always eat at a precise time, who must be in bed by a preset bedtime, who are subtly reminded that they are

being timed and having their lives scheduled, are learning to become Type A anxious people.

The more deadlines imposed on children, the more likely they are to become anxious about life. Deadlines deny them the freedom to be spontaneous, to wander into the unknown, to feel free, because they are restricted by external rules and timepieces. Children need to make their own decisions if they are going to be no-limit people. Let them set their own time limits, their own calendars, and their own sense of what deadlines are important and which are to be ignored. Compulsive children who must always do things a certain way are not innovators. Obsessive children want to know how many hours of sleep they had in order to know how tired they are the next day. They are learning to run their lives on external measures rather than developing controls from within. The more external measures imposed, the more anxiety experienced. To avoid Type A status for a lifetime, teach children to look carefully at their commitments and develop reasonable time constraints, but not to become overly dependent on deadlines, watches, calendars, and external scheduling.

4. *Impatience.* Type A people are always in a hurry. They cannot stop and enjoy the sunset because they are too busy predicting what time the sun will rise in the morning. The sense of hurry sickness is omnipresent in the Type A individual, and it does not escape children, particularly if adults behave that way around them. Examples of this behavior include eagerness to get ahead of the car in front of you, rushing through meals, expressing irritation in lines of people, becoming impatient with those who do not move quickly (such as elderly people and young children), interrupting the conversation of others in order to speak, and inability to listen without talking.

Type A people always have to arrive at a social gathering at a set time, and become increasingly agitated if they cannot leave at the predetermined time. This impatience can take its toll on you as an adult, and if you model it for children, you will see the same behavior expressed by them. They will become impatient with their friends, interrupt constantly, and demand that the younger children be more advanced than their years or suffer the consequences of being yelled at and hit. Because of the hyper quality that they have seen modeled for them, they manifest abrupt speech, a hurry-up attitude in their play and work, an impatience with those who are less or more talented than they are in games, and an unwillingness to simply watch a movie or sit and relax.

Take corrective steps to ensure that the children in your life are not being programmed with undo anxiety due to an impatient quality of yours. Teach them the value of being more patient, with both themselves and others in the world. Help them to relax, to simply meditate on the beauty of the world, to help others rather than to criticize them for being slow, and to stop and enjoy the brief time they have on this planet. Impatience, as described here, is an exceedingly large cause of anxiety in children. In schools, this emphasis on having to get things done fast and to beat everyone else is a major contributor to producing Type A toddlers as well as Type A teenagers.

Dismiss the absurd notion that one cannot ever get ahead without always beating the other guy and without always being in a hurry. Teach children that a person in a hurry is not relaxed, and that one rarely completes any task efficiently when there is pressure to be first, best, and fastest. People who are ultimate achievers are, ironically, the people who are most relaxed at their task. Hank Aaron makes it look easy. Bjorn Borg makes it look simple. The Olympic gymnasts appear relaxed and make it look fun. Pablo Casals played almost effortlessly. The impatient, always striving, hurry-sick individual is only defeating himself. Help children attain the ability to be relaxed inside, to slow down, and to enjoy what they are doing, rather than fighting themselves and their worlds and ending up the Type A losers.

5. *Excessive Organization.* Type A people are often suffering from the need to organize and compartmentalize life. They feel that anything that is out of place represents a personal mission for them to put in order. Their homes are spotless, their drawers fully organized, their lives a model of perfect order. Yet they are suffering from large doses of inner anxiety as a result of this neatness neurosis. They obsessively play by the rules and are extremely anxious when others do not. They are almost always thinking about what has to be done, how it must be done, and the guidelines for keeping it that way. This fixation and organization causes anxiety simply because the world is not wired together in any neat, predictable way. Yet despite the spontaneous nature of our world, where everything does not have a logical place, these Type A's are constantly trying to get everything in order. They want to categorize the birds rather than enjoy their flight and beautiful colors. They want to count and label the stars rather than be awed by their majestic perfection. They want to get the house clean rather than live in it. An ashtray out of place can cause a family uproar. A dirty blouse can create an unseemly family fight. A glass of spilled orange juice is a catastrophe rather than a normal occurrence. When these kinds of organizational neuroses take hold in children, they begin to feel anxious every time they do anything. They will begin to fib to preserve the order. They will change their report cards and lie rather than face the consequences of an uproar over a grade. They will tremble at the idea of making a mistake. This is anxiety, and Type A people create a fertile environment for this kind of anxious thinking.

I believe that dull people have immaculate homes. No-limit people have homes which are lived in. No-limit people know that the purpose of life is to enjoy it, rather than to get everything labeled and categorized. Help children to be neat and organized to the point where the organization serves them and their needs, rather than to where they become a servant of the organization. But be sure to interact with them in ways that emphasize their humanity and their happiness, rather than teaching them to be obsessive compulsive organizers. I once heard it said that "Life is what happens to you while you're making other plans." Do not let life pass by the children within your sphere of influence, and by all means do not let life beat them down by teaching them to count the stars, rather than seeing and appreciating the universe.

Young people are taught to grow up with anxiety, and without serenity, when their lives are filled with a proliferation of guilt messages, worry thoughts, and Type A behaviors which emphasize external striving rather than internal arriving. Before looking at some specific strategies for creating anxiety-free children, I am providing in the next section a look at some specific behaviors which, in fact, help to induce needless anxiety.

Some Typical Anxiety-Producing Behaviors

Children grow up with anxiety and become anxious people as a direct result of the choices they make throughout their lives. Their choices are strongly influenced by the things that you, as an influential adult, reinforce and provide for them. Communication patterns with them, the kind of examples provided, and daily living interactions all serve to influence their choices. To be anxious or not to be anxious? This is a question that you can help them to answer in a no-limit positive way.

Here are *some* of the more common actions between adults and children which encourage children to choose anxiety as a lifestyle. Examine them carefully. Then, after looking at the payoffs for continuing these behaviors, you will have a head start on bringing them to an end. Specific strategies are offered at the end of this chapter to assist you in creating anxiety-free children, regardless of what age they are today. First, however, consider the behaviors defined in the following list.

□ Refusing to acknowledge the merits of a nonanxious lifestyle. Ridiculing such things as meditation, relaxation, contemplative thinking, yoga, mind control, the literature of inner peace, self-hypnosis, and the like.

□ Living a pressure-filled, nonrelaxing kind of lifestyle. Hurrying through everything and demanding excellence and top performance in all areas from children. Putting unrealistic demands on them from the beginning, and rushing them to walk early, to be toilet trained before they are physically ready, to read early, to figure out mathematics early, and generally trying to accelerate the normal developmental pattern that is unique to each child.

□ Not providing privacy for children. Constantly interfering in their lives and monitoring everything that they do.

□ Putting all the emphasis in their lives on being bigger, faster, stronger, and smarter than others. Deemphasizing inner growth and development in favor of those achievements that have observable measures.

□ Emphasizing the children's report cards rather than what they are learning and whether they are content with their performances in school. Similarly, demanding trophies, awards, and other externals rather than looking at what they symbolize.

▫ Comparing your children with other children, particularly their siblings.

▫ Referring to their past mistakes. Recalling how they "can't be trusted after what they did" a long time ago. Reminding them of their shortcomings and mistakes, rather than focusing on their achievements and their capacity to learn from their mistakes.

▫ Using guilt or threat references. "You ought to be ashamed of yourself!" "Just wait till your father finds out." "God will punish you for what you said to me." "You're hurting Mommy's feelings again." "How could you do that after all I've done for you?" "Someday you'll pay for this."

▫ Focusing on a child's self-contempt and putting him down regularly with sentences designed to make him dislike himself. "You're always doing dumb things." "You're so fat, you look terrible in that outfit." "You never could do anything in music."

▫ Being a person who feels guilty and reminding children that you, like them, are loaded with guilt. "I feel terrible—I forgot to push when going through the revolving door." "I know things won't work out for me now." "I should have helped that blind woman cross the street."

▫ Refusing to allow your children to grow toward independence. Telling them how much they owe you, and how terrible they should feel for leaving the nest. Being depressed and sullen when they prefer their friends' company to yours. Fostering dependency rather than independence.

▫ Being a worry example to your child. Using pills for every little ache or tension. Being a sickly parent who always visits the doctor. Taking the children off to the doctor for anything at all. Teaching them to take pride in their "boo-boos" and providing them with overdoses of pity when they scratch their knees, bruise their shoulders, or anything else that happens every day to all children.

▫ Teaching them to worry. "You had better start worrying about your examination right now." "You have a lot to worry about, the way you've been going lately."

◻ Being overly worried about everything your baby does. Classifying too many things as too hot, too sharp, too dangerous, too dirty, or capable of making them sick. Being a bundle of nerves around your young children and teaching them that the world is a hostile and dangerous place.

◻ Using sentences that emphasize fear, guilt, or external judgment. "Never speak to a stranger." "Stay out of the water until you know how to swim." "You should have been home by three o'clock." "He's your puppy and you let him run away." "What would Grandma think if she saw you doing that?" "What will people say?"

◻ Setting unrealistic standards and goals for children.

◻ Refusing to accept children's age-typical behavior. Always insisting that they act older than they are and punishing them for divergence from your expectations.

◻ Imposing punishment on children without explaining why they are being punished, or not having the punishment understood in *their* minds.

◻ Complaining about life in front of children. Encouraging them to complain and whine rather than take some constructive action to correct their problems.

◻ Saying "yes" when you really mean "no." Teaching them to hide their real feelings and "fake it," particularly when they have disagreements with authority figures, including you, their parent.

◻ Accepting children's excuses when you know they are simply avoiding responsibilities, and consequently teaching them to lie and distort the truth.

◻ Constantly correcting children in front of other people and being their critic as a parental role. Always using negative rather than positive reinforcement.

◻ Making objects, acquisitions, and money the most important things in their lives.

◻ Always emphasizing the future and where they will be someday.

◻ Teaching them to always be in competition with others and ridiculing cooperation. Showing them that sharing is not a smart strategy.

□ Placing excessive emphasis on promptness. Running their lives by the calendar and the clock.

□ Being obsessively organized in the home and in their lives. Making them always be clean, neat, and tidy. Teaching them to be afraid of dirt, bugs, animals, germs, and the like.

□ Being impatient with their pace in life. Always expecting them to move faster, and putting pressure on them to keep things moving fast.

□ Not talking with them about their own lives, concerns, fears, and personal issues. Being their judge, critic, warden, and evaluator, rather than their confidante, friend, and advisor.

These are some of the more common anxiety-provoking ways that adults interact with children. The anxious-thinking child soon becomes overwhelmed and behaves in anxious ways. They often are afraid to be spontaneous and find it difficult to give love because they feel unworthy, yet compulsive about doing their duty. They begin to act negatively, becoming depressed, with signs of poor physical health. They can be clinging children who are constantly seeking reassurance and always trying to make amends. You will also see both mental and physical signs of withdrawal with evidence of poor concentration, and ultimately the avoidance of persons who provoke or remind the child of his failings. Anxious children can develop headaches, sweating, stomach disorders, and excessive vulnerability to allergies, colds, flu, and asthmatic conditions as well. Often they experience nightmares or sleeplessness, and a poor appetite—which, of course, leads to weakened resistance and illness.

Type A toddlers, or children growing up with excessive pressures, exhibit certain characteristics early that generally remain throughout the lifetime. In the beginning they have a limited interest in foods, clothes, and toys. They are intolerant of strangers and avoid warming up, other than to authoritarian models. They can become excessively fastidious, upset easily by changes in the environment, deficient in spontaneity, solemn, reserved, and usually impatient with themselves and others. They are prone to outbursts, considered "hyper" by those around them, and lack a sense of humor and willingness to experiment in life. They are often repulsed by nature and dislike spiders, bugs, and anything that might get them dirty. They often complain that it is too hot, too cold, too windy, or too something else for them to be satisfied. They develop prejudices, become insensitive, and find it impossible to "walk in another person's shoes." They grow to respect authoritarian figures and symbols of power, including uniforms, a doctor's white coat, a presidential suite, or anyone with a gun. They can evolve into hero-worshipers and learn to love their toys of power and destruction.

These general characteristics are not always completely observable in all children who grow up with Type A mentality, but they strike enough of a chord to be considered warning signals. You can become a very constructive influence in helping children to grow as no-limit human beings, but you mu. first be aware of the payoffs for raising the anxiety levels of children. Then you must take specific constructive steps to ensure that they have the opportunity to swim through life and enjoy it, without always feeling as though they are in a race without a finish line.

The Support System for Keeping the Pressure on Children

No one would readily admit that he or she derives enjoyment from raising the anxiety levels of children. Nevertheless there are some benefits (self-defeating though they may be) for this type of parenting. Once the payoffs are understood, then the patterns of communication can be changed. Following are some of the most obvious payoffs.

Perhaps you feel that your children's anxiety is worth its price if they are always pursuing some goals. You may have learned that you are not worthwhile unless you are busy, busy, busy all the time. An anxious child is in fact a busy child, even though he may be very busy simply worrying, feeling guilty, and being neurotic. You may feel as though you are doing a good job because busy, frightened, worried, and anxious children are doing what you think they are supposed to be doing. The more productive they are, the better job you feel you are doing, even though the price they pay is an expensive one.

You can definitely feel superior when children are afraid of you. You have the authoritarian power to push the buttons to send children on a guilt trip, or to protect yourself from any potential embarrassment by having them so consumed with worry about disappointing you that they will conform out of fear. Children become your captive audience. It is a power trip that you might get nowhere else in your life, and an anxious child will keep you feeling powerful in your own little kingdom.

You may have grown up believing that doctors know what is best for you and that if they recommend pills then you should take them. Since we dispense over a hundred million prescriptions a year for tranquilizers alone, and they are all prescribed by doctors, then there must be something to this. Pills become the instrument of making you right. You feel better knowing that you are taking some medicine, since you are not capable of any healing yourself. Thus, you can pass this mentality on to your children and feel as though you are doing the right thing. Even if they become little addicts to external cure-alls, at least you will take comfort in knowing that everybody else is doing it—so why should they be any different?

A child who is taught to simply feel guilty or to worry a great deal, is a child who is learning not to take responsibility for changing, but only for feeling bad and helping others to do the same. This kind of child is much easier to manage than a child who is creative and listening to his own inner voices. An easily managed child may in fact be your goal. To some parents, keeping their children in line—being sure that they do as they are told and do not make any waves—is worth the price of having them anxious with guilt, worry, tension, and stress. (Except for those hundreds of thousands of casualties who contemplate and often attempt suicide, become addicted to their pills, or become depressed and full of shame as a result of excessive anxiety.)

Anxiety is an avoidance technique. You can only experience anxiety in this particular moment, be it guilt, worry, stress, or anything else. Thus, being productive is patently impossible. The more of this avoidance behavior you engender in your children, the less likely they are to become doers, innovators, or creative participants in life. Thus, your risk of criticism from your family and friends is reduced when you keep them anxious. Little children who are not heard, who are not treated as complete human beings, who know their place, make you look good in the eyes of your peers.

You can feel secure in knowing that your child is learning to take the safe route in life. He is anxious, yes—but surely that is worth the price of being safe. J. Krishnamurti, in his book *You Are the World*, said, "A mind that is safe, secure, is a shoddy mind. Yet that is what all of us want; to be completely safe. And psychologically there is no such thing." Children will never run into any unexpected traps if they worry everything through. They will never be disappointed if they are totally organized and obsessed about their lives. They will never get hurt if they practice being perfect. And you will help them to do these things and then feel better knowing that they are completely safe. Of course, the price they pay is a heavy one, but it is worth it for you to maintain the illusion that they are eternally safe and secure

Your children can grow up to be just like everybody else, and that has its own built-in reward for you as a parent. They will fit in. They will look good doing the same things as everybody else. They will not stick out or feel conspicuous. Since most of the people in our world are pretty anxious and full of stress, then at least they will feel like part of the majority. (And most of the world is that way because most parents think this way, which is something you might want to consider as you contemplate some of the strategies in the next section.)

Self-pity is a great reward that people receive for their anxious thinking. Feeling sorry for themselves because they are so anxious is the game, and avoidance of doing something constructive to end the anxiousness is the strategy. Children can learn this method early, and your payoff is a feeling of comfort in not having to witness them taking the risks that are necessary to avoid being anxious.

You may also believe that some anxiety is good for them— that all of this nonsense about inner peace is really an illusion, and that no one in our modern world can be free from anxiety and stress. Thus, you raise them to use guilt, worry, and anxious thinking, believing that you are well-intentioned and teaching them to cope with the modern world, which is not anxiety-free by any means. Of course, a careful look at the world reveals that it is a perfect place, a joyful and miraculous place in which to be alive. However, you may not see it that way. You may well believe that the world is a monstrous place, a place that is full of evil and a place where people will take advantage of you. Thus, your anxiety-provoking style fits in with your view of the world.

Some Strategies for No-Anxiety Parenting

What follows are some suggestions for dealing with anxiety-ridden children. These strategies are written with a strong belief that everyone is entitled to feel peaceful within and that happiness and fulfillment are the birthright of every single human being on our planet. Give them a try. See if they work in your efforts with children, regardless of their ages, and even with yourself, since you too have a child inside who wants to come out and enjoy life.

Provide your children with opportunities to learn about serenity and inner peace throughout their lives. Let them read what all great thinkers have said about a more quiet kind of internal existence. Talk with them about what is going on inside them. Do exercises together that will help them to look inward now and then. Take a yoga class in your neighborhood and invite a child you care about to attend with you. Practice meditating together with a cassette tape and instructional materials that are available through your local bookstore or yoga center. Do yoga exercises together in your home and see if you do not feel more relaxed and healthy inside after just a few sessions. In other words, be careful not to discourage children from activities that you know very little about

Learn about self-hypnosis and discover that it is a natural and effective stress alleviator. Examine your prejudices toward activities that could help you and the children in your life to feel less anxious. Once you practice some of the professional strategies and techniques that are available for helping you to feel less tense, you may find that they are much more valid than you had ever imagined. Activities such as yoga, meditation, music appreciation, Zen, mind control, and reading books on inner awareness help them to develop early a quiet mind. A mind that knows how to rest and not always be busy is one that has significantly less anxiety in life, as well as a better chance at handling a busy pace.

Relax in your efforts to have young children get ahead of the game very early in life. It is not necessary to spend endless hours teaching children reading, math, foreign languages, and the like, long before school begins. While it is absolutely wonderful and helpful to allow them to explore everything as young toddlers, the pressure to excel, to be ahead of the other children, to memorize incomprehensible symbols, all in the name of being fast and first at what they do, is putting the anxiety pressure on when they are still in diapers. Children need to develop at their own pace. They will walk when they are ready. They do not need any pushing from you. They will not embarrass themselves in college with dirty diapers simply because they are not toilet trained sooner than other toddlers. It will come. Relax. Do not force them. Allow them to enjoy their young years. Be *with* them rather than *at* them all the time. Learn from them rather than trying to condition them to get ahead. They love to explore, to point, to laugh, to be silly, to look at books, to play, and to simply be in their new world. When you begin to force-feed them Type A attitudes as babies, they accept and carry with them for a lifetime those kinds of pressures to excel and beat everyone else. While it is nice to be highly motivated, it is also nice to be well balanced. Being able to relax and enjoy life is at least equal, if not superior, to being at the head of the class and always being nervous inside because of an inordinate need to be first.

Teach children that stress comes from the way in which they think and not from people or life situations. Do not give them excuses for having stress by saying, "The teacher puts too much pressure on you" or "We are low on money now, so you must be feeling stress." These are cop-outs that allow children to practice anxiety every time a new life situation crops up. Teach them to practice mind control. When you find a child occupied with a stressful thought pattern, see if you can help her to push it out for a sixty-second period of time. Each time the thought begins to invade her consciousness, directly teach her to refuse to think that thought in that one moment. This may sound simplistic, but it is the basis for eliminating self-defeating thoughts: moment to moment, with practice. The stress that children experience will soon disappear when they refuse to think stressfully, but they must begin with small amounts of time, and eventually train themselves to make those time periods longer.

Examine your own life for stress that you may be modeling. Stop trying to be the perfect mother, father, wife, single parent, homemaker, teacher, aunt, counselor, or whatever. There is no such thing as a flawless person, so why not give up that ghost in favor of being a stress-free happy person? You will never be appreciated by everyone all the time for everything you do, and any amount of upset that you have because people do not appreciate you is a waste of your present moments.

Do the things that you do because you choose to do them, not so that you will be seen as perfect. And remove the perfection pressure on children. Teach others to take care of themselves from an early age and you will be doing everyone concerned a big favor. The best role model that you can be is one who is happy, stress free, and feeling good about yourself. If you settle for anything else, and you are feeling tense and upset about not being perfect, then the ironic fact is that you are less perfect when you try to be perfect, and more perfect when you treat yourself well. Remind yourself regularly that your family does not deserve a slave, and that the best thing you can do for anyone is to help him to help himself. Your children will be the benefactors of your reduced stress level as much as you will, so if you cannot do it for yourself because you still see that as selfish, then do it for them. But whomever you do it for, just work each day at doing it.

Work one day at a time at developing an atmosphere of peace. Anything that you are doing which brings about upset and strife, either in yourself or in children, ought to be examined and eliminated. Everyone benefits from living in peace, particularly from reducing anxiety levels in children. If you are picky, fastidious, pushy, arrogant, short-tempered, or have any personality trait that is unpleasant to others, then go to work at changing it. Practice biting your tongue and postponing an outburst for a few minutes. If you eliminate one horrible scene through this technique, you will have prevented some stress. Do what you can to make your environment a fun, pleasant, nonhostile place. If others do not cooperate, and behave in unpleasant ways, they will soon get the message that you are not interested in their surliness because you refuse to engage in any dissonant interchanges.

Just as chemicals do not solve problems for children, the same is true for you. It is imperative that you visit a doctor who is interested in helping you to reduce any chemical dependencies, rather than one who encourages you to take antidepressants and tranquilizers as an antidote to your stress. If your physician does not cooperate with you in your efforts to be less chemically dependent, then seek out another professional who can be of help to you in reaching this goal. At any rate, keep in mind that you want to be off those "anxiety pills" and be in charge of your life, rather than being numbed by consciousness-altering drugs to the point of not being able to handle normal life problems without the aid of a drug. You must give children a solid example of a person who does not think anxiously, rather than showing them one who stuffs a tablet down his throat when the first sign of a problem crops up. If you cannot handle it alone now, then get help in doing so. Everyone will benefit.

Give children an opportunity to have the luxury of a sense of privacy without feeling pressured to be with other people all the time. Children need to learn how to be alone. Teach them very early the joy of books. A child who comes to love books never feels later in life that he has nothing to do. Being able to escape to one's own private space and read (and no one will ever run out of books to read) gives a person an advantage over those who cannot.

Many children complain constantly that they are bored, that they have nothing to do, that they hate leisure time. These are the sentiments of children who have grown up thinking that others have a duty to keep them entertained. They have always had some kind of activity, and if they get bored, then someone will take care of things for them by taking them to the circus or turning on the television or buying a new toy or whatever. This is a child who is growing up expecting action all of the time. This translates to anxiety about having to be alone. Let them play alone; in fact, encourage it. Expose them to books, newspapers, and magazines right from the very beginning. Let them have a place where they can go to be alone, without feeling that they are doing something wrong. Privacy is terrifically important as a way to avoid anxiety, and the child who experiences it when very young, and learns not to be threatened by it, will have a big head start on not feeling anxious when "there is nothing to do." This is true for quiet meditation, or talking with toys, or making up fantasies when alone. These are healthy games that secure children will engage in by themselves if allowed. Children benefit from private peaceful time. If they can play uninterrupted, or be allowed to quietly look through a picture book, or make up their own games with their toys, then they are releasing energy that might otherwise be devoted to being whiny, surly, or demanding. Later in their lives, they will also find that they will not need to talk it out with a therapist or consume tranquilizers. They will be prepared for tranquility by being tranquil of their own volition, rather than reaching for a chemical tranquilizer.

View each child as a unique, complete, separate human being who ought never to be compared with anyone else, particularly his or her siblings. You know how much you dislike being compared with your sisters or brothers. You know how you resent anyone saying, "You really don't look as nice as Margie," or "You're not as smart as Phil," or anything that even resembles such nonsense. You are you—period! The same thing applies to children. The temptation to compare children is almost overwhelming. You saw when the oldest one walked, talked, and poked himself in the eye for the first time. Naturally you see the same behaviors in your younger children, and your first impulse is to make a comparison. Well, stop it! Curtail your natural impulse to make comparisons, and instead see each of your children as unique. The child who is being compared feels a great deal of pressure to live up to expectations of how he should be. This is simply unnecessary anxiety. If a child does not talk until he is three, and his older brother talked at five weeks, all that can be said is that they began talking at different ages. Einstein did not talk until he was four. I assume he figured there was nothing yet to say. Perhaps he was learning everything there was to know, and deciding to talk about it later.

A child hears you comparing him with one of his siblings and immediately feels that he must now live up to these past accomplishments. All children do things when they are ready. Some love butterflies; others love fire engines. Some are neat; others are slobs. Some love schoolwork; others detest it. The point is that you must learn to avoid comparisons, particularly since these comparisons are generally accompanied by judgment. A clean child is better. An academic child is superior. Walking early is better than walking late. While there is no absolute truth in any of these or the thousands of other judgments you make, they become truth for the child, and this is the beginning of anxiety-provoking pressures he will place on himself.

Love your children for what they are. Treat each one as special. Love them a lot whether they are dirty or clean, academic or otherwise, fishing or playing a harmonica, and work each day at avoiding the comparison trap. If you avoid comparisons, you will not hear the guilt-inspired logic of children later, when they will be most tempted to say, "You always liked Michele better than me." If they are going to use these lame excuses, at least do not give them the ammunition when they are very young.

Try to remove the pressure on children to acquire external rewards throughout their lives. Help them to focus on the pure enjoyment of playing baseball, rather than on winning a trophy. Teach them to love baseball all of their lives, rather than learn to avoid it because they are not supremely talented at it. Do not give them early reasons to avoid anything in life, which is precisely what you do when you place the emphasis on achieving external awards, rather than internal fulfillment, from anything they do. Take the pressure off the report card as an index of anything really important. Talk with them about what they are studying, how they can apply it later in their lives, whether they are happy with themselves in school, what they like to study, what meaning they see in it for them now and in the future. Creating all of this pressure to achieve awards, grades, trophies, and the like is really one of the most neurotic and anxiety-provoking things you can do to children. As I emphasized earlier, grades are only scratch marks on a transcript. They may seem terrifically important at the time, but as you go through life you find out how really meaningless they are.

In fact, grades, awards, trophies, and all of the merit badges we dispense, genuinely lower a child's motivation. If they pursue only the award, once they have attained it, they will no longer wish to pursue that area of endeavor. I would assume that you want your children to love athletics, reading, poetry, music, and everything else that can enrich their lives, for a lifetime. Not to get an A in English literature and then put it all behind them in disgust. Not to place a trophy on the mantel and then get fat later in life for lack of exercise. Not to pass the obligatory music class and then disavow any interest in music for a lifetime. Teach them the inner joy of learning and applying what they gain for themselves. Help them to achieve discipline in undertaking any tasks, but not for the purpose of raising up their fingers to indicate that they are number one, or to show off a medal, but for the real joy of feeling positive within at a wonderful achievement. You can help children much more by teaching them to feel unpressured about acquiring external symbols, and joyful at feeling that wonderful sense of serenity that comes from participating in life. *The more things children can do, the greater their opportunity for personal happiness throughout their lives.* Pursuing awards and grades reduces their options and teaches them to only participate in the things that they can excel at, and to avoid everything else, not just for now but forever.

Once a child has been reminded of a mistake and punished, or whatever the consequences, then drop it. Do not remind children over and over again about what they did and how bad you still feel about it. They cannot go into rewind and do it over. They cannot erase the experience for your benefit. They *can* accept the consequences of a mistake and then move on. It is your job as a no-limit person to avoid any guilt trips that you might continue to lay on a child long after the incident is over.

Todd, a young teenager, told me how he had made a mistake one time when his parents left town. He invited several friends over without his parents' permission, and they had some beer and a party. When his parents returned, he was grounded for three weeks. He made a commitment to never do such a thing again, unless he had his parents' permission. He had had a long history of being responsible, and he readily admitted his mistake and took the consequences of his lapse in responsibility. Two years later, whenever Todd wanted to go anyplace or do anything away from his parents, they reminded him of his previous mistake. His father hounded him about the trouble he had caused, and how disappointed both he and Todd's mother were at the time. They simply would not forgive and forget. They wanted to get some extra guilt mileage out of Todd's error. The result: Todd simply withdrew from his parents, particularly his father. He lost respect for them simply because he really did not want to be continuously reminded of how much pain he had caused two years earlier. The more they reminded Todd of his conduct and how much he had hurt them, the more he looked forward to being away from them. Guilt works like that. No one wants to be around someone whose goal is to make him feel worse by reminding him of his wayward ways.

When it is over, let it be over, and remember that love is for-giving as well as for giving. Do not use past reminders to make children feel guilty. The more guilt they internalize, the more re-sentment will be building. Additionally, you will be teaching them to do exactly the same thing in their own relationships. In fact, you will see some of it coming back at you. Todd soon realized that his father was using guilt on him, and he began giving it right back. He took to reminding his father about an affair he had had six years earlier that almost caused a divorce. "How can you ex-pect me to be perfect when you sneaked around on Mom?" he would say in retaliation. Guilt breeds more of the same, and the only way to ensure that you do not get it back is to avoid using it yourself.

Try to avoid the use of all guilt-engendering sentences with children. Below are five examples, with guilt-producing state-ments on the left and sensible statements on the right, which will help children to take responsibility for their conduct rather than simply feeling guilty.

Guilt	Self-Responsibility
You ought to be ashamed of yourself.	You've behaved in a foolish way and you will have to take the consequences.
You're hurting Mommy's feel-ings when you do that.	I don't like that kind of behav-ior. When you act sassy you make yourself look bratty, and no one likes being around a brat, including you.
God will punish you for that.	You might want to look within yourself and see if you really like that about yourself.
How could you do this after all I've done for you?	How do you feel when you treat people who love you in that manner?
Someday you'll pay for this.	You must really be upset to talk like that. Why don't you cool off and we'll discuss it when you are more like yourself.

Keep in mind that no one likes to be insulted, regardless of how young they are. You do not enjoy someone pointing out your deficiencies or telling you how unattractive you appear. The purpose of these kinds of insults is to gain a measure of control or power over another by making him or her feel terrible inside. This is not only an inconsiderate thing to do, but an unhealthy one for children. All too often, adults forget how sensitive children are to criticism. You forget in the daily business of being around them that they can take one of your insults, even if it was not meant to be hurtful, and internalize it for a lifetime. *Your love for them is a huge shield that will protect them from the ravages of anxiety, so be careful not to weaken that shield by sending out contrary messages.*

Get off the guilt wagon yourself and work at being an example of a person who chooses to be responsible for yourself rather than merely feeling guilty. Eliminate your own victimization through the guilt of others in your life. If you are manipulated by your parents, show them that you are not interested in being reminded of mistakes you have made in the past. Be firm, but loving, in your response to their efforts to have you think badly of yourself. Take corrective action to avoid repeating the same old mistakes, rather than simply saying in front of your children how terrible you feel. Be an example for them. Show them that you will not be shaped by the guilt-inspiring efforts of others, regardless of who they might be. If you are a single parent, get on with parenting rather than constantly complaining about how miserable your lot in life is. Refuse to talk badly about the other parent, no matter how much you may be tempted to do so and no matter how right you may feel. Children have two parents, and it is not in their best interest to hate either one of them. Your children did not divorce either one of you. Your children need all the love they can get, particularly the love of their parents. Do not bring children into your squabbles unless you want them to feel anxious, guilty, worried, and generally tense now and later on as well. Squelch any temptation to talk badly about anyone else in front of them. They need to see a model of adults who are loving people, who feel a sense of joy at being alive, who do not feel like victims of their own choices. They need to see highly effective, happy people, rather than bitter, angry, and hostile people who are demonstrating to them how rotten the world and those in it are. Positiveness is a barrier to anxiety, while negativeness intensifies it. Be positive and be careful not to intensify their anxiousness. A separation is one problem, and it is a problem that people can learn to deal with effectively. But parents who are embittered and take it out on their children are making an extremely irresponsible choice to help their children to feel even more anxiety than they should. As Mohandas Gandhi put it, "Hate the sin and love the sinner."

Encourage children in their moves toward independence. The adult role in child development is not to have the children cling to you, but to make any clinging unnecessary in their lives. Every step they take toward their own independence is a step in the direction of being their own no-limit person. Applaud them loudly as little babies when they take their first few steps. Let them know how proud you are when they show you that they can ride a two-wheeler. These are magnificent accomplishments to them. Think back to your own days when you first knew you could swim alone without holding on to the sides, or when you went to school all by yourself for the first time. These are the giant steps of independence. And when they take even bigger giant steps away from you, out of the nest completely, you must applaud just as loudly, and enjoy their takeoffs. That is what the parenting trip is all about. Give them support for their independence, show them that you are not intimidated by their growing away from you, and they will always want to be around you. Show them the opposite—that they should feel guilty for leaving you after all you have done, that you will be alone and empty without them—and I guarantee you that your only "reward" will be that they will want to see you less and less after they leave the nest. No one wants to experience anxiety, and if they know that you want them to feel guilty about their natural choice to move on and away from you, then they will do all that they must to avoid that anxiousness.

Have your own sense of purpose independent of your children. Become active at anything that is exciting to you. Enroll in courses, take on new challenges, try out career choices, take up writing or wiring, but be a doer, a person who does not live your life through your children but has a life of your own, independent of them, just as they do. The more you see yourself as a fulfilled and important human being, the less likely you will be to feel the empty nest syndrome that produces so much of the guilt I am talking about here. You will become lifetime friends and compatriots if you both have your own unique interests, or you will do battle with each other over who owes what to whom if you use the guilt path.

Teach children, through your own example and by helping them, to become more confident in themselves rather than becoming worriers. When a child has a little ache or pain, ask her if she thinks she can get rid of it herself without resorting immediately to a pill or a visit to the doctor. Remind children of the great healing capacity they have with them all of the time, that being their own mind. Talk to them about not thinking sickly all the time. Stop reinforcing their inclinations to be sick by refusing to give heavy doses of sympathy every time they hurt themselves. You may be encouraging them to be more sickly than they would ever have to be by giving them attention and rewards for their illnesses. Tell them in no uncertain terms, "Try not to think about your cold. See if you can avoid telling anybody about it. Perhaps you can even make it go away by not telling anyone how bad you feel." Children have some measure of control over their own health, and they need to learn it from you. Stop complaining to your children about how you feel. Work constructively at being healthy, changing your nutritional habits, and exercising more regularly, and you will feel better. Then, vow to never complain out loud to anyone about how bad you feel. Think of yourself as a healer, and the children will as well. If you constantly talk about illness, and teach them that it is something that only a pill or a visit to the doctor can cure, then you are teaching them to become worriers.

The child who is not thinking sick and who firmly believes that he does not have to stay ill if he works on himself and stops looking for sympathy, will eliminate the need for worry. He will be too busy thinking healthy to use up his present moments in wasteful worry about his health. Be a model of a person who believes in his own ability to be healthy, who only takes medicines as a last resort, and who does not go to the doctor's office for every little ache and pain, and you will see it rubbing off on them. They will not only worry less, but they will become healthier as well. I can personally attest to the validity of this approach. Since I began exercising regularly and stopped thinking sick, I have not experienced colds, influenza, allergic attacks, or any sickness that is worth mentioning in almost ten years. I simply believe that I have the capacity for being healthy within myself, and I talk this way to my children as well. Now, when a minor ache or sniffle arrives in my life, I treat it as a mistake, and do not mention it. I use it as a signal to get more rest or use more vitamins, and the offending little germ or pain is gone almost before I know it. Thinking healthy and teaching your children to do the same is a great anxiety reliever, along with teaching them to become more in control over what goes on in their own bodies.

Whenever you see signs of children taking on worry habits, stop them with this sentence: "I want you to simply sit right here and worry with me for the next ten minutes." The absurdity will soon take hold. No amount of worry is going to help them pass their tests in school, or help them solve a dispute or get on the cheerleading squad. When they are through, ask them if studying would be more productive, or planning, or practicing the cheers, and the message will hit home. Worry is a waste of time, and anything you can do to illustrate this will be helpful.

With babies, try being sensible rather than a worrier, and it will help you and the baby to be less anxious. The warnings to lock up and put out of reach those items that are too dangerous for youngsters are well taken as preventives to tragic accidents and also as a means to avoid constant negative messages from you as a "worried" adult. Foresight rather than worry can lead you to take precautionary measures, reducing mental and physical strain for the adults as well as the children. If you are a nervous rather than a confident person, you will see the results of your behavior reflected by babies. You cannot be optimally effective when you are worried. Worry causes you to make more mistakes, to be constantly checking every movement, and to become paranoid about the baby's safety, cleanliness, emotional stability, and everything else. When you are relaxed, trusting yourself to use your own common sense and taking the necessary precautions to provide a safe environment, then you will not be a bundle of nerves around the little ones. You will be able to enjoy them, rather than always being worried about them. And no amount of worry is going to keep a tragic event from taking place. In fact, worry will make an accident far more likely. Caution, yes; worry, no. Being sensibly concerned, yes; worry, no! You will only succeed in making a baby become anxious and fearful if that is what you model.

Help younger toddlers and preadolescents by teaching sensible lessons of personal safety, without putting an unnatural fear into them. The fearful person is far more likely to be victimized than the confident one. "Never ever speak to strangers" is a pretty silly rule when you give it some thought. Everyone is a stranger until you get to know him or her. If no one ever talked to any strangers, no one would know anyone outside of their immediate family. It is important to reiterate here that you must use some common sense and talk to children about the dangers of being kidnapped as they are capable of understanding such a concept. But a fearful child who is always intimidated by any stranger is learning a terrible lesson: that the world is mean and ugly and everyone wants to do the child harm. This is not the case. The world is full of people, the vast majority of whom are loving and do not want to harm children. The natural outgoing qualities of young children should not be squelched in favor of teaching them to worry about everyone they meet. You must balance common sense with sensible precautions. A very young child must be supervised at all times. Period! You cannot let them out of your sight when they are capable of running off into the street or into a stranger's car. Yet you do not have to scream at them to warn them of such dangers. You know the dangers, and you also know that worrying is not going to help. Watch them, by all means be extra careful in an age of child snatching and baby stealing, but do not make them nervous wrecks about everyone they meet. Remember, your worry will not prevent a tragedy; only sensible precaution will.

As your children get older and it becomes literally impossible to watch them at all times, then you can tell them about not going with strangers, about not walking alone, about being safety minded, without scaring them into becoming raging young neurotics who are afraid of everyone they meet and who begin to see all strangers as potential perverts. They must learn how to protect themselves and how to have confidence in their own abilities to avoid a serious problem, but they must not become so anxious that they lose their magnificent joy and awe of the world. Be specific about what they should do to protect themselves, and insist that they call you to inform you of their whereabouts. Go over the potential dangers, but do not scare them into becoming people who are afraid of life. The fact is that learning to be confident in yourself and to carry yourself in an assured manner, while taking sensible precautions, are far greater deterrents to being victimized than simply being scared, full of anxiety, and a worrywart.

Let children set their own goals for themselves, and stay out of the way of their grandiose dreams except to serve as a positive encourager. Most children are afraid of their own greatness and set their sights too low, or they are the product of parental interference in which the parents, well-intentioned though they may be, tell their children what they should aim for in life. If an eleven-year-old girl wants to be a doctor, encourage her to dream in that direction, even if she hasn't shown what you think are the appropriate aptitudes or attitudes. If she is not going to become a doctor, she will make the adjustments as she goes along, and there is no problem in having to adjust one's goals.

In talking with a young girl who wanted to become a pilot, but whose eyesight was too poor at the age of thirteen, I can remember telling her to go for it anyway. "By the time you are ready to take the examination for your pilot's license, the world will have caught up and they will allow pilots to wear contact lenses," I assured her. The gleam in her eyes was worth it. She told me how her father had told her to think about something else because she had been cursed with poor eyesight. And sure enough, today she is a flying instructor. She wears her glasses and confidently enjoys her occupation. And if the requirements had not changed, then I would have encouraged her to fight that regulation in the courtroom rather than cursing her bad luck. When you tell children that they cannot do something or to be more realistic, you are only teaching them to distrust themselves and to become unnecessarily anxious about something that will surely work itself out.

Keep in mind a child's age when you react to him or her. If you take a four-year-old to a restaurant, understand that that child is not capable of being twelve, any more than you are capable of being a giraffe. Get in touch with the reality of a child's age, and do not try to make him anxious by expecting him to be something that he is not. Two-year-olds act two, all the time with no exceptions. The same is true of every other age. Stop the insistence that children be older and more mature than they are capable of being.

If you do not want little ones to wander around in a fancy restaurant, stay home, leave them with a sitter, or go to a family-style restaurant. If you do go to an elegant place and then sit there fuming all night because the baby is crying and disturbing everyone, or the four-year-old is making faces at the other diners, then you, not the child, needs a head examination. Asking children to be older than they are is putting unrealistic anxiety into their lives. This is not an endorsement of disruptive behavior by excusing them, it is simply to remind you that all children have age-typical behaviors which you are not going to eliminate by being their warden. Two year olds will wet their pants now and then. Three year olds will say, "nah nah na nah na," and call you a "poopy head" once in a while. Four year olds will pick fights with everyone, nine year olds will whine and moan and throw fits now and then, pre-teens will punch each other and you too, now and then, teenagers will be moody and find you impossible occasionally. These are the facts. You did the same thing. So stop with your short memory and instead learn to laugh with them, call them a poopy-head once in a while in jest, playfully punch them in the arm, wrestle with them, ignore the moodiness, forget about the outbursts and let them have their age typical behavior. It will not last forever. They will not call their boss a poopy-head on their first working assignment. They will simply outgrow these things, and you will help yourself and them to be far less anxious if you simply grin inside and move on to more important things.

If you punish a child for anything, be certain that he *knows the reason*. Children will become anxious if they do not know why you are upset. It is not sufficient that *you* know why you are meting out punishment. *They* are the ones being punished, and even if they do not agree with the punishment, at least be certain that they have heard you say the reason why. If possible, ask them to give it back so that it is not misunderstood. "You cannot simply throw a tantrum whenever you feel exasperated and ruin everyone else's right to a peaceful home. You will stay in your room until you can stop making a fuss and ruining everyone else's peace." This is enough. Even if the child continues to scream, at least she has heard why she is being sent to her room. "You have violated a curfew that we both agreed upon. I am taking your driver's license away from you for ten days because you are not living up to your agreement. If it happens again, and you are late without notifying us, then I will take away all of your driving privileges for a month. I want you to learn to accept responsibility for your commitments." This makes the reason for the punishment clear, and you do not then have to remind them over and over about their being irresponsible. But they must, at any age, understand what it is all about. If you simply withdraw privileges over nothing, or you are looking for reasons to be upset with them so that you can exercise your parental power, you will increase their anxiety about living with you, teach them to be suspicious about your mental health, and drive them further and further away from you.

Punishment is something that goes with the territory of a child-parent relationship. But it should be used only sparingly, and to have any benefit it must be mutually understood. At all ages, regardless of your opinions about punishment, I strongly suggest that you use punishment only as a learning device. You should never ever use it to inflict pain, and it should always be something that is reasonable. Taking away driving privileges for a year for a minor infraction only makes you appear to be an ogre. Follow through on what you have agreed, but do not make unenforceable statements. If you do make a threat of punishment that is unrealistic, then back off of it when you have calmed down. "I am not really going to ground you for the rest of your natural life just because you failed science in the fourth grade, but you will have to stay in and study each night until we both are convinced that you are putting in a serious effort in school. Okay?" It is far more sensible to admit to having overreacted than to go ahead with punishment that was obviously not intended to be handed out in the first place.

Allow children to speak their minds, even if they say things that you find intolerable. Children who are fearful about speaking are internalizing their feelings and moving away from you. They will begin to hide everything from you if they know you are intolerant of their ideas. Become excited about their lives rather than refusing to hear about them. Talk to them about their music rather than criticizing it. Ask them about their views on important subjects in the world, rather than treating them as people whose views do not matter. They do matter, and if they know that even though you disagree on many things, at least you respect their right to have an opinion, you will be lessening any anxiety, as well as giving them a place to talk openly about what they believe.

When I counseled pregnant teenagers and suggested that they tell their parents, they almost always said, "You must be joking. They would kill me—I could never ever tell them" This says something very revealing about their relationships with their parents. If your children would not want to come to you when they are in deep trouble, then it must be because they fear being judged or rejected. To whom but their parents or primary caretakers should a child turn when he or she is in trouble? Why would they turn to their parents only when things were going along smoothly? What kind of a one-way relationship has been created when adults can only hear good news? They do not need you nearly so much when everything is running just fine. They need you most when they make mistakes, when they get into trouble, when they stumble. You must create a relationship with your children wherein they come to you with the good news and the bad, knowing that they will be comforted and helped by you when they make a mistake as well as when they make you proud.

It is easy to love people when they smell good, but sometimes they slip into the manure of life and smell awful. You must love them just as much when they smell foul. This can only happen in an open, honest interaction where they know that they can speak their minds and have their opinions respected, no matter how much they may conflict with yours. I want my children to feel that they could always come to me, no matter how muddy they got, rather than looking for help someplace else because I taught them to fear my disapproval, or because I never allowed them to have an open mind. Keep that in mind as you interact with children, and they will know that you are someone they can trust to provide help and guidance in the good times and the bad.

Avoid correcting children in front of others, and ask them to do the same for you. Take them aside if you have something that must be said, rather than giving them an opportunity to be embarrassed in front of others. Keep their anxiety levels low as much as possible by respecting their rights not to be corrected by you.

Be with your children now. Children do not see into the future the way you do. You are much better off to be with them in this moment, rather than always reminding them about where they will be someday. Be with them *now*! Throw the ball with them, now. Take them to the beach, today. Hold them in your lap, right this moment. These are the things that children remember, which comfort them rather than teaching them to be anxious about the future. To a child, the future is something they do not even understand, so don't waste their precious present moments making them anxious about what they will study in college, when they are still in grammar school. They want you to be with them rather than giving them lectures about tomorrow, and it is a wonderful strategy for reducing anxiety. I think this subject is so important that I have devoted all of Chapter 7 to it.

Try to get your children off schedule to some degree so that they can experience some spontaneity in their young lives. While you obviously cannot be making meals at every hour of the day, sometimes it is important to let them eat when they are hungry, particularly if they are capable of fixing their own meals. The notion that everyone ought to be hungry at the same time is absurd, but you need not be the victim here at all. Mealtime often becomes a time of great anxiety in a home. Children fight with the adults about what they have to eat, bargaining one carrot for a dish of ice cream and the like. Stop this nonsense now! By and large, their bodies will tell them what they need. If you do not provide junk, they will not have the option of eating it. If you provide good food and they do not want it that night, try ignoring the situation now and then. Take their bargaining position away by simply not making food a big deal. If you worry over every bite, they will manipulate you by becoming fussy eaters. Worry will not make them better eaters; common sense will. Try ignoring what they refuse to eat, saying nothing about it at all, and being firm about no junk after dinner. Keep the lower shelf of the refrigerator stocked with fruit, yogurt, and vegetable snacks.

The same rationale applies to bedtime as well. Take the pressure off yourself and them, too. Tell them to be in their rooms at night at whatever time you both think is sensible for their rest needs, and then forget about it. Do not keep checking on them. Let them read, play, think, or whatever in their rooms, and if they appear tired the next day, then make bedtime a little earlier the next night. You can remove all of the needless anxiety over these routines by making them unimportant, by showing children that you are not going to get into anxiety-provoking fights about them any longer.

If you rid yourself of some of your own rules and rigid thoughts about what the children need, and determine their needs instead by simply observing their behavior, you will find life much more pleasant at both mealtimes and bedtimes. All children do not need the same amount of sleep. All children do not need to drink milk four times a day. Each one is unique. But most certainly no one needs to have nagging arguments and anxiousness over such simple matters. Give up your rules about what they must do, stop fighting with them about these things, and ignore your worry that they will end up sickly or full of fatigue. Children are absolutely amazing. When they get tired, they sleep, and if they are not tired at nine o'clock they do not pretend to be just because the clock says it is time to be tired. If they need more potassium in their bodies, they will eat a banana if it is there, even if they did not have your planned meal. Let them regulate themselves a bit more, using common sense, and you will all have less anxiety as your reward.

Get your children out into nature as much as possible. Nature is a great reliever of anxiety for both you and your children. Being outdoors is a wonderful way to teach them about being anxiety free for a lifetime. Camping without rules. Walking through a trail with no homework assignments to categorize everything. Sitting in a boat and experiencing the majesty of a lake, pond, river, or ocean. Make every effort to get outdoors as often as possible. A walk through a city park, or through the streets of your neighborhood, is a great way to relieve some tension. With my own babies I have noticed that they cry much less when I take them outside. They smile a lot more on the grass than in the house on the carpet. Young children crave nature, and you can raise them to appreciate it by making every effort to instill a love, and a healthy respect, for the magnificent miracle that is in everything natural.

No-limit children have learned a different response to the same stimuli because they know the world to be friendly. Their behavior is meant "for the best," or at least their mistakes are "honest." Therefore, if an action goes awry, it does not elicit feelings of guilt. Remorse, learning, redoing, and improving are possible responses instead. Rather then worry, a no-limit child sees future events as exciting adventures, opportunities to grow, chances for fun challenges and new experiences. Since self-worth is not tied to performance, the worry about "doing well" is eliminated. Worrying about the plane crashing or "Will Grandpa be there when I land?" does not affect the no-limit child because he knows that the pilot is in charge and the cockpit is an interesting place. If Grandpa is late, he gets to stay with the flight attendants and ask them a million questions. No-limit children are "doers," and guilt and worry do not *do* anything. Thus, it is very unlikely that they would bother themselves with negative thinking or destructive behaviors.

The no-limit child is learning to be here in life, rather than to categorize it. He is excited about the prospects of each moment in each day, rather than trying to find something wrong and complaining about every little detail of life. Life is fun, to be enjoyed, to share, rather than a burden for everyone. An absence of anxiety typifies a no-limit person. This means putting a premium on inner serenity, removing those onerous guilt and worry trips, getting rid of the complaining habit, and learning to slow down and enjoy life. Living is not a race; it is a journey, something to be enjoyed each day. You can do a great deal to help children to understand this important truth, and you will get a nice bonus as well—that is, a lot less anxiety for yourself as part of the bargain.

6

I Want My Children to Have Peaceful Lives

The no-limit person is mobilized rather than immobilized by anger. He "keeps his cool" while fighting for a creative, constructive solution. He is a pleasure to work with and to be around. He goes with the flow rather than fighting life. He thinks, feels, and behaves as a self-master.

Anger manages everything badly.

—STADIUS

There are few if any occasions in our lives when we have been angry or lost our tempers on which we can look back without regret.

—ASHLEY MONTAGUE

You want peace in your life! This is a statement which I can make with almost absolute certainty. Everyone wants a peaceful life. The same is true for children. Every child wants a peaceful life. Peaceful on the outside and peaceful on the inside as well. In the previous chapter I offered you some suggestions for helping your children to grow up with inner serenity. Freedom from thinking anxiously will aid children immeasurably in becoming no-limit people. As I said in Chapter 5, you can help children to become human beings who refuse to think anxiously. So too can you aid them in having a peaceful, serene, optimal living environment. You can do a great deal to ensure that they are not constantly embroiled in, or witness to, violent family fights. You can help them to live in a salubrious environment which is devoid of immobilizing anger and hostility, and simultaneously give them the opportunity to discipline themselves in such a way that they will make their own living environment civil rather than turbulent for those around them.

A positive environment is crucial if you are determined to raise children as no-limit people. You cannot expose them to the vagaries of anger and hostility all the time, and then expect them to cultivate an inner serenity. You cannot scream and holler at them all the time and expect them not to take on violent characteristics themselves. You cannot raise them in turmoil and expect them to be peaceful. You have a choice in what kind of an environment you provide for children. Regardless of what you may have come to believe, or how tough the circumstances of your life may be, you still have a choice about what the emotional environment is going to be. If anger is a major feature, you will have angry children. If fights are constantly erupting, you will see children developing into fighters. If you exercise no discipline over your own emotional reactions around children, you will see undisciplined children emerge.

No-limit people want to send violence out of their lives and out of this world. They see that there is too much anger and hostility in the world. They see the results of hating others, of constantly fighting each other, of a world gone mad with the proliferation of weapons that threaten our survival. And no-limit people are the ones who are going to do something to erase this terrible conflagration of anger from our planet. We not only crave peace, we absolutely must create it if we are going to leave this planet inhabitable for future generations. The world family demands peace. Our national family cries out for peace and shudders at the excessive amounts of anger and hatred in our country. It must all begin with our own personal family units. Your family, whoever its members may be, and whatever their conditions, must take the initiative in bringing about a peaceful environment. If the children in your family unit (and millions more) are raised on peace and serenity, they will become the no-limit people who will live peaceful lives and help others to do the same. Finally, they will take up the cause of bringing ultimate peace to our entire planet. If they are raised without the immobilizing anger and are free from the stress of continuous family fights, they will not choose to strike out at others. If they are raised in peace, they will not know how to be warlike. They will not lash out in anger if they have not been raised on anger. They will be free to tackle the problems of our world creatively, rather than fighting with neighbors and their children in this seemingly endless cycle of bitterness and animosity toward each other.

You can make a difference in the kind of child you raise. It does not matter if you are a single parent or in partnership with your spouse. It makes no difference how old you are or how old your child may be; you can still make a significant difference. It makes no difference what your nationality is, or what your own parents instilled in you as a little child. If, in your heart, in the most honest corner of your being, you believe that anger, fighting, belligerency, and warfare are wrong, then you can do something about children's attitudes, too. Stop for a moment and put yourself into the shoes of those people who are the victims of violence in our world. Then realize that the perpetrators as well as many of the victims are individual human beings who for some reason or another decided to use violence as a means for expressing their desires. Those who decided to kill or beat up someone else were raised in a violent society, be it their families, their cities, their nations, or their universe. It had to start somewhere, where individuals learned to simply act out in hostility. Your children do not have to be that way. They need not grow up seeing anger as a natural mode of self-expression. They need not resort to violence to get their way. There are other methods that are far more effective for solving our differences, and the truth is that it must begin with you, in your own individual family unit. No excuses. If you want the world to change, you must start with yourself, and that is the only place you can start: by making a commitment to have your children grow up in an environment which condemns violence and places a premium on being civil. It will save your children from a grievously unhappy life. It may help save the world from premature extinction. It all begins with you.

The person who grows up with no-limit values places a high premium on solving a problem as opposed to being a part of the problem. The no-limit individual is one who has total control of his own inner world. Anger and hostility erupt from within a person. Usually that person is one who has not been trained to monitor his own angry impulses, and instead simply blames the world for making him angry. But it is not that way in reality.

If you put pressure on someone and he or she reacts with anger, that anger was inside the individual who expressed it. No one else can make you angry. No event can make you hostile. If these emotions come out of you or your children, it is because they are inside you in the first place. If you have no angry thoughts stored up inside, it is impossible for them to get out. Remember the analogy to the orange: When you squeeze an orange and orange juice comes out, it is that way because orange juice is what is inside an orange. Simple but true. And simple but true for human beings as well. Squeeze a person, and whatever comes out does so because of what is inside, not because of the person doing the squeezing.

Problem-solving people (no-limit people) are those who do not store up anger inside themselves. Instead, they know how to process their thoughts in a way which leads them to solve a problem. You want to help children to get to the point in their lives where they know how to process their thoughts in a beneficial way, rather than turning them into anger and hate. This process begins with you taking a hard look at your own attitudes toward anger and fighting, and working at creating a fight-free environment in which to bring up children.

You Can Stop Having the Same Old Family Fights

You have heard it over and over again: "Fighting is only natural." "It's healthy to have a good fight now and then to keep the juices flowing." "People in families just naturally fight with each other—it clears the air." But you know that fighting is not a pleasant activity, and that every time a fight occurs you feel miserable and drained of your life juices. You know that children suffer the most when you have explosive family fights, and that a great deal of venom and ugliness come out that you would rather not have them exposed to on a regular basis.

It is time to challenge the belief that fighting is an inherent component of human relationships. In fact, fighting almost always results in a breakdown of communication, a distancing between the fighters, and intensified physical reactions of increased blood pressure, headaches, insomnia, and even tension-produced ulcers. Take a look at the facts before you justify the old familiar fight scene. Fighting in the form of heated arguments, anger, and especially rage is extremely destructive to all involved, and it is one of the most tormenting parts of family life.

If you find yourself disliking the fight scene in your family, and if you are feeling in any way immobilized by the constant repetition of the "same old fights," then trust your own judgment that this is not fun, or in any way helpful to you or the children. It is sheer nonsense to defend fighting as a natural phenomenon. Obviously people who live together will have many disagreements, and everyone has a right to be assertive about ensuring his or her own personal human rights, but the haggling and fighting that you experience are not only bothersome but just plain destructive. No one likes being in a fight regularly. No one likes being screamed at or, even worse, verbally or physically assaulted. A family fight is something that you should be looking to eliminate from your life, rather than justifying it as a natural part of living together. Disagreements, yes. Fights, no more.

When I use the words *family fights* I want to make certain that you understand what I mean. Fighting can take many forms. It means to participate in verbal exchanges which involve intense anger, rage, and sometimes physical abuse. It also implies orally assaulting each other by rehashing the same old material until someone is so frustrated that he or she becomes emotionally immobilized. Fighting, as I use it here, refers to any exchange among people in a close relationship which is unproductive, and in any way injurious to any one of the participants, particularly when children become involved, either as participants or sideline observers. If the interchanges are directly associated with hassling and intimidating others, then you are participating in family fights whether you like to admit it or not. And underline this in your mind as you think about ways to rid yourself of the family fight scene: *Fighting feels lousy, it makes for a lot of unnecessary pain, it is irritating, it leaves deep scars on your children, it teaches them to use the same tactics in resolving their disputes, and it is never worth defending if you want your children to become no-limit people, or if you are in the least bit interested in having a no-limit life yourself.*

Some Typical Family Fights

Fighting goes on in many families despite everyone's disliking the highly charged atmosphere. Each person in a family has his own set of "same old fights." When they are looked at from an objective point of view, they serve no functional purpose other than to get everyone upset. The same old tired arguments, the hurt feelings, the slammed doors, the storming out of the house, the verbal assaults and thoughtless obscenities occur. And when it is all over, there is the anticipation that it is going to happen again and again and again, because the fighting process does nothing more than intensify the hostility; it does not resolve anything.

Here is a brief list of "same old fights":

the checking account	your room is not clean
taking out the garbage	doing household chores
visits from relatives	doing the dishes
money, money, money	where are we going for the holidays
you never talk to me	you're late again
your past behavior	personality traits (lazy, pushy, fearful)
I want more freedom	you're not the person you used to be
you're inconsiderate of me	personal habits (smoking, drinking, eating)
no one appreciates me	you embarrass me

I want privacy	you drink too much
you won't talk to me	I don't like your friends
this is the curfew	I hate being told what to do
you don't understand me	stop trying to control me

This list could go on ad infinitum, but it serves to illustrate the more common same old fights.

If you genuinely want to eliminate the fight scene in your home, you must come to a decision yourself. Yes, yourself! It does not involve waiting for the children to change. It does not mean waiting for your spouse to come around to your point of view. It means making a decision that fighting is going to be a thing of the past. It means making a vow that you are not going to continue to raise your children in an atmosphere of violence, be it verbal or physical violence. It means committing yourself to giving your children the opportunity to be free from anger and rage, from the sores that ultimately infect them from overexposure to fighting and war. Below are seven guiding principles that you can adopt for yourself to help eliminate the family-style fight. At the end of the chapter I will provide some specific techniques that you can use to help live peacefully, but first examine these principles, which can become the basis for your own family peace treaty.

Basic Principles to Adopt as Guidelines for Eliminating the "Same Old Fights"

1. *Virtually all fights revolve around the absurd thought, "If only you were more like me, then I wouldn't have to be upset."* This is an erroneous assumption about the people in your world. People—including your spouse, your children, your parents, or anyone else—will never be the way you want them to be. When you find yourself upset with someone else, you are really saying to yourself, "If only you were thinking the way I am thinking right now, then I wouldn't have to be so upset." Or "Why can't you do things the way I want them to be done?" Once you eliminate this notion that others ought to be the way you want them to be, and you accept them (not approve, simply accept) for what they are, then you will not be able to be seduced into fighting with them.

Why would you ever fight someone for being what you would expect him or her to be? People are not going to be different simply because you would like it to be that way. If you curtail your expectations for others, and stop evaluating your own personal happiness on the basis of what others are doing, thinking, saying, or feeling, then you will find it almost impossible to fight with anyone. While you may want to put a stop to anyone stepping on you, and teach your children to do the same, you will find it unnecessary to get upset just because other people choose to be the way they are.

2. *You get treated in life the way you teach people to treat you.* You must teach this basic lesson to your children and accept it yourself as a guiding principle. Your willingness to participate in family fights comes from within you. You have other choices, and you must stop blaming others for the way you get treated and instead look within. Your children must also learn that the way they get treated by everyone is a result of what they are willing to tolerate. If you feel that people dump on you, and treat you in an inconsiderate manner, rather than blaming them, you might ask yourself, "How did I teach them to treat me in this manner?" Instead of being mad at others for the way they behave toward you, remind yourself that if you do not want to be victimized, then you must stop playing victim. Resolve to stop sending signals which teach others to treat you in a way that you must resolve by fighting.

3. *Behavior, rather than words, is the greatest teacher of all.* You can talk until you are blue in the face, and you generally will get nothing accomplished except to be upset and further frustrated. If you want to teach someone in your family to put her clothes away, devise behavioral rather than verbal cues. Once you have discussed the matter, and you have discovered that your words are ineffective, then practice new methods. Toss the clothes next to the washing machine, leave them lying where they were dropped, or simply stop washing clothes that are not in the hamper. Do anything but have another long discussion about learning responsibility, which either gets ignored immediately or results in another family fight. Behavior, not words! You can stop conversation after the evidence is in that the child is not listening, and then resolve to teach with actions. Once you teach someone with behavior that you will not tolerate being abused, you will see the

abusive behavior subside. But if you continue to talk about it endlessly, you will not only keep having the same old fights, but you will be teaching children that they can talk or argue their way out of being responsible. You want children to learn no-limit behaviors, rather than how to avoid being a responsible person. Your behavior is the most effective teaching technique you have.

4. *People are more important than things.* If you keep this principle in mind, you will end a lot of the same old fights, since so many of them revolve around objects and money. No *thing* in this world is more important than a person. When you fight about funiture, drapes, cars, money, clothes, dishes, garbage, and so on, you are elevating those things to positions of prominence over people. No "thing" is worth fighting about. People's happiness is what living is all about. When you see the emphasis being shifted to things, and the result being that people are becoming unhappy, you can resolve to not let this happen. Stop yourself when this things-over-people mentality crops up. If others want to do it, fine— you will not be able to stop them by fighting about it. But you can refuse to allow any *thing* in this world to be the source of your own unhappiness, and when you model this attitude for your family members, you will find them getting the message as well. Imagine yourself screaming at a little child for scratching an object. Imagine the foolishness of becoming irrational over a lost toy. Think about the absurdity of beating your child over a torn piece of fabric. These are things. They can be replaced. But a child's inner pain, his realization that his feelings are less important than a toy, his own lack of integrity at being treated lower than an object—these cannot be replaced quite so neatly as a lost toy. People count; things do not!

Do not be surprised if your little ones start beating up on each other if they are recipients of such behavior themselves. As I noted earlier, physically abused children almost always treat their children (and other people as well) abusively, particularly when the abuse they received was the result of making things and objects more important than human beings. While you do not have to endorse destructive behavior, you also do not have to become immobilized when you find others treating objects in ways that you do not like. Keep in mind that the only thing that matters in life is life itself. You cannot get love from a thing. You cannot caress an object and get anything in return. And while you want to enjoy things, and to teach respect for nice things, remember that objects are valueless without people to give them meaning.

5. *Perhaps the most neurotic pursuit of all is the desire to have those who love you understand you all the time.* You, once again, are unique in all the world. What that means is that no one could possibly understand you all the time, because to do so would mean that the other person would have to become you. When you find people not understanding you, instead of senselessly chasing after "being understood," you are much better off to say to yourself, "They don't understand me and they probably never will, and that's okay since it really doesn't reflect anything about me." Once you stop expecting people to understand you all the time, then you will be purchasing a ticket to the sidelines when the same old fights begin to surface. The greatest understanding that you can have is that you do not understand each other, and that it is all right. Children live in their own worlds. They occupy their own unique bodies. They live in a space far different from yours. You cannot understand why they do the crazy things they do—and, believe it or not, they see you as "weirder" than you see them. Accepting the fact that you do not understand each other is a great place to start in building a fight-free environment. Let them be unique instead of like you. Allow them to be "weird," rather than struggling every day with trying to understand and be understood. Why would anyone who is unique in all the world expect someone else who is equally unique to understand her all the time? And why should you have to surrender your uniqueness by demanding to be understood, simply because you are the parent or spouse? Once you accept the fact that you will never be understood all the time, then you will also stop all of the hurt that goes with the insane demand for mutual understanding on every issue in life. More than half of the fights which center on the notion that "You don't understand me" will disappear. You will be teaching children to stop trying to be understood all the time themselves, and to get on with understanding themselves, which is enough of a life's mission all by itself.

6. *Self-confident people seldom participate in the same old fights.* When you are at peace with yourself and you love yourself, it is virtually impossible for you to do things to yourself that

are destructive. You want to treat the people you love with love, not hate, and you must be one of those people that you love, and that goes double for your children. I have devoted all of Chapter 2 to discussing the importance of a child learning to love himself. Having fights is a sure way to reduce that self-love. Why would someone who loves himself do anything to hurt the self he loves? Fighting is destructive and hurtful. If you think of yourself as an important person, you will not allow yourself to become overweight, addicted to foreign substances, plagued with guilt or worry, or wracked with the pain of regular fighting.

Self-love means treating oneself lovingly. If you show others that you love yourself, and that as a result you are going to treat yourself with respect, you will find that they will not be surprised when you simply refuse to go along with their attempts to lure you into fighting. They will soon realize that you think too much of yourself to be filling your precious life moments with agony as a result of fighting, when it is simply a waste of time and the only payoff is distress. Show your children that you respect yourself too much to be reduced to screaming, fighting, or even rage. You will be giving them an important message about yourself, as well as giving them an example to live by: an example of a peaceful person rather than someone who can be bought and sold emotionally by the whims and inconsiderations of others.

7. *All participation in family fights is a choice.* No one can make you fight if you refuse to go along. When you are embroiled in the same old fight, you must remember that you put yourself there, and that you have the ability to avoid this stressful activity. It is very, very difficult to fight with a rational person. By staying rational you reduce the opportunity for fighting, and consequently for being upset as well. When you find yourself in a fight and you dislike being there, remember the message that you are modeling for your children: "You don't have control over yourself." They will learn this neurotic message. They will simply blame someone else for starting a fight because they have parents who also believe the same nonsense. If you practice maintaining your composure, and remember that someone else's behavior belongs to that person and cannot upset you unless you allow it to do so, then you will not become an unwilling target. When your "opponents" see that you are plainly uninterested in joining them in their neu-

rotic pursuit of fighting, and that you refuse to choose an upsetting experience, then you will be out of the fight game with all of these sparring mates in your life. Everything is a choice, and avoiding senseless fights is an excellent thing to practice if you want more serenity for yourself.

Much of the family fight scene is a habit that can be turned around if you are willing to do so. Before looking at the payoffs for fighting and specific strategies for eliminating it from your life and the lives of your children, you must also look carefully at the emotion called anger.

Much has been written about anger. Some claim that it is normal; others, that it is always destructive. Regardless of your position, the statement by Stadius at the opening of this chapter is relevant for you: "Anger manages everything badly." We know that angry people are not as efficient as calm people. We know that anger motivates people to behave in destructive ways, and that we cannot tolerate much more of this anger in our people or there will be no people left to be concerned about. In order to reduce those family fights, you must tackle this thing called anger, and help yourself and your children to change the thought processes that create this rampant anger in the first place. You can help to change and rechannel this angry energy. You can teach your children that you will not be the victim of their anger, and you can teach yourself to eliminate it as well. No one likes being around the impossible person who is full of explosive anger, so let's stop pretending that it is only natural, and get on with replacing it with something far more tranquil and life-enhancing for everyone concerned.

Understanding Anger

You do not want your children to grow up with anger and hatred inside them. You know how awful it is to be around a person who erupts in anger. You know how lousy you feel when you see children having a temper tantrum. Even worse, you know how lousy they feel. You see the anger in their faces and the pain all over them when they go into a rage. You know that it is not good for them to have these outbursts or "inbursts" and that if they continue into adulthood, that person will be as big a victim as those he or she continually victimizes.

To assist children to be no-limit persons, you want to do all you can to ensure that they do not become slaves to their own angry personalities. They will be far more productive, happier, and more appreciative of life if they can eliminate this anger zone from their lives, but first you must understand it, and then you must work hard at teaching them that it is not going to be tolerated by you.

Anger is the result of thinking. Those same old family fights originate with thinking. So too does anger. Angry outbursts by children are almost always used because they work. They are seldom the result of some deep pathological disorder. A tantrum serves to get the negative attention that will ultimately cause you, or others, to give in rather than be the recipient of the offensive display of anger. Children learn very early that an expression of anger is a very effective way to get what they want. From crying with outrage when not picked up instantly in infancy, to a tantrum in the grocery store when bubble gum is denied, the behavior only persists for as long as it works. That is, if it gets them their bubble gum. When you give in to an angry outburst at any time, what you are saying to your child is this: "All you have to do to get your way is to act uncivilized and angry, and then you can have what you want." No matter what else you call it, this is behavior modification. Only it is your behavior which is being modified by the negative influence of anger. Children learn to do it very early, and it is up to you to make sure that you do not reinforce this kind of behavior in them when they are young. Otherwise, they may grow up believing that they can bully others around with the excuse that "I'm a person with a quick temper. I really can't help myself—it's in my genes."

You must take a no-excuses approach to helping children learn that anger is not going to be the way in which they relate to you, or to anyone else. You must not be afraid to confront this anger, and be sure that you do not inadvertently reinforce the very thing that you want them to eliminate in their lives. When you give in to anger, outbursts, rage, tantrums, or irrational arguing, you are teaching children to use these strategies throughout their lives. When I refer to a "no-excuses" approach, I am talking about not simply excusing their unruly behavior with sentences like "He really can't help it—he's just like his father," "He's always been short-tempered," "She really is a sweet child; it's just that she has this demon living inside her that escapes now and then," "All children have temper tantrums—it's only human nature." All of these excuses must go if you want to help your child to be rational instead of irrational throughout life.

If your children are going to make it as no-limit people, they must learn very early that they will do it with their brains. They must learn to take control of their own minds and to take responsibility for how they react emotionally. Children who are raised on anger are being taught quite the opposite. They soon come to believe that it is not really their fault, that they have no control over these outbursts, and that Mommy and Daddy will overlook it anyway. You have many options in helping them to be more in control of the way they think.

Anger does not come from other people or things in the world; it comes from the way in which people decide to view the world. This is an important distinction for children to make. They first think angry thoughts, and then they feel the physical results of that thinking within. If a child is angry because someone played with one of his toys, it was not the toy that made him angry, nor was it the someone who played with the toy. All of this could have happened without his awareness of it. But when he discovered that his favorite toy was missing, he began to think certain things that produce anger in him, such as "How dare anyone else play with my toy! I'll beat the kid up or cry real loud to Mommy." The angry thoughts create the angry reactions. The angry thoughts create the red face, the increased blood pressure, the tightened jaw, the clenched fist. And it is precisely those angry thoughts that you must help children to work on in order to eradicate anger.

I have no problem with anger that mobilizes people to action. Let children get angry over their poor grades and mobilize themselves to improve. Let them be angry at hunger and starvation, and work toward ending it. Let them get angry over injustices in the world, and then mobilize themselves to make a difference. Let them get angry at their own foolishness in leaving their toys around for others to ruin, and mobilize themselves to store them properly. This is what is called the constructive use of anger, and when angry thoughts mobilize children to corrective action, I applaud it.

However, most anger does not work that way. Anger usually immobilizes the person experiencing the angry thoughts, and it victimizes the ones who have to be exposed to the results of the angry thinking. This immobilizing anger is unhealthy and dangerous, and puts a serious limitation on becoming a no-limit individual. It comes from a lack of inner conviction about the rights of others to be free from an annoying bully. It derives from a person who is basically displeased with himself, or who wants the world to be different than it is.

The quick-tempered person (child or adult) relies heavily on fear in order to manipulate others into being the kind of people he thinks they should be. These people know very well that their unpleasantness is something that everyone around them dislikes. In fact, they rely on the typical reactions of others in order to use their strategies most effectively. They know that everyone feels embarrassed around someone who is blowing up at the tiniest irritant, and so they use their hostility to feed their need for power and recognition at the expense of everyone's peace of mind. Teenagers who know that provoking an argument about which television program to watch can get everyone in the family into a squabble, will usually get their way, just to calm things down. Often the quick-tempered young person will pout or scream and throw things around, and everyone simply gives in to maintain the peace, rather than have to put up with these explosions.

The reverse is also true. Children who can provoke you into getting angry have a great deal to gain. While they may have to spend some time in their rooms, look at the tremendous payoff to them. "Wow, I really got to Mom this time—she was ranting and raving. I have complete control of her now, and all I have to do is stay in my room for a few minutes." If you respond to children with uncontrolled anger, you are merely giving them control of your behavior. They will manipulate you with your own anger for the price of a few disciplinary measures. The long-run benefits to them become worth more than the minor inconvenience of a slight punishment. If they control you with your anger or theirs, they will do it forever. Anger is a double-edged neurotic sword. If you allow others to use it on you, you will be manipulated by trying to avoid their outbursts. If you allow yourself to think angry thoughts because of the behavior of others, then you suffer the internal trauma of that anger. There is only one way out! You must teach children that you are not going to think angry thoughts regardless of what they want you to do. And you must help them to make more mature emotional responses to their frustrations each and every day of their lives.

While many of the angry outbursts that typify any family-life situation may seem to be only minor annoyances, this is really not the case. When anger goes unchecked and is allowed to become a family manipulator, children are learning some very basic strategies for bullying their way through life, and for avoiding responsibility for being rational, law-abiding, responsible citizens. Too many outrageous acts of violence are committed in a quick burst of anger, with an eternity of misery immediately following the angry outburst. Too many crimes of passion are excused with "He's really not that kind of a person. He just snapped for a moment. I'm sure he won't do it again." These kinds of excuses ensure that the real-life tragedies which result from angry explosions will continue unchecked forever. Help children to see the folly of using anger as a means of expressing themselves and getting their own way. They must learn to use mental, not physical, energy to get what they want, because ultimately everyone in our society will suffer the consequences of those who are allowed their anger without having it curtailed right from the beginning.

Being able to express one's anger is far superior to keeping it buried inside, where it will eventually spill over. Certainly children must be allowed to have angry thoughts, and to give vent to their feelings. But *never at the expense of any other human being.* This is our ultimate morality. Anything we do should not interfere with anyone else's right to actualize himself. Your child's right to swing her fist stops with my right to decide how I want my nose to be shaped. Period! No excuses. Express your anger rather than suppress it. Allow your children to vent their hostile frustration at will, but not at the expense of another human being. Sulk for an hour, hit a pillow with your fist, or kick the soccer ball. But screaming, yelling, hitting, manipulating, bullying, swearing, or anything else that is aimed at another person, regardless of who it may be, is simply not tolerable in a society where we must all learn to live together.

There is one higher lever that people who aspire to no-limit living endorse when it comes to this business of anger. Expressing the anger you experience in a way that is not harmful or inconvenient to anyone else is healthier than storing it away for a later explosion. And turning the anger to a mobilized outlet rather than letting it immobilize is even better. But the highest position to get to is to stop having the angry thoughts in the first place. Learning to accept people who are different is far superior to being mad at them for being the way they are. Learning not to be frustrated at losing one's keys is far superior to simply expressing the inner frustration. Learning to use one's mind creatively, to avoid the inner pain of anger, to think for oneself in as healthy a way as possible—this is the no-limit way. I suggest that you can help your children up this stepladder of anger: from simply using it to manipulate, to being mobilized, to expressing it in a nonoffensive way, to ultimately, being so at peace with themselves that they do not entertain the angry thoughts in the first place. A clever poet, Isaac Watts, once penned these pointed words, which stand as a monument to what I am writing about in this chapter:

> Let dogs delight to bark and bite,
>   For God hath made them so;
> Let bears and lions growl and fight,
>   For 'tis their nature too.
>
> But, children, you should never let
>   Such angry passions rise;
> Your little hands were never made
>   To tear each other's eyes.
>   DIVINE SONGS (1715)

You want your children to grow up looking at the world as a miraculous place, rather than a place in which to be full of anger. You want them to have control over their own destinies, as opposed to being constantly in turmoil (or creating it) because of their inability to think in peaceful ways. You want them to exercise discipline over themselves through the effective use of intelligent disciplinary measures. This too must be looked at as you help them along the path of inner peace. Not inner anger, but inner peace.

Discipline for No-Limit Living

Children grow up learning that discipline is a negative word. "If you don't do what you are supposed to do, I am going to have to discipline you." "What you need is more discipline to get you to behave." The word *discipline* has come to be associated in a child's mind with the concept of punishment. Naturally, since one wants to avoid being punished, children also learn to avoid discipline. They believe that discipline is something that is imposed upon them by you, their parent. They think of it as punishment, so they seek to avoid discipline whenever possible. If this is the case with your children, it should not be surprising to you that they are undisciplined. They have worked hard to avoid discipline, so of course they lack what they have shunned most of their lives.

Discipline can take on an entirely new meaning. Discipline can be seen as joyful rather than as punitive. When discipline takes on a positive flavor, children become disciplined from the only place where it really counts: within themselves.

I have run eight miles or more daily for the past nine years without once missing. I have avoided eating as much sugar and sodium as I can for the past decade. I have written hundreds of articles and seven (now eight) major books since 1976. I have flossed my teeth every day for as long as I can remember, without once missing a day. Am I being punished? Do I do these things, and many others as well, because I fear what a big person will do to me if I do not write, exercise, watch my nutrition, or floss my teeth? Of course not! I love doing these things. I enjoy exercising each day. I feel very positive about myself when I force myself to sit at the typewriter. Each time I finish flossing I feel a sense of inner pride that I have taken the time to do something that is healthy for my teeth. Discipline is a positive, not a negative, attribute. Children need to learn to discipline themselves for the inner rewards which they will experience as a result of their own discipline. Discipline can be fun, rewarding, and exhilarating, and it can provide your children with a strong sense of their own control over their lives.

Inner discipline, the kind I am talking about right here, is not practiced very well in our culture. Schools talk about the need for strong disciplinary teachers. These are generally teachers who can motivate the students to behave themselves while the teacher is in the room, but when that authoritarian teacher steps out of the room, the entire class is in chaos. A strong teacher is one whose departure from the room causes little difference in the behavior of the children. We want children who will behave whether the teacher is in the classroom or not. Teachers are not always present in life.

Long after a child's school days are over, the importance of being self-disciplined will be clear. If they need a supervisor around all the time, then they are only behaving out of fear, not discipline. And they will always need someone else to tell them how to behave if they learn that discipline is imposed upon them by authoritarian figures. They will not know what to do when the boss leaves for a day. They will goof off when they are not being watched carefully. In essence, they will be undisciplined for a lifetime if they learn to behave out of fear when someone else is providing the discipline.

Children who have discipline imposed upon them by their parents experience the same dilemma. Why and when should they behave? Strictly adult-imposed discipline gives children no reason to develop self-discipline. Then when you leave town for a weekend, you will find that they will go wild. As long as you are around they will behave, but do not take your eyes off them for a moment or you will have chaos. "Our parents are gone, so let's be crazy. Let's drink their booze—they won't know the difference. Let's stay out late—they won't know. We can do whatever we want, because our parents aren't around to watch us." These are the sentiments of children who grow up having discipline imposed upon them. When they leave the nest, they are no more ready to take on mature responsibilities than they were when they were seven years old. Why? Because they did not learn that discipline is an inner code of ethics, something to internalize and use in order to be effective, intelligent, moral, no-limit people. Instead, they learned to avoid discipline because it is associated with being punished, and no one in his right mind wants to be punished. So they learned to stay away from discipline, and it shows whenever they are left unsupervised.

Think of discipline as helping children to adopt an internal code of ethics to guide them throughout their lives. There are many actions which are simply impossible for no-limit people to take regardless of who is watching. They will always return extra money that is given to them in error by a salesclerk, not because they might be caught if they do not, but because being honest is an internal disciplinary rule that they cannot violate. To violate this rule would be to violate their own personhood. Plainly impossible. Furthermore, the same no-limit people engage in acts that others find impossible. They can note that everyone around them hunts for the sport of hunting, but to them it would violate their own sense of inner values, and so they conduct themselves based upon what is inside them rather than what everyone else is doing. Children need to adopt inner discipline in forming their values, and you can help them, or get in their way. It all depends on whether you force discipline on children, or help them to adopt self-discipline as a way of life. It they adopt self-discipline, you are not going to have to be concerned about their conduct when you leave the room, the neighborhood, the city, or even the country. You will know that they have learned to use their own inner values, rather than relying on you to make decisions for them, based upon being afraid of being disciplined if they fail to do what you told them to do.

Effective self-discipline can be learned very early. Obviously with very young children you must simply tell them, "No! You cannot punch the baby in the face," and then give a sensible explanation without imposing fear. "The baby it too little to stop you. No one likes to be hit in the face—you know how much it hurts. I do not want you to hit the baby even if I am not around. We all love each other, and that is much nicer than hitting." Teaching them to internalize the notion of not hitting is effective discipline. Telling them that they will get smacked hard if you see that again, registers this way with your youngster: "I'll have to make sure that Mom isn't around the next time I hit the baby so I won't get hit again." When you use fear, or impose the discipline because you are bigger, then you teach children to be sneaky and to misbehave behind your back. When you help them to understand why, and reinforce that you want them to learn this information and that it has nothing at all to do with being caught, or with anger, but that it is something that they must internalize, then you are teaching effective discipline. This is true for children of all ages. Safe driving and wearing a seat belt ought not to be done for you as their worried parent or for fear of breaking the law, but must be taught as the only way they can avoid accidents or protect themselves in the event of an accident. The discipline must be internal. You do not speed—not because you might get caught, but because it is dangerous and immoral to place your life and particularly the innocent lives of others in jeopardy. You do not snort cocaine—not because I say so, but because your body is precious and you want to take care of it always. If children avoid drugs because you are around, then they will seek them out when you leave the scene. But if they learn to have respect for their own bodies, if they are permitted to ask questions, are not afraid to tell you what they have tried, and adopt their own ethics regarding drugs, then eventually it will not matter whether you are around or not.

Yes, children need guidelines, and even some prohibitions at earlier ages, but always with a sensible explanation—and, most urgently, always with the notion that they, not you, must adopt their own discipline regarding virtually everything they do. You cannot supervise them every moment. You cannot watch them at all times. They will be on their own away from you, much more than they will be around you, at all ages other than infancy and toddler years. It is how they think and what they do when they are away from you that determines the level of discipline they have adopted, not what they do when they are being scrutinized and supervised. If they have a code of ethics securely within themselves, they will always conduct themselves in self-enhancing no-limit ways, but if their ethics are imposed by you, then they will only behave for your benefit. And later, when they need discipline the most and you are not there to provide it, they will become unruly, just as they did when the authoritarian teacher walked out of the classroom for a few moments. Teachers can help their students to become trustworthy when they are not in the room, only by cooperating and creating a democratic environment in the classroom, by sharing with the students the reasons for having a good learning environment. This is also true in the home. Teach children why they are being helped to learn what they are learning, why the rules are applied, and later, when they need discipline the most, they will look within themselves for the guidelines.

Discipline imposed by anger, frustration, fear, or simple strong-arm tactics only works in the presence of the jailer. Family fights rage on and on in the presence of such home-management strategies.

How We Can Inadvertently Create Angry, Fighting, Undisciplined Attitudes

Below are some of the more common tactics that contribute to the use of anger regularly and to imposing external discipline on your children. Look through this list, then examine the self-defeating payoffs that you may be receiving for conducting your family life in such a manner. Finally, see if some of the alternatives offered in the last section of this chapter will be helpful in turning the tide of anger and fighting.

▫ By looking for problems rather than solutions. Keeping the emphasis on what has been done wrong. Yelling about what is already done.

▫ Raising the frustration levels of children through baiting, spying, excessive teasing, and consistent argumentation.

▫ Maintaining an atmosphere of arguing and competition in your home.

▫ Talking "at" children. Treating them as inferior human beings because they are younger and smaller than you.

▫ Exposing children excessively to movie and television violence.

▫ Using hitting, screaming, slapping, yelling, and verbal assaults as a means of enforcing your code of conduct.

▫ Overlooking violent outbursts or excusing them as only normal.

▫ Making all of their decisions for them and allowing them to have no power over themselves. Overprotecting them or displaying a lack of confidence in them.

▫ Thinking for them and not permitting them to have any challenges.

▫ Demanding more of them than they are capable of delivering. Setting their goals for them without consulting them.

▫ Comparing your children with yourself when you were younger, or with each other.

▫ Revering power, violence, killing, and war, and encouraging this kind of thinking in your children.

▫ Valuing things and money more than people and love.

▫ Being a family dictator.

▫ Positively reinforcing a child's inclination to be a bully, to fight, to hurt animals, or to show a lack of respect for the rights of others.

▢ Providing excuses for a child's brazen or hostile behavior.

▢ Overlooking a child's angry outbursts or tantrums in order to avoid a scene.

▢ Permitting angry put-downs and fighting to become a way of life.

▢ Using discipline as punishment to be imposed by you.

▢ Using empty threats as scare tactics for enforcing good behavior.

▢ Failing to follow through on consequences of a child's behavior, or establishing unrealistic punishments and refusing to relent.

▢ Using hate and anger to accompany disciplinary actions.

▢ Being a model of a person who uses anger to get his or her way.

▢ Not allowing for cooling-off periods for your children or yourself.

▢ Not teaching your children about the real source of anger.

▢ Being picky. Looking for something to be wrong or out of place.

▢ Using children as scapegoats for your own frustrations. Taking it out on them because they are smaller.

These are only a few of the thousands of actions that lead children to adopt anger and hostility as a way of life. These, and others like them, create an atmosphere conducive to fighting rather than cooperation. By using such tactics you will raise children who may be fearful and well-behaved when they are around you, but who lack the inner discipline to run their lives on a no-limit basis. Before examining some specific designs for eliminating these kinds of attitudes and actions in your children and in yourself, I offer in the next section what I believe to be the major payoffs, self-defeating though they may be, that accrue to you for maintaining this kind of an atmosphere and allowing fighting and anger to go unchecked.

Your Psychological Support System for Anger and Family Fights

Here are some of the payoffs which I suggest you are receiving from practicing some of the behaviors listed above. Although they do not serve you in a positive way, nevertheless you may use these reasons or excuses to keep you from raising children in a fight-free, anger-free, self-disciplinary manner.

◻ By continuing to participate in those same old family fights, you can elicit pity for yourself. Since nobody in the family really understands or appreciates you, you have a built-in reason to feel sorry for yourself. It is easier to have self-pity than to actively do something to correct the situation.

◻ By turning an incident into a fight, by using your angry outbursts or being outraged, you can manipulate other members of the family into doing what you think they should do, or into feeling guilty for daring to challenge your position.

◻ It is easier to avoid taking responsibility for yourself or teaching your children to do so by participating in continuous fighting. When you fight, you use up the moment and the energy in the process of fighting. Obviously, if you are so busy fighting, feeling bad, and then recovering, you have no time left over for taking constructive action to eliminate the fight scene in the first place. Thus your continual fighting serves to keep you tied up in anguish and gives you a ready-made excuse to avoid the hard work of changing.

◻ You can avoid the real risks that are involved in being different, and in accepting someone else as he is, by simply fighting with him instead. Fighting is a lot less risky than opening yourself up, or changing, or working at accepting the differences between you and other family members.

◻ You can become a blamer rather than a doer by engaging in useless fighting and then creating a scapegoat for the misery that you are currently suffering.

◻ You can feel self-righteous and correct, and even get your friends to agree with you, by participating in fights and then having someone else to complain to about your inconsiderate family members.

□ Fighting in the family can be a useful tactic to implement your own self-worth. If you have very little else to feel positive about, then you can at least feel proud of your fighting ability. This is a neat but destructive little substitution game to keep you from having to take on productive activities in your life. How can you ever grow if you are always so distressed or anguished about your family?

□ Anger is a useful tool for displacing feelings about oneself. It is a way of shifting the emphasis from an unsafe target to a safer one. "I can't get mad at my boss, so I'll just take it out on the children." Similarly, your children cannot express hostility to a friend or a teacher, so they shift it to Mommy, with whom they know they are safe. Mommy will love them even if they act hostile toward her.

□ Anger is a terrific manipulator. It is, quite simply, a way to get other people to give in and do what the angry person wishes. Children can use a tantrum just as effectively to get their way as you can use one to get them to clean up their rooms. Also, a person who is having a tantrum cannot do the dreaded task.

□ The physical effects of expressing anger are cathartic to the body. Although everyone else around you may suffer, you feel better inside after getting all that hostility out.

□ Imposing discipline on children, rather than teaching them each day how to become self-disciplined, is a means of controlling children. Having them fear punishment, which you call discipline, keeps you in control, and you do not want to admit that your children do not need you. We want children to go on needing us because it makes us feel important, so we decide how they shall be punished for breaking the rules that we set as parents.

□ Anger and hostility are great to use for breaking down communication between intimate people. The person who feels threatened by intimacy or commitment can simply come up with an excuse to get angry, and thus shift the focus from the real problem to the anger.

□ When you raise your children in a way that provokes a great deal of anger, you have a built-in cop-out. "Everybody gets angry once in a while; my kids are only human like the rest of us." Thus, you equate being angry, hostile, and participating in those loathsome family fights, with being human.

Some Useful Techniques for Eliminating Those Family Fights and Creating a Harmonious Atmosphere for Everyone

Look for solutions, not problems, in dealing with your children. Below are contrasting responses. Those on the left are from the parent who is looking for problems to provoke anger and to keep the problem from going away. Those on the right are from the parent who seeks solutions.

Looking for Problems	Looking for Solutions
You never help me. You are always so inconsiderate.	What would you do if you were me? If your child talked disrespectfully to you, would you do anything?
You never do anything to help out around here. You're totally irresponsible.	These are your responsibilities, which you agreed to. I will not tolerate you running off to play when you have chores to do. Your work is just as important as your play.
You're lazy and everyone in the house knows it.	You can plan to put in some time this evening on your homework, which you have avoided all week.
I can't stand to see you looking so sloppy. You have no pride in yourself.	You are so gorgeous when you take a few minutes to spruce yourself up. I think you are beautiful no matter how you dress. Do you feel attractive?
You are the world's biggest slob. Your room is an outrage.	Can you make a commitment to pick up your dirty clothes today? I am closing the door to your room so that I don't have to look in anymore.

There are always solutions, yet so often anger and family fights are the results of interacting with your children in such a way that the problem will become intensified. The more you focus on how bad they are, and what you dislike, the more you challenge them to a fight. Think about what would make for a solution, then work each day at speaking in such a way as to make life more positive for everyone, rather than speaking in a way that says, "I'm ready for a fight."

Work actively at deflating rather than inflating potential blow-up points. When you insist on always being right, or in turning a normal discussion into a challenge, argumentation and anger are almost always the result. Allow your children to have their own points of view, and if they refuse to allow the same for you, ignore their efforts to bait you. Simply refuse to become an angry, fighting, argumentative person with children. Your anger comes from the way in which you elect to think and react. If children send out signals that they are being intolerant, then that is their decision at the moment. Your reaction to that signal is your decision at the moment. You can choose to react with anger and you will be taking the bait, or you can refuse to be lured by it and make it go away. One very effective technique is to practice reflecting back what is being offered to you. The following examples apply. "The teacher gave you a rough time in math class, and now you want to fight your little brother over a toy." "You are really scared about your test tomorrow, so you are taking it out on me." "You feel cheated when the other kids get to go someplace and you have to stay home." "You are sulking because I pointed out that you are avoiding your chores. You'd rather I just ignored it and did things for you instead." These are all reflecting-back techniques. They start with the word *you,* so as to keep the focus where it belongs. If the child owns the anger, then be sure to let her know that you are not going to take the bait. The opposite of reflecting back is to take ownership of *their* anger. Here are the same situations with anger-baiting replies. "Don't take it out on your brother just because your teacher gave you a hard time." "I don't know why you are mad at me over this test. I didn't do anything." "I hate it when you sulk. Just do your jobs and quit being a complainer." "I can't take everyone with me on every trip, so grow up."

These are all important reflecting messages. Think about it for a moment. When someone is attempting to bait you into an argument with his anger, use a sentence that begins with *you* rather than *I*. "You are really upset that I didn't do your laundry" is superior to "I didn't do it, and I don't have to." When you begin with *you*, you are effectively placing the upset where it belongs: on the person who is really upset. You are also teaching children that you see what they are attempting to do, and you are labeling their feelings, rather than defending yourself with *I* sentences and getting baited into one of those same old fights. Whenever someone else is upset, always remember that he owns the upset, and that you can refuse to join him. Most of the time, beginning your sentence with the word *you* is effective at defusing a potential fight. When you label how someone is feeling, and you don't join her in her anger or frustration, you present a rational person, whose emotions are under control, and who is consequently almost impossible to fight with.

Simply leave a room for a short time when you feel a same old fight beginning to emerge. Providing a cooling-off space, where you can be alone and where your antagonist can also think it through without you there to remind him of his anger, is a most effective technique. Once you realize that winning an argument with a child is impossible, you will find it easy to simply absent yourself and let the other person have some private dignity of his own. When anger surfaces, there is never a winner in a family fight. People continue the argument just to prove that they are right, and all that happens is that the angry atmosphere is charged even further. The very act of providing privacy for all concerned is often enough to make the fight go away before it even gets unraveled. This is a particularly effective strategy when you sense a rehashing of old material coming up. If you see that you are being baited, and you know that no solution is forthcoming, then getting to a neutral space will quell the encounter before it begins. This is not avoidance; it is a sensible way to eliminate the endless rehashing that causes so much anger.

Make a decision within yourself that you are not going to have a family-fight atmosphere any longer; then work each day on yourself in this regard. You cannot have a family fight if you refuse to participate. That's right. Simply refusing to be a part of a warlike home atmosphere is the surest way to clean up the war games. Work at postponing your anger for short periods of time. Putting it off by counting to ten to yourself, and letting your children know that you are not going to participate in these rituals any longer, make wonderful lessons for children to observe. When you defuse your anger, they will learn from your example. Time yourself for sixty seconds. During this time, talk to yourself and remind yourself that your child's behavior is no longer an acceptable reason for you to be angry or to go crazy. If after sixty seconds you still want to explode, then do so, but away from any human beings. However, the delay process will most likely defuse your anger to the point where you will not need to explode. By doing this, you will be learning a vital lesson in becoming a no-limit person and helping your children to do the same. The lesson is that *you have control of your emotions,* and you do not have to explode with anger whenever someone else decides to behave in angry ways. This is not a case for being scared to say what you feel, but for the postponement of outbursts that will lead to your being involved in fights which lead to nothing but further stress. The delay process gives you time to really consider if you want to fight over any issue, and it gives your children a wonderful example of a person who values peaceful coexistence over destructive fighting and anger.

Try making your adolescent right instead of arguing with him any longer. Yes, I said make him right! Adolescence has been described as the time when children pay you back for all the things they feel you did to them when they were younger. They become extremely argumentative, and logic will never work with an arguing teenager. If you feel that they should contribute more toward keeping the house clean, they will never, and I really mean never, agree with you if you argue. They tend to view your imposition of a cleaning code on them as "telling me what to do," and they will not give in because at this age they cannot stand to have you telling them anything. The more you argue, the more likely you are to be frustrated, and they will move further and further away from you emotionally as the argument intensifies. Try saying something like "Cindy, you are right. I am being an old fuddy-duddy, and I am not sensitive enough to your wishes in this matter. You hate cleaning up, and I simply have refused to accept that in you. You have a right to your opinion, and I have just been

provoking you. I'm really sorry that I was so demanding of you."
This will put Cindy into a state of shock. How can she argue with
you? Later I would ask her, "Cindy, what do you think your responsibilities in this matter of cleaning up after yourself ought to
be?" Almost always she will come up with an even more stringent
plan of action for herself than anything you would devise if she is
allowed the freedom to think it up herself. Try it! You will soon
discover that she only needed to be right. Once you acknowledge
her rightness she will do more for everyone concerned, the arguments will diminish, and your home will be a cleaner and happier
place. Many times when talking to young people who were complaining about their parents or teachers, I would stop my arguing
with them and instead say, "You are right. Your parents don't appreciate you. They are inconsiderate and pushy, and your teachers are really as bad as you say." Before long they would be saying
to me, "Wait a minute! My parents aren't that bad. They really
care about me. I just get impatient. And my teachers have been
really tolerant with me." When you give them the opportunity to
be right without an argument, they will often come up with an alternative of their own to being disagreeable.

With infants, keep in mind that children are not born with
anger inside them. They learn it from those around them. Never—
I mean never—scream and yell in anger at a tiny baby. This builds
up a frightening amount of fear in a baby, and teaches her to ultimately react the same way when she is frustrated. Babies need to
be loved all the time. They crave affection, and any screaming or
yelling that you do directly at your infant will be something that
they store away inside their tiny bodies. Many studies have been
done which substantiate that infants who live in violent environments either become introverted and fearful or take on the violent
characteristics themselves. In the mind of a tiny, frail human being,
a family fighting around the infant, with verbal assaults directed
at the infant, is indeed a violent atmosphere.

Infants can be tremendously exasperating at times. They can
cry for no apparent reason, and they can fuss and make life miserable for you occasionally, but this is not a justification for reacting violently toward them. They are helpless while developing
their own personalities. Loving, kind words are the best teachers
you can provide for them to become no-limit people. If you feel

angry and exasperated, remove yourself for a few moments so that you cannot hear the crying, rather than directing your anger at your babies. Believe me, it is very important for that developing human being that you bring any anger to a halt when dealing with him or her.

To avoid raising your toddlers on angst, try viewing them as complete human beings rather than as miniature people. When you see them as having equivalent value to you and all the other big people, you will be inclined to avoid angry outbursts and ugly scenes with them. You will be surprised at how perceptive these tots really are if you listen to them each day. They are just as sensitive as you are. Try looking in your mirror and making the ugliest, meanest face you can make, and then scream out loud directly at your image. Then ask a friend to stare you directly in the face, looking as menacing as possible, and yell right at you. See how intimidating and frightening this can be, and please note how much you dislike the experience. It is just as unpleasant and frightening for little children, except that you are two or three times larger than they are. You would need a fifteen- to eighteen-foot giant doing the same thing to you to duplicate equivalent feelings. Keep this image in your mind when you raise your voice or act uproariously toward little ones. The more you curtail this inclination, the more you are helping children to grow up without internal anger and the accompanying anxiety that goes with it. Teach them from the beginning to be rational by providing them with that kind of an example.

Remember that images last forever! This is true for both positive and negative images. Television and movie violence that is ingested daily teaches people to see violence as entertainment. We live in a mixed-up world which allows children to witness a woman's breast being sliced off in anger on film, and prohibits them from seeing a woman's breast caressed lovingly. However, you still make a big difference in the way your children view violence. If it is worshiped in the movies, it comes to be idolized internally. If children see enough images of horrible violence—killing, maiming, bullets ripping into human beings, eyes being gouged out, bloodier and bloodier effects—they will internalize these images forever. Certainly they are capable of distinguishing between fantasy and reality on a conscious level. We assume that they know the difference between watching people shoot at each other on the screen and doing so in real life. But the effects linger, and many children cannot make these distinctions properly, or they grow up to be adults who worship violence as a way of life. Every time a mass murder movie is shown in this country, invariably there is a repeat performance in real life, by some borderline person who had too many images to deal with rationally.

We need to teach love to our children, not hate. We need to help them to abhor violence rather than emulate it in their games and try to duplicate it in their lives. You must be careful about what you allow young children to watch, not from a sexual point of view but from a violence point of view. Supervise their selections and discuss what is being shown or suggested. Let them see necking rather than someone's neck being slit. Lovemaking, when it is not related to power struggles, is preferable to abuse. Television, movie making, and all forms of entertainment will react positively to your efforts to keep your children from becoming violence prone if you are selective about what they watch, and let them know that you abhor violence in your life. They will only produce what the people will watch. If enough people stop watching, they will react accordingly. Those mental images are extremely powerful motivators. They are even more powerful when children are very young. You as a parent can help children to have more positive images by carefully screening out the extremely violent material. I do not think that exposure to cops and robbers and some toy guns is necessarily detrimental. Children have many fantasies in their lives. They must be exposed to a fantasy to learn how to differentiate it from reality. But the line between what is real and what is extreme seems to be growing more and more absurd. Keep an eye on what images children receive as youngsters, and remind them with reassurance that "This is a movie. It isn't real. The monsters are only in the movie."

Watch out for the excessive use of corporal punishment. You must be very careful about hitting your children at any time. I personally do not condone hitting, and I have never done so with any of my children, for any reason, with one exception. A slap on the bottom for emphasis—not to administer pain, but for emphasis—is the only exception in my life. When my little daughter would run into the street, where her life was in danger, I cracked her on the behind after a warning, to let her know that Daddy really meant business. I do not believe in beating children and administering pain as a means of punishment, yet I know that many of you do. To me, corporal punishment has no place in raising no-limit children—period. If you feel however, that you must administer regular spankings, or even beatings, I suggest before you proceed that you answer two questions honestly.

1. *Whose needs am I serving?* That is, are you in fact serving your own needs to be all-powerful, to show that you are bigger and stronger, or even to receive some pleasure from dishing out corporal punishment to smaller people? If it is definitely for their benefit, then it should be applied rarely, and only for the most severe infractions. Regular hitting and slapping of children teaches them to be obedient in front of you, to be fearful—and, worst of all, to become angry slappers and hitters themselves. If you truly respect children as people whose value is equal to your own, is physical punishment the dignified recourse you would expect from any other adult equal? We stopped whipping prisoners long ago. Shouldn't children be treated as well?

2. *Am I administering this beating to help them to change or simply to administer pain?* When used routinely, beatings do not help people to change. In fact, children who are beaten regularly seem to become more recalcitrant. The more you hit them, the more they become internally resolved to fight you and prove that you cannot scare them. Violence seems to beget violence, rather than ending it. Children can learn that you mean business without having to be struck regularly.

I suggest that you look very carefully at the effects your corporal punishment has on your child, on you, and on the remainder of your family. This kind of an atmosphere may create blindly obedient children, but not for long, and certainly it is the least effective way to change their behavior permanently. *Parents who slap their children seem to have to do it all the time. If it works so well, then why is it happening all the time?* I suggest that parents who slap around little children are doing it for their own need to assert their power, and that if they really considered what is best for their child, they would give them much more loving and hugging and work at catching them doing things right, rather than hitting them when they catch them doing things wrong.

Be careful not to overlook any violent outbursts that children display, simply out of fear of a scene. You must be firm, teaching them what is tolerable and what is not, and you cannot run away from their violence, since that will teach them to continue doing exactly the same thing in the future. If children use a quick-tempered approach in your life, you can first show them with words, and then with behavior, that their outbursts are not going to receive the desired results, regardless of how much they pout and rant afterwards. A simple statement such as "I have too much respect for myself to allow you to act that way. You are not free to abuse me or anyone else simply because you cannot control your temper. If this persists, you will go to your room and remain there until you have cooled off. Also, your television privileges are going to be examined, and you will not be going out of the house for two days if you don't go to work on your temper." Be firm, and by all means follow up on your promises; do not simply overlook the incident. Later, when he is not angry, I strongly suggest that you have a talk with your child. Try to make these talks as nonthreatening and nonjudgmental as possible. Take the child out for a walk, or to a restaurant where you can be alone. Tell him honestly how you feel when he erupts like that. Explain that you know that he does not like having a quick temper, but that it is really a choice that he is making, not the result of some inherited personality trait. Let him know that you are willing to help him work on it if he would really like to change. Give him support and love, even after he has had an outburst, but *do not give him his way*. There is a big difference between showing someone that you love him when he is angry, and giving him his own way as a reward for being an angry person.

Give children as much control over their own lives as you possibly can. When you make all of your children's decisions for them, you encourage them to be frustrated. You also keep them from learning one of life's most important skills: that is, decision making. Give them more control over their lives and you will find that they experience less frustration. I have made this point in every chapter of this book. Children need to exercise as much control over their lives as is possible without putting them or anyone else in any jeopardy. Everybody hates being told what to do and how to do it. Especially you! You know how meager you feel when someone tells you how to do something, acting as an expert over your life. Your children feel the same at every age of their lives. Two-year-olds protest, "I can do it myself." Five-year-olds say, "Watch me, Daddy—I can dive into the pool." Ten-year-olds say, "Oh, Mom, I know how to make a coffee cake." Fifteen-year-olds say, "I'm sure. I guess you think I don't have a brain." Regardless of the lingo, the message is always clear: "I want to be my own person and have a mind of my own." When you take this control away from them, you raise their frustration levels, and you teach them to get angrier and angrier at you, the tyrant who will not let them do anything. Give them a chance to prove themselves before you take over for them. Talk with them about how to do things, rather than talking at them with your advice. The more control they are given over themselves, the more they respect you for letting them discover their own genius. And, conversely, the more you take over for them unnecessarily, the wider the rift that grows between you. They simply get angry, and as Stadius said, "Anger manages everything badly."

Try to be ever alert to helping children to reduce their frustration levels, and to helping them to act more rationally when they do experience frustration. Frustration is almost always associated with anger and family fights. When you make demands on your children which they are incapable of meeting, you increase their frustration levels enormously. Insisting that a child make the basketball team or dance a solo in a recital may sound like wonderful goals, but children ought to be involved in their own goal setting, with your participation limited to supporting them rather than imposing the goals on them. The child may not want to perform a solo number, but she may feel that it is her responsibility to do it for you. She must instead feel a need to do it for herself, with your blessing and proud support as a wonderful bonus. But only a bonus. A child's drive must come from within if he or she is going to experience a sense of accomplishment and personal worth. You can guide children in setting goals, you can help them to establish self-discipline programs and encourage them all the way, but always be certain that they are doing it for themselves, for their own personal reasons, and not exclusively to please you or anyone else. When you live through the accomplishments of your children, you invariably put pressure on yourself and the children as well. They will want to please you, and when they do not, they will become hurt, embarrassed, disappointed—and, eventually, angry. Not at themselves, but at you, who always tells them what they should be aiming for. As Dorothy Canfield Fisher said, "A mother is not a person to lean on, but a person to make leaning unnecessary." Have your own personal ambitions and purposes in life. By all means help your children to do the same. But always stress that they should be the source of their own goals. Let them know that they can alter their goals at any time without any chastisement from you.

Remember that nothing grates on a child's frustration level more than being compared with someone else. Each child is unique, as I have stated many times in these pages. What you did thirty years ago means as much to them as what Roman centurions did two thousand years ago means to you. Your childhood is ancient history to them. While they may love your war stories, they still do not relate to how it was for you when you were a child. "Yeah, sure, Dad—I'm sure the Vietnam War was really tough, but these are modern times. I'm dealing with the nuclear war threat." "Here come those 'when I was your age' stories. She goes through this phase about twice a month." You've heard your children say such things, or at least give you "the look" that communicates the same sentiment. To them these times are different from your times, and they are absolutely correct. I am quite sure that given the exact conditions which you faced as a child, and having been raised exactly the same as you were, they would have handled their problems ever better. You see, your children have evolved beyond you, just as you have evolved beyond your parents and your grandparents. They are bigger, smarter, faster, and more capable of almost everything than you were at the equivalent age. World records in athletics that were unbreakable when you were a child are now achieved by junior high school students. If you really need to compare your children to you, watch out, because they are at higher levels in almost every category, even if they did not have the same kind of lifestyle. It is not their fault that they were born when they were, and you had to suffer through different times. This is just the way it is. It cannot be changed. In fact, that is precisely how you want it. You want them to avoid some of the tougher times, to have it better than you did. That is what it is all about, making the world better for those we leave behind. Try to treat your children as unique, not in comparison to anyone, especially to you, who lived in those ancient times that are as distant as the Stone Age as far as they are concerned.

Try to shift your emphasis away from violence in your life. Raise your children on love, not hate. Do not let them see you as someone who personifies the angry, spiteful, power-worshiping model. Remind them not to hate anyone when they talk about whom they hate. Long lectures are unnecessary. More effective are simple statements such as "It really isn't necessary to hate someone just because you disagree with him." No more; just a tiny reminder at the appropriate time. If you are a practicing member of any religion, try to live by the real tenets of your religion. Do not be a Christian; be Christ-like. Otherwise you are a phony to them and to yourself. I always ask those who say they are Christians, yet practice hating others, "Would Jesus Christ feel the same as you do? Would Jesus judge another person as inferior?" That is the key question, regardless of whether you are a Christian, Jew, Buddhist, Moslem, or whatever. Would your God or your religious saint behave that way? Do not talk about being a Christian and then conduct your life, for your children to see every day, in a way that would be foreign to the teachings of your faith. Ask yourself, "What would my religious ethics require of me?" Be totally honest with yourself, and then start acting that way. Do not simply give yourself a neat little label that makes you feel fine, and then proceed to behave in quite contrary ways. If we are to give peace and love and worldwide understanding a chance, then it must come from peaceful, loving, understanding human beings. It cannot come from those who worship power and violence and live angry lives. We can solve this universal problem if we set a positive peaceful example for our children, and then encourage them to follow suit. Before you know it, we will change the whole world, but we must start with ourselves and our immediate families if we are to be part of the solution, rather than one more contributor to the problem.

Teach children to be self-disciplined in all areas of their lives. When they are doing homework, ask them how they feel about their progress and how they feel about their report cards. By all means, do not equate the behavior of your children with your own personal worth as a human being. If they receive poor grades, do not make that the source of a same old tiresome fight, by starting out the confrontation from a position of being angry about their lack of motivation. See it as their choice. Help them to understand that they must suffer the consequences of their behavior, and be firm about what those consequences are to be. But never allow yourself to let their behavior hurt you with any immobilizing emotion like anger or depression. Work with them, but do not be mad at them. Allow them to own their behavior and work to help them to become self-motivated, without making it the cause of a nervous breakdown for you. Talk with them about the consequences to *them* of their actions, rather than what they are doing to *you* by not being more scholarly. And if they absolutely refuse to be a better student, then you have two choices.

1. Become insane and upset and create a problem for you and your child.

2. Accept the real-world fact that the child is not yet ready to motivate himself, and stop judging yourself. Teach him to accept the consequences, and be firm about it, but refuse to become an emotional wreck.

There are no other choices. You cannot force someone to do something he absolutely refuses to do. Your child will change when he is ready.

When I was a teenager I was not the world's greatest student. I goofed off, skipped some classes, and generally did only what I had to do to get through high school and get it over with. My mother talked with me about it, laid down the rules about when I could go out, and then basically went on with her life. At the time I was working at a grocery store to help bring in money (poor me, would you like to hear my story?), but I was not internally motivated to be the student I could have been with the appropriate effort. My mother refused to fight with me or any of my brothers about our schoolwork. She knew that her life was too precious to waste being upset over our lack of motivation. She often said to us, "It is your choice, and you will pay the price—not me or anyone else." Well, years later, when I was ready, after spending four years as an enlisted man in the armed services, I became an honor roll student for eight years in college, culminating with my doctorate and a place atop the dean's list.

The point is, I did it when I was ready. No amount of anger, outrageous family fights, and hostility would have made any difference, other than to tear us all apart as a family, increase tension, and very likely deter me from ever pursuing academic excellence when I was ready to take up the challenge. Anger, fighting, and hostility create an atmosphere that diminishes motivation. Sometimes you have to peacefully wait out a child's periods of low motivation, providing her with a loving person who does not push too hard, and who shows support. Then, when your child feels the need deep inside, there will be nothing to stop her. The truth is that nothing my mother or anyone else had to say would have done anything to change my attitude at the time. But when I was surrounded in barracks and ships around the world by people who lacked an education, and I lived face to face with ignorance each day, I then knew, because I experienced it in my gut, that being educated was far superior to being obstinate. The lesson of living often serves as the greatest motivator of all. Some people have to experience what they don't want before they realize what they do want, and no amount of anger on the part of a parent is going to change that fact.

Follow through on your punishment promises to your children as much as possible. If you say you are going to do something, then make sure that you do not back off and show them that you really do not mean what you say. However, be careful to make realistic promises, not outrageous threats that you will not keep anyway. Try to involve your children in ascertaining an acceptable punishment that will help them toward a solution to the problem. A child who simply has to sit in his room for three hours because he hit his sister, is not learning anything from this imposed punishment. But if he is involved in the punishment, even in a minor way, he will learn not to continue the hitting behavior. "I've told you several times that hitting your sister cannot be tolerated. Now, what would you suggest I do to get the message home to you? I could hit you back, but that would be stupid because I've told you that hitting is simply wrong. You think about it in your room for a while, and then we can talk about a better way to get your point across to your sister without resorting to clobbering her when you are frustrated. We will discuss it later when you are calmed down. Meanwhile, I want you to go into your room and stay away from your sister. When you are ready to talk, we will consider such options as not riding your bicycle or not having any friends over for the rest of the week. You must learn that hitting just cannot be tolerated." A brief, to-the-point admonition, allowing for a cooling-off period, and involving your ten-year-old in the process of punishment, rather than a simple command—"Go to your room and don't come out until you are eighteen"—will be effective. If you do make outrageously punitive statements that you know are unreasonable, admit to it later, during a cooling-off period, and get him involved once again. "I told you to stay in your room until you are eighteen, but obviously you have to come out a few times in the next eight years. What can we do together to get you to stop hitting people just because they do something you dislike at the moment?" These kinds of approaches help children to see the reasons for your punishment, and also serve to illustrate that you are human and sometimes say things that you do not mean.

Do not administer punishment when angry. Anger is an immobilizer. You cannot be rational and angry at the same time; therefore, you must give yourself a cooling-off period before attempting to help your child to correct his misbehavior. If you are going to have a discussion with a child, do it when there is no present-moment anxiety. If a child has just spilled a box of nails on the carpet, that moment is the least effective time to deliver a lecture on not being clumsy. Similarly, when your teenager arrives late for dinner, it is most wasteful and fight-producing to launch into a tirade on the importance of punctuality. It is far better to simply record your feelings with a look, or to offer support for the spiller, and then, at a time when there is no personal investment in having to defend oneself, to have a talk about spilling or lateness. Wait until bedtime or even the next day. By timing your talks so that no one is put into a defensive posture, you can help everyone concerned, and you can also eliminate many of the same old fights.

A reminder on the referee syndrome that I have mentioned previously: Refuse to be a referee in your children's daily dis-

putes. If necessary, go into the bathroom and read until the requests for you to resolve petty arguments are over. Do this regularly for two weeks, and you will discover that you are no longer continuously bombarded to referee every little disagreement that surfaces in your family. Most requests to have you settle a petty dispute are nothing more than attempts to get your attention. In order to have a life of your own, you must teach others that you view yourself as too important to be settling disputes all day long. The only way to teach this lesson is with behavior. The most effective behavior is to simply let the children work it out by themselves. Most of the time they will not only work it out and learn how to think for themselves, but you will have avoided one of those impossible situations of being a referee when all parties concerned expect you to rule in their favor. The vast majority of these disputes are staged for your benefit, and you are the supreme victim if you fall into the trap. Model to all concerned that you view yourself as too important a person to be chasing after little children and monitoring all their moves so that you can hand down rulings. I have found that when I absolutely refuse to make a ruling, and I simply state, "I am not interested; you will have to work it out yourselves," then leave, the fighting stops. They have no audience to fight for, and they hate having to fight if no one will intervene, since they could get hurt that way. In a moment or two the dispute is settled, almost always more efficiently and fairly than anything you could have dreamed.

One time my daughter, Tracy, aged nine, and her friend Robin were arguing very loudly in a motel room they were sharing with me. The fight concerned who would sleep on what side of the bed. Tracy said, "I sleep on the side next to my daddy—I have a right to." Sounded reasonable to me. Robin retorted, "Yes, but I was here first and I'm not moving." That seemed equally sensible logic. As they blasted away at each other I decided to go into the bathroom and read the newspaper. I announced that I would not come out until their problem was resolved. Through the door I could hear them sort things out. When they realized that I was not going to intervene, and that I truly was not the least bit interested, Tracy suggested, "Let's put two numbers on a piece of paper. Whoever draws the higher number gets to decide where she sleeps." From my seat in the bathroom I was shocked that they both agreed, and at the simplicity of the solution. However, had I intervened, there would have been a chorus of "That's not fair," "But I should decide," "But I was here first," and so on. Children have the answers within them for almost all of their disputes. They usually fight for your benefit, so if you take away that pay-off, the fighting almost miraculously ceases.

In dealing with any quick-tempered individuals in your home or in your life, it is important to talk firmly to them in no uncertain terms. In quiet moments, when the quick-tempered individual is not hauling out his heavy artillery, tell him how strongly you feel about being verbally assaulted. Do not do it in an argumentative manner. Simply state how terrible you feel when you are treated this way, and then quickly change the topic. You are not interested in winning an argument, but in simply informing the person for the sake of making an impact. Do not keep it all bottled up inside, and then quake in fear when you are about to see the explosion. If you want a fight-free atmosphere, tell the individual how you are going to react from now on and then proceed to do just that. A simple statement such as "I spend far too many hours being afraid of how you are going to react, and in this way I feel like a prisoner in my own home. From now on, when you lose your temper around me, I am not going to just stand here and take it. I hate myself afterward for being so weak, and I am not going to go through my life hating myself any longer. I know you are always sorry afterward, but I am really not interested in your apologies. The next time it happens I am not going to just sit there. I am going to challenge your right to act that way, and if you persist, I will remove myself. I am just not interested in being your victim any longer."

This kind of approach will let the quick-tempered individual know that you mean business, and that you are being as honest as you know how to be. If the verbal assaults still persist, you have at least stood up for what you believe, and now you must make a decision about what actions you will take. If it is a child (of any age) who behaves this way, I suggest that you refuse to wait on her at all, and then let her know at those moments what you are doing. If necessary, you call a strike as far as waiting on any disrespectful family member. No lunches, no washing clothes, no money, no service at all. Each time, you simply explain, "I will not do laundry for someone who abuses me. I won't hate you, but I won't wait on you, either. You'll have to wash your own clothes today.'' Then give a hug, a kiss, or a touch to let the person know that your loving feelings are authentic, but that you will not be serving those who act in a nasty and disrespectful manner. This may sound extreme, but it is important to teach this vital lesson. There will be far fewer victimizers in the world when people stop playing victim. Children will respect your strength, not your weakness, and they will learn that you mean what you say if you follow through.

The following list is a short summation of effective strategies that you can use when your children behave with anger and hostility in the home. I have talked about most of them in detail, but you might want to post this abbreviated list in your consciousness.

- □ When a child is out of control, do not attempt to reason with him.

- □ Hold a child to calm her down, or send her to a cooling-off place.

- □ Let children have inanimate outlets for their anger: kicking a pillow or throwing darts at a board. People do not deserve to be their outlets, ever.

- □ When the child is calm, establish a system and stick to it. I'll tell you once; then you go to your room.

- □ Do not threaten what you will not do.

- □ Arrange conditions in advance. "If you are not polite to me, I won't drive you to soccer practice."

- □ Do not reward abusive behavior. "I have to feed you, but I do not have to take mean kids out to restaurants. I am going. You stay here and eat peanut butter."

- □ Reflect with the child so that he can clarify what is bothering him. "Your friend didn't invite you to her party, and now you want to take it out on others."

- □ When both of you are calm, talk about what the child might be getting out of her tantrums. Explain why it won't really work, and that it just causes trouble for her and everyone else as well.

▫ Use humor, and be good-natured and unbothered when children are trying to get you to join them in their anger.

▫ Do not model anger as the solution to a situation. Traffic, tax audit, or whatever is going on in your life that you dislike, should not transfer a negative lesson.

▫ Identify what is happening. "You are acting loud and mean because you think I will give up and let you do what you want just to get you to be nice again. I told you why you cannot have your way. You can go to your room and act this way if you think it helps you feel better, but I have heard and seen enough."

These are some tips that might help you to help children to replace their immobilizing anger with something far greater: a peaceful, no-limit approach to their lives. Nothing will work always. There will be times when everything you try simply does not work. But do not forget that you are building internal mind sets in these children. The daily reminders, the regular efforts to ease their own anguish, the living by example as much as possible, and the genuine attempt to live in a peaceful environment (in which each person is learning, each day, to exercise self-discipline) are the real techniques that will have a positive long-range effect. I've always appreciated the words penned by William Blake concerning anger and how to resolve it—

> "I was angry with my friend
> I told my wrath, my wrath did end.
> I was angry with my foe:
> I told it not, my wrath did grow."
> **WILLIAM BLAKE**

In our world today, we spend two thousand dollars on war for every dollar we spend on peace. We must reverse this outlay if the world is going to change. You can begin this reversal process by investing two thousand thoughts and two thousand techniques on love and peace in your environment, for every one invested in fighting and anger. If enough of us do it, we will turn this angry world into one of peace and love for everyone. Indeed our wrath must go!

7

I Want My Children to Celebrate Their Present Moments

The no-limit person sees the past in terms of what it has taught him about how to live now, and the future as more present moments to be lived when they arrive. He lives exclusively and fully in the present moment. He is able to make peak experiences out of almost all activities. He prefers not to have "a plan" if possible, in order to make room for spontaneity.

Every choice, action, thought, ambition, fear, dream, whatever, must be a *now* event to be anything at all. The *now* is where it and you always are. The *now*, simply, is the working unit of your life.

—JOHN KILEY

The important question to be asking yourself is "Can I teach my children to live all of their present moments to their maximum benefit?" It is not "Can I teach them to be within the present moment?" because that is not your decision. The present moment is exactly where they and you will always be, like it or not. The present moment is all that any of us ever gets here on this planet. No one can live in the past. Living in the future is plainly impossible. However, it is quite possible for people to use up their present moments being mentally consumed about the past or in anticipation of the future. But everything is done in the now. You feel guilty, only in the present. You experience anxiety, only now. You feel happy, hopeful, elated, afraid, nervous, fearful, and every other human emotion, only in the present moment. One key to being a no-limit person is in learning how to use up all of your present moments in no-limit, fully functioning ways. To learn how to become absorbed in the now. To live in awe and deep appreciation of each moment that you have. You can influence children to learn how to live their present moments fully, or you can teach them to always be concerned with the future or the past. Either way, they will live in the present, but how that present is lived will be dramatically affected by your own perceptions and interventions in the lives of your children.

The Purest Form of Sanity

"Nowness is the purest form of sanity." Keep this little piece of wisdom close to your heart as you read about how to teach children to live fully in the now. The closer you are to living each of your days fully in the present, the closer you get to the ultimate no-limit lifestyle. Think about it for a moment. If you are depressed in the present moment, you are generally using up your *now* being consumed about something or other that has already taken place or is going to take place. Whatever it may be, you are using your inner energy in this moment to feel bad. Were you to become totally immersed in your current moment, doing anything in which you are totally involved, you would not be able to experience depression in this very moment. You cannot be sick in a moment in which you are totally immersed. Undoubtedly you have had the experience of finding yourself so busy or excited by a project that you literally sent away a cold, or becoming so involved in an activity that you forgot about being tired and lived for days on your natural high. You simply were too busy or involved in life to be able to have any sickness or fatigue. You have this capacity within you for losing yourself totally in any project, if you train yourself to live this way. Children have the very same capacity.

Take a look at people who experience lows in their lives, including those in mental hospitals. The further away they are from this very moment and their own reality, the more disturbed they are. The more consumed they become with what should or shouldn't have happened in the past, or what might happen in the future, the more impossible it becomes for them to be fully alive. The now is a magic place wherein you are uniquely capable of being so involved that there is no room for any unhappy or debilitating thoughts. When you learn to live totally in each of your moments, treating them as miracles provided for you to enjoy, you will know the essence of what many seemingly esoteric Eastern philosophers have talked about and experienced for centuries. Children have this magic within them from the very beginning. It is part of their human inheritance. They come equipped with the potential for living each moment fully, very much the same way a baby bird is equipped with the potential for flying. It is there. It is within each of us. Our task is to make sure that we do not squelch it in children before it has the opportunity to materialize naturally.

Living in moments other than the present moment, while plainly impossible within our reality system, is done on an internal basis all the time. One can send himself away from this moment at will. Commiserating in the present over some bad luck, or anguishing in the present about future events, is a choice adults often make, and children do so too if encouraged by teachers and parents. Living in the present moment both physically and mentally, and viewing the present moment as a miracle, is an approach to life that may be foreign to you, yet it is one for you to examine carefully if you want to teach children present-moment living. A child who learns to live fully in each present moment is guaranteed to be as sane as it is possible for a human being to be. To be appreciative of each moment, fully alive in all circumstances, and wonderfully awestruck at even the simplest of life's events is a pure form of sanity. This does not mean an absence of planning or an end to goals. Far from this picture, it is a ticket to having your children become great achievers, free from the taxing disabilities of neurotics and traveling along the path of life in a way that teaches them to be fully alive, rather than fighting life at every turn. They don't have to learn very much from you about living in this *purest of sanity* manner; rather, they need you to stand out of their way, and to have you refrain from diverting them from this most natural path to enlightenment. That is, you must stand out of the child's light and refrain at all costs from being an obstacle in the path to his or her own highest level of no-limit living. This means accepting your children as they are. Children, fully complete, now. Not "going" anywhere.

Accepting Children Where They Are

Children are confronted with a unique set of expectations that is visited on them by the adult world. They are constantly being bombarded with the question "What are you going to be?" Implicit in this question is the assumption: "You are not yet complete as a human being." A child who responded to this question with the answer "I am not going to be anything; I already am something" would be viewed as insolent and disrespectful to say the least. Yet the set of adult expectations that assumes the child to be an apprentice deserves such an answer. We often forget that all people are active, fully participating members of our society for their entire lives, including the period we choose to label childhood. Young people, regardless of their age, are equally significant and need to be viewed by all of us as fully arrived, vitally significant rather than in a period of preparation for life. That is, they are not getting ready for life in any way, but in fact are living it each and every day.

This may indeed be a radical departure for you. Children are little; you are big. They know very little; you know a lot. Therefore, they must be taught to be like you. You may have interpreted your job as one in which you must gradually shape little and helpless people into fully functioning adults, believing that someday they will appreciate your efforts. But there is another way to look at these little people. They are whole now! They are not striving; they have arrived. They are pure and total, just like you, even though they, like you, are changing each and every day. In Chapter 3 I talked at length about learning to accept change. In fact, learning to accept change means learning how to accept yourself, since each of us is always changing. The changes that are taking place within you psychologically and physically are just as dynamic as those that are taking place within your child. This attitude that children are somehow incomplete must be rethought if you are going to have no-limit children close to you.

Consider how much we have to learn from children and you will begin to get the message. We could all save ourselves a great deal of needless pain and suffering in our families if we could begin to view children as partners in living, as people who have as much to teach us as we have to teach them: the adult with his life catalog of experiences and children with their wide-eyed enthusiasm and freshness of appreciation for everything encountered. Indeed, we have much to gain from each other if we alter our perception of children exclusively as the recipients of our teachings, and replace that myopic vision with a view of all children as present-moment miracles who are just as complete as we are in this moment.

This view of children as whole and complete is the first step that you can take in helping them to stay tuned in to the now. If they can keep their childlike fascination with all of the world, if they can hold on to their ability to see the positive in everything, the fun in anything, and the joy in all of life, you will be doing them a much greater favor than if you train them for a so-called real, cruel, tough world that they will someday have to confront alone. They must hold on to that posture wherein their *inner* flame does not flicker though the worst goes before them. To ensure this, you must accept them as whole now, rather than developing strategies to prepare them for life. Instead, use your time with them to help them to continue to appreciate everything in life to its fullest, and still develop the inner discipline to conduct their lives in a manner that is purposeful to them—not you, but them.

We are not very good at accepting children where they are. Parents particularly will constantly be tempted to view their role as one of preparing their children for life. And in many ways it is very difficult to accept any contrary notions about parenting. After all, you know what children need; you have lived longer, and you want to impart your knowledge to them. But this is not possible, and the sooner you recognize that fact, the fewer heartaches you will have as a parent. Look at your own life. Think about the futility others experienced in trying to teach you something that you refused to learn. It cannot be done! How can you get a child to learn biology if the child refuses to do so? You cannot do it! Even if you firmly believe that someday he will need this information that you so desperately want him to learn. Everything that you know, you made a decision to know, and this is equally applicable to children. If they learn, it is because they made a decision to learn. If they do not want to learn, no amount of pressuring and pushing from you is going to sway their resolve. Thus, your role is to help them to decide what is most helpful for them.

Be aware that a child's readiness to learn anything is the most crucial variable in the entire learning process. Readiness to learn! Readiness means now, in this moment; finally, I am ready! The child who knows how to swim does not know any more the day he swims than he did the day before, when he couldn't swim. He was ready on this day to let go of the side and do it. He had the confidence, or the will, or the drive, at that moment, and off he went. You may have provided him with the proper atmosphere, the pool, the equipment, the lessons, even the desire, but the present moment when he decided to give it a try was his. That is the main point of this section. You help children the most by recognizing that they are totally human when they refuse to go under water or refuse to push off in any other way you want them to, and that you must accept such refusals as a part of their full humanity. They are equally complete when their moment for swimming *is* there. You must accept them as complete in all their moments, and stop wanting them to be different than they are. They need your support and love in each moment of their lives. You may give them the keys, but they must unlock the doors. No matter how much you might like it to be the opposite, no matter how desperately you may want them to be something else, they are not. And they will not be unless they make a decision to be. Just as you must try to see your children as whole and complete in all moments, so must you view yourself as a total human being. You do not want the love you crave from those who are precious to you to be contingent upon you changing. The truest test of love was offered by Robert Frost in his famous line, "We love the things we love for what they are."

Accept your children as perfect, as whole, and treat them as though they already are what they can become. Send them messages all the time that they are great, that they are terrific swimmers already. Let them know that you see them as swimmers, but that they do not have to actually do it until they are ready, and you will have a handle on what I am talking about here. Give them no judgments or negative reinforcement for not pleasing you; simply love them for what they are, and treat them as though they already are what they can become. This combination allows them to take control of their lives, and keeps them feeling positive about themselves in each moment that they are here. It gives them goals to shoot for, but it gives them unconditional love and acceptance of wherever they are in the pursuit of any goals they might have for themselves. Believe it or not, they have much more to teach you about living fully in the present than you have to teach them. You may very well have lost your childlike fascination for the miracle that life is, but if you watch them—stop treating them as apprentice people who are on their way to being somebody, and instead enjoy them for where they are—the rest of it will all fall into place naturally. Yes, they know about this business of the present moment, so stop preaching and learn for a moment. This moment will do just fine.

The Joy of Present-Moment Living

The avoidance of living in the present moment can be traced directly to the multitudinous admonitions to "Postpone your gratification," "Save for a rainy day," "Be very careful," "Don't spend all your money in one place," "Sure, school is boring, but it will pay off someday," "If it feels good, don't do it," or "Wait until you are grown-up."

Let's set the record straight right here for children and adults alike. Pleasure is terrific, and you should try to fill your life with as much of it as you can. No conditions, no apologies; a simple fact. Life is to be enjoyed, and if you are teaching children otherwise, you are doing yourself and them a disservice. Do you get mad at your plants because they stretch toward sunlight? Why do they do that? Because sunlight feels good and is necessary to their survival, so they instinctively seek it out. Do you punish your pets when they want to be petted or to romp? Of course not. Why? Because it is just fine for your pets to seek out pleasure and avoid pain. Well, you should at least consider the same privileges for your children and yourself.

This is not an endorsement of grabbing your pleasure at the expense of others. Abandon the idea once and for all that it is bad to encourage children to seek out pleasure. Their lives ought to be fun, and the same goes for you. Schoolwork ought to be pleasant and enjoyable for students, not some dreary exercise in plodding through a painful and boring curriculum. Life need not be thought of as a series of misfortunes, suffering, drabness, or constant misery. It does not have to be serious and grim in order to be relevant. Children are entitled to have as many pleasurable life experiences as possible, and you ought to do all that you can to help provide those experiences. They ought to learn that it is foolish to see life as a suffering experience and that enjoying life and everything they do in the present moment is the healthiest approach they can take toward being a no-limit person. Even the tasks they do not particularly relish can become fun if they learn the attitude of enjoying life for the moment, taking pleasure from each experience that comes their way and forgetting about the pain and suffering that so many others opt for in life. Their road to personal mastery must be strewn with larger and larger numbers of activities they genuinely enjoy; otherwise they will develop a sour, melancholy personality which will eventually ooze with pessimism. While they do not have to develop a phony sense of excitement about emptying the garbage, they also must learn not to be immobilized by these routine tasks and to look for the brighter side in all that they do. No garbage, no food. No food, hunger. Therefore, be appreciative of your garbage. Do not take it for granted, but feel privileged about having garbage to take out!

Living in the present moment is essentially an attitude. It is the way in which a person considers everything that he or she does. Total present-moment living means looking into the present moment, pushing out all distractions or negative thoughts, and becoming totally engaged in what is happening right now. It means not telling children that they must learn to postpone their gratification in order to have something better later on. Instead, they learn how to find joy in what is happening in this moment, and in future moments as well. It means setting goals, but not making the achievement of the goal more significant than each moment spent working toward the goal. A high school diploma is a fine goal, but it takes many days and years to achieve. Enjoying the time spent studying and participating in high school activities is the crucial attitude I am talking about here. Children can learn to see the attending of classes as a joy in and of itself, and not a necessary evil to be endured in order to receive a diploma. Both the striving for and the attainment of the external reward offer equally significant present moments to savor. Once children learn that each moment of life offers them an exciting miracle, they will stop looking for miracles and begin to live one. I will never forget reading this little statement supposedly written by someone much older. It contains a lesson for all of us who are concerned with helping children to be fully alive.

> First I was dying to finish high
>   school and start college.
> And then, I was dying to finish
>   college and start working.
> And then, I was dying to marry and
>   have children.
> And then, I was dying for my children
>   to grow old enough for school
>   so I could return to work.
> And then I was dying to retire.
> And now, I am dying . . . And suddenly
>   realize, I forgot to live.

There is much truth in this paradigm. Children are raised to avoid living today in preparation for a better future. The problem is that the future never arrives; all we get are present moments. The conditioning of always thinking ahead never leaves a person, and consequently people so conditioned will never learn to slow down and accept the pleasure that is inherent in virtually everything they see. Such a child becomes the adult who focuses on dessert while eating the appetizer, who does not savor the first cup of coffee because he is thinking about the second one, and who misses the lovemaking experience in anticipation of the orgasm. This vicious circle can be broken by simply accepting the idea that it is all right to feel good, that pleasure is not something bad, that one can enjoy one's life, including the planning for the future and the reminiscing about the past.

There are adults who specialize in not allowing their children to enjoy childhood. They view childhood as a time of preparation only. School is a necessary evil which children must endure. Being little is the price you pay for getting big. Pleasure is something that will arrive later if one suffers enough now. But now never arrives for these people. This approach creates pessimistic children who soon see life as a testing ground in which nothing is to be enjoyed for what it is. If you want children to develop an appreciation for life, to be happy and fulfilled not only now but always, then you must understand that these are inner attitudes that a child brings to his life tasks, rather than something that he will receive from them. This inner attitude is one which permits him to be exactly where he is in his life, and not preparing for anything greater later on. The joy of living in the present, then, is an inner concept that begins with the suppositions that pleasure in life is not bad, that joy is better than suffering, that everything in life is a miracle, and that living fully now is far superior to planning, planning, planning, and perhaps never arriving.

Take a look at our culture and you will see multitudinous reinforcers of postponing gratification. In a political science course I took in college, I once went back through every single Presidential contest since the formation of our Republic. In every single election, there was this slogan: "This is a time for tightening our belts. These are tough times, and we must all sacrifice together to have a better future for our children." These sentiments have been present in every single election for over two hundred years. Imagine, in two centuries we still have not arrived. We still cannot loosen our belts; we still have to sacrifice for the future. We never arrive in our elections, and we never will if we have to believe that the present moment is something that is a time for sacrificing for a future that never comes. In religion classes children are taught that they must suffer in this life in order to have a better life in the hereafter. In school they are taught to suffer now in order to have the fruits of an education. In our approaches to health we tell everyone that they must not enjoy what they eat, that they have to suffer through kelp and cactus juice to be healthy, that they must exercise to the point of pain to have any benefits. "No pain, no gain." Seldom do we hear that exercising and the fruits of the exercise are equally satisfying, that sound nutrition in and of itself is terrific, that being moral is a wonderful approach to life, and not a punishment or a future reward. We do not hear that we have arrived, that we can finally loosen our belts and enjoy the results of the suffering of our forefathers.

Pessimism, pain, suffering, and an eye toward a day that never arrives seem to be the watchwords of our culture, and they rub off on our children as they set about to repeat the same old mistakes that generations before have succumbed to. Help children to develop a total appreciation for every single moment that they are blessed with in their lifetimes. Avoid being pessimistic about anything that comes their way. Help them to have inner attitudes that give them a sense of joy in being able to live fully in all their present moments. This kind of attitude will not create a child who is selfishly hedonistic and uncaring about his future or about the future of others. In fact, the opposite is much more likely to happen. The optimistic child who looks for the silver lining is much more likely to want to help others to see the possibilities inherent in any moment than to look for dreariness. He becomes a model of hope for others rather than another purveyor of despair. He will help others to look for something positive in their life conditions rather than giving up on themselves.

There is not much you have to do to help children become aware of the limitless joy that is available to them in the present moment. They have it as their human heritage, as do you, if you will only allow it back into your life. Children take great pleasure in a snowstorm. Watch their wide eyes when they look out at the magnificent scene after a fresh snowfall. The adult in you might say, "I have to shovel it, put on the tire chains. Plod through the slush," and so on. And that adult can be very convincing in his rightness. "The kids can afford to love the snow—they do not have to drive in it or put up with the mess." But stop yourself right there. Your sour attitude toward the snowfall will not change anything except how you experience it. Being mad at it will not make it go away. Being "right" about it will not change it. All you get for thinking miserably about a snowfall is your misery. Imagine being able to enjoy driving slower to work. Imagine having fun shoveling the snow rather than cursing it. The child in you wants to do just that, but the adult who knows what lies ahead for him because of that insidious snow usually wins. It all goes back to the present-moment thinking that I am trying to help you to cultivate in yourself and your children. Forget about what lies ahead and *be here now*. Your pessimism breeds an unhappy experience with the snow, but most important of all, it does not change the fact that the snow is here, now.

The more moments you have in your life in which you are totally in the present and not thinking about where you will have to be later, the more your life will be a no-limit one. This is also true for children. The more you allow them to be the appreciators of the now that they naturally are, the more positive experiences they will have, and the more positive experiences they will help others to have in addition. And isn't that what life ought to be about? Making it more positive and enjoyable for all concerned? It is all about making life into one big peak experience rather than an experience of pique.

Toward More Peak Experiences

The term *peak experience* was first used by Abraham Maslow in his pioneering work, *Toward a Psychology of Being*. Notice it does not say a psychology of *becoming*. The emphasis is on being, and that was Maslow's great contribution: a psychology of arriving rather than a psychology of striving. Now, peak experiences are nothing new to those who are familiar with Eastern philosophy. The words may have changed, but the concept is as ancient as man himself. In *The Sky's the Limit* I wrote about the Japanese culture, the experience of *muga*, and learning how to train one's mind to experience one thing at a time in all of its totality. Pushing out all thoughts from the mind and totally concentrating on one thought, one object, one person, one enemy, or one physical task is a part of the training for those who would become Zen masters. My purpose in citing the literature is to encourage you to understand that a Buddhist monk who can push out pain by intense concentration and inner meditation is not some freakish being with magical powers. He is a student of the great powers of the mind. Each one of us has an ability to have peak experiences in any moment of our choosing, if only we would acknowledge our powers and become more present-moment oriented in our lives. I am not asking you to take up meditation necessarily, or to seek out a guru for instruction on the art of *muga*. I am asking you to tune in to your own unique capacity for enjoying life, to stand back and watch unspoiled children to see how it is done, and then to encourage rather than discourage both yourself and youngsters to make all of life one big peak experience.

A peak experience is nothing more than being intensely occupied with all of your being in a present-moment activity. No distractions, no thinking, a quiet mind which is not judging anything, only total "being" in the experience. Women have told me about the process of natural childbirth and how they train their minds to push out everything and only experience what their bodies were telling them. No pain, no thinking, only pure bliss created by training themselves to breathe and simply be with the experience. I have had my own peak experiences more and more frequently in recent years, since I have become more willing to abandon the traditional style of living my life the way others think I should. I have found that the more freedom I allow myself to experience what is important for me without hurting anyone else in the process, the more I seem to have extended periods of total present-moment involvement in my life activities.

I have been able to experience the peak feelings while running eight miles or more a day, and having the incidence of total involvement increase as I become less and less judgmental in my attitude toward my running activity. Instead of thinking about being tired, winded, hot, or anything unpleasant, I let my body take over, and I simply concentrate on my body and the wonderful machine that it is. Before long I have been running for miles without any awareness of the time or any unpleasant sensations. My mind is rested and my body is totally absorbed, and I am without judgment. There is no focusing on when I finish and no thinking about where I have been; there is simply running and allowing myself to flow. This is true for me in writing, where hours will simply disappear while I am totally caught up in the experience of writing. There is no pain, no anguish, no wishing I were someplace else, no thinking about what I will do when I finish; I am simply being in a moment and allowing myself to flow.

You have almost certainly had present-moment peak experiences yourself. Perhaps you were so involved in a project that you forgot about time, hunger, and fatigue. You were enjoying what you were doing and transcending all other judgments. Many people report moments of pure time-lost bliss in sexual experiences, wherein time stood still and they became totally absorbed in loving another human being. Many speak of such moments when they are participating in an athletic event—lost in time, moving without conscious thought. In these moments, rare though they may be in your own personal life, sickness will often disappear. A friend described being given instructions on how to handle a parachute landing on a day he had a runny nose due to a slight cold. While he was listening to the instructor, while he was actually floating through the air, and while he was focusing on his landing technique, he was totally immersed in the experience. Then, driving home in the car he suddenly thought about his cold, and his nose began to run. But during the entire time of the parachute suiting up, instruction, jumping, and landing, he literally had no cold. By putting it on hold for several hours he had the peak experience I am writing about here. I have had similar "lost in the present moment" experiences wherein I sent away fatigue and slight illnesses while playing with my children, walking along the beach, being interviewed on a network television show, reading a novel, and endless other experiences, once I allowed myself to have a quiet mind and to stop judging life and start being a part of it.

Children have this amazing capacity to have peak experiences, and they do it all the time until they are taught to be different. How many times have you told children to "think about what you are doing," and then they mess up whatever they were attempting? Children are natural geniuses at living life in the present-moment peak-experience mode that I am discussing here. They know how to get lost in a moment and to enjoy it fully. A child can spend an afternoon on a waterslide and be there completely for the entire time. She can become totally immersed in a dollhouse, creating her own fantasy world and losing her sense of time and judgment. Children can put their thinking selves on hold and suspend all judgments for the purpose of living totally in the present moment. This absence of thinking, this quieting of the mind, and this ability to not only enjoy what they do, but to actually *be* what they are doing is what it means to be an unspoiled child. You must try very hard to learn from children rather than making them think about what they are doing. Do not teach them to judge it, grade it, learn from it, and take a test about it. Instead they must be allowed to simply be what they are doing, and you can work at doing the same by following their examples. Be a child again! This is what it means to be a child again. Not to be childish, but to be childlike. Be totally involved in a moment, rather than thinking about all the things you have to do before you can enjoy an activity such as an aerobics exercise class. Then at the class you diminish the joy by thinking about all the things you have to do when you get home, never totally losing yourself in your exercise program so that you actually become the exercise.

Children know how to lose themselves in an experience until you work at taking that instinct away from them. They approach everything in life as a peak experience, until they are programmed to think about what they are doing, and then they forget how to totally enjoy life by actually being the enjoyment itself. They then learn to look outside themselves, to practice until they have it perfect, to grade themselves, to compare their performances with those of others, to work at improving themselves in their tasks, and soon they are no longer willing or able to perform. They learn to hate failure, since they equate failure at a task with failure as a person, so they simply avoid those tasks which they cannot perform at a level commensurate with their preset expectations. They learn to organize their activities rather than to simply be their activities without judgment, and unfortunately, they unlearn what made them supremely human in the first place.

Watch children as they go through their daily activities. See how much of what they do is done for the joy of doing it, and how much is done in order to get some kind of grade on it. The younger they are (that is, the less conditioned they are), the more they can get lost in their present moments and have peak experiences. As they grow older, they get bored with life. They worry about how they will appear, what grade they will get, what their friends will think, what the adults will say, and on and on. What I am asking of you is to change your attitude about children and their present moments. The great thinkers who have tried to help others suggest getting back to those childlike *muga* experiences. We can learn from our children and listen to the child inside all of us. Not to become irresponsible, but to take up our responsibilities by actually "being" that responsibility and living it that way each moment. By not asking God to do it, but by being godlike. By not asking our teachers to teach us, but by being the learning experience. By transcending the external judgments and having more and more, rather than fewer and fewer, peak experiences as our children grow older.

When I say that everything in life offers an opportunity for a peak experience, I am not exaggerating. When you tune in to any given moment and see what you have always ignored, you will discover an entire universe before you. Examine a drop of water from a pond under a powerful microscope, and right before your eyes you will discover entire universes containing a multitude of life forms. While it was once only conceptualized as a drop of water, when you become part of it and focus into all of it, you can be lost in the experience of everything taking place within that drop of water. All of life is just like that. When you open up to it, when you encourage children to experience life in all its richness, when you stop and really see and experience, you will find an entire world which was absent from your life only because of the blinders you wore. Watch a youngster study a spiderweb. See how hours can go by as he explores the detail of an anthill. Watch children as they literally become what they are viewing. This is what I mean by a peak experience. Slow yourself down, and instead of telling the children to "get on with your tasks," remember that this childlike fascination with the world is the key to their remaining no-limit people.

Before moving on to practical, down-to-earth information to assist you and your children in becoming more present-moment oriented and peak-experience involved, I want to share a beautiful Sanskrit poem that sums up all of the foregoing on the subject of peak experiences. When I say that each day has in it a total peak experience for everyone if you will allow it, I mean just that. This poem puts it into context on the physical as well as the philosophical plane.

> Look to this day,
> For it is the very life of life.
> In its brief course lie all
> The verities and realities of your existence:
> The glory of action,
> The bliss of growth,
> The splendor of beauty,
> For yesterday is but a dream
> And tomorrow is only a vision;
> But today well lived makes
> Every yesterday a dream of happiness
> And every tomorrow a vision of hope.
> Look well, therefore, to this day.

Read it again!

Now, while reading it try to *be* the words and the message in this day. There is much truth in these words. This day is truly all that you have. Make of it your richest peak experience, and by all means, practice, practice, practice doing the same with children. They know it better than you only because they have not had as long to forget what they already are.

Some Typical Actions That Inhibit Present-Moment Living for You and Your Children

Listed below are some of the more typical things that you might be doing to inhibit your children from growing up within the present moment and having those luscious peak experiences that can be their trademarks as no-limit people. The more they are able to stay here and now, and to wallow around in full appreciation of all that they think and do, the more you are helping them toward total no-limit, fully functioning lives.

□ Not spending time with your children; constantly farming them out to various caretakers.

□ Treating them as incomplete, as if they are residing in the waiting room of life until they are older and bigger.

□ Never playing with them.

□ Having goals for your children and keeping them focused on attaining *your* goals in the future.

□ Reminding them of their past mistakes.

□ Placing more emphasis on their roles and the appropriate rules than on simply doing.

□ Always insisting that they do their "best" at everything they try.

□ Being an example of a person who never stops to smell the roses.

□ Teaching them to have tasks at the expense of appreciating life.

□ Rushing them early in their lives: learn reading at eighteen months, math at two, spelling at three.

▢ Reminding them of what they "should have" done.

▢ Not living up to your promises without a sensitive explanation.

▢ Never praising them directly.

▢ Emphasizing long-range goals as the purpose of life: "Think way ahead."

▢ Establishing moneymaking as the most important purpose in life.

▢ Rushing children through all experiences such as movies, dinner, vacations, and family gatherings.

▢ Being annoyed at delays and taking it out on them.

▢ Refusing to come down to their level.

▢ Telling them that "someday" things will be different and they will understand.

▢ Talking about "the way it used to be."

▢ Not giving explanations to your children.

▢ Giving in to pressures for them to "grow up fast."

▢ Not permitting them to do things for themselves, and instead doing everything for them.

▢ Encouraging them to follow fads and commercial ad campaigns.

These are some of the general categories of actions that keep children from living more fully in the present. They often contribute to creating hurried children rushing through life and ultimately becoming adults who spend their lives contemplating either what is going to happen or how good it used to be. The ability to genuinely enjoy a present moment and to be totally absorbed in the experiences of life in a peak fashion is further stifled by many of these actions. While none of these practices are undertaken to deliberately sabotage children's prospects for peak experiences and more joy in the present moments of their lives, this is often the result.

Some of the Payoffs for Discouraging Present-Moment Living

Before providing some alternatives to the pleasure-inhibiting actions listed in the previous section, think about the reasons why you may be conducting yourself in this manner with children. If you understand the reasons more fully and vow to rid yourself of some of the self-defeating payoffs, you will find it much easier to adopt alternative strategies.

You may have learned a long time ago that hedonism or pleasure for the sake of pleasure is wrong. By teaching your children to always be serious, to keep their noses to the grindstone and forget about enjoying life, you reinforce that the way you were brought up is the way it is supposed to be. Avoiding the present moment helps you then to feel right and proper about your own life mistakes, and it keeps you from having to admit that maybe you have been making a mistake in your own approach.

You may be the product of a "Depression mentality" in which your Depression-era parents (or perhaps you were there yourself) taught you to always save for a rainy day and sacrifice any enjoyment today for a future time. You may be foisting these notions on today's children, never stopping to realize that they are erroneous assumptions. Talk to people who lived through the Depression. Many will tell you how tough it was, but many will also remember fondly how everyone worked together, how great those days really were in testing and building character. The present moment offered them much, but they may not want to admit it.

You may believe that living only for the present is selfish, foolish, and wrong. By discouraging children from being totally alive in their present moments you keep alive your assumption that it is possible to live in any moment other than the present, and that anything that feels good must be bad.

You may have convinced yourself that a child ought to be seen but not heard, should be obedient, and should never speak unless spoken to. If you were raised that way, it may be difficult for you to admit that it is not the best way to raise children. It then becomes more important for you to be right about these beliefs than to perhaps challenge them and see where they may have inhibited you from reaching your own full potential.

When you insist on children behaving in ways which avoid present moments and peak experiences, you yourself have a built-in excuse for not changing. If you are dissatisfied with your ability to get more joy out of life, you can avoid examining your values and behaviors and also avoid the risks and challenges by insisting that your children be the same as you.

If you have gotten into a rut in life and are not having as much fun as you would like to, you can remain unappreciative of life and avoid its mainstream by being lazy and fearful. Rules and guidelines for children can be justified by using yourself as an example. If you refuse to let children enjoy their lives in naturally exciting activities by insisting that they be serious and future oriented, you justify your own feelings of discomfort about your own life. The children's lack of fun becomes your justification for being the kind of human being you have chosen to become.

You can abdicate your responsibility as a parent to provide a rich and varied childhood experience for your children by simply making them be small adults rather than what they are today. If they are working toward something else, then you can avoid being with them in the ways that will enrich their lives the most.

By reminding them of their past mistakes and holding grudges, you can manipulate children into thinking the way you believe they should, rather than having minds of their own. Constantly referring to the past and what they should have done gives you a power over them that you may not have in any other area of your life.

These are some of the neurotic dividends that you may be acquiring for raising your children to avoid the now and all the delirious enjoyment that goes with having peak experiences.

Some Strategies for Present-Moment Living

What follows are some specific tactics that you might attempt if you are interested in helping your children to be fully alive in the present. The same tactics will also help you to view your children as whole now rather than on their way to becoming complete later on in life.

Try looking at your children with new eyes for a few minutes each day. Say to yourself, "She is three years old—period! I will appreciate her today for her three-year-oldness. I will not view her as on her way to being an adult. I will not think about what she will become someday. I will instead attempt to be with her in her three-year-old world. I will be totally with her now rather than judging her for not being something other than what she is." This is a very important mental exercise for you regardless of your children's current ages. They are complete and totally equal to you and all other adults in importance as human beings. They are smaller and younger, but they are still just as complete as you are. Love them for what they are, which is ever-changing people just like everyone else.

This kind of thinking will help you to be more appreciative of your children each day. Revel in their wide-eyed fascination with the world rather than seeking to curtail it. Take joy in the "dumb" things they say rather than correcting them all the time. Love their ability to play with such energy, rather than trying to get them to be more serious or subdued. Practice saying to yourself that they have the same rights as big people, that they are entitled to be treated with dignity and respect even though you and other adults are bigger than they are at the moment. If you talk to yourself this way, you will realize that *everyone is always changing*. Although the physical changes are more obvious in children, adults are also constantly changing. You do not view adults as incomplete largely because once they reach their full physical dimensions they pretty much look the same except for the aging process. Yet adults are changing all the time. They become more mature at thirty than they were at twenty. They are generally more emotionally stable at forty than at twenty-five. Adults have varying degrees of energy, ever-changing attitudes and interests, always shifting styles and means of speaking. Nevertheless, adults are generally treated as though they are complete and whole right now.

Children will be much less troublesome if we stop *preparing* them for life, and remind ourselves that they are just as much a part of life *now* as anyone else. This change is attitude keeps you focused on them now, and appreciating them for their uniqueness. A parent who lost a child in an auto accident once told me that the biggest mistake she made as a parent was to treat her child as incomplete. She said to me, "Tell any parents that you work with to appreciate their children for what they are each day, because if they ever lose one they'll then know that they are special exactly where they are, and how foolish it is to prepare them for something that they might never have." In my view she was absolutely correct. None of us knows if we have a future. Tomorrow is guaranteed to no one. So while you want to provide children with solid guidelines and a terrific example, you also want to be thankful for the miracle that they now are, and appreciate their age typicalness, today.

Spend more time with children in the unique world of their play. If you simply play with children on their terms, coming down to their level, you will soon see why they do it so often. It can be the most gratifying experience of your life to shed your "grownup" exterior and play with children. Hide-and-seek can be just as much fun for you as for them, and when you join them, you send them a message that you acknowledge them as total human beings who do such things as play hide-and-seek, rather than judging them as "only children" who play games all the time. This can be done with your children each day, and at all ages of their lives. A baby who plays peekaboo with you when you take a blanket off of your head is learning to be involved with you as a person. A toddler who wants you to close your eyes and find her behind the dresses in Mommy's closet is doing what is most natural and necessary for a child—playing. When you join the game, you accept the child. When you scoff at it, or simply decide to always read the newspaper instead, you are ignoring the child and communicating, "When you grow up, then I will acknowledge you as a total human being, but for now you really do not count in my eyes." You do not have to play with children all the time, but for a few moments a day it is a terrific way to show them that they count. Playing catch, sitting on the swing together, going to the park, taking a walk, making up your own games, wrestling, and clowning together are extremely important activities for children and you as well. Be a child with them without any rules and you will see a much happier child. As much as they want you to play with them, they also need you to leave them alone in their play. The timing is up to both of you. But if you never play with them, you are treating them as incomplete and unimportant. If you fail to give them independence in their play, you are teaching them that you do not trust them to be alone. The point is that some play with them is tremendously fulfilling for all of you and a terrific way to actually be with them where they are, but, like anything in life, too much of it will ruin the effect.

Take a day to just be with a child in a totally different way than you ever have before. Try to become totally engaged in the experience. A day at the beach can be a wonderful experience of being together totally in the now, or it can be a way of making another day go by. What you get out of a day is up to you and the attitude you have about the present moment. For example, a day spent at the beach in which you and the children (the age does not matter) become a part of the beach can go something like this: Seashells can be examined for hours; the shapes, sizes, textures, and where they came from can be talked about. Sand can be experienced in all its shifting magnificence. Just stand together on the beach and see what happens to the sand as it buries your feet. Pick up a handful of it and tell a child that there are more stars in the universe than there are grains of sand on all the beaches of our planet. The sea life that abounds at the edge of the beach is a ceaseless miracle; turtles, fish, crabs, seaweed, sand fleas, sea gulls, and pelicans are all wonders that you can behold together. The waves coming at you can be experienced together as an awesome miracle to explore. The winds and how they shape the beaches can be felt. Building a sand castle or tossing a Frisbee together can become peak present-moment experiences. Having lunch together at a picnic on the beach is fun for children of all ages, including the child that resides deep within you. Catching a fish for dinner can be part of the beach scene. The excitement of a day at the beach can become something that is a miracle for children each moment they are there, or it can be a way of simply passing the day. The beach will still be there for you to make of it what you will, and what you make of it all depends on how willing you are to become totally involved in the present moment with children.

This same approach to being with children is applicable in virtually everything you undertake. It means slowing down, looking at the miraculousness of every moment with wide eyes and an open heart. It means examining the moment, living fully in it, grabbing everything out of it that is there, and suspending any thoughts about having to get home, be at the office, take a nap, or anything else. Instead, you live one day at a time, enjoying a peak experience with your child. Pick your spot; a beach is only one example. The opportunities for present-moment fulfillment are inherent in every single cubic inch of space. You can find them in a ball game, a walk in the park, a ballet, a lunch together, the rodeo, a bike ride along the canal, a game of kick-the-can—you name it. If you have the willingness to be totally there, you will experience the richness of the moment in childlike fascination. Or you can simply bypass it, and go through life as an observer in a hurry, rather than as a participant. The opportunity to really become involved in life is most available with children, since they already know how to do it. Do it with them and you will see a change in you and especially in your relationship with your children.

Children need as much freedom from you as you need from them, but they are entitled to a sincere explanation when you leave them, particularly when they are very young. You may have a job that requires you to be gone a great deal of the time. This ought never to be a source of guilt on your part. But try explaining to them in as sincere a way as possible why they must have a sitter or go to a day care center. "Mommy has to work to bring home the money to help pay for all the things we have. I also like working and being with my friends, just like you have fun with your friends. I think of you during the day, and I'll be home so that we can make supper together." Whatever the truth is for you in your own circumstances, your children are entitled to an honest explanation of why you leave them.

Do not tell them that you have to work if you are working because you want to. Be honest, but let them know why you are leaving them. When you constantly leave them alone without explanations, you teach them that they really do not count as total human beings. You demand explanations from them, yet you never offer one yourself. They want to know where you are and that you are safe, and when you will be back, just as much as you want the same courtesy from them. Let them know through this process, without guilt, that they do count, that you do appreciate their feelings and their concern, both for you and for themselves, and talk about why you do the things you do, even if you are leaving for your own need to be alone, which is a fine and healthy thing to do. Say something like "When you want to be alone, you can go into your room and close the door. I can't do that because I have to watch the baby, or be available whenever one of you needs my help. I like to get away and be by myself just like you do, so I'm going to get to the mall for a few hours. When I get back we'll spend some time together." This is an honest approach which teaches children that you consider their feelings but that you are still entitled to, and are going to take, some time for yourself. When you give them the consideration which you demand of them, you will find that they will return it much more readily than if you have two separate codes of ethics.

Take the emphasis off any long-range goals you may have for your children and focus instead on having mutual goals that are attainable in short periods of time. When you tell your children that you want them to be something much later on their lives, you are really treating them as if they do not matter very much today. Children must be involved in the setting of goals. If you tell a six-year-old that he should study hard in order to get into college, you are ignoring his six-year-oldness and imposing a standard on him that has absolutely no meaning to him, even though your intentions may indeed be honorable by your standards. However, they are indeed dishonorable in terms of accepting your child for what he is now. Studying in school ought to be done for the internal benefit that it presents to children, not for some external reward like a college admission credential. Children, not you, will someday decide about college for themselves. If they go, it will be the result of their own daily approaches to school, the daily study habits they develop, their own perceptions twelve years from now, the economic condition of the world in a decade, and a thousand other factors that are the result of living in a certain way within the present moment. You will be of much more help to children if you are with them in the first grade, talking to them about what they are doing in school *now*, and helping them to develop positive attitudes toward schooling and the joys of being educated. Let the long-range stuff take care of itself. Be with them where they are, and they will learn to handle everything that comes along. Goals that you have for them are only going to intensify the distance between you and them if they are not in agreement with those goals. Imagine how you would feel if I suddenly told you what your goals were to be. Despite your objections to the contrary that you know what is right for your children, and that they are too young to know any better, they feel precisely the same indignation that you would.

Avoid placing roles and labels on children. Telling them that they can only do certain things and are limited in other ways keeps them from trying new behaviors now, today, in the only moment they have. If your daughter has learned that she cannot play football due to being a girl, she will miss out on many present-moment fun times because of that limited perception. Encourage her to play touch football, show her how to hold the ball, let her kick it, and take her to a football game. Don't allow the label of "unfeminine" to inhibit her throughout her life when so-called "masculine" activities are taking place. The reverse is also true. Why shouldn't your son learn to bake cookies or prepare a lasagne dinner by himself when he is nine? Wouldn't he get just as much enjoyment out of the activity as your daughter? No activity need be eliminated from the menu of a child's life due to any label. The more things they can choose to do in any given moment, the more they will get out of this wonderful experience called life. Take away all the silly labels like "You're too young for that," "You're too little," "Boys never do those things," "We don't like those kinds of things in our family," "You haven't the talent for that," "No one in our family ever did that," "You're too frail to do those kinds of things." All of these labels, and endless others, should be abandoned. Instead, children should be encouraged to experiment with life. "No one in our family has ever tried skiing, so why not be the first?" "I've never seen a girl runner before, but if you want to try it, go for it." "Even if you are short, I'll bet you'd be a great basketball player if you really want to be." "I'll bet you are strong enough to lift both bags of groceries." Encourage and praise, rather than the opposite, and you will have a present-moment peak-experience person right in front of you.

Get rid of the sentence "Always do your best." No one can always do his or her best. Having to always do their best keeps children doing only those things that they can do well. If you want them to enjoy life and be totally alive in their present moments, encourage them to simply *do!*

"On a few things you will want to give 100 percent effort, particularly those which you want to pursue with all your heart, but in the rest, simply do." "Don't worry about falling down. Even when you fall you are better off than the person who sits on the sidelines of life and never fails." "Sure, you could run faster than you are presently running, but that's not what's important. The fact that you are doing it is what impresses me the most. Your time will improve if that becomes important to you later on; for now, simply enjoy the running." "I don't care if you are really terrible at making candles. The fact that you made it yourself is what matters to me. I'll always treasure it." "Sure you can wrap your own presents for Christmas. However you think they should look is great."

I trust you get the message. Be a doer. Try virtually anything and do not worry about how it looks to others. Their best will come later in some areas—and if it doesn't, at least they are doing something rather than sitting around. I have mentioned this in earlier portions of this book, and it bears repeating here: The child who must always do his best—or who learns that if he does not do everything well, then he should not do it at all—is really learning to restrict his efforts to those areas where he excels. He is learning to avoid failure, to fear the disapproval of others, and to be an observer rather than a participant in life. There is nothing wrong with going for an average walk in the park, or a mediocre bicycle ride. It is far superior to watching others do the walking and the cycling, and if someday he wants to take up Olympic cycling, then at least he will know how to do it. For now, doing it is more important than getting a grade on it.

Be an example of a person who lives in the present moment and appreciates all that life has to offer. Try to avoid grumbling about your hard luck in front of the children (or in front of yourself, for that matter), and instead try to find something positive in each day. Examine spiderwebs; show the children how spiders capture insects and wrap them up for meals later on. Watch a special on public television together, and then talk about it with them. Go to the zoo together—but instead of thinking about what time you have to get home, try to stay totally in the present moment at each exhibit. In other words, slow down a bit yourself and show children an example of a person who really appreciates everything in life. Even if they think it is dumb or boring, tell them how exciting it is for you. Tell them stories about what you did as a child, and what they did when they were much younger. Children love to be involved in stories, and when they are the principal characters, it is even better. Those little moments in which you send a signal to children that you are a person who really loves life in all of its magnificence, teaches them to stay more present-moment oriented, and ultimately to enjoy everything that life presents to them. The more time you take to just appreciate and be with them in the present moment, regardless of where you are or what you are doing, the more you give them the ability to enjoy the precious moments of their lives. Even as simple an activity as getting a haircut can become a fun learning experience if you approach it with vigor, rather than as a boring routine task that has to be hurried through.

Get rid of the notion that children who do things early are way ahead of the game of life. Teaching your children to read at age two, and putting them through practice drills as pretoddlers, often intensifies their anxiety levels rather than doing them any positive good. You might be interested in a few summaries of statistical reports, discussed in much more detail in David Elkind's *The Hurried Child.*

- □ Adolescents who were introduced to reading late were more enthusiastic, spontaneous readers than were those who were introduced to reading early.

- □ The majority of children can, however, learn to read with ease if they are not hurried into it.

- □ Generally it is parent need, not a child's authentic wish, that pushes children into team sports at an early age. School-age children need the opportunity to play their own games, make up their own rules, abide by their own timetable. Adult intervention interferes with the crucial learning that takes place when children arrange their own games.

The message is clear when you study the facts. Hurrying children into advanced activities represents the adult's need to have a precocious child rather than the best interest of the child. Let them be infants, toddlers, and little children. Allow them to make up their own rules, to argue among themselves, and to figure things out themselves without adult intervention. If anything, join with them and be a participant without interfering or imposing your adult mentality on them. Remember, the unspoiled child is the closest example you will see of a completely no-limit person. Do not impose limits on such children. Stand back and learn from them, and let them enjoy the path of life, rather than pushing them along at a hurried pace.

If you have to break a promise to a child, give the child a sensitive explanation. While she may act upset with you, at least you convey to the child that she counts when you tell her why you had to change plans. Avoid promising anything you know you cannot deliver. Apologies wear very thin very fast. If they come too frequently, children will begin to view you as untrustworthy and phony, and they will be right. You are much better off to simply keep your mouth shut, rather than to continuously make promises which you will be unable to keep. It is important for you to model integrity to them if you expect them to have integrity. The child who grows up being constantly disappointed by adults learns to view the world as an untrustworthy place, a place that promises much but delivers little. Apologies soon become even greater sources of displeasure.

Of course there will be times when plans must be shifted. When such an occasion arises, an intelligent, honest explanation will do more than anything to keep up a child's trust in you, as well as to help him to handle disappointments effectively. "I know I promised that we would go fishing on Saturday, but I will be unable to make it due to an unexpected meeting that I must attend. I would much rather be fishing than traveling, but this meeting has to be attended. We'll make it up within the next few weeks." This is not an empty apology; it is an honest declaration that gives your relationship to the child the priority that it deserves. Be a person of integrity and offer children the same courtesy that you would want from anyone who was breaking an important appointment with you.

Make sure to praise your children at every opportunity. I want to remind you again in this chapter that praise is the world's greatest teacher. Praise helps children to appreciate the moments of their lives. Praise is essential in raising no-limit children. You know how good it feels when someone tells you something positive, and how awful you feel with negative criticism. Negative reinforcement has been shown to be the absolute worst way to motivate a child. The more you criticize, the more likely you are to extinguish your children's desire to improve, and the more likely they are to give up on themselves and on you as a trusted confidante. I know you have heard the old saying a million times, and you have probably used it yourself over and over again: "I am only criticizing you for your own good." Well, don't you believe it for a moment. Virtually all criticism, especially when directed at children, has behind it this message: "I think you should be doing what you are doing *my* way. *I* know better." And, unfortunately, this does not work. Children are unique, and they are not going to emulate your way of doing things regardless of how much you force it. They are going to do things in their own ways, and if you want to help them to improve, try motivating them with praise rather than with criticism. Remember, no one likes to be criticized!

When they are doing something that you disapprove of, try out a strategy like the one that follows as an alternative to criticism. When a two-year-old has just thrown an apple core on the floor rather than putting it in the garbage:

Criticism	Praise
How dare you do that! You have no right to be such a slob! You pick it up and then go to your room for being so nasty.	You know where the garbage can is. I know you like the room clean, just like the rest of us do. Put it where it belongs; I know you can do it. (Then leave and give the child a chance to think about it on his own.)

In this little scenario, the criticism simply makes the child more determined to win, even if he must endure punishment. In the praise strategy, the child learns to behave properly without being told that he is a bad person because of his behavior.

If you give direction and praise, and then allow a few minutes for the child to consider what has been said, with you absent, he will most likely pick up the apple core and throw it away. A child wants and needs your praise in order to build a self-image of being a terrific person. Criticism makes the present moment a foul place and detracts from growth, while praise almost always has the opposite effect. This is true for children of all ages and for adults as well. Always look for the good in children and reinforce that part. "You are beautiful. Do you really want to mess up your natural beauty by not grooming yourself?" "You are normally so careful about not ruining things. What happened this time?"

Start out with something positive and praiseworthy and you will see how much more pleasant the present moments of your life are for you and your children. Stick to criticism and you will teach them to lie and be afraid of you. Worst of all, you will lower their motivation for improving, which is precisely the opposite of what you intended.

Give children plenty of opportunities to be around the friends of their choice. The present moment is made more glorious with the inclusion of friends. Make your home into a place where children feel comfortable having their friends over. Allow them to "take a friend" when you go on a short trip, shopping, or to any special occasion. I have found that children are much happier when they can have their own friends around. In addition, they seldom need to be reminded of how to behave, and everyone has a better time. If your home is a place where your children do not feel comfortable bringing their friends, you would do well to examine why this is so. Children tend to congregate where they feel the least pressure, where they are free to be themselves, where it "feels right" for them. If they avoid your home, something is missing, and no amount of insisting that they bring their friends home will change it. The atmosphere itself must be conducive to their wanting to be in your home. This means being less judgmental and more open to them. It means permitting them to play or congregate in a place which is theirs to enjoy. Most neighborhoods have a few homes where children of all ages feel welcome. Look at the parents in these homes and you will find people that the children like to be around and who have earned the respect of the children as well. These parents feel most at home with the children, often treating them just like their own personal friends (because that is precisely what they are), yet their homes are not places where young people can be irresponsible and destructive. When children want to bring their friends into the home to be around you with their friends, to have them stay overnight at slumber parties, or sit outside and eat pizza together, with you right there to enjoy it with them, you have then created a home environment which allows the children to be just that: children in the present moment. The more activities in which you can include friends, the friendlier everyone will feel, and you will be raising children in the present moment as well.

Deemphasize money and the cost of things in front of children. Obviously you must be conscious of living within whatever financial means are available to you, but this need not be the focus of your life. Try to keep money references to a minimum, and emphasize instead the things that you can do in the present that require very little money. It does not take money to have a positive attitude. It does not cost a cent to go for a walk together, to talk about a good book, or to go to a museum for the day. Whatever your financial picture at home, it is not necessary to constantly remind children about the cost of things. Raise them to respect money but not to be made servants to it. A child's entire lifetime can be spent in worrying about what things cost and avoiding being fully alive if he or she is always being reminded about the cost of things. Try to take off the price tag of life with your children; instead enjoy what you can afford.

Encourage a child to earn her own way in life and make it a pleasant experience for her as well. A child with a paper route or a job bagging groceries or babysitting is not only having a terrific time in her present moments, but is also learning a valuable lesson in each one of those moments. Children love to be independent, and that goes for finances as well. They feel important when they have earned their own money. When they participate in a carwashing day to raise money for a school activity, they can work, have fun, and feel that they are making a contribution as well. This is true around the neighborhood also. Encourage them to figure out ways to make money for themselves, and thus eliminate the hassle of always talking about a shortage of money. Children of all ages are capable of figuring out ways to earn something for themselves. They love doing this, and it gives them an opportunity to learn about accounting, mathematics, banking, interest rates, saving, and other important lessons of life. A lecture about interest rates is meaningless compared with having a child go down to the bank and open his own account, experiencing interest rates for himself. Help children find ways to feel responsible and important, recognizing that working in any small way will contribute to that feeling of importance. Children have the ability to fuse the work-play dichotomy. When they are making money at what they are doing, work becomes play, as it should for all of us. Making lemonade and selling it, standing out in the hot sun, counting up their earnings—all of this becomes fun. But picking up their clothes can be "work" which is accompanied by whining and complaining. Why? Quite simply, because the lemonade stand is their idea and the picking up of clothes is your idea. The important message here is to allow children to have an inner feeling of self-importance about their life tasks. If they do, then the whining is replaced by experiencing life as both work and play simultaneously.

Work at having more spontaneity in your life with children. Take the planning out as much as possible and simply do things together. Go on a vacation in which you make no plans other than to travel. Stop whenever you feel like seeing something, camp out where the mood strikes you, take time to look at the local sights, enjoy a meal without a reservation by asking the local people where they most like to eat. One of Jackson Browne's songs contains a line that tells a lot about the enjoyment of life. "The times we were most happy, were the times we never tried." Not trying to have a good time is often the best way to make it happen. Keep this in mind as you do things together. Spontaneity—just doing something without having to spend half your time getting ready for it— is one of the most important ingredients in the no-limit life. Teach children through your example that being spontaneous is not only allowed, it is encouraged. Use words like "Why not? We've never done that before," rather than "We can't do that—we don't know what to expect." Not knowing what to expect is exactly what makes a funhouse fun! It is also what makes a funlife fun!

These are some of the strategies you can employ with yourself and your children to get on with living more fully in the present moments of your lives. Raising children within the present moment means that as they grow older they will not think about all the things they wished they had done yesterday; instead they will do them today and enjoy all the moments of their lives. The present moments are nothing more—or less—than the precious currency of their lives. As Kay Lyons reminded us, "Yesterday is a cancelled check; tomorrow is a promissory note; today is the only cash you have—so spend it wisely." Children do well to learn this valuable lesson. They can plan all they want to, but it can only be done in this moment, and the same may be said of reminiscing. All of life is in this day. Help your children to stay in it.

8

I Want My Children to Experience a Lifetime of Wellness

The no-limit person pursues physical "superhealth" with minimal reliance on doctors and pills, knowing it is all in his power to preserve and strengthen himself. He loves his basic animal nature and is in awe of how beautifully his body functions. He exercises for the physical joy of it and appreciates aging as the universal medium of life and growth. He recognizes that a sense of humor is vital to all aspects of life.

The art of medicine consists of amusing the patient while nature cures the disease.

—VOLTAIRE

Believe it or not, most children are raised on sickness rather than on wellness. You have a wonderful opportunity as a parent to aid your children to live their lives relatively free of illness. You may believe something quite the contrary. Most likely you have come to believe that the general state of your children's health is in the hands of a much higher authority than yourself. You may believe that your children's health is a matter of luck, or genetic distribution, and that your input is largely irrelevant.

I suggest you examine a relatively new concept in the field of medicine, one that is beginning to be introduced into the training of physicians in the world today. It is called wellness or behavioral medicine, and it has as its foundation the belief that the practice of medicine ought to be for the purpose of helping people to become as healthy as they possibly can, rather than primarily to assist people to eliminate illnesses. Imagine that. An approach to medicine in which the paramount function of the doctor is to help each person to become superhealthy and to maintain superhealth throughout his or her lifetime.

The concept of wellness embraces some simple notions which I would ask you to seriously consider. Basically it is an approach to health that embraces the belief that we have a great deal of control over our bodies and their current states of health. It begins with the premise that we are all capable of maintaining maximum health by means of our everyday living habits, and that being well is a natural state for our bodies. Illness itself is something that receives very little attention from the wellness-oriented person. The inner system of the wellness-oriented person is one which adopts a belief that being well is the normal state of affairs for all of us, and that being superhealthy is our destiny. Sickness itself is viewed as unnatural, and it is always unexpected and unplanned and receives no reinforcement. You reinforce instead a positive wellness attitude toward the miracle that is one's body and the belief that children will not get sick. The important consideration in teaching children wellness is the development of an attitude, and that means getting rid of all beliefs that support sickness and illness as normal conditions of being human.

Developing a Wellness Attitude with Children

To help children grow up on wellness, you must first stop making sickness so attractive. You can help very young children to establish a total wellness attitude right from the very beginning. You can minimize the amount of attention you provide for sickness, and help a child to adopt an attitude of having much more control over his or her own health than you have ever imagined. Below are some examples of how sickness gets reinforced and a look at how wellness might be used as a viable substitute in each example.

Sickness Orientation	Wellness Orientation
If you don't wear a scarf you'll catch a cold and be sick.	You are too strong to catch a cold, but here is a scarf to keep you nice and comfortable outside.
It's the cold season, so button up.	You are so strong inside and so healthy that you probably won't catch a cold, even if the other kids do.
You will get really tired if you stay up late, and then you will probably get sick with the flu.	Even if you don't get as much sleep as you are used to, you won't get sick if it only happens occasionally.
If you don't take a nap, you will be tired later on and then you will get grouchy.	You know how much better you feel after you have rested.
You always get these headaches when you have so much homework.	I'll bet you could send those headaches away if you stopped worrying so much about your schoolwork.
You always get cramps this time of the month. It's only natural.	I'll bet you could work at not having those cramps by paying less attention to the unpleasant side of having your period.
You need your allergy medicine every day this time of the year.	I'm sure you could send those allergies away with less medicine.
Don't go outside. You are too sick to be running around.	You look fantastic! You are sending those germs away all by yourself. Let's go for a walk together.

Take a look at the attitudes being conveyed to children by the two contrasting approaches to sickness and wellness. If you believe that children have the capacity for maintaining wellness and you reinforce that belief each and every day, then you are helping by eliminating the unnecessary babying that goes with a sickness approach to life. The more you feel sorry for a child, conveying to him that he is sick and must stay immobilized and take medicine, the more you teach him that he has no control over his health, and the more you encourage him to stay sick. His reasoning goes something like this: "I get much more attention when I am sick. They listen to my complaints. They get worried and stop everything else to pay attention to me. They take me to the doctor and buy me medicine. I don't have to go to school. I can lie here and just soak up all this attention. I am really in the limelight. I think I'll opt to hang on to sickness for more of this good stuff called attention." This is actually what is going on in most cases involving "normal" illnesses, and the more attention you provide, the more likely children are to develop and maintain these kinds of sickness attitudes for their entire lives. Study the responses on the right-hand side of the page very carefully. You can stop providing attention for sickness—and, more important, you can help children to stop expecting to become sick. You can get the focus off colds, headaches, the flu, cramps, allergies, asthma, the "cold season," tummy aches, "boo-boos," and the like, and shift to a new approach that reinforces being well and using the body as the healer.

This is what I call a wellness approach to life. It means talking to children as if they have control over what goes on in their bodies. It does not mean being irresponsible and acting as if the child does not have a fever when he does. It means talking to the child and explaining what a fever is, and then saying, "This will go away. You won't feel bad for very long. You can even help it to go away by resting and drinking lots of juice and actually visualizing its being gone." Wellness stems from the supposition that each person has the capacity to send illnesses out of his life, and that a minimal use of medicine is far superior to teaching a child to become addicted to pills and medicines early in life, foregoing his own inner capacity for healing. Wellness stresses the individual's strongly believing that he can stay well, that colds and influenza are not necessary evils, and that being sick is quite unacceptable as a normal state of affairs.

Developing a wellness attitude involves taking a stand against sickness thinking. R. William Whitmer, in *Whitmer's Guide to Total Wellness,* a book I strongly recommend for an in-depth look at this subject, stresses five major points that differentiate wellness from sickness. I present Whitmer's five points and comment briefly on how they pertain to parenting.

1. *"Wellness is taking aggressive, positive action rather than a passive role in dictating and directing your health destiny."* This means that you must help children to become the directors of their own life habits. Reinforce the belief that they do have control over their health. With proper nutrition, a sound approach to regular exercise, and a belief that they can be superhealthy rather than simply without symptoms, they can expect to avoid illness forever. The very expectation that they will not get sick, and the absence of your reinforcement for being sick, will do more for them than anything else in aiding them to be wellness people. This is something that you can help them to cultivate, not only by your own example but by changing your expectations for them. As usual, I will provide you with many specific examples of how to do this toward the end of this chapter.

2. *"Wellness is total comprehension and acceptance of your own responsibility for staying well."* Put the responsibility for staying well on your child, regardless of her age. You do this by saying, "I see you have decided to feel lousy," rather than "It must be that time of the month again." No blame, no guilt—simply helping the child to come to believe that her own health and how she feels each day is basically up to her. You do not want children to think that feeling lousy is "something that is going around," whatever that means, but that it is a choice. The more responsibility they feel for being sick, the more they will be inclined to eliminate sickness from their lives. The mind is a powerful instrument in the healing and health processes, and the more children learn to use the miraculous powers of their minds, the more you will be helping them to grow up on wellness and to live longer.

3. *"Wellness is the systematic recognition and elimination of all your negative lifestyles."* Children can learn that negative lifestyles are choices that contribute to their sickness. Excessive consumption of sweets is something that they should come to see as contributing to a sickness approach to life. Very early you must keep candy away from them or hand it out only on rare occasions, but later on they must understand that it is their teeth they are destroying, their metabolisms that are affected, their headaches that result, and so on. As they grow older they must see that smoking cigarettes is their choice to opt for sickness and not something from which they must refrain because you forbid it. Alcohol and drugs need to be seen as inhibitors to wellness and not as social evils. The emphasis must be on the child's own negative lifestyle and how it impinges on his health rather than on regulations imposed by you. Teach children from the beginning, but beginning right now, that any negative lifestyle action is something which they are choosing. With very young children you obviously just keep them away from negatives that affect their health adversely. They usually do not want them anyway, since they are perfect animals who opt for health instinctively. No child likes the taste of straight Scotch whiskey, yet they all crave the taste of pure spring water. As they grow older and have negative lifestyle habits imposed on them through your habits and beliefs, they soon adopt sickness rather than wellness approaches to life. You can help them by emphasizing wellness at all times, and also by teaching them to avoid making social decisions to have a negative lifestyle at the expense of their own wellness.

4. *"Wellness is a way of life which results in maximum longevity and enhanced quality of life."* A child's life will obviously be improved in direct proportion to the reduced number of hours and days spent being sick. The more children learn from you to rid themselves of attitudes which foster sickness, the more you are helping them to enjoy life each day. They will actually live longer and more productive lives if they learn wellness as very young children. The development of an ulcer is directly related to the amount of worry and stress that a child learns to choose for himself. Learning how not to be a worrier is learning to avoid an illness-oriented life. This is equally true for the minor inconveniences called colds, aches, cramps, feeling awful, and tiredness. The less thinking in this direction, the less expectation to have these inconvenient illnesses, the more improvement in quality of life. The new research on serious illnesses and attitudes suggests that even cancer and heart disease are strongly related to the inner attitudes

toward wellness that a person possesses. Regardless of what the research tells us, we know in our hearts that if we do not think sickly, we are less likely to be that way, and that having the *will* (attitude) to live is a strong indicator of how successfully one will emerge from any serious bout with illness. Knowing this is enough of a reason to help children cultivate wellness beliefs from the earliest possible moments.

5. *"Wellness is feeling better and living longer."* All caring adults want children to feel better rather than worse. By helping them to maintain wellness attitudes as children, you are improving their ability to enjoy life. And if you reexamine what I said in Chapter 1, you will note that what virtually all parents want is for their children to feel better, be happy, and live longer, fuller, more productive lives. Wellness thinking will accomplish just that. But you must give children a shining example of someone who strongly believes in these principles.

How to Model Wellness

More than any other component of no-limit living discussed within the pages of this book, becoming an example of wellness is absolutely crucial if your children are going to come around to this point of view. While I strongly endorse modeling all of the no-limit behaviors, this one stands head and shoulders above the rest as most significant. If you are a sickly thinking person your child will very likely have the same attitudes. If you reinforce their sickness by babying them, and if you think and act sickly yourself, complaining all the time about how terrible you feel and demonstrating hypochondria for them, you will be teaching them—inadvertently, perhaps, but teaching just the same—that they should develop sickness thinking as opposed to wellness thinking.

Make a commitment to yourself to take charge of your own health. This means approaching your health from a wellness point of view and demonstrating to children that you think enough of yourself to make yourself as healthy as you possibly can be. When they see you behaving in these ways and living a wellness life, they will naturally adopt similar attitudes for themselves—or, at the very lesat, they will not have the excuse that "You don't do it, so why should I?" A commitment to wellness for yourself involves thinking of health in a new light. Rather than thinking that everything is all right with you if you have no symptoms of illness, you must shift your emphasis to "How can I get to absolute superhealth for myself and stay there?"

When you think in wellness terms you are not satisfied to simply have an absence of symptoms. You want to be way beyond that point in your life. For example, you might feel just fine normally, but find yourself tired and breathing heavily after walking up two flights of stairs. While you have no symptoms of illness, this is a clear sign that your cardiovascular system is out of shape, you are not exercising sufficiently, your diet may need adjusting, you are probably overweight, and you have work to do on yourself to be at superhealth. Similarly, you may not feel ill but you may find if you take your pulse that your heart rate is excessively high. Your heart may be working two times harder than it ought to. Here again, you have work to do on yourself. It may be difficult to walk briskly for an hour, and you may be able to pinch more than an inch of fat on your body, indicating excessive body fat. Tests may show that your cholesterol level is too high and that you are deficient in vitamins and minerals. Your skin may show symptoms of stress with eczema or psoriasis. You may consume too much alcohol or smoke cigarettes, and you do not need a lecture from me to tell you how bad those substances are for your health.

Adopting wellness thinking for yourself and modeling it for children involves a commitment to your excellence as a human being. It does not require arduous work or painful exercise regimens each day. It does not mean eating seaweed, drinking exotic extracts, and abstaining from everything that feels and tastes good in life. It means simply being as healthy as you possibly can be, and being determined not to allow your wonderful body, the place where your mind currently resides, to deteriorate unnecessarily. Once you make the commitment to the kind of superhealth I am talking about, you will find that it will become a tremendous source of joy. Once your body is as slim and attractive as it can be, you will wonder how you ever allowed it to get so out of shape. Once you start becoming conscious of your diet and nutritional habits, you will be shocked at what you used to put into your body. It all begins with the kind of commitment to wellness that I am presenting in this chapter. That commitment, once in place and carried out on a daily basis, becomes a way of life rather than just another long-range diet and exercise program. And, keeping the purposes of this book in mind, it will rub off on your children in ways in which you never dreamed possible.

Assuming that you want to make a commitment to your own wellness and that you want to model it for your children, how do you go about doing it? The answer is you simply do it, beginning now! You can call a nutrition center and go in for testing and nutritional information if you wish. It could help you a great deal, and the address is in your Yellow Pages. You can consult a physician who specializes in a wellness medical practice or look up the address of your local wellness center in your phone book. Or call your local American Medical Association office and tell them what you are interested in. They will give you the names of wellness practitioners. You can pick up a book on wellness in the library or bookstore. I recommend *Whitmer's Guide to Total Wellness*. You can begin your own regular exercise program with daily objectives if that is your style, but the important thing is to begin to work on yourself right now. You will never be sorry for getting your entire human mechanism into the best shape you have ever been in before. Even if you do not want to do it for yourself, your children demand it from you. It is your responsibility to raise them to stay as healthy as it is possible for them to be. That is your duty as a person who brought a child into this world. It begins with you. The need for wellness in your children is greater than you imagine.

Why Your Children Need Wellness

As you read on about wellness and consider the specific suggestions I offer at the end of this chapter, keep in mind that children need to begin thinking about this approach to their health right now. It is much easier to educate children in this kind of thinking and behaving than it is to get adults to change after they have become set in their ways. While I believe that anyone can change at any time in his life if he is willing to make the daily commitment to his own excellence, it is far better to get in the habit of wellness while young. If your child becomes convinced very early in life to avoid bad health habits and to stay away from a debilitating lifestyle, he or she will remain convinced for a lifetime.

Some of the recent studies on the absence of wellness thinking in young people point out that almost half of all nineteen-year-olds are moderate to heavy drinkers. Teenagers become alcoholics much more readily than do adults, and it is not at all unusual for teenagers to become confirmed alcoholics six months after their first drink. In other studies it is reported that 25 percent of children of smoking parents are themselves smoking regularly by the age of eight. Moreover, one-fourth of the children in our country in grades one through seven are obese. Many studies indicate that young people have no regular exercise habits and that cholesterol levels of children who eat junk food on a regular basis are causing premature heart problems in as many as 40 percent of our young people. The statistics can go on and on, but the message needs to be brought home clearly to you. You may be the finest parent in the world. You may be teaching your children to have high self-esteem, to live fully, to be free from gulit and worry, to develop a strong sense of purpose and an appreciation for the highest values of humanity, and still be doing them a large disservice if you are not tuned in to a wellness approach to their upbringing. The strongest mind will still succumb to a body that is diseased and not treated properly. You need a strong house to store that beautiful mind of yours, and so do your children. Hopefully our schools will begin to see the need for teaching wellness thinking right along with the three R's and self-control.

Children need to be brought up on wellness. Take a look at the bodies you see the next time you are on the beach. Notice how many of them have excess fat, are slouched over in poor posture, and are consuming poisons in the form of alcohol and cigarettes. You do not want your children to grow up developing such sloppy habits about their perfect creations called human bodies. You can literally transform them into models of wellness if you believe that it is important. While I have not included all of the medical data on how wellness affects such body parts as the heart, liver, pancreas, stomach, lungs, bladder, intestines, and so on, the evidence is available if you care to examine it. Dr. Herbert Benson, writing in *The Mind/Body Effect,* provides ample evidence for the connection between how you think and a physically healthy body. Dr. John Harrison, writing in a new book called *Love Your*

Disease, puts it this way, "Those people who are generally happy to be themselves and who satisfactorily resolve childhood conflicts, WILL BE HEALTHY." The growing body of evidence that supports a wellness approach to life as a tool to being a happier, more productive, and less neurotic individual is available for you to examine. It is not my purpose to provide extensive research data, but only to help you to adopt a new approach to your health and the health of your children, and to inform you that the research is out there in the literature if you care to study the matter. I am writing about this subject because I believe it to be extremely crucial to becoming a no-limit person.

Some years ago I was thirty pounds overweight, living on a diet that was a nutritionist's nightmare, and totally unaware of what the word *wellness* meant. I turned my life around—began a regular approach to exercise, began walking almost everywhere every day rather than driving to the store for a loaf of bread, took up vitamin therapy and became aware of my nutritional intake—and I can honestly say that I have never felt better in my life. My weight has stayed down around 170 pound (I am six feet, two inches tall), and I run eight to ten miles each day and walk another five or six. I have eliminated most sugar and salt from my diet, and yet I still enjoy every meal I eat. Exercising is not a task for me; it is simply a way of life. I never tell myself that I am too busy to run or walk. Instead I say I am too busy to get sick, so I must take time for exercising. I have not had a cold in eight years, the flu season seems to pass me by now, and fatigue is a thing of the past in my life. I cannot imagine going back to being overweight, smoking, and being tired. I have forgotten how to have colds, and I cannot imagine returning to them ever again in my life. But the most important payoff for me has been the impact that my wellness attitude has had on other people in my life, particularly my children. When they see me exercising each day and taking the time to go for a run, they too want to take up exercise. Even the little ones emulate Mommy and Daddy exercising. My children have become more aware of the importance of good food and solid nutritional habits because I have adopted these habits for myself. The junk food is out of the house, so they naturally reach for a plum or an apple instead.

If you get your wellness act together, everyone you love will benefit, especially your children. Those are essential reasons for doing it: first, because it benefits you, and you must take good care of yourself since no one else can do it for you, and then for the spin-off value that it will have for your children. You owe them no less than teaching them to be well for the rest of their lives. Dr. Harrison tells us in *Loving Your Disease* that "Predispositions to disease are often not passed on in a physical sense but rather through the messages parents give their offspring and the living habits and diet they pass down." Keep this in mind as you read on about this new way to view health and how it pertains to the raising of your children. The living habits are what you have control over. You can pass down a legacy of wellness if you think more positively about these habits, and make that all-important commitment to wellness that is crucial for you and everyone in your family.

The obvious elements of wellness that all medical practitioners consider include diet and nutrition, exercise and physical fitness, eliminating negative lifestyle habits (smoking, excessive alcohol, drugs, and the like), and becoming aware of what one does for one's body. But an equally important area of wellness revolves around two attitudinal elements that will help children as much as the more obvious physical components just mentioned. These include the ability to use visualization in their approach to being healthy and the importance of having a sense of humor and being able to laugh regularly. To me, these are just as significant as their diet and exercise habits.

Using Visualization for Wellness

I have discussed positive imagery and visualization earlier in this book, particularly as they pertain to helping your child to develop a strong mental picture of a worthwhile, capable, attractive, human being. The use of mental imagery is one of the strongest and most effective strategies for making something happen for yourself and for children. The more you can help a child to actually have a mental movie in her head about what she would like, and then act as if that picture were in fact a reality, the more it becomes impossible not to have the image become a reality.

The practice of imagery is particularly useful in helping everyone, including children, to think in wellness terms for the rest of their lives. A picture in your mind of you being as superhealthy as it is possible for you to be is just as useful to you as a strong exercise regimen and a balanced nutrition program. In fact it is more significant. The picture in your mind's eye is the one thing that will automatically force you into a wellness approach to life. Store away a picture of yourself as healthy, trim, internally perfect, attractive, highly energized, and powerful, and that image will soon become your reality. You cannot help it. The image gets stored away in your robotlike subconscious (your inner mirror, if you will) in precisely the same manner as your external picture in the mirror. The more you visualize yourself in the way that you want to be, the more you will begin acting in the ways that will bring about the picture you have stored away. It is a law of the universe. Albert Einstein put it this way: "Imagination is more important than knowledge, for knowledge is limited, while imagination embraces the entire world."

Using creative visualization is nothing more than putting your imagination to work for you to help you to achieve what you want. In wellness thinking, it is simply picturing yourself as healthy and never wavering from the image. With children, it is helping them keep those images of healthy wellness always uppermost in their minds and never permitting them to believe that they are less than superhealthy or at least capable of being as healthy as they want to be. Shakti Gawain, whose book *Creative Visualization* is the clearest writing I have seen on this subject, says this about the process of visualization for wellness:

> Imagination is the ability to create an idea or mental picture in your mind. In creative visualization use your imagination to create a clear image of something you wish to manifest. Then you continue to focus on the idea or picture regularly, giving it positive energy until it becomes objective reality . . . in other words, until you actually achieve what you have been visualizing.

This business of visualization and imagery may be foreign to you, and in fact you may be quite skeptical about putting such a theory into practice for yourself. I too had many reservations many years ago about simply using mental imagery to make something happen for myself. I must say right here that I am no longer a skeptic. I know that when I practice with images I can improve any skill I want. I have taught myself to hit a backhand in tennis through mental imagery. I have visualized myself before an audience, being alert and sharp and having a wonderful time with everyone, and it always works out that way for me when I do it. I have visualized myself without lingering colds, actually creating a picture of the cold disappearing and never permitting it to get a foothold, and for me it works. Let me share one exciting experiment devised by Dr. O. Carl Simonton, a cancer specialist who has written a great deal on how thought processes can alter the progress of cancer growth in the human body. He would actually show slides of how cancer cells operate in the body to large groups of cancer patients. He demonstrated how cancer cells would gang up on healthy cells and defeat the healthy cells. Then he showed a dramatization of how healthy cells work against cancer cells. He then instructed his patients to visualize their healthy cells working to defeat the cancer cells, rather than vice versa. I am presenting here only a sketchy view of his remarkable experimentation, but he reports significant remission rates among people who actually use this visualization process. This is wellness thinking at work in the research laboratory, and it is becoming a more and more viable strategy for treating people with serious illnesses. Norman Cousins' inspiring best-seller of a few years ago, *Anatomy of an Illness*, clearly demonstrates the powers of the mind and visualization in curing what used to be thought of as incurable diseases. I recommend it strongly.

If imagery and visualization can be used successfully in the treatment of serious illnesses (and there is much evidence to support this belief), then it seems evident that this same process can be used in the *prevention* of illness, and in making people more conscious of their own capacity for achieving high-level wellness. Think about the pictures your children have of themselves as healthy, capable human beings. Think about all the ways that they have come to view themselves in sickness terms, and exactly what kinds of pictures they have in their heads regarding their own abilities to be superhealthy. Think also about the ways in which you may have encouraged them to have sickness rather than wellness images. Then open yourself up to the possibility of turning those sickness pictures into images of pure wellness.

Even if you are skeptical, read the last sections of this chapter with an open mind. In the pages that follow I will be offering some specific alternatives to sickness thinking. Along with visualization, I would also like you to consider laughter and a sense of humor as a potential magnet to attract a wellness attitude for you and your children. Yes, laughter may be one of the most powerful tools you have for this purpose, and it may have escaped your attention until now.

Wellness and a Sense of Humor

People like to laugh! We all need to laugh! Yes, I said *need* to laugh. Maintaining a sour attitude is one way to ensure that your body will stay in a constant state of disrepair. Notice children when they are playing with other children. Take note of how much laughter and silliness goes on. It is instinctive and necessary for their well-being, both physically and emotionally. Ask children who their favorite teacher is, and almost always they will tell you about someone who has a sense of humor, who can laugh and take classroom life a little less seriously. If you are a person who takes life seriously, who seldom laughs and who cannot have fun with your children on their level, very likely you are adversely affecting their physical health to a greater extent than you realize.

Laughter is a healer. We are discovering this over and over again in medical treatment today. Norman Cousins' famous *Anatomy of an Illness* illustrates how a prescribed dosage of humor and heavy laughter each day actually became a part of his treatment for a disease that was considered fatal. He tells us:

> It worked. I made the joyous discovery that ten minutes of genuine belly laughter had an anesthetic effect and would give me at least two hours of pain-free sleep. . . . I was greatly elated by the discovery that there is a physiologic basis for the ancient theory that laughter is good medicine.

When children laugh they are actually releasing into their bloodstreams chemicals which are necessary for the prevention and cure of disease. When they go through life believing that everything is serious, that one should not laugh but instead keep his nose to the grindstone, they are not only enjoying life less but contributing to their own physical letdown as well.

Assist children in sustaining their natural inclination to laugh and have fun. You can tease with them and allow them to play a joke on you rather than ignoring their efforts to be funny. You know how much they like to ''get'' you when they play ''knock knock'' with you, and how much they laugh when you pretend that you have never heard their answer before. You know how much fun it is for them to hide and have you pretend that you cannot see them, and then jump when they ''scare'' you by suddenly lunging at you from behind a curtain. You know how they love to tease you and make believe that they are going to splash you. You know how they love to wrestle and punch and play hard, and laugh when they get the opportunity to show you how strong they are. All of this laughter and fun is necessary to keep them in their own wellness category. A child who laughs and has a sense of humor, who lives in a household where laughter is frequent, and who can laugh at himself, has a much better chance at total wellness. Create that kind of environment by not taking yourself too seriously and by making a deliberate attempt to bring more laughter to your household.

E. T. (''Cy'') Eberhart, a certified hospital chaplain in Salem, Oregon, has been successfully using humor on hospital patients for five years. ''A sense of humor prevents us from becoming tragic figures,'' he says. ''That is, it keeps us from becoming wrapped up in the tragic side of life, concentrating too deeply on misfortune.'' Dr. Rufus C. Browing, a psychologist in Silver Spring, Maryland, tells us, ''It helps us get over the worst in our existence. And that makes it an ally worth cultivating—by consciously looking for the inanities in life, the crazy contradictions, the jolly aspects of everyday situations.''

These are words to remember when you decide to raise children on wellness. Be a little crazy, act nutty now and then, laugh as much as you possibly can, and by all means, do it with your children each and every day. Play their games. Be a ''monster,'' let them scare you, chase them around the yard, toss them in the air and generally have a ball with your children. Even if you think it is contrary to your nature, try to change your nature instead of giving in to a sourpuss approach to life. You know it is good for them, and you know how much better you feel when you laugh, so make it your commitment to help them to have as many laughs as they possibly can. Each genuine belly laugh, each time you hear them really laughing hard, means they are helping themselves to be more physically sound. It is wellness in action, and it is the cheapest and easiest medicine you can administer.

Children who have not been encouraged to develop a sense of humor, to laugh at themselves and at life, often are uncomfortable with humor, silliness, or teasing. They do not have the ability to help others to laugh, and quite often they are the ones who do not get the joke. They tend to sarcasm with remarks that degrade or insult and exhibit anger whenever the joke is on them. Look carefully at this ability to create laughter and to poke fun at oneself and the absurdities of life. Children who cannot appreciate humor, or seem to be immune to it, are often candidates for more sickness than they ought to experience in life. The person who is laughing cannot be upset or growing an ulcer at the same time. Laughter and fun are the most natural of human actions. Play and fun are ways of learning interaction and physical skills. Using limericks and puns and punch lines creates a complicated playtime for the mind, and helps children to unravel the complexities of our language.

Developing a sense of humor and experiencing laughter and fun through playing and teasing is a powerful force for uniting you with your children in a bond of love that transcends the more serious approach to life. Basically children want to be teased if they are allowed to tease back. It makes for a fun life, and it helps them to think and behave in ways which contribute to their own wellness. Do not underestimate the value of this often overlooked parental responsibility of helping your children develop an ability to laugh a lot in life, to see the fun side of everything, and to be a little crazy now and then. When I finished some work in a mental institution with a group of people who had been labeled zany, they all got together and presented me with a gift. Their spokesman told me, "We like you better than the other doctors." When I asked why, I received one of my greatest compliments in life. "Well," she said, "you're more like one of us."

This, then, is wellness simplified. It is the cultivation of an attitude toward health that takes the emphasis off sickness and puts it where it belongs: on the opposite of sickness—that is, wellness. This attitude embraces new approaches toward nutrition, exercise, fatigue, negative lifestyle habits, and everything that affects physical health. It embraces visualization, positive affirmations, laughter, and a wellness attitude toward everything in life. Yet it is nothing new. Ancient peoples practiced these approaches to life, but somehow they have gotten lost in our contemporary world. The literature on the subject of wellness is growing every day. You can be a part of this renaissance, but before you join the movement, you must be aware of the little ways in which wellness is discouraged in you and your children. The next two sections describe some of the more common anti-wellness positions that you may have been taking, along with the payoffs you receive for acting in those ways. Once you review them you can begin to use some of the suggested strategies for getting on with a total holistic wellness approach to the raising of your children.

Some Common Anti-Wellness Parental Actions

Here is a list of some of the typical things we often do with and to children which encourage a sickness rather than a wellness approach to living.

□ Expecting your children's illnesses to get progressively worse and telling them so with warnings.

□ Raising children to think sick and to be wary of life.

□ Providing children with negative affirmations such as "Life is suffering," "Sickness is a part of life," "Something is going around and you will catch it," "You are frail so you have to be extra cautious," "Everybody carries disease germs so stay away from people."

□ Taking a child to the doctor for every complaint and dispensing pills and medicine as a regular part of life.

□ Teaching children to accept a flabby lifestyle by modeling the same.

□ Not using preventive techniques to ensure the health of your child.

□ Staying uninformed about nutrition and positive lifestyle advances.

□ Being an excessive drinker and smoker.

□ Refusing to discuss certain issues—such as drug usage, abortion, or birth control—because they are simply taboo subjects in your home.

□ Making life a serious enterprise and always insisting that children remember their place. Believing that life is work, not fun.

□ Watching television and sitting around as your main source of activity.

□ Being a complainer about your own health. Talking about your aches and pains as a way of life.

□ Accepting your children's illnesses and giving them reinforcement and attention for being sick.

□ Filling your home with junk food and dispensing it regularly to your children.

□ Excusing your children and yourself for being out of shape. "We are too busy. We have no time to exercise."

□ Putting too much emphasis on eating and mealtimes.

□ Giving a child a label of sickly, overweight, low energy, a thinker rather than a doer, an endomorph, a Leo or Capricorn, as an excuse for poor health.

□ Encouraging children to miss school for minor ailments and giving them the baby treatment when they have a complaint.

□ Telling a child to take it easy whenever he or she has an ailment.

□ Staying uninformed about fats, proteins, carbohydrates, salt, sugar, cholesterol, fiber, hypertension, caffeine, vitamins, and everything having to do with healthy living in general.

These are some of the more prevalent anti-wellness stances that are common to parents. Whatever the age of your children, you can reverse the anti-wellness stand you may have inadvertently taken by first coming to an understanding of why you continue to parent in these ways, and then systematically making a commitment to a new wellness campaign with your children.

Your Support System for Not Promoting Wellness

Here are the most common payoffs you receive for ignoring wellness in your parenting responsibilities. While you obviously do not deliberately set out to keep children from attaining and maintaining superhealth, you do receive some rewards for avoiding a total wellness approach to child rearing. Keep in mind that if you did not receive some payoff you would not allow anything other than total wellness to be your style. When you eliminate the "neurotic" reward system, you eliminate the need to stay as you are in a way that is self-defeating for your children and for yourself as well.

Let's face it—it is easier to sit down and do nothing than it is to get up and be active. This is the number one payoff for maintaining a non-wellness approach to life. It is just plain easier. Easier to give them anything to eat rather than to learn about the benefits of consuming healthier food. Easier to take a nap than to get out and exercise with the children. Easier to light up a cigarette than to take a stand against poisoning your body. A sickness approach to life is a lazy approach, and opting for the easier method keeps you from having to do something that requires more effort. You simply do not know how great it is to be on total wellness, so you fool yourself by staying with the only method you have known until now.

If it was good enough for you and your parents, then it is good enough for your children as well. This is a terrific excuse to keep you off the wellness path. Never mind that your parents may have had far more illness than they needed, never mind that you may be out of shape and feeling poorly—you can still say that you do not need these newfangled ideas and that you are going to opt for tradition rather than anything new.

It's too complicated to figure out all this wellness stuff. Who wants to count calories, become concerned about fiber and cholesterol, think about exercising, and learn about glycogens and glucose? Just give me a cheeseburger and a soft drink and I'll be fine. And order one for my kid, too—he loves those greasy shiny buns with his cheeseburger.

I don't want to have to think health all the time: I have too much to do already without having to be concerned about my body and the superhealth of my kids. If I eat the wrong foods, I'd rather die a few years early than worry about my diet for the rest of my life. Besides, those health experts drop dead, too, so who knows what is the right thing to do.

There is too much conflicting information to take any of this wellness stuff too seriously. One day you eat only kelp; the next day it causes cancer. One day you're supposed to jog; the next day it will kill you. I'll stick with what I like and let the good Lord decide my fate.

I enjoy smoking and drinking and even being a little bit overweight. I think all those health experts look like walking cadavers. I'll take my smoke and my booze and leave the wellness crap for others who look like they belong in a cemetery anyhow. If I have to give up everything that feels good, life won't be worth living.

You can't help getting sick occasionally. It's only natural. There's no need to get all excited about a little illness now and then.

I'm too old to change now. If my kids want to be superhealthy let them go for it, but I'm staying with what I've grown accustomed to all these years.

There they are. The reasons, payoffs, psychological support system—or *excuses,* as I call them. Choosing a sickness approach to life definitely has its rewards, and if you are choosing this kind of lifestyle, I am quite sure that you saw some of your own statements in the preceding inventory of excuses.

If you would really like to change your sickness thinking, and if you want your children to have a wellness approach to life, then try out some of the strategies and suggestions offered in the following list.

Some Techniques for Implementing Wellness in Your Child Rearing

Teach children, through your own behavior toward them, to expect to be well rather than ill. When they have anything "wrong" with them—such as a cold, fever, ache, or bruise—say out loud directly to them, ''This thing will be gone in no time'' or ''You aren't really sick; you've just allowed this thing to take hold of you for a few hours'' or ''I know you can get rid of this little thing in a really short time if you don't keep thinking about it.'' Use words that convey your belief in the child's ability to send away infirmities. You can teach little children not to expect to be sick for very long by always talking to them about how strong and healthy they are, and how much power they have over their bodies. ''You are such a big girl now. You don't get sick when all the other kids do. That's because you are healthy and strong.'' ''You don't want that cold to last, and you're so terrific that you'll probably have it gone by this afternoon.'' With older children, teach them to expect their physical ailments to improve rather than to get worse. For example:

Sickness Attitudes	Wellness Attitudes
This cold is in my nose now, but by tomorrow it will be in my throat.	I can send this cold away before it even thinks about spreading.
I only got four hours' sleep. I'll really be tired today.	I'll sleep later. Now I've got work to do, and I refuse to think about being tired.
I feel like I'm going to catch something—it's just a feeling I have.	I don't care if everyone else is getting sick—it's not going to get me.
I'll just have to wait for this fever to run its course.	I expect this thing to be gone really soon. I'll rest and make sure that I don't have it tomorrow. I'll feel better before I know it.
With this twisted ankle I'll be tied up with crutches for at least six weeks.	I'm going to try to get off these crutches as fast as possible. I think I can have my ankle better really fast.
It takes months to recover from these kinds of injuries.	I refuse to be tied up for months with this. I know I can be back to normal in no time at all. I'm really going to work at my own recovery.

These are the attitudes of expectations that you want to convey to children, regardless of their ages. Have them think well—but, most important, have them expect to *be* well, rather than ill.

Do not reward illness; instead, praise wellness. Just as I suggested that you look for children to do something right and then give them praise, the same holds true for wellness. Catch them being well and give them plenty of praise for it. Do not make illness something that you positively reward, unless you want them to seek out illness. If they know they are going to get presents when they are sick and be showered with affection only then, you can expect them to want to be sick a great deal. After all, the rewards are nice. Instead, take a new approach and discourage illness in favor of encouraging wellness. When they are sick, give the illness as little attention as possible other than to provide remedial medical care. But praise wellness. "You are the healthiest kid in the city!" "You are the only one who never has to be sick when everyone else is, so here is a present I brought for you just because you are such a good example for everyone else." "I can't believe how terrific you are! You must be so healthy because you seldom get sick like the other kids. Let's go to the park today and celebrate how strong you are by having a picnic together." "You didn't complain about hitting your head and scraping yourself. You are some terrific kid, I'll tell you." In other words, take the opportunity to praise them for being strong and well, and minimize the attention you give to sickness.

Give children ammunition within themselves to believe in their abilities to do anything in life when it comes to wellness. Talk to children about how strong they are and what their bodies can do. Show them how their own bodies heal a cut, and what a scar represents in the healing process. Allow them to grow up believing in themselves and their own abilities to heal themselves, rather than to think that the world is a place to be wary of, a place where they can catch diseases all the time. Reinforce within them that they are strong, that their bodies are magnificent and perfect creations that have superb powers for achieving and maintaining wellness, and that they need not be sickly. Give them a set of beliefs about their own health and their bodies which encompasses wellness doctrines rather than sickness dogma. "I can avoid illness" rather than "Illness is inevitable." "My body is a healing genius" rather than "My illnesses always linger on." Help them to cultivate an attitude of wellness and a strong belief in their own bodies as perfect healing machines. Teach them to respect their bodies' abilities rather than to doubt them. Any suspicion or fear that they possess about their own health or the frailty of their bodies will be a detriment to their wellness. Believing that sickness is inevitable is tantamount to having a sickly life. Conversely, believing that wellness is inevitable is equivalent to having a healthy life. The belief system is much more influential than you might have imagined. Do not let children blame the disease for their troubles; let them believe in their abilities not to have disease immobilize them.

Teach children about the importance of positive affirmations in their lives. An affirmation is nothing more than a statement of belief about how things are. Negative affirmations bring about negative results, while positive affirmations tend to help people to healthy results. Teach children to say:

"I am strong and healthy."

"I have a perfect healing machine in my body."

"I believe in health, not illness."

"I know I can stay healthy even if others around me are getting sick."

"I have a lot to offer, and I refuse to let illness get in my way."

"I am willing to be happy and healthy."

"The world is a beautiful place."

"I am growing more and more healthy each day."

"I don't need to be sick in order to get attention."

"I don't have to please everyone else. I believe in my own abilities."

These are called positive affirmations, and they work! By saying these things to yourself and teaching your children to positively affirm their own unique wellness, you are taking a step toward giving each of you the *will* to live a wellness life. The will to live is extremely important for a patient facing major surgery—just ask any surgeon. This same will is crucial in helping children to live well so that they might avoid illness and even possibly avoid that major surgery forever.

By all means utilize the benefits of modern medicine when necessary. Taking an antibiotic to halt a disease process that has taken hold makes a great deal of sense to me. Do not overdo the emphasis on medicines and doctor visits to the point where they become crutches and unnecessary habits. Try to resist using medicine for everyday aches and pains that really are inconveniences rather than illnesses. Try resisting a trip to the doctor for every little ache and pain. The more trips you take to the doctor with your children, the more you teach them that "the doctor makes you well." In fact, you have probably said these very words to your children. Teach them to take more responsibility for their own wellness, rather than to believe that there is a pill for every complaint and that a doctor visit is part of every cure. Use good sense in determining if your child genuinely needs medical assistance, but use good sense as well in determining if he or she doesn't need it.

If your physician is not a practitioner of wellness then talk to him about it. If you feel that you are participating in a sickness approach to children's health, then say so. If prescription drugs are being recommended all the time, and your doctor believes that all illnesses are unavoidable, then think seriously about looking for a doctor who practices medicine from a wellness point of view. There are many fine physicians, and many dentists also, who have wellness approaches to their practices. In dentistry, the emphasis is now on preventive treatment. Teach your children to avoid cavities by practicing healthy oral hygiene habits. Teach them about what they are eating, plaque, fluoride, flossing their teeth, and the like. The dentist's office is now a place you go to primarily for the prevention of dental disease, and only incidentally to fix up what damage has occurred. So too should your physician's office be a place that is primarily wellness oriented, and prevention rather than administering drugs for treatment ought to be the major focus. I recommend that you seek out a physician who subscribes to a wellness approach to life. If you cannot find one, then search for your nearest wellness center and get recommendations. A doctor can be the most important person in influencing a child to believe in her own unique ability to be healthy. If your physician is overweight, a smoker, unwilling to talk to you, or doing anything that violates your precepts of wellness, then be skeptical and seek a doctor who meets your expectations about health. More and more physicians are beginning to practice from the wellness perspective, and you want one who reinforces the ideas of being well and preventing illness rather than one who works from the opposite philosophy.

Get your own act together regarding your health. Provide children with a model of a person who takes care of his body and thinks wellness rather than illness. Show them that you are sincere by being what it is you are asking of them. Set aside time each day for exercise, preferably with your children if at all possible. Practice wellness together! Make a commitment to get rid of any excess weight you may be carrying around. Talk to your children about your own health and show them each and every day that you are a person who is practicing what you are preaching. Children will be exceedingly proud of your discipline and commitment to your health. They like to brag to their friends about how terrific someone they love looks and how that person stays in shape. Then, when you are encouraging them to be healthy, they won't be able to look at you and say, "Why should I listen to you? You can't even take care of yourself." If you are a smoker, make a challenge of quitting and provide your children with an example of someone who is stronger than a nicotine habit. As with everything in relating to children, the more you can provide them with a real live example, the more authentic you become in their eyes. In addition, you are giving them a daily reinforcer for wellness, rather than providing them with excuses. Regardless of your age or your daily responsibilities, a flabby lifestyle is inexcusable. All of your reasons for being out of shape are nothing but excuses you make to yourself. It is a habit to be flabby and out of shape, and it is a habit to be as well and physically fit as you can be. And habits come from the choices you make each day and nothing more.

Make an effort to learn more about proper nutrition. Lendon Smith's *Feed Your Kids Right* and Adele Davis' *Let's Have Healthy Children* are excellent sources, along with many fine nutritional guides available in any health food store. Become informed about what you are putting in your body and the bodies of your children. Talk to them about the effects of sugar, salt, minerals, vitamins, carbohydrates, cholesterol, and everything else. Take the opportunity to have an analysis of how diet affects the personalities of you and your children. Any nutrition center will be happy to give you the necessary information. Get the junk food out of your home. Period! Simply refuse to buy food that you know is lacking in nutritional benefit. You owe your children at least that. Even if they crave junk foods, do not have them in your home. Soon they will be reaching for an apple instead of a candy bar. Get the soda pop out of your house and teach children to drink water. Water is a great cleanser of the body, and children who are given water when they are very young drink it regularly throughout their lives. Even your teenagers who eat junk and drink soda pop will change gradually if you provide them with cold fresh water and healthy foods, and eliminate the junk from your refrigerator. Even if you know nothing about nutrition you can take this moment to begin getting informed. You will be surprised at how fascinating the entire area is when you begin learning about it, and your new knowledge will automatically result in better eating habits for everyone. Once you become more informed, you will wonder how you ever permitted those bad habits to creep into your life, and your children will be forever thankful to you. If they do not say thank you right away, their healthy bodies will say it for them.

Have open-ended discussion sessions with your children at specific times of the day to discuss any topic they want. Bring up subjects that are of interest to them, and listen to their views regardless of how silly they may sound. A child who knows that he can talk about anything with you is one who becomes better informed and who builds up trust in you as well. Any subject that your child wants to know about ought to be fertile territory for discussion. Sex, abortion, birth control, drugs, and anything else that may crop up. If you are uninformed, seek the answers together from other resources. The child who knows that he can go directly to someone who will not shy away from these subjects develops a healthy, honest attitude about everything which is of interest to him. Wellness means being informed and having a healthy body as well as a healthy mind. The uninformed mind is not at all well; in fact, it is the basis for prejudice and misinformation. Look at the word *prejudice*. It means to prejudge. When you prejudge you are making a decision about something before you have enough data on which to base a conclusion. You do not want your children to prejudge anyone or anything. A prejudged attitude about sensitive subjects teaches a different kind of illness from a runny nose or a bellyache; it promotes mind illness. Remember, wellness is of the body and the mind, and raising children on wellness means that you encourage them to discuss anything and everything without fear of you prejudging them for wanting to know about things which you are uncomfortable discussing openly. If you make your home the place where they go to talk about these areas, then they will not have to sneak around learning misinformation from other uninformed children. A wellness mind is one which is open to everything. The more they talk about and feel free to express their views with you, the more you are promoting a wellness of the mind, which is just as important as a wellness of the body.

Take the seriousness out of life with your children for at least part of every day. Put more emphasis on having fun, playing games, just being together, and enjoying life, rather than constantly working, working, working. A child who is being raised on wellness is one who is encouraged to laugh a lot, who can tease and play and include his parents in the fun as well. He does not fear you, but instead respects you and comes to you as someone with whom to enjoy life, as well as someone to answer his questions. The more your offspring feel as if you are able to understand them, as if you are someone who knows what they are going through, someone who can laugh at their silly mistakes and not take everything so seriously, the more they will be growing up on wellness.

Virtually anything in life can be made into fun with the proper attitude. But a child who believes that his place is to stay quiet, to stop asking questions, and to work hard toward some future time when he will finally be able to assume his right place as a real person, is someone who is going to be phony around you and only give you what he knows you expect from him. He will fear being authentic because he will know that he is violating his assigned place in your eyes, so he will give you what he thinks you want him to be. If deep inside he feels scared about asking a girl for a date, but he knows that you do not believe he should ever be frightened, he will pretend to be brave around you. If she is worried about how far she should go with her new boyfriend, but she knows that you disapprove of such goings-on altogether, she will simply avoid that topic and be artificial around you. Children must know at all ages that you can discuss these topics with them, that you have been there yourself and you know how they feel, that you are not going to chastise them, or judge them to be something less, simply because they express themselves honestly around you. Wellness means loosening up and never judging your children; it means an open environment in which your children trust you not to make it impossible for them to be genuine. Give them this environment, and your reward will be wellness along with a closer relationship.

Make an effort to limit the amount of time your children sit in front of a television, without adopting strict authoritarian rules on the subject. Make it your own personal goal to use the television as a source of entertainment and education, but not as a babysitter for your children. Television offers a great deal of positive value; however, it also continuously reinforces many negative values simultaneously. Continuous watching of television programs and commercials reinforces smart-alecky behavior (virtually all situation comedies use sarcasm and wisecracking as their basis for humor) and conveys the idea that being empty-headed and having a jiggly body is what women are about, that pleasing others and achieving status are the primary purposes in life, and that happiness and success are external qualities that one purchases. Moreover, the continuous watching of television keeps you from interacting with your children, which is the primary reason to shut it off more frequently and be with them in the ways I recommend throughout the pages of this book. When you turn off the television set, or even better, when you provide alternatives, the children will ultimately turn it off themselves. Give children the opportunity to try new things, to create new friends, to take charge of their world, and to develop their minds and bodies in the wellness fashion being recommended in this chapter. The less time they spend sitting and being entertained by others, the more time they will have for taking responsibility for their own health and happiness. It is easier to get flabby and disinterested in life in front of a television set, so try to limit that input as much as possible.

Stop talking about your aches and pains in front of your children, and learn to suffer quietly if you have chosen to suffer at all. Simply refuse to tell children how poorly you feel for one day. Give it a try. If you start to complain, simply stop and keep it to yourself. Often your pains are there because you want something to complain about, and when you take away the verbalizing you take away the reason for the pain. But, more important for your children, you will be showing them that you are not someone who uses up present moments feeling poorly, which will give them a model of how to act themselves. Feeling bad is often nothing more than a verbal habit. When someone asks you how you feel, try to reply, "Great, fantastic—never felt better!" Even if it is not 100 percent true, forget about telling others that you don't feel well, and before long, feeling well will become a habit, replacing the complaining habit. When children regularly complain about how they feel, it is because you have either given them an example of someone who does the same thing, or have been willing to listen and commiserate with them over their poor feelings. Minimize this kind of interaction and complaining, and you will be helping them to live on wellness each and every day.

Do not accept excuses from children for their being out of shape, overweight, or anything else which you know they can control quite readily. Refuse to go along with them when they say they do not have time to exercise. Reply firmly but lovingly, "You have chosen to be overweight, and I don't buy those excuses. You may want to fool you, but I want you to know that I can see right through those excuses. I can't force you to shape up, but I'd like to help you if you're willing to stop making excuses." This kind of talk will be respected by a child, even though she may create a scene and complain that you just don't understand. They want you to show the kind of interest that the above statement implies. They want you to come down hard on them and help them to adopt the self-discipline to be healthy. They may not admit it, but when they do get in shape, feel fit, look terrific, and feel better each day, they will thank you a million times over for being so helpful and concerned. If you love your children, do not let them bulldoze you with any song and dance that will keep them off the wellness cycle in life.

Take the pressure off mealtimes and make them more joyous occasions. Stop fretting about every meal and worrying about whether the children eat enough. They have perfect bodies that will generally eat plenty, and enough of the proper foods if that is what is provided. If they do not feel like eating, then do not force them. If they only want a few bites and then feel full, don't worry about getting so much bulk into their bodies. The human body is an amazingly perfect creation that knows how to stay fit. Little children know instinctively not to eat things they dislike, not to stuff themselves, and not to eat simply because someone else has decided that it is mealtime. Provide plenty of good food in the house and let them decide on their own portions. If they are finicky about their eating habits as they grow older, then let them prepare their own food and forget about having to have a special mealtime when everyone must eat. You do not have to be a cooking servant for each of your children. As they grow up it can become increasingly difficult to have everyone eat at the same time. With varying schedules and individual growth rates, some are hungry all of the time, while others hardly feel like eating. Make eating a natural experience, rather than a forced feeding time characterized by arguing about what and when to eat. The more you take the pressure off, the more likely they will enjoy mealtimes. The less pressure there will be on you as well. If you believe in no dessert if one does not eat the veggies, then simply state it, live by it, and do not get into a baited argument about it. Be lovingly firm and mealtimes can be great times for all.

Teach children to be tough inside and out when it comes to illness. Going to school with a terrible runny nose or an obvious case of influenza is not fair to anyone concerned, including the other children at school, but staying home every time they feel like they are coming down with something is a weakling approach to wellness. Being active is one way to get rid of impending sickness. Forgetting about it, refusing to give in to it, and staying resilient and busy are very often the ways that a young person can banish sickness before it even has a chance to take hold in the body. Teach children to be tough on themselves rather than to always give in to a minor ailment. Encourage them to try going to school or to work even if they do feel poorly. Tell them that they will probably feel better once they get going with life. The mere suggestion of probably feeling better will give them the spunk they need to fight their minor infirmities. Do not be the ''big ear'' parent who listens to every complaint and then dispenses pity for your ''poor little babies who don't feel so well today." Respond with "I know you'll feel better soon. Give it a try, and if you honestly feel that you absolutely can't function in school, then come home and rest." If they do opt for illness, then do not let them party and play all day as a reward for giving in to their illness. If they must stay home, then let them stay in bed and rest, and not be rewarded for being sick. Always make the rewards for wellness, not sickness, and you will eventually see children who want to be well much more than they opt for illness.

Talk to children about visualizing themselves as healthy when they are not feeling well. Encourage the child to actually see himself as active, healthy, feeling well, and on his way toward the perfection that is his body. When he is old enough to understand, talk to him about the connection between his mind and his body, and be specific about asking him to form mental pictures of a healthy body and mind. In *Creative Visualization,* Shakti Gawain offers this bit of wisdom regarding being healthy: "The body is continuously changing, replenishing, and rebuilding itself at every moment and it has no other pattern to follow in doing so except the guidance to it by the mind." Teach your child that the illness she is experiencing at any given moment is simply a powerful and useful signal to look more deeply at what is being done inappropriately to the body to make it malfunction. If children grow up believing that they can visualize healthy pictures and that their minds are capable of healing, they will be on the wellness road. If you emphasize always that healing comes from within, they will have a handle on eliminating illnesses before they even get started.

Try to eliminate some of the admonitions below and replace them with a more lighthearted and fun approach to living. Laughter and humor are tremendous healers, and the ability to find joy in every moment is the real test of the no-limit person. Making their lives joyless, with humor constraints imposed by a serious and funless adult, simply deadens their natural instincts to be a little whimsical and fun loving. For example:

No-Humor Approach to Life (Sickness)	More Fun Approach to Life (Wellness)
No laughing at the dinner table.	You are so funny all the time. It's great to see everyone having a good time.

Don't be silly in front of guests.	You're such a silly person, but if the guests enjoy it, why not help them to laugh also.
Stop clowning! Act your age.	I guess you will always be a clown. I hope you enjoy the spotlight and know when to turn it off.
Show some respect!	I know this is hard for you to accept and that joking makes it easier, but this is not the time.
If you make faces yours will stay that way.	You are a person of a million faces. I wonder if you can do a ghoul.
Don't laugh—you'll just encourage her.	Isn't she something the way she can make everyone laugh? I adore her.

Take children on a visit to a wellness nutrition center in your community. Show them what goes on in a wellness center, and explain that proper nutrition can make their insides feel much better. Get them involved very early in their own health, talking to them and showing them examples of how they can make themselves live a long and healthy life. Purchase books and tapes on wellness, and give them the study guides that are offered at life-enrichment centers in your community. Let them view real pictures of human lungs that have inhaled nicotine for a lifetime or visit emphysema patients in a hospital. The field of wellness is exploding with new discoveries every day. Magazines publish phenomenal scientific information related to healing, nutrition, prevention of disease, cytotoxic testing, food allergies, and the physical need for exercise and an active lifestyle. Subscribe to such magazines and have this material available for children to explore. Get them self-teaching materials about their own bodies and have them grow up being knowledgeable about everything that affects their health. The more information you have in your home, and the more you combine it with a total approach to wellness through visits to centers and health food stores, the more your children will simply ingest the information on wellness automatically. Keep them informed and involved in this process and they will make a commitment which will serve them throughout their lives.

Do not impose your own lack of information and experience in the area of wellness on your children. Review those tiresome excuses that I detailed in the previous section of this chapter, "Your Support System for Not Promoting Wellness." Examine them with an unbiased eye and you will see that you are refusing to let your children have the opportunity for total wellness only because you know so little about it. Just because you were ignorant of the facts about wellness as you were growing up is not a reason to deny this information and opportunity to your children.

If you want to stay as you are—perhaps being out of shape, maybe drinking too much, maybe smoking cigarettes—to the detriment of your health, you certainly have that right. But to deny your children the right to be as healthy as they possibly can be, and to raise them to be ignorant of the facts about their own ability to stay well for a lifetime, is to ignore your responsibility as a parent. You want what is absolutely best for your children, and refusing to become informed about wellness is to literally deny that to your children.

What I am talking about in this chapter is perfectly consistent with my approach throughout this entire book. A no-limit person is one who is in charge of all aspects of his or her life. No-limit people control the connection between mind and body, just as they control the way they choose to think about themselves, and just as they take charge of their emotions and thoughts about everything in life. Being in a state of wellness and using all of the techniques available to stay at the superhealthy level is what a no-limit person opts for in his or her life. Children deserve this opportunity. One last quote from Shakti Gawain's wonderful little book, *Creative Visualization*, sums up this point of view quite nicely.

> The natural outgrowth of this point of view is a more constructive attitude about illness. Rather than thinking of illness as an inevitable disaster or unavoidable misfortune, we think of it as a powerful and useful message. If we are suffering physically in some way, it is a message that there is something to be looked at within our consciousness, something to be recognized, acknowledged, and changed.

If you believe that you have this power within you to avoid illness and to maintain wellness as a lifestyle, then work each day to have your children grow up with this attitude as well. Too often we discover some basic truths quite late in our lives and our children do not get the benefit of these insights. In the case of wellness thinking, I suggest that this awareness of your own capacity for healing and staying healthy through using your mind more effectively is indeed one of those latter-day discoveries. If you are beginning to believe in this idea, then by all means give your children an opportunity that you never had as a child. Give them the opportunity to think wellness, the opportunity to heal from within, and, most important, the opportunity to make each day of their lives one in which they are in control, having no limits imposed on them by anyone or anything external to themselves. As you look at this word, *disease,* which I have written repeatedly in this chapter, take a closer look at it: dis-ease, not being at ease. That is what makes for disease. Wellness is putting people at "ease" with their perfect bodies to eliminate the negative prefix forever.

9

I Want My Children to Be Creative

The no-limit person has no sense of ownership toward others with whom he is associated; recognizes that the best way to lose anything is to try to hold too tightly to it; is virtually immune to jealousy; takes a cooperative approach toward thinking through any problem; is never upset by labels people stick on him or others; understands the truth in seeming opposites; takes joy in the successes of others and rejects the comparison/competition game as a whole. He has no specific heroes and recognizes that for every famous hero there are millions of unsung heroes; sees a hero in everyone, but is too busy making his own contributions to live vicariously through anyone else. He places no positive value on conformity for its own sake and is able to get around petty rules and customs as easily and quietly as possible. He approaches others with pure, childlike honesty and always lets his own creative imagination loose in any situation, approaching everything in life from a creative point of view.

If you see in any given situation only what everybody else can see, you can be said to be so much a representative of your culture that you are a victim of it.

—S. I. HAYAKAWA

Imagination is the beginning of creation. You imagine what you desire, you will what you imagine, and at last you create what you will.

—GEORGE BERNARD SHAW

A great deal has been written on creativity and children, with a particular emphasis on pointing out that some children are blessed with being creative and others are not. I take a contrary position regarding the creativity of children. It is my very strong belief that all children are creative, and that we encourage or discourage that natural creativity by the ways in which we relate to children. Natural creativity will blossom when it is stimulated and fostered. Raising children to be as creative as they can be is important, because it will make a large difference in how they grow to approach virtually everything they do in life.

What is Creativity in Children?

Creativity means uniqueness. It means to attack any problem or encounter in life from one's own unique perspective. It means tackling the chores of life in a way that you as an individual decide to. The literal meaning of creativity is "bringing into being something new." Creativity is not limited to artistic or musical interests. You can be exceptionally creative and be doing anything that interests you. Making a salad can be a creative enterprise. Fixing a bicycle can be a creative task. Doing a double flip off the side of the pool and twisting into the water can be a creative exercise. Children who are allowed to use their own matchless selves in their life experiences and who attack everything from their own unique perspective are behaving in a creative fashion.

The opposite of creativity is not "mechanistic" or "dull"; it is *conformity*. Children are being discouraged from being creative when they are expected to only do things the way they are taught. To color within the lines and not use their own imaginations, to emulate the adult rather than figuring out their own method, or to "fit in" and do as they are told, without applying their own uniqueness to their life activities. All children have their own uniqueness. Each one is a special individual and never before in the history of our planet has anyone looked out from behind those eyeballs and seen the world in precisely the way that he or she does right this moment. The willingness and the ability to use that matchless self in all of life's undertakings is the measure of creativity. Unfortunately, many pressures are brought to bear on children which, while claiming to stimulate creativity, in fact do quite the opposite. Earl Nightingale, in his Direct Line Cassette Program, has this to say about creativity and your children:

> A child's actions may be based on false assumptions. . . . . The way most children are raised in home and school is to give them a completely cockeyed picture of what life in a free society can be like. They are taught to play it safe, to avoid the risks of getting hurt, to conform, to fit in, to be one of the group, one more sheep in the herd, to tiptoe through life instead of dancing and running through it. Consequently they don't know what is available for them.

Children raised in such a way as to encourage natural creativity are children encouraged to be their own selves, to feel free not to fit in or not to live life only as others do. They are brought up to understand that it is impossible to be just like everyone else and still have anything to offer. They learn very early that conforming and adjusting to life are not worthwhile goals, and that it is all right to challenge established authority, to ask why, and to try new ways of doing things. Seldom will you hear a parent say, "I do not want my child to be creative." Yet, most parents' actions would support that assertion almost all the time. You may want a creative child, yet you may be discouraging the very attribute you desire by insisting that the child stay within the lines and do things the way he or she is expected to do them by all of the established authorities.

The exact components of creativity are simply not definable. Experts have made many efforts to define precisely what creativity is, and there is still no universal agreement on what we mean when we say "creativity." Yet we use the term all the time, and it is pretty much accepted that a child who is creative is to be much admired. I will give you my components of creativity, and they will not look like anything you may have read in a "Childhood and Creativity" textbook.

It is my purpose in writing this chapter to help you foster creativity in children by not putting out the sparks before they have a chance to ignite that creativity fire within. Give a great deal of thought and positive action to helping children maximize their creative urges, rather than determining to raise a conformist child. As you read this chapter, particularly the suggested strategies for helping children nurture their instinctive creative impulses, keep in mind the words of one of our most creative writers, Ralph Waldo Emerson.

> There is a time in every man's education when he arrives at the conviction that envy is ignorance; that imitation is suicide; . . . Whoso would be a man, must be a non-conformist.

These are powerful words, and they are at the very heart of what it means to be a creative person. The freedom to apply the unique self to all thought and action as long as it does not interfere with any other person's right to do the same is precisely what I mean by being a creative person. Children can have this wonderful opportunity each and every day of their lives—or they can work at conforming, imitating, and doing as they are told. The approach to life, creative or imitative, is largely dependent on what is encouraged and permitted. The seven central ingredients of a creative approach to raising children, in my no-limit way of looking at creativity, are as follows.

1. *A sense of independence.* The creative process involves bringing something new into being, or attacking a problem from a new perspective. In order to be able to create, children must feel a strong sense of their own unique independence. They must know that it is unnecessary to please you or anyone else in order to do the things that are important. If you are raising children to depend on you, to need your approval, to seek out your permission, or to follow rules and learn to live the way you feel they should, then you are at the same moment stifling their creative impulses. Encouraging independence does not imply condoning irresponsibility. It simply means looking at children as totally unique and special, and encouraging them to seek out their own matchless approach to everything as often as is feasible. For toddlers, fostering independence means allowing them to make up their own games without interference from you. To preteens, allowing independence means letting them write their own stories in school and pick their own friends. To teenagers, it means allowing them to express their own opinions, to worship as they choose, to experiment with new recipes or different cuisines.

The creative human being is one who is fiercely independent.

He cannot and will not allow someone else to think or act for him. If you want children to grow to be as creative as possible, then allow for sensible independence and the freedom to think as they choose, and encourage them to experiment in life, to try their own methods, and to throw out the ways everyone else does it if it does not apply to them. The dependent child, generally speaking, has had his creativity squelched by a parent's need to be depended upon.

2. *An absence of labels.* The creative process requires being open to new experiences, having an open mind about everything and a willingness to wander into virgin territory in virtually every endeavor of life. This means that parents must refuse to place labels on children and instead reinforce their natural inclinations to be anything and everything, depending upon their whims and the whims of the universe. This means ridding yourself of labels like the oldest, middle, or youngest child, or the smart one, her father's daughter, pretty, uncoordinated, lazy, a slow learner, a bad seed, black sheep, rebel, neat, slob, mama's little soldier, shy, artistic, bossy, a little mama, or anything else you might use. On any given day, the creative child can be all of the above or none of the above. In the course of one day a child could try handball, put a puzzle together, then feel lazy, later want to draw, and then play soldier: lethargic in one moment and highly energized in the next. This diversity seems to be very important for those who measure high on the creativity scale—that is, the opportunity to experiment with all of life, without being compartmentalized in any way.

Parents seldom allow more than one child to occupy any category or label they place on their children. These labels often stick with children despite the child's efforts to change them. As soon as children accept the labels you provide for them, they give up on themselves and become the noncreative people they genuinely do not want to be. Their internal logic tells them, "Why fight, when I'm always perceived this way by everyone anyhow?" Before too long they become the labels you have given them, and their creative juices soon stop flowing in favor of living up to the tags you have assigned. Creativity demands that children see themselves as capable of doing everything rather than being restricted to a label.

3. *Growing up on personal integrity.* Creativity is inextricably intertwined with personal honesty and integrity. To be able to

apply her uniqueness to any task in life, a child must possess unconditional trust in herself as a person of integrity. If she is honest with herself, then she will be free to use that personal honesty in life and all of its undertakings. The child who fools himself, who lies to others and lives a cover-up kind of life, will attack problems from the perspective of needing to protect the ruse which he has created. Consequently you will see him behaving in ways which are designed to win the approval of others and to maintain his active lie, rather than being honest. Children who must live up to some internal expectations of their own which are based on being artificial, behave in artificial ways. And creativity can never be fostered in a child who is living a phony lifestyle.

The creative child needs to feel at peace with himself even if he makes mistakes. He needs to know that what is important is that he apply his uniqueness to the running of his life, and that maintaining a "put on" posture is not only silly but will interfere with his own creativity. Being honest with oneself is a vital ingredient in the creativity process. Children must learn early the lessons of being honest with themselves. Use sentences with children such as "You may feel a need to fool me, or even your teachers, but be honest with yourself" or "Only you know if you are working at your full capacity and if you are satisfied and genuinely pleased with your effort" or "In your quiet moments, when you are alone in your bed, have a conference with yourself and see if you are really being honest with yourself." The more you support children in helping them to face themselves honestly without fear and without being concerned about what you or anyone else thinks, the more you are helping them to trust themselves. The more he trusts himself as he grows older, the more willing he will be to use his own unique approach in everything he undertakes, and that is precisely what separates a creative child from a noncreative one. The entire process of teaching self-honesty begins when children are quite young, when you praise them for telling the truth rather than punishing them for being honest, or when you expect them to live up to Shakespeare's famous dictum: "This above all: to thine own self be true."

4. *Never fearing one's own greatness*. Creative children are unafraid of their own greatness. They are encouraged to think of themselves in ways which are never limiting. They are not taught to believe in heroes or to make other people more significant than themselves. Creativity and risking go hand in hand. Children need to know from the very beginning that they have genius and greatness residing within them, and that they can choose to allow those qualities to flourish. How a child perceives his heroes is important in the creative process. If he believes that he could never be as great as a sports figure or a musician—or that any hero is bigger, stronger, and better than he is—then he will begin to fear the very greatness which exists within him.

Make all heroes normal yet unique for your child. The activity of raising creative children is deeply rooted in helping them to dream about their own greatness, rather than living vicariously through the accomplishments of their heroes. It means meeting senators, business executives, artists, authors, entertainers, and anyone else whom they admire, but only considering such people as examples of what they can achieve if they really choose it for themselves. They must see the greatness within themselves and want desperately to allow it to rise to the surface. They must see the examples of others as lights that are being lit for them to follow their own inner illuminations, rather than assuming that others are inherently greater than they are. The child who learns about great inventors should also be asked about inventing something herself someday. "What would you like to invent? How about a machine to make us go to another planet by rearranging our molecules? Do you think it is possible? Do you think you might someday invent something that will help people? I'll bet you could do anything, you're so smart and always coming up with special ideas." Talking this way to very young children helps them to feel that they too can be great, and that those who have lived before were not supermen but normal people just like themselves—not heroes, but role models who can lead them to discover their own greatness in any area of their particular choosing. Creativity means believing you have greatness, and you can do much to help children believe in their own greatness.

5. *Intensity of awareness*. Creative people have an intensity about them that is not shared by those assessed to be noncreative. In *The Courage to Create,* Rollo May tells us, "Absorption, being caught up in, wholly involved, and so on, are used commonly to describe the state of the artist or scientist when creating or even

the child at play. By whatever name one calls it, genuine creativity is characterized by an intensity of awareness, a heightened consciousness." Training children to persevere, to be persistent in what they find interesting and exciting, and to feel the intensity that Rollo May describes is the same as raising them to be creatively alive.

Young children at play become intensely involved in the games and fantasies they create. Support this involvement by asking them about their stories and the characters in their imaginations. They should be encouraged to put on plays and dance exhibitions, to find excitement and praise in your eyes when they develop their own skits and games. The intensity of those creations will flow naturally into their later endeavors. The more they are supported for their involvement, the more you are helping them with the building blocks for creativity. Take their genuine excitement and intensity in their games to a new level for them, at whatever age they may be.

When your children are infants, concentrate with them as they grab at a toy or stare intently at an object. Talk to them about what they see, praising them when their eyes follow your finger, or laugh out loud with them. For toddlers, the nature of their inquiring minds is to be intense about almost everything. The more that intensity is praised, the more creatively you are helping them to think and act. The Strawberry Shortcake doll which they imagine as a mommy with her little babies can become an adverture in their wondrously imaginative minds. The endless hours of arranging and rearranging a play area, or examining bugs in a field, should be supported and encouraged by you, even if you find it tiresome at times. The more you allow young children to have their intensity without constantly being interrupted or discouraged, the more you are fostering a central ingredient in the creative process.

Preteens have a phenomenal sense of imagination and intensity within their lives. They can create their own clubs with various roles for each member. They will take hours of delight in writing a screenplay or creating their own version of *The Dating Game* for you to enjoy. They want to perform, and their total involvement and attention to detail bring out the creative process and teach them that it is perfectly acceptable and praiseworthy for them to be as wildly imaginative as they choose. Teenagers, too, become intense in their creative efforts. In their school reports or field trips they can become vitally involved in a learning project. They talk endlessly to their friends with a degree of excitement and intensity that is generally unknown to adults. They love to squeal in delight over who really likes whom. They dream up scenarios that they discuss with each other, and the more intensity they display, and the more you are supportive of these actions, the more you are teaching them that they are perfectly wonderful, and that they can be trusted to rely on their own unique selves to determine their interests. This is creativity at work. The more you reinforce that intensity and refuse to criticize it, regardless of how silly or immature it may seem to you, the more you are putting your children on the path to thinking for themselves. And that is the essence of their creativity: thinking for themselves in as intense a manner as *they* choose.

6. *Allowing for persistence.* Once creative people become involved in a project, they attack it and stay with it until they have exhausted all of their energy on the subject. The quality of persistence is as important an ingredient in creativity as any I have mentioned above. One of my very favorite quotations describes the importance I place on perseverance in terms of accomplishing anything in life, and it applies to me personally more than any other quality in whatever success I have attained. I know that others are more talented and better educated, but I have yet to meet anyone who has the dogged persistence that I possess when it comes to going after what I want. Here is the quotation. Keep it handy when you look at your children and think about helping them along their own unique creative paths.

> Nothing in the world can take
>   the place of persistence.
> Talent will not; nothing is more
>   common that unsuccessful
>   men with talent.
> Genius will not; unrewarded
>   genius is almost a proverb.
> Education will not; the world
>   is full of educated derelicts.
> Persistence and Determination
>   alone are omnipotent.
>
> AN UNATTRIBUTED MOTTO
> TAKEN FROM *DAILY PLANET*
>   *ALMANAC*

You can help children to have persistence, though the desire must come from within them. Help them not to give up, ever, on the things that are of great importance to them. Help them to never think in impossibility terms, and to see the value of staying with a situation until it is resolved. Young children often need a little encouragement to persist with a problem, and if they receive it from you, then they will be taking those necessary steps early in their lives to follow through on their own goals. Asking young children to "Stay with that puzzle until you get it, even if you appear stuck right now" is the kind of encouragement I am talking about. Help them to seek answers in unconventional ways, rather than trying once and then quitting. "I know you can find the answer. Stay with it, and try thinking about a solution in new ways." "You'll be a great soccer player—I know it. Let's practice controlling the ball with your left foot for another half hour, and I'll bet you'll have it before long." "You've made a ten-week commitment to the jazz class, and I want you to stick it out and give it all you've got. Then if you want to quit, by all means do so." "If you sign up for tennis lessons I insist that you continue even if it gets tedious. Giving it your all for the period of the lessons is just as important as having talent, which you have plenty of." These and other verbal encouragements to be persistent and not become a quitter are significant for developing creativity in children. When they learn to stick with an endeavor, to give it their all, and to refuse to give up on the projects which they choose, then you must help them to persist even though they might find quitting an easier road to take. As they develop this quality of persistence, they will then apply it to their most significant undertakings later in life, and this is when the creative juices will flow. I have found that if I persist with my writing, even if I feel like quitting, the actual "sticking to it" helps me to write more creatively than at any other time. The more I continue my work, the better I feel about my output, and creativity will naturally come out of your children when they practice this persistence regularly in their lives. Encourage them to be *doers* and the creative part will come almost automatically.

7. *Independence in thought.* There is more to being independent than simply not being attached too closely to one's parents. Creative people think in unique ways which allow them to create. They perceive the world according to their own inner voices, and

they think in ways which do not permit them to simply categorize and compartmentalize the world. Creative people see the whole as made up of seeming opposites. They know that the world is not divided into mere dichotomies, with black being on one side and white on the other. They look to fuse the seeming opposites and to see beyond what common thinking generally dictates. Creative people think in ways that are nontraditional. They are not satisfied to simply put a label on something and then dismiss it; they want to look beneath the surface. They know that one cannot neatly divide the world, but that one must explore at previously unexplored levels. William James, a great contributor to modern psychological knowledge, defined genius as "the faculty of perceiving in an unhabitual way." This is what separates those who are creative from everyone else: thinking in unhabitual ways. They are not creatures of habit. They want to know more. They ask why over and over again. If that why is met with a tired glare or is dismissed by you because you do not have time for those questions, you might kill any further interest in asking questions. Certainly if you ignore inquiries often enough children will seek out answers from other sources or lose the enthusiasm for the pursuit of knowledge.

Creative thinking and thinking in nonhabitual ways must be encouraged by adults. Teach children not to attach labels to others by discussing with them how all people are made of many contrasting qualities. Show them that exploring a question and admitting openly when they do not know an answer is much better than trying to fake it. Help them to use their own minds rather than simply accepting something that any so-called expert tells them. Encourage them to ask questions of everyone, to challenge anything that they doubt, and to avoid blind obedience in life. Creative thinking means questioning all the time. As a parent you are in a position to either encourage or discourage that process. Even if you do not know the answers, you can still look things up together. Teach children to doubt everything that they are told when it is presented as an absolute. Investigate and check out the sources of others. To believe in the integrity of their own minds is a great lesson to teach children, and it is one of the cornerstones of a creative person's approach to life.

Little ones will ask you "why?" almost every hour of the day. Encourage it. "You're so fantastic—you always want to know the answers. What do *you* think about it? Why do *you* suppose the sky is blue? Where do *you* think heaven is?" In other words, be supportive of their inquiries, and give a problem right back to them to solve. If there is no clear answer to a question, admit that you do not know and then speculate with them, so that they learn early to stimulate their own brains. In later years, ask them to find opposing points of view and to figure out their own truths. Support them in questioning the teacher's interpretations. Teach them to question the "experts" and to come up with their own theories. The more they learn to think in inquisitive, open-minded, non-judgmental ways, the more they will apply that thinking to the creation of their own truths. And that is what creativity is all about: finding one's own truths without thinking in habitual ways.

These are the major components of creativity. The more you can help children to grow in each of these seven dimensions, the more likely you will be able to say, "My child is really creative." It will not be because he likes art, music, literature, or inventing, but because he approaches his world differently from the habitual ways in which most people have come to live. Creative children are indeed quite distinct from those who are described as noncreative. Before going into some of the specifics for helping children to grow up on a steady diet of creativity, I am presenting my brief portrait of what a truly creative child is like as she travels through the everyday business of living her life. Some of these qualities may surprise you, yet they seem to run consistently through those children who are truly being raised on creativity.

A Brief Portrait of Creative Children

Creativity is an approach to life. It is an attitude that leads us toward more and more personal fulfillment because it allows us to apply our own special selves to all of our undertakings in life. The creative child is not simply one who learns to play the piano at age four or shows a strong interest in painting or classical music. Creativity does not imply precociousness! Every child has the potential for creativity. The extent to which they are permitted to actualize that potential is the determining factor in whether children live creative lives. Not the genes, not the chromosomes, not the family background, and not the financial picture. Creativity crosses all of these elements. It is your attitude toward children and how you relate to the special uniqueness of each one that is largely the determining factor. While many children may grow up to have special talents and abilities which transcend whatever the parents do, the creative child, by and large, is one who is not only permitted to be creative, but is encouraged to be so throughout his life by the significant people to whom he relates daily. Here is a brief look at what these everyday, regular, normal, but highly creative children are like.

Creative children are those who love to play and invent new games. They seem to take great enjoyment in making up new rules and inventing characters for everyone to assume. They delight in asking questions about everything, and their curiosity seems to know no boundaries. They are interested in everything that comes along, and they want to try new things, rather than fearing the unknown. These children are most happy when they can be spontaneous and invent new ways to have fun. They will enjoy just about anything you give them to play with. A garden hose becomes a fountain; a tin can is something to kick and play catch with, or the "ball" in a new game of kick-the-can. An old tire can easily become a swing seat or something to roll along the street with a doll inside. A house under construction is an entire world for exploration, with the wood, the bricks, the mortar, and all of the exciting materials to experience and enjoy for what they are. The lid from a garbage can becomes a shield and two sticks nailed together become a sword, and before long you have children who are playing King Arthur or Prince Valiant. A spool can become a doll with a little paint, and aluminum foil and paper cups can make for magic moments of creating decorations. Creative children do not need to have a computer, an intercom, a shortwave radio, and a television set in order to be entertained. They can find entertainment with an old bed sheet, a big stick, and some rocks; before long they have built a tent and are making a clubhouse.

Creative children ask "Why?" all the time, and they are encouraged to do so. They are confident within themselves of a positive outcome regardless of what they are undertaking. If you ask a creative child if she can ride her bicycle to a town forty miles away, she will say, "Sure, I'll try it if you'll let me." Creative children know that they have unlimited potential within themselves, and they are willing to take the necessary risks without fearing failure. They trust themselves, and that trust comes from applying themselves in a unique way in everything they do. They will try jumping off the thirty-foot diving board, knowing that they will be all right. Why? Because they know within themselves that they can do it. They will try jumping off the edge of the bed onto the chair at eighteen months of age, and they will keep trying it until they make it—unless they are told that it is too dangerous and that they should be afraid of taking giant steps. They will work for endless hours on a high school float for a Saturday parade, adding their own unique brands of creativity to the design, and love doing it. They will dress up in adult clothes, put on makeup, talk to their dolls in their very own language, and generally try anything that pops into their heads.

Creative children do not know about censoring their ideas; instead, they give vent to them. They have not learned to be extra careful; instead, they are willing to take sensible risks. They are infused with an internal spirit that is boundless in anticipating a picnic, a day at the beach, a game of softball, or a birthday party. They want to go! They do not want to sit through life as spectators; in fact, they can't wait to get there. "Are we there yet? When will we be there?" And all the while they are waiting, they invent games and fun things to pass the time. "Let's look for license plates from every state." "Let's make up new songs." "Let's play slapping our hands and see who flinches first." "Let's arm wrestle. No? How about finger wrestling?" They are doers, their minds are always going, and they want to participate in life rather than watch it go by.

Creative children often prefer to learn or work alone. They do not want to be interfered with every few minutes. They are often regarded as eccentric, and can be mislabeled "underachievers" if they are not challenged and encouraged. Many times they are labeled "troublemakers" because they ask too many questions or won't sit still and do what everyone else is doing. A creative child can be called the class clown or even the loner, but these labels often are applied by noncreative people. Creative children love a variety of resources rather than having one narrow point of interest. They love books and are fascinated as youngsters by pictures of farm animals or *Sesame Street*'s Big Bird. They also are fascinated by most of what they see on television (particularly commercials). Music of any kind is a joy to creative children, and they will often dance and mimic the words and rhythm while still in their pretoddler years. They find everything exciting, with no judgments about what is good or bad. They will take notice of everything outdoors. Birds, ducks, worms, cats, dogs, flowers, wind, rain, snow, and everything else outside is fascinating to creative children, and they never seem to tire of wandering around in nature, discovering and inventing their own explanations for why things are as they appear to them. They find toys everywhere. Sticks are magic wands, laser guns, conductors' batons, or anything they want them to be. A sugar bowl can instantly become a spaceship or a place to hide the "cooties" and scare a little brother. Generally speaking, they have dirty hands and it is difficult to keep them clean and tidy. Their experimental nature makes it so.

Creative children love puzzles, building blocks, mazes, and toys which challenge them to make their unique minds work overtime. They are masterful at figuring things out when left to explore, and when they are not given a lot of rules and regulations about how they should be playing. They love to draw their own pictures, invent their own stories, and work creatively with glue, paste, scraps of paper, glitter, and objects which you may think of as trash. In fact, a trash can is not just a trash can to a creative child. It is a place with a million treasures, as well as the home of Oscar the Grouch. Creative children will read extensively for a project that they find interesting, going to the library and looking up new resources, talking to experts to learn more about their new discoveries, and yet they may refuse to do routine class assignments, such as answering the questions at the end of the chapter. When they have their interest piqued, they have unlimited energy, yet they will not participate in mundane tasks that everyone has to do precisely the same—or, if they relent, they will do a less than enthusiastic job of completing a routine assignment. They love challenges and learning new things, but they also need to apply their own creativity to their projects, and when they are treated just like everybody else, they become quite incensed quite readily at the apparent indignity. Allow a creative child to experiment and try out his own solutions and you will have a happy, enthusiastic child on your hands. Tell the same child to sit up straight, answer the questions, and simply do what everybody else is doing, and you will have a problem on your hands before you know it.

Creative children wear their emotions right on their faces for everyone to see. If they are angry about how they are being treated, you will absolutely know how they feel. They might not know how to keep those emotions in check at the earlier ages, so they will shout, scream, and often create a mess for themselves. But you cannot get them to reform just because you would like them to be different. They are sensitive and unwilling to be phony about how they feel. They are quick to show their anger and equally quick to show their love. A creative child will hug you and do a million wonderful things for you in one afternoon, and you will wonder what you ever did to deserve such a perfect child; then in the next moment she will flail her arms, shout some obscenity, and run into her room crying. They are unique inside! That fact you must keep uppermost in your mind at all times. Creative children have creative insides. They think uniquely, they feel uniquely, and they behave uniquely. Those feelings or emotions are precisely what make them so creative. They cannot temper their emotional reactions to things just because it would be nicer for you and for them. They are inwardly honest, and if they feel hurt, you will see their tears. If they feel joy, you will see ecstasy in their eyes, their hands, their jumping feet, their big smiles, and their "I love life" looks that defy definition.

Creative children are often called oddballs. They love to read maps and dream of faraway places. They will study the dictionary and try to use an adult vocabulary long before they are mature enough to understand the total meanings behind their utterings. They will invent new taste sensations such as peanut butter on asparagus spears, or a special Monte Cristo sandwich made of bananas, mayonnaise, and honeydew melon slices on pumpernickel bread. They love to tell stories after hearing stories read aloud, and their creative imaginations can run rampant if you encourage them to make up intricate plots with strange and wonderful stories. They only need a little prodding for the stories to become fanciful masterpieces of children's fairy tales. If you give them free reign in the kitchen, they will have a wonderfully exciting time inventing their own original meals. They will try adding curry powder and garlic together even if you've never done it that way. But only if they get the opportunity now and then.

Creative children love new situations and are never reluctant to experiment, unless they are taught reluctance. They are not enticed by cliques and belonging to the in crowd. Instead, they are able to get along with all of the various subgroups in their neighborhood and school. They will not stay only with the boys or only with the girls in a group, opting instead for playing with everyone. They know no prejudices, and their natural desire to be experimental encourages them to learn about everyone rather than prejudging anyone. They will show remarkable maturity of thought as teenagers, since they have had exposure to so many new ideas and people, and since that very exposure discourages prejudices. They consequently become open to everyone and every idea as well. They have learned through living that there is nothing to hate in anyone else, and little to fear. Sensible, yes—afraid, no! They know that most people fear what they are uninformed about, but they have been blessed with the opportunity to become informed because of their inquisitiveness and their uninhibited personalities. They are willing and desirous of finding out about everything. From the time they are very tiny, until well into their teen years, they are lovers of life, encouraged to learn and unafraid of failing.

Creative children will sometimes try things that you may disapprove of, but they must try before they are convinced it is not something they want in their lives. Yes, a creative child will likely try smoking a cigarette, but not to be one of the gang. Instead, she wants to know what all the fuss is about for herself, firsthand, and until she has given it a try, she will not be satisfied. When she tries it, and finds it distasteful or inappropriate or too dangerous, or whatever, she will likely leave it alone. But creative children will experiment and make their own judgments about what is right and wrong for them, based both upon the information and guidance you provide for them and, more important, upon their own needs to find out for themselves. Yes, they will probably try drugs at some time in their lives. Yes, they will do some things that you disapprove of—and yes, they will disappoint you sometimes, and even disappoint themselves. But they must have the opportunity to investigate life for themselves, and no amount of your wanting it to be otherwise is going to make a difference.

Creative children learn very quickly from their mistakes. They know what will inhibit them from their own creative desire to excel, and they will not—I repeat, *not*—become addicted to drugs, engage in petty criminal activities, or otherwise disgrace themselves, since they have extremely strong creative impulses to be successful and fully alive. They will see very quickly the folly of allowing a drug, or a persuasive person who does not have their best interests at heart, to control their lives. Their own creative impulses for survival and happiness will win out, as well as the moral and ethical lessons which you have provided for them. But you cannot keep a creative person from inquiring into what all the fuss is about. They have their own unique minds (that is what makes them creative in the first place), and they must find out for themselves.

A creative child makes his choices based not on having been "drilled" on "Do what is right" or "God is watching" or "Your grades are more important than you are," but on his desire for self-improvement and his loving regard for others. Creative children are fascinated by the differences that exist in the world, rather than subscribing to arbitrary assignments of what is absolutely right and what is unquestionably wrong. They are not fearful of being different; in fact, they are proud of what makes them unique and special. They love being their own people and generally are quite unaware of what everyone else is thinking of them. While they are sensitive and easily hurt when chastised or criticized, they take great inner pride in being who they are and not having to be just like everybody else.

Creative children seem to know no bounds when it comes to what interests them. They are willing to try virtually any sport; they are eager to learn to ride their bicycles as soon as possible. They will talk to anyone who will listen, and generally are not concerned about wearing the appropriate designer labels. They can be sloppy or neat depending upon their moods, but they do not become immobilized because they do not have the "right" item, the "in" hairdo, or the current popular "label" on their clothes. They are curious and persistent about life, and they often demand parent and teacher attention to get answers, since they will not ever settle for "Because I said so!" This may shut them up, but it will not shut out their anger at having been treated to such authoritarian responses from people who are older or bigger, but otherwise have nothing on them.

Creative children will learn for the sake of information and the pleasure of solving problems as much as or more than for approval and external rewards. If a creative child becomes fixated on a particular problem, nothing you can say or do will get her to abandon it until she has a resolution. Creative children have inner needs to find out which transcend any external rewards they may be offered. They do not need or covet "stars" on their papers. In fact, they know how well they are progressing, even in the earliest grades, and often they will view the handing out of "stars" as something that teachers need to do, rather than something they should get all excited about. A creative child can learn from a janitor, a crossing guard, a secretary, or a cafeteria worker just as much as she can from a teacher, and she will often be found making friends with these people. A creative child becomes absorbed in her own projects all the time, and while she may stay with a teacher's lockstep approach to teaching, she will often be checking out books in the library and progressing at her own speed without even telling anyone about it.

A creative child has a sense of humor. Such children can make you laugh and are good at helping others to do the same. They do not resort to forced clowning in order to hide any insecurities they may have about themselves, nor do they engage in sarcastic humor or picking on others from the safety of a group. Often a creative child will be the only person in the crowd to "defend the absent" or to put a stop to gossip and ridicule. They are not stopped by failure, but they are usually surprised by it. They will learn very quickly what hurts, and try even harder to omit that behavior on the next try, which is usually coming up in the next moment because of their uncanny perseverance at proving they can be anything they want to be.

Creative children are those who will rescue stray puppies. They see virtues in everyone rather than looking for flaws. They love competition, but they emphasize their own progress rather than having to defeat others. They like their own looks, and while they seek to improve their appearances as they mature, they are not overly critical of themselves. They do not see themselves as too short, tall, dark, light, fat, ugly, or skinny. They love the challenge of self-improvement but are creative enough within to know that their value does not come from how they look to others, but in the quality and content of their actions and characters. You will find creative children enjoying solitary entertainments such as reading, playing solitaire, jogging, and learning to play a new instrument. While they are social and gregarious, that creative flame is always burning inwardly. They love life and everything in it. They are willing to try anything and everything, but only if they can be permitted to apply their own matchless selves to their undertakings. A creative child may become a rebel in your eyes and in the eyes of the established authorities, but regardless of how you view him, that inner flame burns for him and he will always be led by his own light. The creative child is an enigma. He may cause you the most headaches, but he will also make you the proudest.

If you saw your children in this description of how creative children live, I am not surprised. As I said at the beginning of this chapter, all children are creative. It is up to you to cultivate and nurture and encourage their natural creative instincts. As you read on about the typical ways in which we curtail our children's creativity, and consider some of the strategies which I have offered to help you to raise them on creativity, keep in mind what Norman Douglas said about children, particularly if you want them to be as creative as is possible: "If you want to see what children can do, you must stop giving them things."

Some Typical Ways We Inadvertently Interfere with Children's Natural Creative Inclinations

Obviously you do not deliberately set out to interfere with a child's creative development. Yet in some of the ways we interact with children we are doing precisely that. Here are some of the more typical interaction patterns that you might want to examine to help you to refrain from any such interference.

◻ Encouraging children to become overly dependent on you and not permitting them to apply their own unique solutions to their problems.

◻ Raising children to be just like everyone else: to conform, to fit in, and to avoid being different. Teaching them to think in habitual ways and comparing them with everyone or anyone else when they are behaving inappropriately.

◻ Discouraging questions by ignoring their persistent requests of "why?" or shrugging off their inquiries and letting them know that you are not interested.

□ Teaching them to be always on the safe side and to avoid risks at all costs.

□ Not taking the time to interact with your children each day: to read to them, have discussions, and answer their questions.

□ Teaching them to "stay within the lines" when they color, write, tell a story, play a game, or do anything.

□ Punishing them for telling the truth.

□ Letting children believe that they are average or normal, and that they do not have greatness and genius within them. Letting them think they are not talented.

□ Discouraging creative exploration by criticizing or putting down their creative efforts.

□ Not providing them with a role model of a person who pursues his or her own creative interests with excitement and abandon.

□ Teaching children that you do not trust their opinions because you consider them too young to have formed any valid viewpoints.

□ Constantly monitoring their lives and interfering in their play by the imposition of advice, rules, and restrictions.

□ Talking to children in a condescending manner, treating them as inferior, or using baby talk as your principal means of communicating.

□ Giving them an excessive amount of toys and filling their lives with gadgets, television, and a houseful of things to keep them occupied.

□ Taking complete responsibility for making sure that they are not bored, by regularly inventing activities to fill their time.

□ Not providing them with an opportunity to have privacy whenever they choose it.

□ Taking the position that children are wrong and adults are right in any disputes that arise in their lives. Or always taking a position against theirs. Not letting them think for themselves and work out solutions.

□ Keeping them indoors and observed most of the time.

▫ Forcing team sports on them very early and relishing the fact that they are learning to compete.

▫ Encouraging children to always be obedient to please you, rather than developing internal codes of ethics that they take with them for a lifetime.

▫ Discouraging them from exploring life because it will get them dirty or in trouble or be an inconvenience for you.

▫ Not providing praise for their "weird" inventions or unique solutions.

▫ Praising only the rewards they receive and not the activities. "Wow, you got a star!" "Terrific! You won a trophy." "Sensational! You got the highest mark in the class."

▫ Putting labels on children. "You're big, so you have to be tough." "Girls don't do those kinds of things."

Your Payoffs for Keeping Children from Developing Their Creativity

Keep in mind that you receive some kind of payoff for virtually everything you do in relationship to your children. Try to look objectively at the explanations below to see if maybe you fit in here someplace. Once you understand what it is that you get out of discouraging creativity in your children, perhaps you will be more inclined to use some of the strategies for helping them to become more creatively alive at all stages of their development. You must grasp the *why* of your behavior toward your children before you can utilize the *how to* in bringing about positive change. Just as your children are constantly asking "Why?" and attempting to get a solid hold on how to do things, so too must you be asking that big "Why?" Below are some of the payoffs that might give you the answers.

You may find that it is actually much easier to raise your children in such a way as to minimize their creative aspirations. A child who is doing things in a unique way is much more difficult to control, and control may be what you are after with your children. If you permit them to think for themselves, they will begin to challenge some of your established beliefs. It is easier to have them all obediently do as they are told than to have to deal with each child being his or her own unique self.

Answering questions all the time can be annoying, particularly when your three- and four-year-olds are asking "Why?" to virtually everything they see. By telling them to stop asking so many questions you can get them off your back and you do not have to admit that you do not know the answers to most of their questions.

You may feel that raising creative children is too physically taxing for you. Creative children are full of energy, and they want to know about everything and to try everything. You may find it exhausting to allow them to pursue their own interests since they never seem to get tired, so rather than allowing them to pursue their interests without you, perhaps you simply discourage them from being so exuberant around you. It keeps you from having to muster up energy that you do not seem to possess, and it quiets them temporarily as well. Rather than changing yourself if you cannot keep up with them, you simply force them to slow down and stop being so inquisitive. Also, you may be telling yourself that you simply do not have the time necessary to raise them on creativity.

You may be telling yourself, "I don't want any oddballs for children. They can grow up like I did and like everyone else in the neighborhood. That creative stuff is all right for little Mozarts, but my kid is going to work in the mill and he does not need to be confused by dabbling in a lot of foolishness. He can slow down those creative impulses and learn to make a living like the rest of the world." This kind of attitude makes it easy for you to keep children from being different and unique in what they do. If they can get along and do what everyone else does, they are a lot better off. This is the logic of "What's good enough for me and everyone else is good enough for them."

Perhaps you have convinced yourself that raising children to be creatively alive is akin to being overly permissive, and that eventually they will develop problems if they are not disciplined to fit into the world. This kind of logic may work for you in keeping children from becoming too creative, but it defies the fact that anyone who is going to make a difference in the world, or make a contribution to improving the world, does not think and act like everyone else. "But," you may say, "I don't want my kid changing the world. I just want him to learn how to get along and not develop into a crazy person like all of those so-called 'creative' folks." Such reasoning will give you the rationale you need for discouraging creativity.

Perhaps you like maintaining your children's dependence on you. It makes you feel wanted and needed, and that is a powerful motivator to keep them from doing things on their own in their own unique ways. The more they need you to think for them, to get permission, to do things for them, the more important you feel and the more you feel as though you are really doing a good job as a parent. You may very likely believe that if you allow them to exercise too much of their natural creativity, they will be more likely to get into trouble. This kind of reasoning gives you impetus to maintain their dependence on you for as long as possible.

You may have convinced yourself that creative children are incapable of making a living for themselves, that this is coddling and spoiling them, and that if you raise them on creative methods they will end up in the poorhouse. "I've seen those artist types. They're all hippies who end up on welfare. I want my kids to know how to make a buck, and they are too young to be able to figure that out for themselves. I'll train them right from the beginning to be practical and skilled in one area, and they'll always be able to get a job."

It is much less risky for you to keep your children from becoming too creative in their young lives. If you know what they are doing, if you keep tabs on them, if you monitor them closely, then you will help to keep them out of trouble. You will be able to eliminate worry by knowing where they are and what they are doing. They are "safe," so you can relax. The more they are raised on conformity and obedience, the easier your job of parenting, and you want to do all you can to keep this enormous job as simple as possible.

These are some of the payoffs you may be coveting for keeping your child's creativity profile low. However, if you would like your children to have heavy doses of creativity, believing that the more they become all that they are capable of becoming, the more likely they will enjoy a successful and happily fulfilled life, then read on for some specific strategies and techniques that you might like to include in your relationships with your children at whatever ages they are *today*.

Some Sample Strategies for Raising Your Children on a Regular Diet of Creativity

Keep in mind as you read through these strategic offerings that I am not talking about overly permissive supervision in which you simply allow children to run wild through whatever thoughts enter their minds. The creative child is not a spoiled or ignored child. Indeed, creativity implies teaching children a kind of self-discipline for themselves so that they will not behave themselves to please you but because it is the most effective way to conduct their own lives. The more you help children to a creative kind of life, the more you are equipping them to be able to handle anything that comes along. Creativity does not mean irresponsibility; it means applying one's own thoughts and ideas to any problem or life activity without worrying about what everyone else will be thinking.

Most people believe that if you make a lot of money you will then be successful. This is faulty logic. It works quite the opposite way in real life. Successful people are the ones who make money and know how to earn a living at any time, regardless of economic or other conditions. Successful people bring their successful attitudes and their unique selves to any project in life, and if you take away all of their money and send them off to a new city or even to a foreign country, you will find them on the positive side of the accumulations ledger. Successful people are, without exception, creative people. The more a child learns to rely on himself, to trust himself, the more he will bring his unique self to his life's work.

Do not mix it up as you read about creativity. Do not for a moment believe that a person must go out and make a lot of money to be successful. It's quite the reverse. Be successful inside as a person, and the rest will flow to you regardless of your undertakings. Try out some of these suggestions if you want to see creativity blossom in your children.

Work each day at developing patience with your children so that they might learn from their own perspectives rather than de-

pending upon you as their parent to think and act for them. Creativity essentially means that a child is thinking in his own unique manner. I suggest that you silently count to ten before interfering in anything that your child is doing. Give yourself a few moments to be aware of the need for children to work things out in their own ways. When you see a two-year-old trying to put the pieces of the puzzle in backwards, count to ten silently before correcting and see what the child's personal solution is. If he works at it for a few minutes longer, at least he had the opportunity to do it himself. When a four-year-old is trying to get on a bicycle and is doing it from behind rather than from the side, stop yourself before correcting her. Maybe she will invent her own unique method for mounting a bicycle that suits her just fine. Let her be creative rather than dependent. When a ten-year-old wraps presents for the holidays, and the ribbons are twisted and the seams not quite straight, stop yourself with a silent ten count and let her have her moment of design creativity, and praise her efforts. When a fourteen-year-old is writing his first composition for English class in high school, avoid correcting his choice of words and encourage him to write in his own fashion. When a seventeen-year-old is singing off key, stop yourself, and remember that it is far better to have singing than to have silence for fear of being out of tune. Stop yourself from offering to think and do things for your children, and interfere only if they become so frustrated that they get stuck, or if they ask for your help. And when they do ask for your help, respond with "What do you think?" "What is your opinion?" "How would you do it?" Let them know that you value their opinions and solutions and that they have the choice to do things in their own way even if you would do it differently.

Allow children to be unique without becoming nonconformists for the sake of nonconformity. Anyone who is deliberately trying to be different from everyone else is still being controlled by what everybody else is doing. The truly creative no-limit person functions in the ways that are most effective for him or her without being concerned about what everyone else is thinking or doing. Try to remove any inclinations to compare children with each other. Here are some contrasting examples that provide you with some specifics on ways to encourage creativity and ways that encourage conformity.

Encouraging Conformity	Encouraging Creativity
Why can't you be like everybody else and just get your homework in on time?	You are really hurting yourself with your pattern of always being late with your homework, and you are the only one who suffers the consequences.
Your sister never gives me a hard time. Why can't you be the same?	You sure do like to argue. I wonder what you get out of always provoking arguments. Can you think of any way we can both get along better without fighting?
If you would just look around you, you would see that you are in the minority.	I understand that you don't want to be just like everybody else, that you like to do things your own way. But is your way working for you or against you?
No one else is complaining!	What is it you dislike?
We've always done it this way in this family.	Maybe you do have a better way of doing this. Tell me about your idea and maybe we can all try it.
Can't you ever do things the way everybody else does?	I've always loved the way you stick up for your own point of view.

Eliminate references which encourage a child to behave in ways that everybody else is behaving. There are ways to get children to look at their behavior, to examine what is working for or against them, other than to plead with them to simply fit in and go along with what everybody else is doing. Remember, "If they act just like everybody else, what do they really have to offer?"

Take a unique approach to their persistence when they are young and always asking questions. Take as much time as you can to provide answers that show that you are interested in their inquiries. Remember, the question "Why?" does not require a detailed answer. Generally they just want your attention and to know that you care enough to respond. Keep in mind the old story about the little boy who asked his mother where he came from. She went into a detailed analysis of the sex act and the reproductive organs and her pregnancy, worrying that she might not be providing the child with a correct reply. Her little boy's response was startling: "I know all about that sex stuff, Mom. It's just that Billy said he came from Cleveland, and I wondered where I came from." They do not need detailed explanations as much as they need to know that asking questions is a sensational thing to do and that it should never be discouraged. After the fourth or fifth "Why?" I have always asked them right back, "Why do *you* think? I'll bet you already know the answer." A good-natured interaction encourages children to be inquisitive. However, when you shrug them off, or ignore them, they learn very early to stop asking questions. When they stop asking questions, the creative process is stifled. Without an inquiring mind, you will not be dealing with a creative child for very long.

Remember that creativity and risk-taking go together. As I've said previously in this book, a sensible approach to risk-taking is always in order, and you must obviously do all that you can to ensure that a child does not put himself in a position of danger to himself or others. However, and this is a big *however*, children must not grow up always on the safe side of everything they do. Sensible risk-taking is an ingredient of creativity. The person who is never able or willing to take risks is not going to have a creative approach to living. Being safe means doing what everyone else is doing. Risk-taking means challenging established authority when it seems appropriate to do so. Risk-taking means trying something new, being innovative, experimenting, going against established tradition, and wandering into the unknown now and then. A young child can learn to do homework the way everybody else does it, or can be encouraged to talk to the teacher about trying a new method of completing the science project. A teenager can either go along and follow all of the rules, even if they do not make sense, or make an attempt to change them.

When I was in the Navy, stationed on Guam, I was told that one never challenges established military policy. However, I found it unconscionable that Guamanian citizens who worked for the United States government were being discriminated against because of their nationality. The mainland American civilian employees were permitted to shop in the military stores, while the dark-skinned Guamanian employees who were U.S. citizens were not permitted the same shopping privileges. I entered a letter-writing contest and published my opinion on this matter. Ultimately, after some threats of a court-martial and reprimand, the policy was changed to eliminate the obvious discrimination. Had I not been encouraged by my mother to stand up for my opinion and to speak out about what I perceived to be injustice, that policy would have remained in effect.

A child must learn very early that she will suffer some setbacks and some difficulties for stating her point of view and fighting for it, and that there will always be risks involved. Children must be encouraged and praised for such behavior, rather than told to sit back in the safety of the do-nothing majority. Children will display signs of wanting to try new things, to think in their own ways, to challenge silly rules, or to come up with new ways of doing things. Whether they are two, twelve, twenty, or anywhere in between, try to encourage and praise them for being risk-takers, and help them to see the consequences of their behavior. But by all means, if you want your child to be creative, do not try to get her to be one more sheep in the herd, bleating away to a tune being orchestrated by someone else.

Take a few extra minutes each day to just be with your children and listen to them. If you have more than one child, arrange for special minutes alone with each. If they are very young, show them a picture book for a few minutes each day and talk with them about what they are seeing on the pages. Creative children, without exception, love books, and exposure to books helps them develop their creativity early. With toddlers, go for a walk alone with them, holding hands and conversing. At bedtime, sit with them for a few moments and talk about their day and what is coming up for them. Talk to them about their interests, their feelings, their fears, their anxieties, their loves. Just a few moments a day. I know you are busy, and so is everyone else, but a few moments each day is a wonderful commitment to make to your children. With preteens and post-toddlers, take a moment out to be alone with them and become a learner in their lives. Here are a few starter questions that you might ask in a nonprying way that will help you to convey to them that you care about them, that they are important, and that you consider their special, unique, and creative ideas to be worthwhile and interesting. "What do you do all day in school?" "What's it like to change classes in the middle of the day?" "What's it like on the school bus?" "Who are your favorite people in school?" "Why do you like them so much?" "Were you scared when the teacher called on you?" "What's it like to learn long division so early?" "Is it hard for you?" "Do you think you're doing well in school?" "Did you like playing with Mary today?" "How come you like your Cabbage Patch doll more than your other dolls?" "Will you swing on the swing set tomorrow like you did today?" "What would you like to do more than anything?" "You seemed upset today. Is everything all right? Are you worried about Grandma in the hospital?"

The idea is to become a learner in their lives. Let them share their unique lives with you. Let them open up about what they have to say, and show them that you are interested in the one thing that they are complete experts about: that is, themselves. No prying, no demanding, simply being with them with a held hand or a kiss, and letting them talk about their own important lives. This "being a learner" technique takes you out of the advice-giving expert authority-figure role, and lets the child be the expert. It shows them that they are important to you, not as people to boss around, feed, and take care of, but as unique human beings. The more they feel unique and special inside, the more they are likely to apply those unique selves that they trust to the tasks of their lives.

Allow children the freedom to just be themselves in as many areas of their lives as possible. When they are quite young, do not place a heavy emphasis on staying within the lines when they are coloring. Let them scribble, and be as artistic as they choose to be. Creativity does not mean being neat, orderly, and meeting the approval of others. It means scribbling at first, then learning color formations, then whatever they choose. They are not graded on their early artistic endeavors. It is far more important that they have opportunities to simply express themselves in whatever forms they desire. The actual process of grading and criticism (which is nothing more than comparing their work with their peers' performances or with standards set by others) impedes the creative process. Creativity, it must be remembered, means allowing them to create from their own perspectives. They must be free to try it in their own ways. Their early coloring scribbles are not an indication of future artistic talent as much as a determiner of whether or not they will ever pick up crayons or a paintbrush later on in life. If the child feels constrained, or graded, then that endeavor will cease in the name of pleasing Mommy or Daddy by doing things the parents' way.

Creative people never stay within the lines of life. They do things their own way. They innovate. They go around the lines that confine the average person, and create their own no-limit pictures for themselves. Children must learn early, with loads of praise for their own styles, that what they try out is not only all right with you, but it is also sensational in itself. This is true for virtually all of their activities. Avoid imposing rules on them when they play. Let them come up with their own rules and stay out of their light. Learning to reach an agreement with their friends and siblings is a part of the creative process. Encourage them to state their own ideas in writing and not to give in to the demand to write in the same old tired way that everyone else does. They may suffer some setbacks along the way, in the form of reduced external approval or even lowered grades, but in the long run, it is the writer who can be creative with his words, who can make his sentences come alive as no one has ever done before, who will make the real difference. By all means they must learn the rules of the game—in writing, coloring, playing, working, and everything else in life—but they must never learn that those rules are to dictate to them what they can do or become.

The creative person cannot be confined by the rules that apply to everyone else. That is what makes him or her so special. The more you permit children to bend the rules, to experiment with new approaches, to try out their own unique styles, the more you will be fostering that creative spirit I am writing about in this chapter. There are some early setbacks to going one's own way, but the more it is praised and encouraged from the earliest moments, and the more children are taught to take disapproval with a grain of salt and not to make a disapproving look or grade anything more than one person's opinion, and certainly nothing to become immobilized about, the more they will learn to trust themselves and get on with being doers rather than critics in life. Creative people are doers, not critics. There are thousands of statues erected to creative people in every discipline. I have yet to see a statue honoring a critic.

Children need to grow up with the sounds of their own greatness ringing in their minds. The only real barrier to their no-limit living is within themselves, and they need a great deal of confidence about their own abilities in order to accomplish anything that they choose. The way to help them avoid fearing their greatness is to give them plenty of reinforcement for maximizing their own potentials. Children are all geniuses in their own right. They are unique, special individuals who are potentially anything they genuinely set their sights on. Be sure to allow them to set their sights based upon a belief that they have greatness inside. Here are several examples of parental interactions which encourage children to experience their own greatness, and those which teach them to fear that same greatness.

Fearing Their Own Greatness	Believing in Their Own Greatness
You haven't applied yourself enough to ever get into nursing school. I suggest you think about something else.	If you can put your mind to it, you can do anything. You may have to go at it the hard way, but I know you can do it if you want it.
Your SAT scores are too low for you to go to college.	SAT scores mean nothing to me. I know you can be great at anything. Take the test as many times as you need to and I know you will get what you want.
You are too little to run a 10k race, but maybe when you get older you can try it.	If you think you can run ten kilometers and you are willing to train for it, go ahead and give it a try. Nothing would surprise me about what you can do when you really put your mind to it.
I doubt that you will discover a cure for cancer.	If anyone is going to discover a cure for cancer, I'll bet you'll be the one. You are so smart and persistent, and I have complete faith in you.
You're not the right build to be a model, but maybe you could work in advertising.	As gorgeous as you are I know you'd make a terrific model. Don't give up on it if that is what you want.

| Acting is a very tough business; you'll never get a job because there are millions of unemployed actresses already. | If you love acting, go for it. With your talent and determination I know you'll be a sensational actress. |

Whenever you are confronted between the choice of praise or criticism, opt for praise and administer it often.

As much as I have talked about the value of praise in this book, it is important for you to see its connection to creativity. The more praise, the better, if you want children to be creatively alive. Your tiny infant should hear how beautiful she is every few hours. Hold her and talk to her about how terrific she is. Get in the habit very early. Studies show that infants only a few days old respond to praise and love, and as they develop they will have an inner sense of being valuable which will encourage their creative exploration throughout their lives. When they show you a drawing or a piece of writing, find something to praise before being critical about anything. "You are really something, Stephanie. Most children your age never even consider writing a paragraph, and here you are writing an entire story. That is really great. You express yourself well on paper; I'll bet you will do great when you get into composition classes later on. Do you want me to offer any suggestions on other ideas to include?" Give praise first, then ask the child if she wants corrections, rather than simply telling her what words she has misspelled or how ungrammatically she writes at the age of eight.

Remember, praise works to encourage children toward more creative pursuits, while criticism only serves to discourage them from doing anything else. Avoid criticism as much as you possibly can, and when you do offer any criticism for their creative efforts, be sure to ask first if they want it. Your heavy dosages of praise eventually turn into their own belief systems about their abilities. I can remember my music teacher in the third grade telling me, "Wayne, why don't you just mouth the words during our presentation to the parents. You have no ability in music, and I don't want you to ruin the concert for everyone else." Thirty years later I could still remember those words and I literally left all musical pursuits and interests behind. While my music teacher may have been correct about abilities in the third grade, who is to say what will happen later on in a person's life? Edison was very hard of hearing as a child, but he made record players later on. Einstein couldn't even talk at the age of four, but he had plenty to say as an adult and the whole world listened.

A child's creative potential is virtually unlimited, but his desire to pursue a given area can be abandoned forever by criticism. Even if a child seems to display zero talent in a given area, anything he does and asks you to look at it should receive a great deal of praise if you want him to continue with creative pursuits for a lifetime. Besides, creativity is not something you can grade. It is an attitude, an approach to life, that you want to reinforce as often as possible.

I have reminded you in every section of this book on no-limit living that you must provide children with a viable example of a human being who enjoys your own creative pursuits. Show them that you do not always have to follow the recipe book. Demonstrate your own creative touch when cooking a meal or playing a game of catch with them in the street. Stop being a person who is so rule conscious that you forget to add your own touch of creativity. Wear the clothes that you love rather than what some fashion experts dictate, and tell your children that it is more important for them to feel good about the way they dress than it is to fit in and be just like everybody else. Involve them in your creative efforts and in learning new things. Take up a painting project and ask for their opinions. Involve them in decorating the house, using your combined creative flair. Let them see, each and every day, a creative person. Do not quote rules to them as reasons why they have to do things. Let them see that a creative approach to living involves making one's own decisions about most everything they do, and that other people's opinions, while they may be nice to know about, are not the determining factors in how they ought to conduct their own lives. Be an example of a person who does things in a unique way, who pursues creative interests with flair, and they will have that same creative attitude rub off on them.

Do not talk baby talk to your children if you want them to develop a healthy sense of creativity. The more you talk down to them, treating them as inferior or incapable of understanding adult conversation, the more you teach them to doubt themselves. Children who doubt themselves will not make attempts at anything that requires individuality, since they distrust the individual who would be doing the creating. A one-year-old child understands perfectly when you say to her, "Please bring that blanket over to me, my beautiful girl," rather than "Pease bing you bankey to Mommy-poo." Similarly, if the child speaks in a way which misuses the language, do not constantly repeat the erroneous language pattern, even if it is cute. If the child says, "Me gots to go to the bathroom," respond with "I'll help you to go to the bathroom," rather than "Mommy sees you gots to make a doo-doo." Talk to them as people throughout their lives. They can understand everything you say to them in normal, loving, fun ways, but they do not need to hear that silly *wee-wee, boo-boo, ca-ca* talk from you.

In addition, avoid talking to your older children in condescending tones. I can remember an elementary school teacher who always talked down to us in the classroom. Everything seemed to be on the order of "Now, children, we are feeling bad today because we didn't eat a good breakfast." All of that condescending language only served to turn us off. We discussed the silly way she talked to us, and we felt less than complete while in her presence. The more you talk in condescending tones to children, regardless of their ages, the more you discourage them from feeling competent and grown-up. A teenager who is talked to as if she is a helpless little girl resents the implication and also learns to distrust herself. This is equally true for twelve-year-olds and six-year-olds. They want to feel grown-up, mature, important, and creative, and the more you talk to them as if they were nincompoops who are incapable of comprehending adult language, the more you teach them to turn you and themselves off. Use the very same language tone with your children throughout their lives as you would in talking to any friend, and you will avoid interfering with their creative development.

If you want to help children to develop creatively, then give them an opportunity to explore the world without a houseful of toys. If you provide them with a toy for every occasion, then how can they possibly learn to use their own creative imaginations? Give them some time to invent their own lasers, rather than buying them cheap toys that they will come to rely on. Allow them to make their own clubhouse, rather than having it prebuilt out of cheap plastic. Let them learn the joy of building their own swords, rather than buying them battery-equipped toys that send off electronic lights to destroy their imaginary enemies. Allow them to invent their own games, rather than always buying them games that they soon tire of. In other words, give your child an opportunity to use his or her creative genius, rather than supplying it courtesy of a manufacturer. While you are at it, turn off the television for several hours each day and encourage the children to get outdoors and get involved with life. If you fill up all of their moments with gadgets and programmed entertainment, you are dulling their senses and teaching them to rely on someone or something else in order to make their lives fun and interesting. Allow them to express their creative urges by letting them have free rein without a large supply of toys and gadgets. A child who watches television all day long soon thinks that television keeps him from being bored. In reality it is causing boredom. The creative child needs to learn to take care of his own needs and never know boredom. Certainly some television is not harmful, but when you consider that the average child in this country spends far more time just watching commercials than he does in creative enterprises, you might want to consider allowing your children to rely on themselves more frequently. While toys are wonderful, they are not the source of creativity. The application of the toys and the ability to invent one's own toys are the true marks of a creative child. Be creative when buying gifts. Get them logs and blocks that they can use to build their own castles, art equipment and blackboards to make their own creations, or puzzles and books that will stimulate rather than dull their creative urges. You make a big difference in a child's creativity, simply by the purchasing decisions you make, so use your own creativity to its maximum when shopping for children.

Do not be afraid to say, "I don't know." And even more important, teach your children to say the same words when it is appropriate. "I don't know, but I'll try to find out." When children feel a need to answer questions even if they do not know the answers, they will soon begin faking answers and engaging in self-deception. Teach them the value of these three important words: *I don't know.* Creative people are motivated by these words, since they then want to seek out the knowledge. Noncreative people will fake it, or make up an entire story to gloss over the fact that they do not know something. The more your children hear you saying these words, and the less pressure they have on them to always give a correct answer, the more you will be helping them to a creative approach to life.

Give children ample opportunities to figure things out for themselves in life. It is not an adult responsibility to keep children occupied at all times. In fact, it is your responsibility to help them to figure things out for themselves as much as possible. You do not want to be a person that they come to lean on, but rather a person who helps to make leaning unnecessary. If they tell you that they are bored, do not buy in to that trap which will put responsibility for entertaining them on you. Let them know in no uncertain terms that you are not obliged to fill up their days with exciting activities. If you refuse to take their bait, before long they will be inventing something on their own and developing their creative powers. Train them to use their own creative imaginations to keep themselves occupied.

I have never felt obliged to play with my children. Although I love doing it, it must be a choice for both of us. Sitting in the house and playing checkers has never been something that appealed to me, although it does to my wife. Therefore, the children play checkers, Chutes and Ladders, Strawberry Shortcake, and other indoor games with Mommy, and everyone is happy. I love to wrestle with my children, to play ball, to read, to go for bike rides and walks, and to go out for lunch together. I feel no sense of obligation to be playing games that I dislike, any more than they would ever consider doing things they disliked for me. If they do not like something, they make it clear that they are simply not interested and then go about their business. I feel that as a parent I have the very same right.

The things that you do together with your children ought to be mutually satisfying. If you want to play with them, but you do not enjoy swimming or walking, then suggest alternatives that are mutually enjoyable. If they insist on doing what they want, then by all means encourage them to do just that, and not to victimize you into doing anything that you dislike, any more than you would do the same to them. When you do play or work together, make it mutually satisfying. Do not feel any guilt about telling them to figure out their own creative approaches to filling up their lives with activity to eliminate their boredom, and tell them not to expect you to be their source of entertainment in life.

Allow children the right to have space of their own to create, to think, to just sit, or to do whatever they feel like doing. Creative people need privacy! Do not always ask them, "What's wrong?" or "Why don't you share it with all of us?" or "I'm your mother—you can tell me." The very same child who comes running to you with a cut knee at the age of nine, wanting you to soothe her, will run into her room three years later, slam the door, and become indignant if you want to help her or talk to her about her scrape. You are the same parent, only three years have gone by, but for that child, a full 25 percent of life has transpired. She now needs to be alone, to think about things herself, to figure out her own responses, without a "meddling" parent (who is really motivated by love) interfering. If you see this scene developing in your home, instead of being upset that the children do not come to you anymore or believing that something is wrong, murmur a private blessing to yourself. "I've done something right. They are learning to handle their problems by themselves, and that is what parenting is about: teaching them to think for themselves and to figure out their own unique solutions." If you attempt to crowd your children and insist that they tell you everything, or if you spy on them by going through their possessions while they are out of the house, you are violating a strong principle of effective creative parenting. They need privacy; they need a place that is theirs which is not subject to arbitrary inspections. As long as you are trying to help them to cultivate a sense of personal creativity, do not interpret their desires to be alone as having anything to do with rejection. It is normal, healthy, and absolutely necessary for them to want to be alone.

As a person who has spent the greater part of his life in creative pursuits I can attest to my need to a lot of alone time. I need time to think without having someone inquiring about what I am doing and whether everything is all right. I need time to be alone for the purpose of concentrating on my life's work: to think things through without any interference or distractions, to be by myself in order to apply all of my creative juices to my work. I have tried doing it with others around, and for me, it simply does not work. Unless I can get away by myself—to think, to write, to study, to be frustrated, to tear up my notes, to start over, to sit around unshaven and undressed at my typewriter—without any prying eyes or inquiring minds, then I simply do not create. Your children are very much the same. Give them space and time alone if they want it, and do not assume that something is wrong when they just want to be alone. It is usually a sign of increased maturity. Remember as you fret over their alone time that "People who cannot stand to be alone, usually cannot stand the person they are alone with." If they want privacy for being creative, you know that they must have a strong, healthy self-image; otherwise, they would be lonely rather than simply alone now and then.

When you provide praise for your children, try to put the proud part on what it means to them, rather than teaching them to only go after external rewards. Teach them the value of pursuing their own excellence, rather than striving for merit badges, trophies, stars, and approval. For example:

External Reward	Creative Praise
You got the highest mark in the class. I'm so proud of you.	Just think, you can spell fifty more words than you could last week.
You came in first place. That's great!	You are such a terrific athlete! All that practice is paying off for you.
You got the highest SAT score in your school. That's quite an achievement.	You certainly are terrific at taking those tests. I always knew you were a genius.
You won a trophy for your school attendance.	I'll bet you are proud of yourself, not missing one day of school.

The major emphasis should be on what an achievement means to a child, rather than keeping the focus on whom they beat or how they compare with everyone else in the school. Creative people have internal standards that are only important to them, and they are generally immune to what everyone else is achieving. Thus, the more you can keep the emphasis on what every activity means to the child personally, the more you will be encouraging that child to strive for his or her own internal excellence. This is also true of excessive competition. Remember that a child who needs to beat someone else in order to feel like a winner, or who is always looking over his shoulder to see how the competitors are faring, is actually being controlled by the performances of others. This is not creativity. The child is judging himself by how he stacks up against others. If his competitor falls down, that makes him a winner. This is really a losing mentality. If you have to beat everyone else all the time, or be number one at all costs, then you will be a loser for a lifetime. No one—I repeat, no one—can be in the number one position all of the time. This standard for personal excellence makes losers out of everyone.

A different approach is to look within for personal standards. Be competitive and work as hard as possible in given areas of life, but never judge yourself a failure simply because you lost to someone else. Creative people are those who do not compare themselves with others; instead, they cooperate with others and use their own creative minds in ways that are satisfying to them. You can encourage this in children by deemphasizing the need to defeat others. Give children the opportunity to play their own competitive sports without the need for any adult interference, to make their own decisions while playing, and to argue out their own disagreements rather than having them all resolved by adult arbitrators. Let them start out each day with a new game, rather than being reminded of their place in the standings as a result of last week's play. In other words, let the children, not you or some other authority figure, create their own play, and leave the overly competitive athletics to those who are going to make careers out of being athletes. Children need time to play, to grow, to make decisions. They do not need adults organizing their uniforms, game schedules—and relegating less coordinated children to the benches until the game's outcome has been decided.

Keep in mind that creative children are not necessarily clean and neat children. If you insist on keeping them spotless, you might as well forget about their creative development. They need to explore, to play in the dirt, to get down into the earth and grovel around. They will get scratches, cuts, bruises, and—most of all—dirty hands and faces. Accept it, rather than fight it. It is very unlikely that they will want to keep their rooms clean and spotless, and the less pressure you put on them to organize their lives around your adult principles, the more likely they will be to develop more healthy creative habits. Creativity does not have anything to do with putting everything in its place and having life organized like an accountant's ledger. Creativity means being loose, free to think and explore, sloppy now and then, and certainly not regimented and orderly. Remove the emphasis on keeping their lives neatly organized, and allow for as much spontaneity as possible. Telling them to clean their rooms is a contradiction in terms. If it is truly the child's room, then you ought to keep your eyes off it and let the child decide how it is to be arranged. As long as there are no cockroaches scurrying from under the door, and there is no hygiene problem, then let the child's room be just that—the *child's* room! Children's rooms are their creative places, and just as you would not want anyone telling you how to organize and live in your room, they have the same right. It will save you a million fights if you just learn to shut the door and ignore the mess. After all, if they are unique individuals, then why should they want to live in their rooms the way that you think they should?

There you have some ideas for helping children to maximize their creative potential. Keeping in mind that creativity is an attitude toward life, and that it is something which simply defies definition, you can do much to help children along this no-limit path. The more you stay in touch with just what is unique about each of your children, and the more you can do to praise and encourage that individuality, rather than stifling it in the name of fitting in, the more you are raising them on creativity. Creativity cannot be measured, graded, or otherwise evaluated by anyone else. Eliminate those external attempts to quantify and evaluate your children's creativity. Here is a quote from Wolfgang Amadeus Mozart, who in only thirty-five years of living was considered one of our most creative geniuses.

> When I am . . . completely myself, entirely alone . . . or during the night when I cannot sleep, it is on such occasions that my ideas flow best and most abundantly. Whence and how these come I know not nor can I force them.

Keep these words in mind, "When I am completely myself," for that is the essence of all that I have written in this chapter. Children allowed and encouraged to be completely themselves will creatively shine like the noonday sun. For that, after all, is what creativity is, and nothing more: simply being oneself and applying that unique self to being alive. Raising them on creativity does not require any more of your time or energy, only a different attitude—a creative attitude, if you will.

I Want My Children to Fulfill Their Higher Needs and to Feel a Sense of Purpose

The no-limit person displays a strong sense of purpose in most or all areas of life. His holistic world-view allows him to see meaning everywhere. He is primarily motivated by higher human needs and values. His search for truth, beauty, justice, and peace are always uppermost. He decides what pattern of growth he wants to pursue next for himself and lets others do the same. He is completely global in values and self-identification, and is able to take pride in local accomplishments when they contribute to the good of humanity. He is intellectually motivated by his natural curiosity and instincts to seek the truth for himself in all possible life situations. He follows his own internal lights in all things, pursuing work that is meaningful to him rather than for external monetary rewards. He never measures anyone's worth in terms of money. If he gets rich, it will be "by accident" in pursuing his purpose. He sees the whole world as beautiful and wonderful and therefore has no limits to its varieties of beauty. He sees all people as intrinsically beautiful even if their actions or creations sometimes are not. He sees all life as sacred and all human lives as of equal worth. He believes war, violence, famine, and plague can be eliminated if humanity chooses, and devotes his life to improving the lives of everyone and ending injustice.

Man is a being in search of meaning.

—PLATO

Our number one goal needs to be centered on helping children to feel a strong sense of inner satisfaction in leading purposeful lives. Without that strong sense of meaning, the individual feels lost, aimless, and unsure of why he is here. While this may sound like more of a philosophical discussion than the final chapter in a book about raising children to become no-limit people, I assure you that there is much that you can do in a practical way to help your children to grow up with purpose and higher values in their hearts at all moments of their development.

It is crucial for you to understand that in order to be able to feel a strong sense of purpose, children have to learn to transcend their personal wants and become engaged in the service of other people. One must learn how to get past himself, to stop focusing exclusively on his own physical wants, to eliminate the concern about what is good for "me, me, me" and how I will be affected, to what is good for others. Children gradually have to learn to stop thinking about themselves and how they are personally affected by everything they do, and to shift their focus to their activities and how those activities will help to improve the quality of life for others. One generally feels most purposeful in life while helping others in some way, but it has nothing to do with denying oneself, putting oneself down, or thinking of others as more important. It works on a completely different level altogether. A person who is vitally involved in his own work, who is literally lost in what he is doing, has no time left over to worry about what the effects will be on himself. He is not focused on how others will think about him, nor does he do what he does for any attention or recognition from those around him. He does what is important to him because it makes him happy and fulfilled inside to be so engaged, and all of the external rewards and opinions of others are of no interest to him at all. Getting to this point—wherein you are conducting your life based upon your own inner lights, where you are excited about your activities and completely involved in your everyday actions, where what you are doing is somehow helping to make this world a better place for at least one other human being—is actually what it means to feel a sense of purpose in life. But in order to reach this place, you and your children will have to go through the steps that lead up to a strong sense of purpose and meaning.

Children must have so much self-love and self-respect that they are givens, not things that they are constantly looking over their shoulders to receive from others. They will have to proceed through the "selfish" steps of self-interest and become at peace with themselves before they can put all of that to rest and get on with their life missions. They will have to be so filled up with love and respect for themselves that they will have plenty of the same to give to others. Each child must be absolutely certain about his or her own integrity and then have enough of it stored away within to use for the betterment of others. They will have to get to the place where they will be as equally delighted to see friends receive gifts as they are to have them themselves. In fact, they will ultimately learn to feel better about the good things that others receive and to not even care about receiving things themselves.

A sense of purpose can be cultivated in a child from the earliest beginnings, and it can also begin today regardless of the present age of your child. Developing a sense of purpose is really nothing more than helping children adopt attitudes toward themselves and their work (the work of children is play) that revolve around the theme of "getting outside oneself" and becoming completely absorbed in all of life's activities. You can help your children to arrive at that glorious place in life where they know why they are here and are thrilled to be doing exactly what they are choosing to do. It is the greatest joy that a human being can experience, and your children have every right to be there throughout their lives. Feeling purposeful is what no-limit parenting is about. If you get yourself on track as a parent, and if you see parenting as not only helping each child to learn and experience his or her own sense of purpose, but as a real part of your own purpose in life, you will begin to feel an inner glow of satisfaction about your reason for being here. By helping each child to cultivate his or her own sense of purpose, you will be partially fulfilling your own. As long as you are in the service of others, including your own children, you are making a difference in the world, and that is the big key to feeling purposeful. Making a difference. Making this place better for those we leave behind.

Climbing the Ladder of Needs That Ends with a Sense of Purpose

Abraham Maslow, the famous psychologist who first wrote about human beings optimistically and in terms of their magnificent potential, rather than developing theories based upon their weaknesses, provided us with a wonderful paradigm for looking at our own parenting behavior. He called this design mankind's hierarchy of needs, assuming that each human being must start from the bottom and fulfill his basic needs, moving up to the very top, which he called "self-actualization" and which I call "no-limit living." In order to reach this level of self-actualization, a level I have been writing about in each of the chapters of this book, a person must first satisfy a ladderlike progression of needs. The higher one goes on this ladder, the more fully one is able to function at a neurosis-free, purposeful, and happy level of existence.

Without going too deeply into each of these needs levels on Maslow's hierarchy, I am going to share with you the basics of his theory. I have found Maslow's work to be most significant for me; it certainly had a profound effect on my own personal and professional development. Maslow departed from all of the previous researchers on human behavior in his positive approach to man's unlimited potential. What he did was to study the greatest achievers, rather than examining those who were loaded with neuroses and psychoses, in order to create his theory, which he called "a psychology of being." He based his theory on the fact that man can be motivated by growth, rather than by his need to repair his deficiencies. Consequently, a person can accept himself where he is in any given present moment as perfect, fully alive and fully functioning. With this acceptance of oneself, a person is capable of being motivated by his desire to grow. Yes! Perfect in the moment, yet at the same time capable of growth. Thus, one does not have to admit to being deficient in order to have a goal. This was a radical departure, but it was the basis for an entirely new approach to helping people to become no-limit people. After studying hundreds of people who seemed to function at the very highest levels in all walks of life, Maslow developed his theory using this logic: "If some human beings are capable of high-level living and fully functioning lives, then let's study these people and learn all that we can from our very top-functioning human beings. Let's see how they think, what they do, what they are made of, and let's assume that human beings can reach those highest levels by giving them something to shoot for." In other words, be motivated by our greatest people of all time, rather than studying the sickest people and trying to help others by having them overcome their deficiencies.

Thus Maslow's hierarchy of needs was developed, and it is most relevant to you as a parent, in that you can look at where you are leading your children on this path. You can see if they are going to be stuck at a lower rung for long periods of time, or if you are going to encourage them to climb ever higher. The very top of this hierarchy is that place called *no-limits,* a brief description of which you have seen at the very beginning of every chapter in the book you are now reading. Here is that ladder as I interpret it, and what it means to you as you help your child to climb the bottom rungs and work at living in the very highest levels. It is only at the higher rungs that you will find the hard-to-define place that I have described as a sense of purpose. Also, it is only in the higher elevations of this hierarchy that you will see children develop the most gloriously important and self-fulfilling values that will keep them from ever having such a thing as a depressing day, an anxiety attack, or any of the "normal" neuroses that so many people experience because they stay rooted on the rungs closest to the safety of the ground. Examine these rungs on the ladder in terms of how you can help children to be constantly climbing, while simultaneously enjoying right where they are as well. To be motivated by their desire to grow. To love every moment of their lives, but to still have dreams and imagination to help them to climb without disliking the place where they currently find themselves.

What Maslow offered was a psychology of arriving (as I talked about in Chapter 7) as opposed to a psychology of striving. Here are the various levels. See if you are on target in your goal of helping your children to reach and stay at that magical place at the top called no-limit living. Remember, they must move through the lower levels as children in order to move on to the next level. It is like hitting a triple in baseball. Just because you will end up with three bases does not mean that you can simply head directly for third base, without touching first and second bases.

PHYSICAL NEEDS

It is obvious that we must first learn to take care of our basic physical needs if we are going to survive even for one day. You will begin early to help your children take over the responsibility of providing for themselves in this vital area. The purely biological needs that children are absolutely entitled to as a function of their humanity include the needs for air, water, food, shelter, and sleep. Without any of these vital commodities, the child will die. These are called "needs" because the organism requires them for its very survival. When you participate in bringing a child into the world, you have an absolute responsibility to provide for that child's needs, and most importantly to provide for his or her physical survival needs. We all have a responsibility to provide these vital needs for children in the world, regardless of where they might be located on our planet. No child ought ever be denied air, water, food, shelter, or sleep. If any child on our globe is starving, then all of us in a very real sense are also starving. First you must take care of your own physical needs, then those of your own children, and then all of the other children of the world.

While this may sound like an enormous burden, it is also a big part of your purpose here on this planet. You do not have to feed them all in East Africa or Bangladesh, but you can do your own bit for making sure that you are sending out the appropriate loving and caring messages to the world. If every single person simply did what he was capable of doing, and behaved in a responsible way toward all the rest of us here on this planet, then the problems of not providing the bare essentials for all human beings would not even exist. Every child would be provided for. Thus, you can do whatever you are capable of doing, and you can accept that responsibility each day, first with your own children, and then for all of the others in the world as well. I know that I cannot feed and shelter everyone, but I can write about it, I can speak about it, I can donate what I can, I can help others to think about their contributions, and before long, my one single voice becomes a part of an idea whose time has come. And as Victor Hugo once said, "An invasion of armies can be resisted, but not an idea whose time has come." I know that I am departing on a more global sidetrack here. However, I feel strongly that any person who cares about his or her own children must also make a commitment to all of the children. This is most urgent in the area of providing basic needs.

You know that each person in the world needs to have his or her basic survival needs met, and you also do not need me to tell you how to go about doing that for your children. By and large, if you provide them with healthy food as I suggest in Chapter 8, and if you provide for only minimal facilities for sleep and shelter, and a supply of fresh water, then they will pretty much be able to take care of themselves after leaving the infancy stage of development. What you probably did not know is that more than half of all the children on our globe do not have their minimal standards of physical biological needs met. Half and more of our children are undernourished. Far too many have no place to sleep, and no fresh water to drink. A huge percentage of the world's children do not have adequate shelter, and with the increase in air pollution, better than half of our children are condemned to breathe polluted air. So, you see, all of us are directly affected when we do not take an active role in helping to ensure that every single child has the opportunity to have his or her physical needs met in a salubrious environment.

You certainly do whatever is necessary for your children to have their biological needs provided for in an appropriate surrounding, but are you aware of your responsibility to ensure that everyone has the exact same opportunity? This must be your concern and the concern of your children as well. On the matter of the horrible conditions that exist for young children in all corners of our planet, your opinions are essentially trivial. That is right; I said your opinions are trivial. Only your commitments make any difference in the world. What you do will speak much louder than what you say. A commitment to do something about the most trivial of problems is far superior to a strong opinion concerning the most profound problem. You will find your sense of purpose when you remember the importance of your own commitments, and also as you remind yourself that having an opinion is basically irrelevant in doing something of value. The karmic principle "That what goes around comes around" is of great importance in this section. The more you give away to help to provide for the basic needs of all human beings wherever they may be, the more you will receive back from your commitments. The more you do nothing but expound about how terrible it is, the more nothing will come back into your life, by way of an empty feeling of powerlessness.

There is one final point concerning the basic physical needs of your children (and everyone else's children as well). A child who is on this bottom rung of the hierarchy of needs, and is not being provided with enough food, water, shelter, and the like, will soon die from malnutrition or exposure. However, as you read on about the higher rungs on this ladder, keep in mind that when an individual is provided with the opportunity to go right to the very top of this ladder, to the point that I call "no-limits," that very same individual can make the *choice* to fast, and survive at a high level with even smaller amounts of food than would have been required to keep him alive at the bottom rung. Keep this thought uppermost in mind as you consider your efforts to help a child to attain the very highest rungs on this ladder of life. When a person has a choice, he can make literally anything happen for himself, but if he is deprived at the very earliest rungs, he will have had choice taken away and he will die. To take away choices from children is literally to kill them before they can ever make a decision about survival. This was the great lesson of Herman Hesse's classic parable, *Siddhartha*. Here is a brief excerpt, but I recommend that you make this one book that you reread yearly. It is one of my all-time favorite books, for it speaks to me about my own purpose, and I learn something new from it each time I read it. Listen in as Siddhartha, who has temporarily given up all worldly possessions in order to experience total poverty firsthand, talks to a merchant.

> "That seems to be the way of things. Everyone takes, everyone gives. Life is like that." [said Siddhartha]
>
> "Ah, but if you are without possessions, how can you give?"
>
> "Everyone gives what he has. The soldier gives strength, the merchant goods, the teacher instructions, the farmer rice, the fisherman fish."
>
> "Very well and what can you give? What have you learned that you can give?" [the merchant asks of Siddhartha]
>
> "I can think, I can wait, I can fast."
>
> "Is that all?"
>
> "I think that is all."
>
> "And of what use are they? For example, fasting, what good is that?"
>
> "It is of great value, sir. If a man has nothing to eat, fasting is the most intelligent thing he can do. If, for instance, Siddhartha had not learned to fast, he would have *had* to seek some kind of work today, either with you, or elsewhere, for hunger would have driven him. But, as it is, Siddhartha can wait calmly. He is not impatient, he is not in need, he can ward off hunger for a long time and laugh at it. Therefore, fasting is useful, sir."

Had Siddhartha not achieved some degree of enlightenment, the absence of food would have killed him. We must all provide food *and* enlightenment to all the children of the world so that they will not have choices taken away.

You can give what you have. Even more important, you can teach your children to do precisely the same thing. You can teach them the lesson of giving, sharing, and making a difference in the world. You can help them to internalize the values that will allow them to reach out to assist others in having their physical needs met, and in the process they will help others to do the same. This can help to make all the difference in the world, much like the snowball effect, growing and growing because of the power of an idea whose time has come. In just a brief time, with enough of us practicing helping others to fill their own needs, that snowball will become a mass of caring, overtaking the selfishness and greed that have created the conditions whereby children must perish because their essential rights as humans have been denied. It is through this very change in consciousness that the world will be transformed, and nothing will be able to halt that avalanche, when you make it part of your purpose and help your children to do the same.

LOVE AND BELONGINGNESS NEEDS

Your children's basic survival needs must be met each and every moment of each day they are alive. Yet, as you move up the ladder, the remaining needs of children are equally important for their survival. While the effects of having love and belongingness denied to a child may not be as dramatically evident, and the results take somewhat longer to become manifest, nevertheless, without a sufficient amount of love and belongingness, children will perish just as surely as if you deprive them of food and water.

Love is needed by all human beings in order to feel a sense of belonging. In studies of children who have been denied all forms of human love, such as being isolated in closets, it has been learned that children cannot recover from such ordeals, and that eventually they perish if that denial of love has been too extreme over a protracted period of time. Love is a basic human right. If you bring a child into the world, you are obligated by moral laws higher than any that have been written by man, to provide the basic survival needs for that human life, as well as seeing to it that your child receives sufficient amounts of love. This book has been filled with provocative suggestions for bringing more and more love into the lives of your children. Every technique that I have written about throughout these pages has been designed to provide for the love needs of your children. They need to know that you care about them, that you have the self-interest of each of them at heart, that you want them, and that you appreciate them. They need to feel deep within themselves that you are raising them to become all that they are capable of being. As I said previously, early in their lives you must give them excessive amounts of touching, holding, kissing, stroking, massaging, and basic human contact. If you feel that this goes against your nature, then change your nature for the good—no, for the survival of your children. If you say that you cannot change your basic nature, change that phrase to "will not" and then examine yourself as to why you would choose to abdicate your responsibilities. You have a free will to be the kind of person you elect, and there is no "cannot" for free-willed people.

As children pass through infancy, the need to be touched and held does not diminish. In fact, that need never diminishes; only the forms that it takes change as children proceed through their development. Your children still need to feel loved. It is important to give them plenty of genuine love throughout their lives. It should be in the form of touching and talking—and then, of course, the real payoff comes in the actions that you display toward your children on a daily basis. Saying "I love you," "You are terrific," "I think you are the most gorgeous child ever," or "I adore you" are the important kinds of affirmations for children right from the time they are born until you leave the planet. We are beginning to amass evidence that saying these things to tiny infants in a loving way gets through to them the message of comfort and belonging. We are learning that children who are held, touched, comforted, kissed, and talked to in loving ways can be reached even while they are sleeping, and that this kind of reinforcement helps to build a strong sense of self-worth and positive feelings toward themselves for a lifetime.

The more love you can send to your children, the more you are helping them to become filled up with love themselves. Obviously, the more love they have within, the more they will be able to give away. And, conversely, they cannot give away what they do not have. If you traced the causes of virtually all of the major problems that confront human beings today, you would find that the answers to these problems are so patently obvious and simple that it is mind-boggling that we do not solve them. The answers to all of the social problems that confront us as a human race are to love each other as much as we possibly can, from the time of conception, and never straying from that path.

Yes, love is really the answer. It is not a corny expression from a gushy idealist; it is genuinely the answer. First, examine the people who get themselves into difficulties, and end up in reform school, prison, or even ultimately on death row. The history of people who run seriously afoul of the standards that are necessary for a society to function, can always be traced to a lack of receiving or feeling love. The young street tough who starts by stealing cars and ends up with a drug habit and a handgun to do his bidding, was once a lovable little infant, with an opportunity to grow up to be a no-limit person and to feel productive and useful to the world. What goes wrong someplace along the way is an absence of love. While I do not believe that the prisoner can sit in his cell blaming others for his predicament, since taking responsibility for one's life is the very heartbeat of being a fully functioning person, nevertheless, with healthy dosages of love, feeling important, and having learned to give love rather than hate away to others, there would be little need for prisons at all. The judge who first had to sentence the young boy who was stealing cars, was not showing love or respect for him by being permissive. From the earliest beginnings, when a youngster begins to act toward others in a nonloving way, regardless of the causes, that young person needs more than anything to understand that there are consequences for acting that way. He needs to learn that acting hatefully is totally unacceptable, from the first time he slaps his little sister, or swears at his mother, or steals a candy bar or an automobile. The message should be "We love you enough to let you know that you cannot do such things." The acting out hatefully toward others comes from an absence of love inside. Similarly, when you squeeze a person and hate comes out, it is because that is what is inside. We must all work together to help our young people to have only love inside. Then, when they are "squeezed" or pressured in any way, it will be love that they will express.

As you think about the serious problems that face our world—including war, crime, famine, disease, and injustice—what we have is an absence-of-love problem. People who grow up loving humanity will not shoot at other people in the name of God, or in the name of anything else. People who feel loved and significant will not need to use or abuse others in order to feel dominant and important. When famine strikes, people who have love in their hearts go to work immediately to fix it. With enough people mobilized by love, a famine becomes a temporary inconvenience rather than a catastrophe. While I am not suggesting that if you simply love others our problems will all go away, I am suggesting that if you begin with your own children to practice giving love away, and then extend your giving to all of those with whom you come into contact, you will be making a big difference in the world.

The big, big problems of the world are not war, crime, poverty, starvation, injustice, or anything else; they are *people* problems. People who grow up with love do not want to commit crimes; they want to work and make the world a better place. People who grow up with love do not turn their heads and look away from starving people or poverty; they want to dig in and help out. *It is people who commit injustices against people*. It is people who shoot at each other, and it is people who build nuclear weapons to kill other people. Imagine a whole generation of people fed a diet of love and you will also be able to imagine a whole world working together. It all starts with you. Instead of breeding revenge and anger, hate and greed, you can vow to give all of your children, regardless of their current ages, heavy doses of love, in whatever way you are able to give it, forgetting about the negatives and your own personal wishes, and you will be making a giant step toward that universal love that I am writing about here on these pages. Love can definitely mean being firm, and not tolerating the opposite of love. Giving love can mean being honest and having integrity, but always it means not using anyone else for one's own advancement or self-interest. It always means thinking about what is good for your children and consequently for all the rest of God's children. I believe it is true that we can change the world if we all start with ourselves.

The ladder toward living at the highest levels must be traversed one rung at a time. Those lower rungs contain needs that absolutely must be met in order to get onto and stay at the higher levels. The need for giving and receiving love is as basic for all the children of the world as the need for having adequate amounts of oxygen. Practice giving love and turning hate out of your relationships with everyone each and every day, but especially with your children. Wherever you have any anger or hate within you, or whenever you act in such a way with your children, is the place for you to begin working on yourself. That is the very beginning place! And I am talking about you working on yourself, rather than focusing on what is wrong with your children—or with anyone else in the world, for that matter. Instead of saying, "He is just no damn good" or "She is plain and simple a stubborn brat," try thinking in a new way. Those kinds of sentiments, whether you want to hear it or not, are *your* problems, not those of your children. Those sentiments reflect judgments and feelings that are located within you. Even if you feel that they are absolutely true and that you have the evidence, they nevertheless reside in you, and that is where you must begin as a parent. You too are like that orange, and when you utter ugly statements, or harbor hateful thoughts, it is because they are inside you. Send love when your children show troublesome behaviors—firm, yes; no-nonsense, yes; but always love—and they will grow up with love inside them. Remember what Gandhi once said, which is perhaps his greatest contribution as a holy man: "An eye for an eye, and soon the whole world will be blind."

Think carefully about this business of sending love out. Your children must have it if they are to survive. Your children must have it if they are to grow, to mature, and to feel a sense of belonging, first to themselves, then to their own families and communities, and ultimately to the world and universe. Those who run seriously afoul of humanity, and who harbor anger and hatreds instead of love, simply do not feel as if they belong anywhere, and consequently they strike out at others to reflect their own self-contempt. The more love that is sent to replace that hatred, the sooner they begin to sense that they do belong, and when that occurs, the need to strike out hatefully not only disappears, but the need to behave in such a way is forever banished from their lives. If this strikes you as liberal nonsense, talk to anyone who has ever worked with hardened criminals or even with those who appear to have been hopelessly labeled as mentally defective or insane. When love replaces the hate, and when love and respect are used as a tool, and if enough of it is distributed, then even those who were once considered unreachable seem to come around.

There is even evidence that young people who have been tagged with the labels of schizophrenic, autistic, insane, and other cruel categorizations can be reached with overly powerful treatments of love. I suggest that you read *Son Rise* by Barry Kaufman as a starting point, for more on reaching the unreachable "stars." Think of love as a basic right of your children. Think of giving love in all of your interactions with your children. Think of love as the way to heal ourselves and our planet, and then simply do what comes naturally. You do not need a course in how to dispense love to your children; you simply need to overcome your resistance to the idea that it is the basis for our survival as a human species. Give it away, and it will come back to you a thousandfold. Give anger and hate away, and they too will come back in the same proportions. This is true for you, and for your children, and it will be true for the way in which they raise their children. You can actually break the chain that binds all of us to the practices of the past by dispensing love when you might otherwise have been tempted to disburse the opposite. You alone can make a big difference in the lives of your children, and millions of children to come, by giving as much love as you can possibly muster each and every time you interact with children and all other life as well.

THE NEED FOR SELF-ESTEEM AND ESTEEM BY OTHERS

The next rung on the ladder toward "no-limits" is self-esteem. It is all quite logical. First and most obviously we must provide for the needs that will sustain life. Then we must have love, which is equally, but not quite so obviously, necessary if children are to survive. Then, when children become filled with the love that you give to them, they begin to feel worthy of being loved, and they transfer the love you provide into self-love. It is another of those ironies that seem to run our lives that in order to be able to have self-love, one must first receive plenty of love from others. When we become filled with that love, we turn it into self-love, and from there, we are able to give it away without any danger of it ever diminishing. To be loving persons, children must feel love for self, and to feel that, they must receive love from you and others.

As you give heavy amounts of love to your children and help them to feel wanted and to have a sense of belongingness, they develop their own images of themselves. The more that self-image is one of being positive and feeling like a terrific person, the more of those kinds of feelings the child will develop toward all other people with whom he or she comes into contact. If children have self-contempt they will be filled with contemptuous feelings, and that is what they will give away to others. If they are filled with self-love, that is precisely what they will have inside to give to others. The building of a strong self-image based upon self-esteem is an absolute need for each person. It is called a need, because without it, a person will turn on himself and others in destructive ways, and ultimately be unable to function either alone or in a social fashion. I believe so strongly in helping children to have powerful self-images that I devoted the entire second chapter of this book to providing you with specific techniques for helping your children to always have strong positive views of themselves. I suggest that you reread that chapter and see how neatly it fits into this hierarchy of needs that children must master if they are going to have a sense of purpose and mission throughout their lives.

GROWTH NEEDS (FREEDOM, JUSTICE, ORDER, INDIVIDUALITY, MEANINGFULNESS, SELF-SUFFICIENCY, SIMPLICITY, PLAYFULNESS, ALIVENESS)

As your children proceed to the higher rungs on the needs ladder, they will have been developing a positive self-image, in which they see themselves as lovable, important, and belonging exactly where they happen to be. The next rung includes the need to grow and develop into functional human beings. Children will develop a sense of purpose provided they are motivated by the desire to grow rather than from a position of having to repair their deficiencies. Abraham Maslow described this phenomenon in his classic book, *Toward a Psychology of Being,* in this way: ". . . there is a real clinical difference between fending off threat or attack and positive triumph and achievement, between protecting, defending, and preserving oneself and reaching out for fulfillment, for excitement and enlargement." The deficiency-motivated child is always motivated by the need to overcome some basic flaws in his life; thus he sees himself as unworthy and is motivated to become worthy. Growth-motivated children accept themselves as valuable, significant human beings who have worth because they exist and are motivated to grow and acquaint themselves with other areas of life. These "meta" needs are crucial to the development of a strong sense of purpose for your child. They include (in no particular order of importance) the needs for freedom, justice, order, individuality, meaningfulness, self-sufficiency, simplicity, playfulness, and aliveness. Each of these words symbolizes a specific need that children have as their self-esteem grows, provided the basic needs for safety and security and the purely physiological needs for air, water, food, shelter, and sleep have been satisfied.

As they proceed up the ladder toward personal mastery, children must have opportunities to feel free to be choice-makers, to know that they can have justice for themselves and that they will not be unfairly persecuted because of the whims of others. They need to have some sense of order to their lives and consistently loving parents on whom they can rely for solid advice and examples of what they are growing into. They need always to feel appreciative of their own individuality and to avoid being compared with others. They need to learn how to take care of themselves, to really feel self-sufficient, and to be praised regularly and authentically for their achievements and for their personal uniqueness. They need to feel playful and to see life as fun, and to have you joining in on this approach to fun living. And mostly they need to feel creatively alive, to have a burning sense of desire and appreciation for everything in life. To eschew boredom and dullness, and to glow in the excitement of each and every day. It is not some farfetched ideal. It can be a reality.

In all of the previous chapters of this book I have alluded to these growth needs, and I have provided many techniques and guidelines that I believe will help to shape the thinking and inner worlds of your children so as to have them focused clearly on being motivated in everything they think and do by their desires to grow, rather than to fix up their deficiencies. I do not believe children have deficiencies. I believe they are valuable and significant at all times, but that growth is always possible, and that they can grow and still enjoy being where they are. This belief is summarized in the statement that I have used many times in my writing and my speaking, "You don't have to be sick to get better."

Keep this hierarchy in mind. As you help your children through your daily interactions, keep in mind that these growth needs, while not as present-moment crucial as food and shelter, can be equally as significant to their inner development as an absence of food is to their physical development. Beyond the growth needs mentioned in this section, you proceed up the ladder to what Maslow called the "higher needs."

HIGHER NEEDS (TRUTH, BEAUTY, AESTHETIC APPRECIATION, GOODNESS, SPIRITUAL AWAKENING)

Children have needs that transcend even those growth needs described in the preceding section. As your children climb through these various phases, and are having their needs met at each developmental stage, they ultimately reach the point where they will begin to feel a very strong sense of purpose and meaning in life. It is in the higher needs that too many parents drop the ball, figuring that these are no longer needs we are talking about, but merely belief systems or choices in faith. According to the work of Maslow and many scholars, the higher needs also constitute a need structure, if the child is going to reach the top of the ladder and live that neurosis-free, purposeful life I described in the beginning pages of this book.

Keep in mind that we are not talking about children simply learning to cope with life, to get along with the environment. We are talking about raising children as no-limit people, children who will never have "anxiety attacks" or feel lost and depressed in life. We are talking about children who will grow to become masters of their world, where they are to their own lives like a great artist is to his masterpiece, shading and shaping the canvas so as to create precisely what they want from their lives. Awareness of these higher needs, and the highest need of self-actualization described in the following section, represents the real difference between simply getting along in life, and creating one's own life. The higher needs that it is crucial for children to internalize in their inner worlds include truth, goodness, beauty, aesthetic appreciation, and spiritual awakening.

Once again it is important to understand that children must be operating at a mastery level with the lower rung needs, in order to be able to get to this place in their lives. When they begin to have their aesthetic and spiritual needs met, they will have mastered the purposefulness that is lacking in almost everyone else's life. It is in these higher need categories that the real dilemmas faced by most people are resolved. Whenever people tell me that they do not know what their purpose is, or why they are here, or that they are still looking for a purpose, I realize that they are still searching because they are fixated in the more basic need categories described in the preceding sections. Once such a person is able to forget about himself and begin to see the need for truth, spiritualism, goodness, and beauty appreciation on our planet, then every single thing he sees or does becomes a part of that mission. When one wants to make the world a better and more beautiful place for everyone, one does not concern oneself with lower needs; they are met automatically. One becomes an example of that beauty, and instead of looking for how to do it, literally lives it. When one knows the importance of truth, one does not try to spread it around or to find it; *one is it*. Yes, a person can stop looking for it all, and instead *be* it all.

This is one of the most difficult areas to write about, and yet it is crucial that you understand what I am saying right here in these sentences you are now reading. A sense of purpose is not something that you find; it is something that you are. Truth is not something that you look for; it is something that you live. Your children need truth for survival, just as they need oxygen and water. Imagine having to live in an atmosphere in which no one ever told the truth, in which everything was lies. How could you believe anyone, how could you function, if no one spoke the truth? Soon one would go crazy trying to figure out what was real and what was a lie, and then when one finally had it resolved, someone would say, "I was lying—that isn't the truth at all." In many environments, where lying runs rampant, people develop such a strong feeling of mistrust that living sensibly becomes impossible. Yes, truth is a need, but it must be something that children grow up to be, rather than to search for and find in someone or something else. This applies to each of the other higher needs as well. The need for beauty appreciation can be seen when you expose people for long periods of time to ugly, deteriorating, filthy environments. Survival becomes impossible when there is no opportunity to have some beauty appreciation in one's environment. The ultimate in meeting the higher need for beauty is not in being able to appreciate a great painting, or to enjoy a classical concert, it is in *being* appreciative within. It is having the capacity to appreciate anything for its own unique beauty, and the internal attitudes that allow for seeing the beauty in everyone and everything. One carries this appreciation inside oneself, rather than trying to find it in anything else. One has it and lives it, rather than trying to find it. This kind of approach to beauty appreciation fits into the psychology of being, rather than into a psychology of striving for higher and higher places.

As you examine each of these higher needs, you will find that the same approach applies to all of them. Goodness is not a quality that one discovers in something outside himself; it is a quality that one must live. Thus, as parents, you can help your children to feel good about themselves, to appreciate the goodness of this world, and to always be looking for the good. Then they will *be* goodness and they will see it everywhere, and their mission will be clearer. They will know that spreading that feeling of goodness is far more important than trying to become a goody-goody person who is only trying to feel more positive about himself by pleasing everyone else. They will *be* what they choose, and goodness is something that they will bring to life, rather than trying to get it out of life.

Finally, the higher need of spiritual awakening will fit into their lives in the same manner. Again, this is a matter of *being* spiritual, rather than attempting to attain spiritual awakening through a certain religious orientation, belonging to a particular church, or practicing religious beliefs imposed by someone else. Attaining spiritual awakening means being willing to be spiritual, rather than asking for guidance from above. It means carrying around spiritualism and all that it implies everywhere one goes, and bringing it to one's life mission, rather than attempting to find it from an outside source. Spiritual awakening, like all of the higher needs, is an inner process. People who have it as part of their humanity are not necessarily proselytizing for an organization, but are instead filled with the awe and wonder of the entire universe. They become people who give love away, who respect all other life, and who accept that everything happens for a reason and that the universe is a perfect place, with no mistakes.

Being spiritual is quite different from attempting to be a religious person, or a good Protestant, Catholic, Jew, Buddhist, or any other organizational label. It means being Christ-like, rather than being a Christian. It means being Buddha, rather than labeling oneself as a Buddhist. Being spiritual means one does not kill, defame, defile, or act immorally regardless of who is telling one to so conduct oneself. Being spiritual is a way of living, not membership in an organization. It is a part of you and your children, and no rules, laws, patriotic duty, or anything else can transcend one's basic spiritual belief in the sanctity of life, the need to send out love, and the need for all creatures to live in harmony. There is no killing in the name of God, and still claiming to be spiritual. There is no fighting and hate carried out in the name of religion. There are only actions, and as is written in the New Testament, "Our love is not to be just words or mere talk, but something real and active; thereby we know that we are of the truth." Notice that it says, "of the truth." That means *being* truth, beauty, spirituality and goodness, not simply talking them, or joining an organization and believing that such membership makes one spiritual. It is the being part that is the crux of the higher needs and values, and while I have written much in this book about attaining no-limit living, this part about *being* is the most important lesson you can teach your children. When they get these higher needs resolved, they will never again ask about their purpose, nor will they ever wonder why they are here. It will be as much a part of them as their faces, lungs, feet, and everything else that makes up an individual's essence.

Progressing up the ladder does not stop with these higher needs, as you will see in the last section of this chapter, on techniques for helping children all the way up the ladder. The highest place on Maslow's hierarchy is what he called self-actualization, and what I call *no-limit living*. This is the place where children are living in a neurosis-free, fully alive space each and every moment of each and every day of their lives. It is a special place, one that will attract some criticism but one which will leave them full of awe and excitement about their entire universe, including themselves.

THE TOP OF THE LADDER—NO-LIMIT LIVING: A SUMMARY DESCRIPTION

At the beginning of each chapter with the exception of my opening statement, I have included a brief description (taken directly from *The Sky's the Limit*) of the no-limit person as a goal or objective for you to keep in mind for your children. Below is a recapitulation of each of these descriptions. This is the top of the ladder; it is the place where purpose, mission, fulfillment, excitement, and appreciation for being part of the universe take place.

The no-limit person is self-fulfilling; has great enthusiasm for himself, with no regrets or reservations. No time or need to be conceited. Recognizes that love and respect come to the person who cultivates them; is genuinely loved and respected by all who can return his original openness to them; does not worry about others rejecting him.

The no-limit person seeks out the unknown and loves the mysterious. He welcomes change and will experiment with almost anything in life. He views failure as a part of the learning process. Success comes naturally in the fulfillment of life projects and practice at things he deeply cares about.

The no-limit person pursues his own individual destiny by his own best internal lights. He feels every moment of life as one of free personal choice. He never wastes time blaming anyone for his own faults or the woes of the world. He depends on nobody else for his own identity or self-worth.

The no-limit person knows that worrying only inhibits performance, and he sees nothing in life to complain about. He never manipulates others with guilt or allows them to manipulate him. He has learned to avoid anxious thinking. Is as happy alone as with anyone else. Seeks out privacy. Cultivates the art of relaxation and recreation. Is expert at attaining total relaxation at will.

The no-limit person is mobilized rather than immobilized by anger. He "keeps his cool" while fighting for a creative, constructive solution. He is a pleasure to work with and to be around. He goes with the flow rather than fighting life. He thinks, feels, and behaves as a self-master.

The no-limit person sees the past in terms of what it has taught him about how to live now, and the future as more present moments to be lived when they arrive. He lives exclusively and fully in the present moment. He is able to make peak experiences out of most all activities. He prefers not to have "a plan" if possible, in order to make room for spontaneity.

The no-limit person pursues physical "superhealth" with minimal reliance on doctors and pills, knowing it is all in his power to preserve and strengthen himself. He loves his basic animal nature and is in awe of how beautifully his body functions. He exercises for the physical joy of it and appreciates aging as the universal medium of life and growth. He recognizes that a sense of humor is vital to all aspects of life.

The no-limit person has no sense of ownership toward others with whom he is associated; recognizes that the best way to lose anything is to try to hold too tightly to it; is virtually immune to jealousy; takes a cooperative approach toward thinking through any problem; is never upset by labels people stick on him or others; understands the truth in seeming opposites; takes joy in the successes of others and rejects the comparison/competition game as a whole. He has no specific heroes and recognizes that for every famous hero there are millions of unsung heroes; sees a hero in everyone, but is too busy making his own contributions to live vicariously through anyone else. He places no positive value on conformity for its own sake and is able to get around petty rules and customs as easily and quietly as possible. He approaches others with pure, childlike honesty and always lets his own creative imagination loose in any situation, approaches everything in life from a creative point of view.

The no-limit person displays a strong sense of purpose in most or all areas of life. His holistic world-view allows him to see meaning everywhere. He is primarily motivated by higher human needs and values. His search for truth, beauty, justice, and peace are always uppermost. He decides what pattern of growth he wants to pursue next for himself and lets others do the same. He is completely global in values and self-identification, and is able to take pride in local accomplishments when they contribute to the good of humanity. He is intellectually motivated by his natural curiosity and instincts to seek the truth for himself in all possible life situations. He follows his own internal lights in all things, pursuing work that is meaningful to him rather than for external monetary rewards. He never measures anyone's worth in terms of money. If he gets rich, it will be "by accident" pursuing his purpose. He sees the whole world as beautiful and wonderful and therefore has no limits to its varieties of beauty. He sees all people as intrinsically beautiful even if their actions or creations sometimes are not. He sees all life as sacred and all human lives as of equal worth. He believes war, violence, famine, and plague can be eliminated if humanity chooses, and devotes his life to improving the lives of everyone and ending injustice.

Some Specific Techniques for Helping Children to the Top of the Ladder and to a Sense of Purpose

Debaters may disagree about whether or not purpose in life can be found through employment or leisure activities, but few will contest the necessity for having a sense of purpose to make life meaningful. A sense of purpose must be established early and constantly reinforced through adulthood.

Childhood is regarded by most adults as a carefree, idyllic period. But childhood autism, schizophrenia, drug abuse, and suicide give evidence that some children are unable to find inner ways to handle difficulties and require specific and skillful interventions to acquire a meaningful life. Other youngsters, less severely impaired by lack of self-esteem, still struggle over the question "Why was I born?" There are some neurotic answers:

To carry on the family name and bring pride to the long line.

To entertain my bored mother.

To allow my father to live vicariously through my adventures.

To prove myself worthy, since I was an unwanted accident.

To take care of other siblings or my parents.

To play out a particular role (the comedian, the nice one, the smart one).

To be the "son" because they already had a "daughter."

To provide the family with a black sheep.

One basis for a sense of security while searching for a purpose in life is the feeling of welcome a person receives from the world. While adults may be strong enough to deal with rejection because their self-worth remains intact regardless of external judgments, babies have a *need* to be wanted. They are sensitive to the manner in which they are held, fed, talked to, cared for. Studies have been conducted which indicate that an unborn child is aware of light, sound, movement, and the chemistry connecting it to the mother. Her attitudes toward the pregnancy alter the physical environment that affects her child for nine introductory months.

Genetics and environment both have an impact on the infant who is already busy bringing the world into focus and balance. The more nurturing, positive data the baby can gather, the more firm and secure the belief that the real world is a good place to be. An infant willingly expands and grows more able to give as well as receive. Some children will approach this widening world skeptically and fearfully, and rarely initiate contact. Some will hesitate and be curious enough to be lured by the tantalizing evidence that exciting things are happening. No-limit children have already discovered that they are ring-masters in a three-ring circus where the performances start when they open their eyes and only sleep brings down the curtain. Life is absolutely jolly, and the main purpose is to experience everything possible.

In the encouraging environment of most babies, this learning from pleasurable activities goes on quite smoothly. However, the notorious "terrible twos," or "troublesome threes" mark the era when parents have fed in enough "no's" to get them back from the junior autocrat who thinks the show must go on just because he likes it. This battle of wills is universal. It is sensible that young children understand limits imposed for health, safety, and social harmony. The difficulty is that some parents get stuck in the authoritarian mode and say "no" as a personal convenience. "Because I say so" is also universally recognized for the thin rationality it presents in the eternal disputes between the two-year-old and his parents. One must keep in mind that early authoritarianism can inhibit them in later defining their own purposes.

Many people have difficulty defining a purpose in life. It tends not to be what a person does (as in occupation) so much as how a person learns to live (attitudes). If the purpose of life is to be happy, the understanding extends beyond self-satisfaction to realizing that personal behavior may not impinge on the happiness pursuits of others. The ethics and values of a no-limit person are not selfish, but generous. Since allowing or ensuring happiness brings inner satisfaction and an outer atmosphere conducive to future sharing, no-limit people thoroughly enjoy seeing other people's happiness and consider it as enriching themselves as well.

Many people focus on material things as a measure of attaining a meaningful life. Accruing a hoard of possessions defines their level of success. Even when the goals are lofty (for example, to make the world a better place), if the orientation is external, the evidence of progress must be physically measurable. No-limit people believe the world is already perfectly wonderful. It is in the way that people think and ultimately misuse our perfectly wonderful world that the sense of purpose that eludes most people will be found. You have the opportunity to develop in your children a respect for freedom and independence as you model behavior based upon your own inner goals toward your own purpose in life. Modeling is the most effective means of molding the values of children and helping them to understand their mission and live by the values expressed in the higher rungs of the ladder that leads to self-actualization or no-limit living. Ethical behavior teaches a great deal more than moral preaching.

Keeping these thoughts in mind, I offer the following suggestions for assisting your children, regardless of their present ages and positions in life, to adopt higher values, to meet their higher and highest needs, and to feel purposeful. As they adopt some of these "higher behaviors" you will see your children maturing into human beings who know their purpose, who never question their value, and who will spend their lives helping others to use the bountiful gift that is life, and the magnificence of this planet, to eradicate suffering and foster fulfillment for all of those who will follow. It is in this spirit that I offer these techniques and suggestions.

In helping very young children to meet their own basic survival needs, allow them as much freedom to make decisions for themselves as you possibly can within the limitations of their own safety. Let them decide when they will eat or nurse, for they are natural geniuses when it comes to their own instincts. They know what they like, when they want it, and when they do not. A tiny baby knows when to take water and when to push it away. Babies instinctively know when to sleep and when to wake up. They will let you know what they need; remember that they are absolutely perfect creations, with abundant intelligence to survive if you will listen to them. As they grow older, allow them to have as much control over their basic physical functioning as you possibly can and still feel comfortable. Avoid forcing foods on them, avoid demanding that they sleep according to your schedule, and avoid telling them when they are hot or cold, hungry or thirsty, sleepy or otherwise. While you do not have to be a slave to their whims, you can certainly permit them to take charge of their physical needs and learn to become independent. As they grow into preadolescence, allow them to prepare their own meals, to set their own bedtimes (within sensible limits), to monitor their own nutritional habits, and so on. You will be surprised at how effective children are at meeting their own physical and biological needs when they are encouraged to do it naturally, and if there is no arguing or fighting in these areas. Once you remove your power trip from your children, and simply allow them to be in charge of their lives to the extent that it is sensible and healthy to do so, their own perfect inner warning systems will help each one to choose a balanced diet, a balanced sleep pattern, a naturally healthy exercise program, and the like. If you believe that they simply are not capable of such control over their lives, ask yourself if this is so because you have always taken charge yourself or used these physical needs areas as a bargaining chip to get them to behave and do your bidding. The more you permit them to have control of themselves as early as possible, the more you are teaching them to move up that ladder quickly and intelligently.

Place as much emphasis as you can on the quality *of life for your children, rather than teaching them to grab as much as they can and accumulate as many possessions as possible.* Be with them in nature and let them experience it firsthand. Praise their efforts to enjoy something, rather than praising their efforts to beat others or to accumulate more stuff. Encourage them to appreciate everything that comes along, first by being a person who is high on the quality of life yourself, and then by refusing to be seduced into being upset when others around you do not seem as appreciative as you think they should be. Point out the beauty of a sunset even if your children scoff at it the first few times. Sentences like "Wow, I never get tired of seeing those mountains" or "I love to watch the birds flying in formation—I never ever think it's boring" will unwittingly teach them to become more appreciative of the quality that life offers. Many times they will say, "Yuk, it's so boring—I'd rather play a video game," and that is fine. "I know you love your video games, and this beautiful sunset is just as exciting to me." In other words, do not try to convince them that they are wrong; simply acknowledge that they have a right to like what they like, and that you are pointing out the ability to find quality in life, even if they have no coins for an electronic machine. Point out quality in their lives, and teach them to find enjoyment in everything they encounter. Eventually, they will be able to enjoy everything that comes their way, and that is a big part of what it means to feel purposeful in life.

Teach your children the importance of this statement if you want them to feel purposeful throughout their lives: No one knows enough to be a pessimist. Be optimistic even when they are looking at the dark side. No lectures, no long-winded speeches, simply optimistic outlooks. "I believe things always happen for a reason; maybe you will learn something really important from this accident." "I always feel that things are going to work out, even if it doesn't seem that way right now." Over and over you can be a model for helping your children to begin to look for something good, to see the glass as half full rather than half empty. The pessimists of the world learn their attitudes from those around them. Those who see the world as a grim place generally have been taught to so view their circumstances. As always, teach your children first and foremost by your own example, and then be a constant reminder of someone who is grateful for being alive, who expects things to improve, who believes in taking charge of one's destiny rather than sitting back and simply letting things happen. This is essentially an attitude, and it is an attitude that definitely can be taught to children in a gentle, effective way. Of all the people I have met who seem to have a strong sense of purpose in their lives, I have yet to see one of them be a pessimist who expects things to get worse. Purposeful people believe that things will improve, and it is that very belief system that helps to bring it about. When you expect things to deteriorate, you are setting them up to happen just that way. Therefore, purpose and optimism and positive expectations all work together.

Help them learn how to "defend the absent." This is mighty important if your children are ever to adopt those higher values and meet those higher needs that I outlined earlier in this chapter. Teach them not to talk badly about anyone who is absent from the scene, and adopt this as a code of conduct for yourself as well. If you want your children to master justice, truth, goodness, and meaningfulness, then remind them not to be gossipy or to fall into the trap of talking badly about anyone who is not there to defend himself. Remind them that what goes around, comes around. Sending out ugly thoughts or saying disparaging things about others will come back to them, but if they defend the absent, regardless of what others are saying, they will receive that same defense when they are absent and the butt of peer criticism. They can learn this very young, and again it does not require any lengthy sermons on your part. Just a reminder like "I really don't want to hear anything bad about your friends. I don't think it's right to talk badly behind someone's back." Or "None of us like to be talked about unkindly when we aren't there to defend ourselves. I'd like you to think about that." Or "I know you are all mad at Sally, but I think she is a terrific person. We all have some traits that irritate our friends sometimes, but I wouldn't say anything bad about Sally without giving her a chance to defend herself." The fact is that young children love to do this sort of thing, and they also need regular reminders that talking disparagingly about others is exceedingly small behavior that only reduces their own integrity. Gossip can be a painful experience for your young children, and teaching them not to participate in it will help them to see early the value of justice, goodness, truth, and meaning in life.

Use praise with children for the regular events of their days. Do not assume that a sense of purpose is something that they will someday attain; remind yourself and your children that each day of their lives is equally important, and that they are indeed being purposeful right now. "Learning to add and subtract is very important work for you. I'm so pleased that you understand it already." "Taking those cookies over to the neighbor was a lovely gesture. If everyone were as thoughtful as you, the whole world would benefit." "Fixing that radio is fantastic. I'll bet you could go into the repair business right now if you wanted to. You could not only make money for yourself, but just think how many people you could help at the same time." Everything your child does is important *now*. Children will feel purposeful later in their lives if they are taught to do so throughout their lives. And you can be a terrific reinforcer of just that, if you take the time to point out how much you value their work and play efforts, and how good they make other people feel when they do things for them. The child who takes cookies and milk to an ailing older person, is one who will later want to help eradicate suffering, and this kind of purposeful behavior needs to be positively praised and encouraged from the earliest moments, right into their adult lives.

Give children the gift of understanding what it really means to believe that all people are created equal. On a firsthand basis, you have an opportunity to help your children to understand that no one is any better than anyone else on this planet. You can remind them firmly that prejudging others is not what high-level people do. You can correct them when they are inclined to use slurs that will make others appear to be inferior. You can encourage them to always think positively about everyone, and remind them that no one asks to be born in parts of the world where there is little food and almost no opportunity. You can get children involved early in projects that are designed to help them to help others, to reach out to be of assistance rather than to sit back and be a critic or a do-nothing person. Show them how to have commitments early, and keep that uppermost in your parenting posture. Purposeful people want to help others to find their own purposes; they are not able to prejudge and malign others. Many young children have learned to put others down, to judge others of a different racial or religious or ethnic background. They will only continue to do that if it is overlooked or encouraged by you. If it is your mission to make sure that they do not learn hatred, then you are *obliged* to make sure that your children do not think in "superior" ways. Teach them that where they happen to be is merely an accident of birth, and that they could very well be one of those people wandering through the desert looking for roots to eat, were it not for their particular shake of the universal dice. Teach them to be grateful for what they have and to want to reach out to others, rather than to be a person who seeks approval from a peer group by laughing and making fun of others. Let them stand out early as individuals who stand up for others, rather than knock them down, and when they know that you encourage such a stance, they will carry out that mission for a lifetime. They need moral lessons from you, not in the form of preachy sermons, but in the very actions that you encourage them to stand up for when they are young. It is part of your mission as a parent to help end the schism between the haves and the have-nots in the world, and the only way to do it is to be an example of a moral person, and to encourage your children to stand up for these principles, praising them for it it even if they are singled out and laughed at temporarily by others.

From the very beginning of their lives, you must be on guard to help your children control their tempers and to discourage any striking out or displays of hate and anger. You can take very positive steps to ensure that your children do not become positively conditioned to violence. You can monitor carefully what they are exposed to on television, and absolutely refuse to allow them at impressionable young ages to watch murders, knifings, rapes, or violence of any sort. When you see children strike smaller ones or hurl obscenities, you must take firm, quick, and definite action. "You can get as angry as you like at yourself, or even at your sister, but you will never be permitted to strike her or anyone.

That simply does not go here. You will now go to your room and remind yourself that you cannot ever strike anyone in anger." This must be done each time the behavior crops up until the child gets the message. You can then love them, put your arms around them, and remind them that they are not bad because they behave that way. It simply must be reinforced in their young minds that being peaceful is the only way we can all get along in this family, and in this world as well. A firm scolding is mandatory, a reminder that bigger people do not hit littler people and beat them up, just like parents do not beat up on children simply because the parents are bigger. I cannot overemphasize the importance of reinforcing peace rather than anger and hatred when it comes to how children interact with each other as human beings. It is not necessarily a fact that all children, particularly siblings, must constantly be fighting and hitting and screaming at each other. Children can have peace and love and cooperation reinforced, and they can learn to channel their frustration and explosions of anger onto objects, or by themselves. There is nothing unhealthy about a temper tantrum, and certainly I support allowing your child and yourself to express the frustration that inevitably builds up when people live together. But it must not be directed at other people. This is a law of the universe, and it is an important one for the survival of all people, as well as for helping them to climb that ladder toward those higher values. Be ever alert for signs of violence, and be ready to step in when you see it surface. This is not to say that you must monitor and referee every single disagreement. It is only when you see ugly violence—temper tantrums or striking at others, vicious statements of hate directed at you or others in the family, and the like. These are nothing more than frustrations that are being expressed in an unacceptable manner, and the earlier children learn that such behaviors will not be tolerated, the sooner they toss those reactions away and learn to check their tempers. Also, it is important for you to avoid being seduced into one of their fights, as I recommended in the techniques section of Chapter 6.

Read to your children passages from books which encourage them to think about their higher needs, and to develop a healthy appreciation for beauty and love in their lives. Sit with them and read *The Little Prince, Jonathan Livingston Seagull, Alice in*

Wonderland, Gulliver's Travels, Candide, Gifts from Eykis, A Wrinkle in Time, and other parables that send out important messages for them to hear. At various ages of their lives, select passages and discuss them together. I can remember reading *Siddhartha* to my daughter when she was only eight years old. Although she did not understand every passage, she nevertheless internalized much more than I even believed she was ready for at that tender age. Let the children stretch rather than reaching down to them. Let them hear poetry and concerts, and see plays and movies that have a message, along with playing video games and going to amusement parks. They can learn a great deal from any and all experiences, particularly if they can discuss them with you. The more you give them games, puzzles, and books, and provide "stretching" activities for them that will challenge them and encourage them to ask questions and to learn the higher values, the more they will have these higher needs met early on in their lives. Do not be afraid to join in with them and learn from these materials yourself. Build a library of "higher needs" materials for your children at all of the various stages of their lives. You can also take them to current movies which emphasize the positive higher values, purchase cassette tape programs on self-development and personal motivation, and involve yourself in providing them with positive higher needs input at all ages. Take your teenager to any movie that will give them inspiration, and talk to them about what you are watching. Make this a regular part of your life with your children, and participate with them in both the viewing and the discussions afterward.

Get in the habit of regularly helping out those who are more needy, and involve your children in these efforts. At holidays, take time to purchase a few extra turkeys, hams, gifts, canned food, or anything that you can afford, and take it to a church or other organization in your community that distributes goods to those most in need. Let your children do the shopping and distribution right along with you, and talk to them about the importance of giving and being generous. Show them that only their actions count, that simply feeling bad or having opinions is a trivial means of dealing with a problem. Remind them, as I have reminded you over and over, that opinions do not make problems disappear, but commitments do. Get them to make a commitment to helping others. Involve them in aid programs to foreign countries where people are living under horrible conditions, and have them make their own commitments to give a small percentage of what they receive to those who are more needy. If enough of our children adopt these attitudes throughout their childhood years, we will make a significant dent in these massive social problems that confront us. It starts with you and your children, and it is a valuable way to teach them about the highest values on that ladder of self-development.

Keep in mind that positive thoughts actually emit different endorphins into the blood system than do negative thoughts. The chemistry of positive thinking is unassailable, and if you teach your children to think in happy, productive ways, they are actually doing something important for the maintenance and health of their bodies. Remind them that they are healthier when they think in uplifting, laughing, fun ways, and that negative thoughts actually increase the likelihood of sickness. Teach them to look at the positive side of everything by being an example of a person who refuses to be depressed in your thinking, and by praising their positive approaches as well. Teach them about the chemistry of their thinking and help them to understand that anger is a strong stress producer and ultimately a killer. Use little games with them to remind them not to make themselves sick with their thoughts. Show them how much better they feel when they look on the bright side, and that it is because they are releasing positive chemicals into their blood through their brains. The more they know about controlling their thoughts and the ability to have control of their destinies, the more likely they will be to send out those unhealthy endorphins from their systems forever.

Be ever aware of the need for all children to respect their own individuality. The essence of this entire book is in helping you and your children to be unique, to trust your own inner lights, to be individuals and not just part of the herd. Put a neon sign in each of their heads that says, "If you are just like everybody else, then what do you have to offer?" Praise them when they try things in their own ways, even if they fail miserably. Give them encouragement to wander from the path that everyone else is taking, and support their efforts to innovate and be creative. The person who lives on higher values and respects his own higher needs is one who is not trying to fit in and be just another sheep bleating away like everyone else. You can reinforce in your children throughout their lives the importance of being unique. I realize that I have made this point many times in the chapters of this book, but it really bears repeating. The route to higher places is one that is traversed best by those who are willing to risk, to try out their own formulas. If you respect and encourage your children to be unique at all ages, regardless of the outcomes and inconveniences to you or to them, then they will be on this higher path and will enjoy the fruits that come to those who feel purposeful. Remember, you cannot feel purposeful if you are emulating others.

Do not allow yourself to tolerate any abuse from your children. There are many times when the raising of children is absolutely exasperating. Regardless of how well you raise them and how much you teach them about the principles of no-limit living, there are still going to be many times when they are going to act nasty, inconsiderate, and outright bratty. You need to know that you are entitled to a break, and that you are not consigned to a position of having to be their victim because they are opting for obnoxious behavior. You do not have to put up with any abuse from your children, and you should be willing to have a plan for such occurrences. You can go into your own room and take some quiet time. You can explode and let out your built-up tension, as long as you remember not to direct it at any other human being. You must be willing to let your children know, in no uncertain terms, that you are working on your own higher needs, and that taking a break from them is just as important to you as having space away from you is to them. Take the space. Take the time. Announce firmly that you are taking a break and that you are not the least bit ashamed or guilty about wanting to have your own interests away from your children. The more you program in regular breaks away from each other as a normal part of living, the more you and your children will appreciate each other and the less you will have to fight for your space to be creative and work on your own higher needs.

Keep uppermost in mind that people are more important than things. That ideas are more important than accumulations, and that peace is worth virtually any price. When Harmon Killebrew, the great slugger from the Minnesota Twins, was being interviewed upon his induction into the Hall of Fame, he told the story of how his mother once yelled at him, his father, and his brother because the three of them were tearing up the grass while playing a game of touch football in the back yard. Harmon always remembered his father's response to his mother, and used it as a guiding principle in raising his own family: "We are raising boys, not grass." Keep this principle in mind. People count; things are replaceable. Conduct yourself this way with your children and you will be helping them to meet their own higher needs for aliveness, playfulness, meaningfulness, and self-sufficiency. When you get upset about things, remind yourself that you are raising children, and that their welfare, happiness, success, and fulfillment are the real purposes of parenting. In all of your interactions with your children, and with all of the children of the world, always remember that people are more important than things.

Allow your child to create her own special order in her unique universe without you constantly interrupting or interfering with that need for order. The need for order does not mean that you can provide it for your children. From the earliest moments of their lives, on through their adult years, and well into old age, human beings need to feel a sense of control over their environment and a sense of order that they control for themselves. A child's room should really be her room, and you are helping her by staying out of there unless there is a health hazard. Children need to go through sloppy stages in order to find out if they want things to be kept a certain way. They need to have dirty clothes strewn about sometimes just so they feel that they are in control of their worlds to some extent. By the same token, if they cannot put their clothes in the hamper when it comes time to wash clothes, then by all means allow them the privilege of washing their own clothes as well. Keep in mind that each of us, regardless of age wants to have some large measure of determination about what goes on in our world. The more you allow for that, and keep out of your children's business unless your interference is absolutely necessary for their safety, the more you teach that self-determination is not only okay, but is encouraged by you, the most important person in their lives.

Help to simplify your children's lives by reducing the number of rules in the house to an absolute minimum, and only imposing those that make sense to all concerned. We all crave simplicity as a higher need. Your children are no exception. You can allow them to do chores in their own ways, at their own paces, in whatever fashions they create, as long as the result is basically within reason. For example, if your son is painting the fence and you think it should be from top to bottom, and he prefers the opposite, let him find out for himself what works best. Tell him why you paint the way you do, but only as a suggestion. You simplify his life by standing back, biting your tongue, and allowing him to learn from his own mistakes. You cannot put your adult head on his adolescent shoulders. Everything that you know, you learned from experience, and the same will go for your children. Keep life simple and uncomplicated as much as you can. Let children experiment with their own approaches, and keep in mind that they genuinely want simplicity just as much as you do. Try to avoid overexplaining to them, and instead let them dig in and learn the hard way. Let your daughter work on her bicycle without you taking over and telling her how to fix it. Stay away from their homework unless they specifically ask for your help, and then minimize your involvement in their schoolwork. Their schoolwork is just that: *their* schoolwork. You can offer to be of help, but if you take over, you are teaching them to rely on you to do their work, and you are setting yourself up to be criticized by them whenever you do not do it the way they, or their teachers think it should be done.

An important reminder here: Make the truth the cornerstone of your relationship with your children. If a child breaks something in the house and is afraid to tell you for fear of being admonished or punished, then you have set up unwritten rules of conduct that discourage the truth. Let your children know that you value truth more than anything in life, and they will come to appreciate the importance of having a parent to whom it is never necessary to tell a lie. A completely truthful environment is the healthiest and most secure place to raise a child. Think back to the times in your life when you were forced to tell lies, for whatever reasons. Think about the accompanying anxiety that goes with such a life condition. The old maxim that "The truth will set you free" is not just an empty homily. It is truth itself. Praise children for telling the truth. Talk to them about their lying whenever it surfaces, and do not think that you are doing them a favor by ignoring any lying that they might do. Be open enough with them that they will come to you should they ever really need help, rather than avoiding you because they might fear your reaction to the truth. You want them to seek out your guidance in the event that they get into trouble, and they must know that it is okay to tell you anything. If you find your children lying to you, rather than viewing this as their problem, first ask yourself, "What is it about me, that I have created an environment where my child is afraid to tell me the truth?" Then go to work on that. Talk about the necessity of truth in making your relationship work. Talk to them about the value of integrity, explaining that facing up to one's failures or mistakes—honestly admitting to having "screwed up"—is far more advanced and admirable than trying to convince others you are something that you are not. Being authentic is crucial for no-limit living. The highest need on the ladder of self-development is the need for truth. Be a parent who is unafraid of any truth, and tell your children straight out, "I promise not to punish you for telling the truth, and if you ever get into serious trouble, regardless of how it happened, I want you to know that you can come to me for help. I may not approve of what you have done, but I will always respect you for telling the truth. We must not have any lies between us, and I will do the same for you as well."

Raise your children to be respectful of all living things. Teach them from the earliest years about the sacredness of all life. If you see them killing ants for pleasure, remind them kindly about the right of an ant to live without having someone killing it for pleasure. When you see your child wanting to kill a moth that has flown into your home, show him that you have a respect for life by letting the moth fly back outside. While I do not necessarily believe that one need get extreme with this position, I think it is essential for your children to learn a strong and healthy regard for all of God's creatures. In Maslow's study of highly functioning people, he found that without exception, they had a tremendous reverence for the sacredness of all life. Teach children to practice respecting everything that is alive and having the same reverence for other lives that they have for their own. If they see any creature in distress, have them take a few extra moments to help. To this day I can remember something I did on the beach several years ago. A tropical fish had been washed up on the shore and was obviously about to die. I picked up the fish and threw it back, but the incoming waves were so strong that it could not swim out, and it washed ashore again. This time I took the fish out over the waves in my hands, and I kept prodding it to "hang in there" and make it. After ten minutes, the fish seemed to regain its strength and ultimately swam sharply out to sea. While it may seem like a silly and insignificant thing to do, I swear to you that I felt as though saving that fish's life was something I was destined to do. I have never forgotten the feeling of triumph and inner satisfaction I got from staying with that fish until I had helped him (her?) over the hurdle of death. The reverence for life can extend throughout all of the animal kingdom. We are all here together, and when we help each other to become more independent and to stay more healthily alive, I believe that we are fulfilling one of the major purposes of our being here in the first place. When your children adopt the attitude that all life is sacred, they will genuinely feel more purposeful and consequently happier and more content as human beings. If you see them doing cruel things, gently ask them, "Don't you think that beetle has a right to live?" or "Why should that little spider die just because you enjoy killing it?" Reinforce that anything that has life in it is part of the purpose of this whole universe, and that killing for the sake of killing is a violation of the very life that we have been given as our gift, temporarily, while we reside here on this beautiful planet.

These are some of the techniques that I would recommend you employ with your children, regardless of their present ages. The higher needs that I have been writing about in this chapter, along with cultivating a sense of purpose, all revolve around the creation of a special attitude in your children. You want to be on guard each day to expose them to the beauty in virtually every object they see, the goodness that is inherent in all people, and the importance of thinking in positive, exciting, respectful ways. The attitude that I have been writing about here is fundamentally one of growth and a belief that the world is essentially good, that people are quite wonderful, and that everything in life is a miracle. The lesson of seeing life as miraculous and living a miracle each day, rather than searching for one, is what this sense of purpose is all about. When you *are* these purposeful ideas and begin to have your children meet their higher needs, their sense of purpose will ultimately begin to own them. Instead of trying to obey the Ten Commandments, they will be the Ten Commandments, and then it will be impossible for them to violate them, because they will be living *of the truth,* rather than searching for it.

Appendix

I Want My Children to Be Able to Someday Write This Letter

Imagine, if you will, a future time when the children are fully grown adults, and each of them sits down to write a letter to the people who have made a significant impact on his or her life. It does not matter if you are the parent, grandparent, a teacher, a minister, a special friend, or a caring person of any description. If it was your destiny to receive a facsimile of the following letter, it would make your efforts at helping children to be no-limit people all seem wondrously worthwhile. As you digest all of the ideas and suggestions offered in this book, and contemplate all that you are doing to help make your children's lives more complete, guiding them to their own greatness and giving them an appreciative attitude toward their lives and the lives of others, think about the contents of the following letter. It is written to you, with the writer's license to peek ahead into the future, knowing that these words could someday be a reality, even though in the present moment the children are not capable of putting down these thoughts for you to hear. It would be nice to hear them as you are influencing and raising your children, but it does not work out that way. I write this imaginary letter for you to have some sense of your mission while you are performing it.

Dear Special Person(s):

It is time for me to write to you and say thank you. I owe you a great big all-encompassing thank-you for all that I have been able to become in my own life. I look back throughout my entire lifetime with a deep sense of appreciation and awe at all that you have been for me. It was when I had children of my own that I began to realize what a phenomenal person you have been for me. I realize now what a stupendous undertaking this entire business of parenting is. As I attempt to raise my children to become no-limit people, and to help them to realize their wondrous potential, I am grateful for having had such a perfect model. I have the will, and I aim to have the energy, the drive, the excitement, and the determination to do it as magnificently as you have. I want to be specific and tell you exactly what I appreciate, now, as a parent and as the child who loved growing up with you.

I want you to know how grateful I am to you for helping me to be able to enjoy life. You were always such a positive person, even in the face of difficult times, and you helped me to look always at the positive side. Thank you for not spoiling me and for not always giving me what I asked for. I now appreciate being able to get things for myself without "expecting" things to always come my way. Many of my friends and acquaintances suffer from a disease called "more." They do not know how to do without, largely because they had parents who believed in handing them everything, rather than allowing them to earn their own way in life, and to experience the word "no" now and then. I can remember one holiday season when you told all of us straight out, "You will not be getting a lot of presents this year because we simply cannot afford it. We'll still have a wonderful Christmas, and maybe next year we'll have more money to buy you some of the things you would like." None of us collapsed, and no one complained. I know now the value of hearing the word *no,* and I wonder if my children hear it enough. As much as I love them, I find it difficult to deny them things and to allow them to earn their own way. I am grateful that you did that for me, and that you encouraged me to work for what I received, and taught me not to look into the pocketbooks of other people with envy, but to fill my own with earnings from hard work.

I can think back to so many positive things that you did. You never demanded an explanation from me for my mistakes or inappropriate behavior. You always seemed to know that I did not even know why I did some of those things I did, and you did not demand explanations or force me to lie to you by taxing my honesty too much. You made it easy to be honest, by expecting honesty, by living that way, and by never giving me an opportunity to have to lie to you. You knew when I misbehaved, confronted me with it, but never took pleasure in trying to trick me in any way. Before long, even as a youngster, I knew that lying to you was simply unnecessary. You accepted me for what I was and helped me correct those deficiencies, rather than trapping me in my own mistakes and taking advantage of me because I was little. Today I feel a strong sense of my own integrity. It is because you were able to do the same for me all of those years. Today, in my work and with my family, I never try to catch others doing things wrong. I run my company based upon the belief that people are good. I live in my family with the same set of beliefs, and it makes relating to people a pleasant rather than a nerve-racking experience.

You never did things for me that I could do for myself. You always encouraged me to try new things, to "go for it," to not worry about failing but to always focus on doing and not complaining. You were the world's greatest encourager, and to this day I have found that I practice encouragement with almost everyone I meet. Just yesterday, I told my little girl not to worry about falling down and to go ahead and try climbing the backyard tree. I recalled you encouraging me to be a climber rather than a whiner, and I still see you there prodding me to make the effort, rather than assuming the worst. You taught me the value of relying on myself, and I know now that it must have been difficult for you to permit me to take all those risks. I credit those risking experiences for my success and the way I feel about my life. You always said, "Forget about what everyone else thinks. What do *you* think?" I will be eternally grateful to you for using that sentence with me so many times, even though at the time I wondered why you were not like everybody's else's parents, who always tried to get their children to be just like everybody else. You gave me an opportunity to have a mind of my own, and I now am helping my children and my employees to do exactly the same. They do not always understand or agree with me, but I know that someday they will be grateful for the greatest gift of all: a mind of one's own.

You were always so "fanatical" about not letting my bad habits get your attention. You instinctively knew that this would only encourage me to continue acting that way. Often you would wait me out while I was acting unruly, afraid, or simply bratty. You would wait and wait for me to do one small thing well, and then you would lay on the praise. It wasn't long before I learned to stop the dumb behavior and do something that would get your attention. Your attention only came when I stopped the nonsense. At the time I hated that, because I wanted you to notice me, but the more I tried being bratty, the less you paid attention to me. What a fantastic way to get me to stop acting dumb, and today I thank you from the bottom of my heart for only giving me attention for doing things well. You seemed to know that I wanted and needed that attention, but that you also could wait to give it to me for having good rather than bad habits.

You were quite firm with me, and I want to thank you for that as well. I always knew where I stood, and I preferred it, even though you would not know by the way I sometimes acted. You were a rock of stability when it came to helping me to make myself a more powerful person. I can recall how you would never buy in to my excuses, even though you would not correct me or try to prove how superior you were. You never nagged me, and I want you to know how much I appreciated that. I saw so many of the other children acting as if they did not even hear their parents, largely because they were always being followed, mistrusted, nagged, and bothered. You treated me as a complete human being right from the very beginning. Regardless of my age, you always gave me the same respect and attentive ear you gave the other adults in your life, and all of the older children as well. I know you believe that children are whole and complete where they are, at any given stage of their lives, but I did not know it then. You listened to my problems rather than trying to solve them for me, and you encouraged *me* to look for solutions. You seemed to know that I needed to feel just as important as the big people, because it was never really an effort for you. I always believed that you thoroughly enjoyed my company and that you were thrilled to have me in your life. I never had to demand your love; it was always there for the taking. I never felt like a little person, and to this day I never feel small or compare myself with anyone. I have you to thank for this wonderful gift, and I shall try to pass it on to my children.

I also want you to know how much I appreciate that you never tried to preach to me. You seemed to believe that I knew the difference between right and wrong, and instead of preaching, you would just ask me to be honest with myself and not try to fool myself. I can remember how you once told me that I could probably fool a lot of people, including you, but that I should never try to fool myself. You were a paragon of honesty yourself, and you modeled it for me throughout your life. I appreciate the example, and I know today how extremely valuable it is to be honest in everything I do. You would talk *with* me rather than *at* me, and you always stressed self-honesty. Today, I feel I can never thank you enough for teaching me that as long as there is any dishonesty in my life, I will not have peace.

You never used force with me. You never laid a power trip on me, even though you certainly could have if that had been your desire. You were always a gentle person with clear values and an unwillingness to compromise on those values. I appreciate how you disciplined me, although I must admit I would get so frustrated sometimes at not being able to goad you to blow up and simply smack me. I'm sure I would have died of shock if you had ever laid a hand on me in anger. Instead, you always let me know that my anger was my problem and that you were not interested in owning any of it yourself. When you would leave the room, or send me to mine, I knew in my own mind that it was useless to go on with my tantrums or my irrational behavior. I was not going to get to you, and you taught me that very early. After a while, you showed me that respect for myself was the problem with me, and that as long as I did not respect me, others would not either. But you always did, even when I seemingly did not deserve it. It seems as though you respected me just because I existed and that you were trying to get me to do the same. Today, I see so many parents striking their children in anger, and when I talk to them, it seems that they were always treated the same way by their parents. You never needed to hit me, only to get me to discipline myself, and you showed me that you have too much respect for yourself to allow any disrespect from me. I always respected you, and I know you always respected me, but what is most significant, and why I want you to know I am grateful, is that I also respect myself today, and I teach those around me to do the same. I can see now that if enough adults treated children as you did, all of this abuse, anger, hostility, and forced discipline would soon be gone from our world entirely.

I want to thank you again for always living up to your promises. You never disappointed me without consulting me first and explaining why something that we had planned, needed to be rearranged. You always treated your promises to me as contracts, and you taught me to respect my own word and not to give it without meaning it. I can remember how you insisted that I not quit a paper route that I had agreed to take over for one of my friends while he went away for three weeks one summer. You knew that I hated to get up in the morning at 5:30, but you insisted that I keep my word. "A promise is a promise, and if you don't keep your promises, then what good is anything you say? You stand for nothing if you can't keep your word." I hated those early-morning deliveries, but you insisted that I live up to it, and you also reminded me that it was up to me to get up and get going in the morning. I have made my word my bond today, and you served as the model.

It was not really necessary for me to try to get away with as much as I could, since you were always consistent with your values and beliefs. I knew in my heart that you did not merely believe in truth, that you were truth. I knew also that you did not just talk about your higher values, you actually lived them. It did not take very long before I realized that you did not compromise when it came to your own values. You *always* talked nicely about others. You *never* spoke from prejudice or hostility, and you lived integrity, rather than spouting words about it. It was quite apparent to me that I did not have to try to sneak around you with my childhood pranks, because you lived tolerance and understanding rather than simply talking about these ideas. I always knew I could talk to you about a problem or difficulty I had gotten myself into, and I knew that you would tell it to me straight if I was at fault. I was often surprised when the other kids told me about lying to their parents, or sneaking things past them, because it was never necessary with you. If I screwed up, you would say so and ask me to correct it rather than punishing me for telling you the truth. When I needed to be alone, you were never threatened. You were always so busy with your own life projects that you did not seem to have to cling to me or be upset with me when I disappointed you in one way or another. I always knew that you had a high regard for yourself, and that my problems were not going to destroy you emotionally.

I always respected the fact that you had such pride in yourself, that you had many outside interests, that you wanted to make a difference in the world, and that you were always thinking about ways to help other people. I appreciate that we had no taboo subjects in our family, and that you were willing to be open and hear new points of view, even though you obviously disagreed with some of them. Your openness made living with you such a joy, and your willingness to listen to all points of view made being unprejudiced simply the way it was for me as I grew up. It seems that when I respect me, and when I expect others to do the same, I almost always receive the respect I seek. I learned from your examples that you would never tolerate disrespect from me, regardless of how annoyed or troubled I was at the moment. I can remember hearing you say more than once, "No matter how irritated you are, or how right you may think you are, you do not ever have the right to be disrespectful to others." The many hours that I spent alone, thinking about your words, helped me immeasurably in taming my own instinctive temper and in directing my anger away from other people. Occasionally, when I would say, "I hate you," or something equally vicious, you seemed to know that I did not mean it, and that I was really only trying to get you to pay attention to me. You seemed to know that I would only say that to you because I trusted your love enough to let the worst come out in front of you. You were not threatened, you were not intimidated, and you simply but firmly reminded me that you did not expect to hear these kinds of sentiments and that I could think about them on my own, away from those who wanted to act civil toward each other. When I finally came around, you were always there to put your arms around me, to forgive me, and to let it be forgotten. You did not remind me forever of what a twerp I had been. You let it go. Today I can appreciate how valuable you were to have around when I slipped into some of my crass behavior.

You never made me squirm like so many of my friends' parents by correcting me in front of other people. I still appreciate how you would take me aside and talk to me privately, rather than overwhelming me in front of my friends or other members of the family. Your sensitivity to this made a big impact on me, and today I use the same strategy on my children. For you, however, it was not a strategy; it was your natural way of respecting the dignity of a little child. You knew instinctively that being corrected in public was embarrassing, and you only had to remind me once in my life, when I slipped and corrected you at a restaurant dinner party. I still remember how you asked me to go out to the car with you for something or other, and how you said, "I have never corrected you in front of your friends, and I expect the same courtesy from you. Please try to keep that in mind." Then you did something that you always did after being firm; you put your arms around me and told me that you loved me, and that we all slip sometimes. I was only seven years old, and yet I remember it still as if it happened yesterday. Thanks for the great lesson. You taught me that mistakes are not sins, they are only mistakes, and that we have to learn to make mistakes without feeling that we are bad when we do. Somehow I always knew that making a mistake was not a big deal, and that you always loved me even when I seemed to do the worst things. It wasn't long before I knew that you were one special person. Most of my friends' parents would stay mad at their kids for weeks at a time. They would hold grudges, say hateful things, and do things that I never experienced. Perhaps that is why our house was the place where all my friends wanted to hang out. They knew you were a friendly person, that you liked us all, and that you would be fair and fun to be around. I can remember how my friends' parents would scream at them for not putting out the garbage, and how they would do anything that you asked of them without ever even thinking about complaining. My friends loved you as much as I did, and they could not do enough to please you. Once they even scrubbed the kitchen floor and cleaned up the entire house while you were at work, just because they wanted to return some of the appreciation that you always extended to them. I guess you were right when you told me that we get back from the world exactly what we put out to the world.

How well I remember how you used to encourage us to experiment and try things out in life. Our basement always had several science projects going, animals were always welcome, there was a basketball hoop made from an old basket in the yard, a hockey rink in the winter, a party almost every month, and always you seemed to be happiest when I was trying out new things. You seemed to know that I learned from experimenting, and that even though it was often an inconvenience to you, it was important for me to try new things, to wander into the unknown a bit. On vacations, you always made it exciting by including us in the planning, and trying out new adventures. You seemed more occupied with allowing us to enjoy life, rather than learning the rules and doing as we were told. You cannot possibly know how much that has added to my life, and how I love to do practically anything new, to experiment, to make life into a fun trip, rather than memorizing a lot of rules and don'ts, like so many of my contemporaries.

You never really expected me to get sick, did you? It was almost as if you taught me to program myself to be well. You always told me that I could take an aspirin if I wanted, but that was not really going to make my aches go away. You taught me about thinking healthy all the time, and you never gave me attention for little tiny ailments. While you did not ignore me, you always said, "You can make this get better much faster by thinking healthy thoughts. Forget about the bruises; they'll disappear faster if you ignore them." Sometimes I thought you didn't care, but I noticed that you did the same thing with yourself all the time. You once told me that you had no time for being sick. I did not really understand it then, but now I do. You simply did not think sick thoughts, and you seldom got run down, or had colds or the flu, like all the other people in our neighborhood. To this day I attribute my own solid exercise program and my lack of illness to what you taught me so many years ago. Again, I owe you one big thank-you. I have avoided many sick days in bed because of those early teachings.

One other thing: You were really special for me around report card time. I can remember how all of the other children were afraid to take home their report cards for fear of what their parents would say. I knew one boy who actually changed his card and lied to his parents about his grades every time the dreaded report card day came. For me, report card day was the time when you asked me if I was satisfied with my own progress. You used the report card to help me to set some realistic goals and even to help keep me focused on what I was doing in school in the first place. You never went into a rage when I worked below my capacity; it was not in you to make yourself upset over my lack of motivation. Instead, you were calm, honest, and helpful to me by insisting that I put in more effort where required. You were not always worrying about my schoolwork, my athletic teams, how I stacked up against the others in my school, or any of these things. You let me know that these were my private concerns and that you had no business prying into all of my activities and introducing stress and anxiety into my life. You did not attend my athletic games, usually because you had your own activities, and I never once thought I was deprived. In fact, I would have been embarrassed to have you at one of my football games. I remember how you discouraged me from organized athletics and told me to go out and have fun, and then if I really wanted it, that I could go for the coached teams, the standings, the uniforms, etc. I learned early that I did not want to be a part of the organized leagues, and that getting together and choosing up sides in a vacant lot was much more important.

I want you also to know how much I appreciate your teaching me to stand up for my beliefs, even when I ran into stubborn rules and archaic policies. I remember so well how I had to sit in the principal's office for three days because I challenged a rule that would not allow me to hold hands with my friend on the way to school, outside of the school property. You thought it was an outrage that such a policy existed, and you did not tell me to simply grin and bear it. I remember your words exactly: "Fight the rules if you think they are wrong, but do not expect me or anyone else to come and fight your battles for you. You will have to take the consequences, but you will probably get the rule changed eventually." You were right. I sat there for three days, and finally, when they made you come into school in order to reinstate me in classes, you stood up for me right to the principal. You told him that he really did not have a right to tell children what they could or could not do on their way to school, that you saw nothing wrong with holding hands, and that you would never insist that I apologize for what I believed in so strongly.

I want you to know how much I value the listening that you always provided for me when I wanted to talk about something. It made me feel important then, and now I know that I still feel that way because of you. Listening is such a wonderful tool. You always seemed to be learning from me, rather than trying to teach me something, and I cannot tell you how good it felt then to know that you really cared enough to listen to me. I did not realize it then because I just came to expect it from you, but now I feel that you must be commended for your wonderful quality of an open-ear policy toward me all the time. I respect your kindness toward me that showed in so many little ways: the lunches that you always provided, the folded clothes, the concern about my getting the proper nutrition, the waiting up to make sure that I got home safely, the fun of bowling together, and all the little things that I only took for granted back then.

I respect your never interrupting or contradicting me, and I have only lately come to realize what a wonderful quality this is. I marvel at the courtesy and patience you demonstrated toward me all the time. You never screamed or treated me rudely, even if I would slip into those behaviors occasionally. Somehow it just was not in you to treat another human being that way. I recall how so many of the other parents would actually make fun of their children around others, and I was always so grateful that you never resorted to such tactics. Today, I know that my own self-respect was built on those respectful attitudes that you always displayed toward me, not just for the benefit of others to witness, but at all of the very private times of our life together. You simply had no meanness in you, and you were so tolerant of me that any mean streaks that surfaced in me soon disappeared. It just was not necessary for me to be mean in order to get your attention, and today I have such positive regard for all other people. In fact, I respect all forms of life—largely, I believe, because you taught me by your own example to have such a reverence. When I see other people being cruel to each other, or to animals, I know that they did not have the benefit of your wonderful lessons in respecting rather than destroying life. I will always treasure you for helping me to learn this invaluable lesson. It seems that when you lost your temper with anyone you would always go off by yourself for a few minutes and get yourself under control. You did not take it out on your children, or nag us to death because of your own frustrations. I wondered a lot about what you did when you disappeared, especially when I knew you were upset. Now I know you were cooling off and talking to yourself, so as not to take it out on other people. That is the strategy of a saint, and I will always celebrate your saintliness in this regard. It taught me, by such a magnificent example, to look within and cool off, before striking out in anger either with words or weapons. Thanks for such a useful strategy in life.

You seemed to be ever mindful of the need to praise and encourage me. You never picked at my shortcomings, even though others around me did quite regularly. Somehow I believe that you were blind to my shortcomings, and that you knew a few words of praise and encouragement could get me to overcome those temporary flaws. You were right. I just needed to hear you say, "I know you can improve; I'm sure you can do better" or "If you can get one right on a test, then you know it. Now you just need to practice." You always looked for that one small thing to praise, and by doing so, you helped me to feel encouraged about my own abilities. To this day I always look for the good in everything I see, ignoring the bad, and I encourage others to believe in their abilities. You were really something with all that praise. It works—it really works.

You always seemed to know that I was a child, never expecting more from me than I was capable of giving. In restaurants you knew that when I was four I was going to act like a four-year-old. You knew when I was a teenager that I did not have the same judgment of an adult. Always you helped me to stretch toward better judgment, but you never punished me for being a child and acting like one. You had this uncanny ability to help me to want to grow up, without being ashamed of being a child. I was always relieved that you did not blast me, like so many other parents, for making the typical mistakes. Instead, you always required me to take responsibility for any mistakes that I made. When I broke the neighbors' window you did not scream and lose control. You did not punish me. You said quite simply, "When you are careless playing ball, and you break a window, you have to take responsibility for yourself. I want you to replace the window for them. Then I'd like you to be a bit more careful about where you play ball." And that was the end of it. My friends were all in shock. They thought I would be grounded for a week. You simply taught me to look for solutions, not problems, and to take responsibility for my mistakes. That is a wonderfully important lesson in life, and I must say that I use it every single day of my life. Your way was simply to not rob me of the opportunity to learn from my mistakes. You did not rescue me; you always turned mistakes into learning adventures, and it made living my life as a child with you a wonderful pleasure.

Each day of my life I am reminded of the phenomenal lessons you offered me by your example. Each time I hear a boat whistle blast I remember how you stopped to appreciate the passing freighters on the river, and how you were always entranced by them, even though you had seen them thousands of times. Each time I see a beautiful sunrise, I remember how you always exclaimed at the beauty that God provided for us. You never seemed to tire of the beauty around you, and you helped me to become a person who stops to see the beauty in everything and everyone around me. You had no unkind words for anyone, nor do I today. You had no malice in your heart toward anyone, nor do I today. You genuinely enjoyed your mornings, daytimes, and evenings—every one of them, as I recollect. As do I today. When we talked about God, religion, or the mysterious in life, you told me the most important words I have ever heard: "If you don't have a temple in your heart, you'll never find your heart in a temple." Today I have a temple in my heart, and I thank you for helping me to put it there.

I could go on and on with this letter to you, but I think you know now precisely how I feel. You were the shining light that gave me the opportunity to glow all by myself. You always gave me an example rather than a lot of preachy words and lectures. You knew what you really wanted for your children, and you lived it, for me to see each and every day. I owe you so much, and yet I feel I owe you nothing. You did not do it to be repaid; you did it all because you knew in your heart exactly *what you really wanted for your child*. Thank you. I love you.

Index